EDMUND J. AMIDON, Temple University
JOHN B. HOUGH, Syracuse University

EDITORS

INTERACTION ANALYSIS: THEORY, RESEARCH AND APPLICATION

With an Introduction by Ned A. Flanders

ADDISON-WESLEY PUBLISHING COMPANY
READING, MASSACHUSETTS · PALO ALTO · LONDON · DON MILLS, ONTARIO

This book is in the
ADDISON-WESLEY SERIES IN EDUCATION

To Peggy and Honey

PREFACE

These are exciting times for those interested in studying the dynamics of instruction and in applying the knowledge gained from their study to the training of teachers and the improvement of instruction. Recent developments in techniques for classification and analysis of the instructional language of the classroom have made possible research on instruction and innovations in the training and supervision of teachers which just a few years ago were not even considered by most educational researchers, teacher educators, and instructional leaders.

Of the recently developed systems for analyzing the instructional process, interaction analysis is the one that is currently best known and most widely used. There is much literature available which describes the system of interaction analysis, the social–psychological theory which forms its basis, the research which has established its empirical validation, and the application of interaction analysis to teacher training. However, much of this literature is in the form of monographs, papers read at meetings of professional associations, and doctoral dissertations, few of which are readily available to students and practitioners in the field. Until the publication of this book, there has been no single source dealing with theory, research, and application of interaction analysis to problems of teacher training. This book was developed to fill the need for a representative source to which students and practitioners could turn.

In selecting papers to be included in this book we chose only papers which dealt with the system of interaction analysis. Much creative work has gone into the development of other systems, and this work has resulted in a number of provocative insights into the teaching process. Therefore the decision to exclude papers describing these systems was not an easy one to make. It was made, however, on three bases. First, many of these other systems are still highly experimental and lack theoretical and empirical support. Second, many of these other systems are highly complex and require an intermediate recording or a typewritten transcript of the classroom interaction, and thus are less useful for training purposes. Third, to have dealt in depth with a representative sample of the other systems would have resulted in a very large and unwieldy volume. Thus it was decided to create a single-focus text dealing with the system of interaction analysis, rather than to attempt a broad general survey of the many systems currently available for the analysis of classroom verbal behavior.

Once the decision was made to limit the book to interaction analysis, we had then to decide which papers and articles on interaction analysis should be included. We chose the three unifying themes of theory, research, and application because in the behavioral sciences the development of principles of behavior often follows the path of theory building, instrument development, hypothesis testing, and, finally, applications based on findings. Under each of the three major headings of theory, research, and application we chose papers that were representative of the work done to date in these areas. Most of the papers were drawn from four sources: journal articles, papers read at professional meetings, abstracts of doctoral dissertations, and selections from larger works such as monographs and books. In addition, however, we have included several papers that were written specifically for this book. Our intent was to be representative, and at the same time to create a book that would be optimally useful to students and practitioners at various levels of sophistication.

The development of the original system of interaction analysis was primarily the work of Ned Flanders. Indeed, the system is often referred to as the Flanders System of Interaction Analysis. The editors, however, were the first to use interaction analysis in undergraduate teacher training and have continued to use it in research on student teaching and other aspects of the pre-service preparation of teachers. In recent years many colleagues have joined in this effort, and from their work have come research findings and innovations which have made possible significant insights into the analysis and improvement of instruction. To Ned Flanders and those colleagues and students who have authored papers included in this book, we are indebted. We would particularly like to express our appreciation to authors and their publishers who have given us permission to reprint their articles. Rather than attempt an extensive listing of such authors and publishers in this preface, we have given appropriate acknowledgments throughout the book. Special thanks are due to Evan Powell for his extensive assistance in the preparation of the final manuscript and to Robin Nelson for her aid in proofreading and help in preparing the figures.

Philadelphia, Pennsylvania   E. J. A.
Syracuse, New York   J. B. H.
June, 1967

INTRODUCTION

This book contains selected readings about early and current efforts to code verbal statements during spontaneous classroom communication and to compare the frequencies of different kinds of coded statements to other measures of the classroom situation. This collection of papers will serve as a useful reference for those interested in particular research projects, for those who wish to learn the skills of systematic classroom observation, and for those who are interested in some primitive theories about teacher influence in the classroom which are based on interaction analysis.

Not very many readers will turn to these pages from an interest in history, albeit inconsequential, but it is to this aspect of the book that these short comments are directed. It was in a makeshift office that overlooked the harbor of Wellington, New Zealand, sometime during July of 1957, that I first studied a ten-by-ten interaction analysis matrix. It was tabulated from some code numbers collected a few days earlier in an elementary classroom. The purpose of tabulating a matrix was to estimate the amount of interdependence between successively coded statements, an issue which had been raised during conversations with a New Zealand statistician by the name of John Darwin, a descendant, by the way, of the famous naturalist. The short observation and tabulated matrix had already served its purpose, which was to prove that the interedependence did exist between coded events. As a consequence, Dr. Darwin became interested in applying Markov Chain Theory to the Statistical analysis of interaction data which was later published.

In spite of the beauty of Wellington Harbor, the movement of ships, and other distractions, the tabulated matrix held my attention for several hours. This display had isolated each shift from one category to another and had formed a pattern which was not easily understood. The notion that the numbers in certain rows and cells could explain a teacher's influence pattern became apparent only gradually. What happened at the termination of teacher praise statements? What was the first type of statement made by the teacher when the pupils stopped talking? What kinds of teacher statements, besides questions, triggered statements by the pupils? These insights did not burst into full bloom, suddenly; they sort of crept into the matrix, one at a time.

Today, some ten years later, systems for coding verbal statements in the classroom are barely coming of age, so to speak. Where three or four researchers were at work, there are now thirty or forty. The progress made each year in the technical aspects of observation, in the knowledge that we are gaining about what a teacher does while teaching, in efforts to help a teacher change his behavior, and in knowing how to create more effective classroom learning continues to increase. Here are some predictions which should be realized during the next few years.

Coding systems with as many as 100 categories will be plotted by computers into matrices that contain 10,000 cells. In effect this will be a 10,000 category system. It will be possible to code with this many categories at higher rates and reliability than were possible with John Withall's seven categories back in 1948. Such systems will prove of interest to researchers, but may have limited practical application.

Observers, whose purpose is to help teachers understand patterns of their own overt behavior, will be trained to use a half-dozen different category clusters. A teacher wishing to study certain cognitive aspects of classroom discourse will request those clusters which provide the information desired. Another, wishing to improve his utilization of ideas expressed by the pupils, will request a different cluster. With these different category clusters to choose from, fellow teachers or older pupils who are trained can code interaction in order to provide the observed teacher with a perspective of his own behavior that otherwise could not be obtained.

New technical equipment or "hardware" is already at hand and ready to be put together, if this has not already been done. The new push-button telephone bases can send ten different electrical impulses over a telephone line at the touch of a finger. This line can be connected with a small memory system, off the main line of a shared-time computer system. At the end of the observation, the computer will hum for a few seconds, and then the remote typewriter will begin publishing the matrix, down at the teacher's lounge, to be ready in the time it takes the teacher and observer to walk from the classroom. When this system is complete, we will have instant feedback to be washed down with the instant coffee or tea.

In the meantime, there is much that remains to be done with the tools at hand. Nearly all the research reported in these pages should be replicated with different populations and under different circumstances. Such replications will serve to build confidence or cast doubt on the conclusions reached during this first active decade of research on spontaneous teacher influence.

From the point of view of history, the earliest papers will be found in Chapter One. The work of H. H. Anderson, of Lewin, Lippitt, and White, of Withall, and of Flanders appears to be originally motivated by a desire to prove that certain preferred patterns were superior for just about anything. The concepts "integrative–dominative," "democratic–authoritarian," "student centered–teacher centered" and "indirect–direct," all spring from a conviction that most teachers could be more effective if they would interact with pupils rather than direct them. This sounds innocuous enough, but a disposition to prove one relationship can hide others. A small step toward a broader view, away from a single-value orientation, can be found in the introduction to the concept of "flexibility of teacher influence." This movement toward a more objective description of teaching behavior has not yet run its course. I believe that the balance between "initiating" and "responding," to be found in both teacher and pupil statements, will become a focus for further research.

The material in Chapter Two is more technical and serves as background for the training of observers. It is to be hoped that, once the basic ten categories presented in this section are learned, a person will feel free to experiment with subdividing the categories whenever he wishes to make a distinction hidden by the standard, broader categories. Thus, should an observer and teacher be interested in pupil questions, special sub-categories should be used. The same could be said about the other categories.

Chapter Three reports work on the intriguing thought that interaction analysis information might be used to help a prospective teacher or an experienced teacher change his behavior. In terms of the long-range development of observation techniques, these efforts are probably premature. Yet, as each stage in the development of observation systems is reached, it is difficult not to turn to practical applications "to see if the new system is useful." There are two current developments which will provide the impetus to continue this kind of research. First, we are learning a great deal about social-skill training exercises which can be combined with interaction analysis to the benefit of both. The most effective pre-service and in-service applications of interaction analysis must await the full development of such training experiences. Second, improved technology in processing interaction analysis data will make any program less tedious and more intensive. Both of these trends should make the experimental treatments more powerful in studies of behavioral change.

Those who read this collection of papers will do well to remember that the work reported includes initial, modest efforts to explore a promising area of research. At the present time, the field is surely in what will be considered, just a few years from now, a primitive stage.

With regard to building new theories and techniques in this field of research, it would be wise to recall that Charles Darwin had the patience to reflect on what he saw with imagination, common sense, and some invention over an extended period of time, before he wrote *The Origin of the Species*. He has been quoted, from his *Life and Letters*, as saying:

> I have steadily endeavored to keep my mind free so as to give up any hypothesis, however much beloved (and I cannot resist forming one on every subject), as soon as facts are shown to be opposed to it.

The University of Michigan   Ned A. Flanders
Ann Arbor, July, 1967

CONTENTS

3. The application of interaction analysis to problems of teacher education

Contents *xiii*

BACKGROUND AND THEORY

CHAPTER OVERVIEW

Teachers have never had an empirically verified instructional theory to serve as a basis for their classroom behavior. Yet, perceptive teachers have sensed that the quality and quantity of teacher-pupil interaction is a critical dimension of effective classroom teaching. Without a theory, teachers have usually been unable to generalize principles of instruction from specific instances. Without a way of objectively describing the nature of classroom interaction, teachers in the past have had no way of capturing the elusive phenomenon of their instructional behavior, the climate that it creates in their classroom, and the effect of this climate on student attitudes and achievement.

Interaction analysis is a technique for capturing quantitative and qualitative dimensions of teacher verbal behavior in the classroom, but as an observational system, it clearly does not measure all that occurs. Interaction analysis views the dynamics of the classroom through a particular lens. What interaction analysis captures is the verbal behavior of teachers and pupils that is directly related to the social–emotional climate of the classroom. It is not by accident that this is the view that interaction analysis takes of the classroom. Interaction analysis as a classroom observational technique was developed by Flanders out of social psychological theory and was designed to test the effect of social–emotional climate on student attitudes and learning.

In the behavioral sciences, principles of human behavior are often derived as a result of a specific pattern of activities. An overall conceptual framework is first proposed from which hypotheses are formulated and tested. The development of this framework as a first step is important in that it gives both substance and direction to the process of formulating and testing the hypotheses. When hypotheses are accepted, the data from such research provide the basis for the formulation of a theory. When principles of human behavior can be derived from theory, then theory gives direction to action. Specific instances can then take on generalizable meaning.

Research on classroom climate and its effect on pupil behavior, attitudes, and learning has followed the approach just described. Chapter One of this book contains six articles each of which has made a major contribution to testing hypotheses and/or developing a theory of classroom climate and its effect on human behavior. Though the approach of each of the authors of these six papers has been somewhat different, there is in each paper a common hypothesis that is being tested or further explicated. This hypothesis deals with the concept of social–emotional climate and its effect on human behavior. In each of these articles the basic terminology differs, but the concept of social–emotional climate remains consistent. The reader should note the conceptual similarity that exists between such terms as integrative, democratic, inclusive, student-centered, and indirect on one hand and dominative, authoritarian, preclusive, teacher-centered, and direct on the other.

As early as the late 1930's, researchers in education became interested in analyzing classroom interaction. One of the earliest approaches to the analysis of teaching behavior was that used by H. H. Anderson. The first paper in

Chapter One describes Anderson's classic study in which he assessed the integrative and dominative behavior of teachers in their contacts with children. His ideas and his basic categories of integration and domination are, in a significant way, forebears of Flanders' concepts of indirect and direct influence.

The autocratic–democratic dichotomy presented by Lewin, Lippitt and White was another precursor of Flanders' concepts. The second paper reports the results of an intensive study of the effects of leader behavior on children's groups. This paper presents a discussion of research on group climate that was conducted in a context somewhat removed from the formal classroom situation, but the inherent hypotheses are basically the same as those tested by Anderson.

John Withall was the first of the early researchers of classroom climate to measure classroom interaction by means of a category system that classified teacher statements. The categories used by Withall are in many ways similar to those that are embodied in the Flanders system. From the work of John Withall came support that classroom climate could be assessed and described by means of a category system. The third article describes the results of Withall's study designed to test his climate index.

Although Morris Cogan did not directly observe the behavior of teachers and students, he did analyze the perceptions that students had of their teachers in order to provide a framework for conceptualizing teacher behavior as inclusive, preclusive, or conjunctive. The results of his work are presented in the fourth paper. They indicate that there is a relationship between the way the teacher is perceived by his students and the amount of self-initiated work that the pupils report doing. Cogan's research along with the other research presented in this chapter provided Flanders with a theoretical basis for conceptualizing the relationship between teacher influence and the behavior and attitudes of pupils.

The work of Robert Bales is clearly in the mainstream of attempts to develop a theory of social–emotional climate. Interaction Process Analysis as a research technique has been widely used by Bales and others in research on small groups. His search for an improved understanding of the relationship between the behavior of group members and the productivity of groups has done much to further the development of a theory of classroom climate. Many of the theoretical principles discussed by Robert Bales and Fred Strodtbeck in the fifth paper in this chapter have direct application to the study of classroom climate referred to elsewhere in this book. The focus of this article by Bales and Strodtbeck is on a system of Interaction Process Analysis which they used to determine and analyze phases in group problem solving.

In the final article, Ned Flanders summarizes many of the ideas presented in the other papers in this chapter and relates these ideas to the theory underlying his category system for assessing the social–emotional climate of the classroom. He also presents a number of hypotheses which form the basis for much of the research reported in subsequent chapters of this book.

In summary, papers included in this chapter provide a basis of support for a theory of social–emotional climate.

THE MEASUREMENT OF DOMINATION AND OF SOCIALLY INTEGRATIVE BEHAVIOR IN TEACHERS' CONTACTS WITH CHILDREN

HAROLD H. ANDERSON[1]

This study reports the extension into adult–child relationships of measures of domination and of socially integrative behavior that were developed in previous studies of the interplay of preschool children (Anderson, 1937, Anderson, 1937a).

What is dominative behavior? And what behavior is socially integrative? The terms in the title of this paper are merely convenient labels for two techniques of behaving that have been experimentally demonstrated to be psychologically different. In the initial investigations it was assumed, for example, that there is a psychological difference between snatching a toy out of a companion's hands so as to play with it oneself and asking the companion if one may borrow the toy for awhile. It was assumed that there is a psychological difference between a command and a request, between "tellin' 'em and askin' 'em."

The use of force, commands, threats, shame, blame, attacks against the personal status of an individual are called dominative techniques of responding to others. Domination is characterized by a rigidity or inflexibility of purpose, by an unwillingness to admit the contribution of another's experience, desires, purposes or judgment in the determining of goals which concern others. Domination is behavior that is based on a failure to admit the psychological inevitability of individual differences. Domination stifles differences; domination attempts to make others behave according to one's own standards or purposes. Domination obstructs the natural growth processes of further differentiation through the interplay of existing differences. Domination is, there-

[1] The writer wishes to make grateful acknowledgment to the George Davis Bivini Foundation for financial aid and to express his appreciation for the help given by Joseph P. Brewer and Dorothy Walker Loeb, research assistants. This article is from *Child Development* 10, 1939, 73–89. Reprinted by permission of the journal of *Child Development* and the author.

fore, antagonistic to a concept of growth. Domination is consistent with a concept of self-protection. But growth is self-abandoning; it is giving up of the present structure or function, a yielding of present concepts, standards or values for new structures, functions, concepts, standards or values that are in process of emerging. Self-preserving, however necessary it may be under circumstances of extreme insecurity, is something decidedly less than growth at its optimum. Domination may therefore be said to be the behavior of a person so insecure that he has to be self-protective rather than self-abandoning, that he has to maintain a status quo rather than voluntarily enter and participate in a changing situation. Domination involves force or threats of force or of some other form of the expenditure of energy against another. Domination is behavior of one who is so insecure that he is not free to utilize new data, new information, new experience. Domination is an attempt at atomistic living; the desires, purposes, standards, values, judgment, welfare of others do not count; it is rugged individualism of a highly ingrowing order. Domination is the antithesis of the scientific attitude; it is an expression of resistance against change; it is consistent with bigotry and with autocracy. It is the technique of a dictatorship.

If, instead of compelling the companion to do as one says, one asks the companion and by explanation makes the request meaningful to the other so that the other can voluntarily cooperate, such behavior is said to be an expression not so much of pursuing one's own unique purposes as attempting to discover and get satisfactions through common purposes. For such expenditure of energy in common purposes, for an attempt to reduce instead of augment or incite conflict of differences the term integrative behavior is used. The person who can change his mind when confronted with new evidence which has grown out of the experience of another is said to be integrating differences. Integrative behavior as the term is used here is consistent with the scientific point of view, the objective approach. It designates behavior that is flexible, growing, learning.

The term integration is not used here as it has been used by some in contrast with differentiation. It is believed that the two processes are inseparable and are merely different aspects of the same psychological or biological phenomenon. With the integration of differences something new is created that never has existed before; this emergence of originals through the integration of differences is itself a differentiation.

Integrative behavior is thus consistent with concepts of growth and learning. It makes allowance in one's own behavior for differences in others. It is behavior that makes the most of individual differences. Whereas domination stifles or frustrates individual differences, socially integrative behavior respects differences, advances the psychological processes of differentiation. Integrative behavior is flexible, adaptive, objective, scientific. It is an expression of the operation of democratic processes.

In addition to the assumption that domination and integration are psychologically different techniques of responding to others another assumption advanced at the outset in the experimental program was that domination and integration would offer different predictions of subsequent behavior. Both in the previously published research on the behavior of preschool children and in a recent study of domination and integration in the behavior of kindergarten children (Anderson, 1939a) data have offered only consistent evidence in support of the hypotheses that:

1. Domination incites resistance, which is itself dominative.

2. Integrative behavior induces cooperation or integrative behavior in a companion.

3. Domination is not only different from, but where a potential avenue of escape is left open, it is dynamically unrelated to integrative behavior.

It should be pointed out that there is no relationship short of the extermination of another individual that is entirely dominative and no situation in which the interplay is entirely integrative. But many situations arise in which the techniques of responding to others can be reliably said to be expressions of domination or integrative behavior.

AIMS

The purpose of the present study was to develop reliable techniques for recording in terms of dominative and integrative behavior the contacts which teachers have with kindergarten children.

METHODS AND PROCEDURE

It was expected at first that an experimental situation would need to be devised but it was shortly discovered that the teachers' contacts both with individual children and with the group occurred with such rapidity as occasionally to tax the abilities of the observers to record them.

With criteria already experimentally established for recording in terms of domination and integration social contacts of paired preschool and kindergarten children with each other it still was not easy to adapt these criteria to the contacts which teachers had with children. Preliminary observations were made in a number of different schools. The teachers were for the most part soft-spoken, attentive, patient, and considerate of the children. In a number of rooms there appeared to be a complete absence of commands or of other evidence of obvious domination in the teachers' responses to children. Teachers, to be sure, told children to do certain things and not to do other things. But all teachers do that. To do so in a casual sympathetic way may seem an inherent part of schoolroom procedure. The whole school curriculum is in a sense a systematic statement of environmental demands to be made on the child.

If a teacher in introducing the music period said, "I am going to sing you a song," it was felt that that was definitely a social contact with the group, and as such should be recorded. It was not clear at first whether it could be checked as dominative or integrative nor was it clear what difference it made what one called the contact. It was with much labor that the experimenters were able to devise criteria and arrive at definitions that would record reliably domination even if expressed in a "soft voice." It seemed that a key to the difficulty could be found by checking the teachers' remarks against the criteria of *conformity by the child* versus *joint participation by the child or by the group*. Did the teacher tell them or ask them? Did she base decisions on her own desires or judgment or did she allow some measure of interplay for the child's desires, the child's judgment?

It did seem as though for each isolated remark it made little difference whether the teacher told them that she was going to sing a song or asked them whether they would like a song or, if so, what song would they like to hear? It seemed logical to expect, however, that an accumulation of tallies that would record such simple differences would make a distinction between some teachers and others, that in some schoolrooms there would be a great deal or a preponderance of teachers' contacts in which the teacher *told* the children what to do, what she was going to do, or what the activities were to be. And on the other hand, it was conceivable that other teachers would have much lower frequencies of such techniques and might perhaps be found to be giving the pupils a proportionately higher number of opportunities to use their own judgments.

Domination in the present study includes social contacts in which the activity of the child or of the group is determined out of the experience or judgment of the teacher. Such a contact is psychologically different from the contact in which there is a democratic interplay, in which the determination of the child's activity comes from a broader experiential base that includes the judgment or choices of the child himself. The psychological assumptions are that the child "learns" and he grows less in other respects to the extent that the teacher decides what is to be done and how and when to do it. Telling them is assumed to be not only psychologically different from asking them, but in general it is assumed to be less propitious for growth, learning, and problem-solving.

THE OBSERVATION BLANK

An observation blank was devised to contain five minutes of observations. Each blank bore the identifying information showing the school, grade, section, date, observer and teacher and in addition the name of the activity in which the group was engaged, the time the observation period began and ended and the elapsed time of the observation period. The blank which was adopted after experimentation with two other forms is shown in Fig. 1–1. It had the names of the children at the tops of vertical columns and the names of the categories of teacher contacts on the horizontal rows. The categories were arbitrarily defined for convenience in recording. It will be noted that there are no categories for numbers 11 to 14 inclusive. These numbers designated categories on previous experimental forms of the observation blank which were finally combined with other categories. Because the experimenters had memorized the other cate-

					Unidentified
Anderson
Form 3   Department of Psychology, University of Illinois
May 1938   Observation Blank

School ....Grade........**Kdgn**......Section........**P.M.**.....Observer...Date...............................

Teacher ....Activity.............................Observation began......................Ended...................... Elapsed Time...............................

Rank Order					Unidentified
Activity	Time	Group			
1. Deter			1	1	
2. Direct Ref			2	2	
3. Relocates			3	3	
4. Postpo			4	4	
5. Disappr blame obs			5	5	
6. Wrn thrt cond-pr			6	6	
7. Call grp act att			7	7	
8. Ration material			8	8	
9. Le Method			9	9	
10. Q Le Method			10	10	
11.					
12.					
13.					
14.					
15. Perfunctory Q or S			15	15	
16. Apprvl			16	16	
17. Accepts diff			17	17	
18. Extend Invit			18	18	
19. Q or S re I or A			19	19	
20. Build up			20	20	
21. Per Jt Act			21	21	
22. Sympathy			22	22	
23. Permission			23	23	
24. Undetermined			24	24	

FIGURE 1–1

gories by number and by relative position on the blank, the numbers and original spacing were retained on the final observation blank. For aid in recording categories quickly two additional columns of guide numbers were inserted in the blank.

THE SCHOOLROOM SITUATION

From eight different kindergarten groups from which data have been gathered findings are presented here for three groups: morning and afternoon groups of children from school X, both groups taught by teachers A and B; and a morning group from school Y taught by teacher C. In school X the head teacher, teacher A, took the leading role with the children much more frequently than did the assistant teacher, teacher B. The assistant had charge of the music period during which time most of the contacts of teacher B which entered the data were recorded.

METHODS OF OBSERVATION

The observers were instructed to observe the teacher who was playing the major role with the children. The frequencies of teacher contacts thus represent those of the one teacher most active at the time but by no means all the contacts which the children received from both teachers during the observation period.

The observer marked the blank by placing in the child's column one tally for each contact which the teacher had with that child individually. If the contact was directed to the group rather than to an individual the tally was recorded in the "Group" column.

If the teacher made some contact with a child or with the group, but the nature of the contact was not clear, the observer recorded a tally under category 24, "Undetermined." If the nature of the category was clear but it was not known with whom the contact was made, the tally was placed in the "Unidentified" column at the right-hand side of the blank. This column collected not only a few contacts which occurred when the observer for one reason or another failed to see or to hear, but a number of such partially disguised contacts as "Some little boy forgot to remember what we said about hands—or eyes—or feet."

SUBJECTS

The subjects were 55 kindergarten children attending three groups. In general the children were superior in intelligence. In school X, an attempt had been made to enroll younger children in the morning group. The enrollment in school X was 23 in the morning group, 21 in the afternoon group and in school Y, 11. In the three groups the girls had the respective numerical superiority of three, three and one as compared to the numbers of boys.

DEFINITIONS OF THE CATEGORIES

The full titles of the categories together with examples of teachers' contacts which they include are given below. Actual observations of teachers' behavior constituted the basis on which each category was constructed and defined.

Categories 1 to 8 inclusive record dominative contacts of the teacher. Categories 15 to 23 inclusive record the teacher's integrative contacts. Categories 9 and 10 which had low frequencies were regarded as ambiguous hybrids, not clearly classifiable as domination or integration. It is believed, however, that the majority of contacts checked in category 9 belong more properly in the group of dominative techniques, and that contacts checked in category 10 would fall more properly among the integrative contacts.

The establishing of categories was an arbitrary matter of convenience in recording the teachers' contacts and also a means for a preliminary search for more refined analyses of teachers' behavior. Analyses of the data have been made to show the consistency with which two independent observers recording simultaneously were able to record teachers' contacts by categories. But in the treatment of the data to show the contacts of the teachers with the individual children and with the group all the dominative and all the integrative categories respectively are combined.

CATEGORIES

1. *Determines a detail of activity or acts for the child in carrying out a detail.* Includes the instances where T (teacher), in order to rush through to an end, goes ahead and does things for the child.

    T: "You will have to fold yours like this."
        "We won't play that game any more."

2. *Direct refusal.*

    T: answers "No" to a direct request.

3. *Relocating, reseating, or placing* children in different relation to each other or to property, i.e., different from the relation which the children have themselves selected.

    T: "Henry, Janet, Sam, please sit down."

4. *Postponing, slowing up* the child.

    T: "Not now."
        "Wait just a minute."
        "Later on."

Holds back the fast ones.
Obstructs differentiation, originality, individual differences, variability within a group.

    T: "Betty Lou, go back and wait until I come around."
        "Wait at your place until I give you one."

5. *Disapproval, blame, or obstruction.*

    T: "Hurry up" implies disapproval.
        "I'm waiting."
        "One little boy—I don't see his eyes at all."
        (Check "unidentified.")

6. *Warning, threats, or conditional promises.*

    T: "I don't want to speak to Henry, Sam, and Janet again."
        "Now if we all sit nicely and keep our hands to ourselves, we might have two stories."

7. *Call to attention or to group activity.*
   Call to attention during group activity.

    T: "Girls and boys - - - - - -."
        "Let's see who is listening."

8. *Rations material.*

T makes decisions as to amount, kind, etc., e.g. amount of paste, amount of grass for rabbit nests. (Implication is that rationing of materials is psychologically more than an administrative convenience; it deprives the child of an opportunity to exercise his own judgment, to decide for himself how much it will take for the job at hand; and for this reason it is an expression of T domination.)

9. *Lecture method.*

T gratuitously defines a problem or anticipates the question and gives the answer. (The "sez you" category.)

e.g. T, passing out paper:

T: "The paper is to keep the paste off the tables."
(If there was a problem of keeping the paste off the tables, the children might have contributed from their experience in defining the problem, especially since only the children got paste on the table. As a matter of fact, the tables were made so paste could be washed off. Paste actually got on the tables, and as a later part of the routine a child with great enthusiasm did wash the tables after the children were through pasting.)

T: "You won't need your scissors." (check #9)
(But) "Don't get your scissors." (check #1)

10. *Questions: Lecture method.*

Questions where the answers are in the back of the book or in the teacher's experience.

T: "What did the birdie say?"
If there is only one answer, then check #10.
If the child is permitted to give an imaginative answer, then check under #19 or #20.

11–14 inclusive deleted on the blank.

15. *Perfunctory question or statement.*

Indifferent "Thank you's."

T: "Isn't that interesting?"—a bare response, but a response nevertheless.

16. *Approval.* Includes rewards, prizes, competitive favors.

T: "I think that's fine." "Billy's row is standing the straightest."

17. *Accepts difference.*

Observer must be alert for negative votes, declinings, expressions of difference, conflicts of difference. Whenever T makes an offer or gives an invitation, and the child declines, some category should be checked for T's response: She either accepts the difference (#17); or she reproves (#5); or she renews her request (#18). e.g.

T: "Jimmy, would you like to sing this one (song) up here? (beside T)"
Jimmy declines.

T turns to another child. (Check rank order for Jimmy, #18, Extends invitation; check the other child, rank order for #18; check Jimmy for #17, Accepts difference.)

18. *Extends invitation to activity.*

> T: "Who wants to be a pony?"
> "Who would like to be a robin?"
> Call for a show of hands. The choice rests with the children. It must be obvious that there is no element of exhortation and that a child can still decline. Under few circumstances will an *invitation* be made more than twice without obvious attempts to exhort; in which case check #1. A teacher's contact in category #1 cannot be declined without further exhortation or disapproval.

19. *Question or statement regarding child's expressed interest or activity.*

Carries no presumption of opposition, antagonism, disapproval or urging.

> T: "Dickie, are you waiting for paste?"
> "How are you getting along?"

Includes the ice-breaker conversation.

> T: "Do you have a dog at home?"

20. *The build-up.* Highly integrative behavior.

Includes instances where T helps child to arrive at a better definition of a problem or a better solution, without giving the final answer.

21. *Participates in joint activity with children.*

Offers help, offers to participate. (Children playing ball. Ball rolls over near T who returns it.)

22. *Sympathy.*

> T: "I'm sorry you hurt your finger."

23. *Permission.* T grants permission to child's request.

> e.g. "May I get a drink?"
> "May I pass the cookies?"

Since a series of research studies into different age levels and different situations is contemplated, the problem of reliability of two observers became an end in itself. A more extended analysis was made of the difficulties in recording than would have been undertaken if the objectives had been merely to study these particular schoolrooms.

The observers attempted to record at an appropriate place on the blank every "contact" which the teacher had with an individual child or with the group during the period of observation.

How reliably could the observers identify instantly and record the contacts in individual categories? How accurately could they assign these contacts to individual children or to the group? Could two independent observers record at the same speed? Could they agree in their definitions of a contact or would

Table 1–1

Coefficients of Correlation between Observers M and N for Total Numbers of Contacts per Observation Period for 73 Observation Periods

Teacher	A & B	A & B	A	B	A & B
Session	A.M.	P.M.	A.M. & P.M.	A.M. & P.M.	A.M. & P.M.
r	0.95	0.96	0.97	0.96	0.96
P.E. r	0.01	0.01	0.01	0.01	0.01
N.	35	38	44	29	73

they come out with greatly varying numbers of tallies? Could they observe and record the contacts of one teacher more reliably than they could the contacts of another teacher? Could they observe dominative contacts more reliably than integrative contacts? These were some of the questions that have been answered in the analysis of the data.

Seventy-three pairs of consecutive and simultaneous records of five minutes each by observers M and N were analyzed. All the tallies on each observation blank were totaled and these totals correlated for the two observers. Table 1–1 gives the coefficients of correlation for separate combinations of observation periods showing respectively contacts of teachers A and B combined for the morning and again for the afternoon, contacts of teacher A for the morning and afternoon combined, and likewise for teacher B, and contacts for all of the 73 periods combined.

These high coefficients indicate that as far as the speed of recording was in question there was virtual identity in relative number of tallies recorded per observation period. This consistency of speed is shown whether the observations are for one teacher or the other; or whether they are made during the morning activities or during the afternoon program. These coefficients show also a very high agreement between observers in using the definitions of a "teacher contact." Moreover, during these 73 periods covering five hours and 45 minutes of simultaneous observation, observer M recorded 1,897 teacher contacts and observer N recorded 1,893.

Table 1–2 shows coefficients of correlation which indicate how reliably two observers recorded for individual children the dominative contacts, integrative contacts, and total contacts of the teacher.

Ten coefficients of reliability of two observers for teachers' contacts with individual children for total numbers of contacts of all kinds were 0.87 or above, six of the ten being 0.94 or above.

Ten coefficients of reliability of observers for teachers' dominative contacts with individual children (categories 1–8) were 0.80 or above, six of the ten 0.93 or above.

The coefficients of reliability of observers of teachers' integrative contacts with individual children (categories 15–23) were based on lower frequencies and were low but consistently within a narrow range.

Table 1–2

Coefficients of Consistency of Observers for Teacher Contacts per Child with Categories Grouped. (One tally on the scatter diagram represents, e.g., tallies in categories 1–8 for one child.)

School	Teachers	Session	Total contacts 1–24			Groups of categories Domination 1–8			Integration 15–23			Total time (min.)	Mean time of correlated periods (min.)
			r	PE_r	N	r	PE_r	N	r	PE_r	N		
X	A & B	A.M. & P.M.	0.94	0.00	688	0.93	0.00	574	0.46	0.03	271	342.5	4.69
	A & B	A.M.	0.94	0.01	319	0.94	0.01	259	0.44	0.05	111	155.5	4.44
	A & B	P.M.	0.94	0.00	369	0.93	0.01	315	0.46	0.04	160	187.0	4.92
	A	A.M. & P.M.	0.89	0.01	411	0.84	0.01	319	0.48	0.05	191	204.5	4.65
	B	A.M. & P.M.	0.96	0.00	277	0.95	0.00	255	0.50	0.06	80	138.0	4.76
	A	A.M.	0.87	0.01	197	0.87	0.01	148	0.53	0.05	91	99.5	4.52
	B	A.M.	0.97	0.00	122	0.97	0.00	111	0.10	0.23	20	56.0	4.30
	A	P.M.	0.91	0.01	214	0.80	0.02	171	0.44	0.06	100	105.0	4.77
	B	P.M.	0.96	0.01	155	0.94	0.01	144	0.53	0.06	60	82.0	5.13
Y	C	A.M.	0.89	0.01	131	0.87	0.02	114	0.29	0.08	66	65.0	5.00

There was considerable evidence that in spite of the high degree of reliability of the two observers in recording total contacts of the teachers, the observers were at times unable to record the contacts at the speed with which they occurred. This would account in part for the lower coefficients of reliability for integrative contacts which by their nature must often be identified by their context, are therefore less specific and more difficult to record.

The most rigorous method of analyzing all the data for reliability of two observers in which teachers' contacts were correlated child by child and category by category showed for 1,560 squares on record blanks for school X a coefficient of 0.78; and for 378 squares on record blanks for school Y a coefficient of 0.77. These coefficients are sufficiently high to make the data in this study acceptable as measures of teachers' behavior.

NUMBER OF TEACHERS' CONTACTS PER HOUR WITH INDIVIDUAL CHILDREN

The speed or rapidity with which teachers make contacts with children raises some pedagogical and mental hygiene questions. The complaint has often been made at home and at school that children are unable to concentrate, that they cannot carry on activities by themselves or hold to a given purpose without adult encouragement or stimulation. The complaint though frequently made is not very clearly formulated. Studies have been made of the attention span of preschool children and of others, but as yet there are no standards or criteria against which to evaluate either the performance of an individual child or that of a group. From experience in clinical psychology one has often suspected that children have been unnecessarily interrupted in their serious purposes by well-meaning adults. In some cases the "over-supervision" has been so unrelenting as to make it seem as though the child could do little or nothing by himself. In fact the greater amount of "free play" or freedom to inquire and to explore one's environment is one of the chief criteria by which the nursery school is distinguished from public school education.

But as to how much free play a child needs; how much supervision is a "good thing"; how many contacts with an adult a child should have; when supervision ceases and "over-supervision" begins; what mistakes and how many a child should be permitted to make without adult interference; for answers to these questions there are only unreliable clinical generalizations. It is obvious that before one can speak reliably about "too much" he must first have units of measurement. This study constitutes an important first step in providing such units of measurement.

Table 1–3 shows the mean number of contacts per hour which each teacher had with individual children, the mean number of dominative and integrative contacts per hour and the total observation time in minutes on which are based the respective rates of contacts. The Domination–Integration ratio is obtained by dividing the mean number of domination contacts per hour by the mean number of integration contacts per hour.

It can be noted that the highest frequencies for all contacts for separate periods show for teacher A 421.3 contacts per hour; for teacher B 474.5 contacts per hour; and for teacher C 489.8 contacts per hour. When morning and afternoon contacts are added together and the means per hour per child computed, teachers A and B are nearer together in frequencies, showing respectively 401.3 and 431.7 contacts per hour. This represents for teacher A a rate of 6.7 contacts per minute for 11.9 hours of observation and for teacher B a rate of 7.2 contacts per minute over a period of 3.5 hours of observation, with the presumption in both cases that a considerable though undetermined number of contacts is unrecorded.

Table 1–3

Mean Number of Individual Contacts per Hour for Teachers A, B, and C

School	Session	Teacher	Children	Total obs. time (min.)	1–24 Total contacts	1–8 Domination	15–23 Integration	D-I ratio
X	A.M.	A	23	362.0	421.3	244.2	115.7	2.1
		B	23	98.5	384.4	278.4	55.4	5.0
	P.M.	A	21	352.5	380.8	210.4	97.5	2.2
		B	21	109.0	474.5	350.6	71.6	4.9
	A.M. &	(A		714.5	401.3	227.5	106.9	2.1
	P.M.	(B		207.5	431.7	316.3	63.9	4.9
Y	A.M.	C	11	440.5	489.8	292.4	126.3	2.3

Another pedagogical as well as psychological problem is presented in the comparison of the teacher in school Y with the teachers in school X. There were 23 children enrolled in the morning session of school X and 21 enrolled for the afternoon. In school Y, however, there were only 11 children present during the period of observation for this study. It can be seen in Table 1–3 that for teacher C there are no great proportional divergences in frequencies of contacts as compared with the frequencies for teachers A and B who had larger groups of children. It can be noted that the rates of integrative contacts and of total numbers of contacts of teacher C exceed in all cases the rates for the teachers in school X while the rate of dominative contacts of teacher C exceeds all rates except for teacher B for the afternoon and for the combination of morning and afternoon.

Is one to draw an inference that teachers are themselves responding at a "capacity rate" whether they have one dozen or two dozen children in the room? Or stated in another way do teachers regardless of numbers of children before them respond at a fairly constant rate? These data raise a further ques-

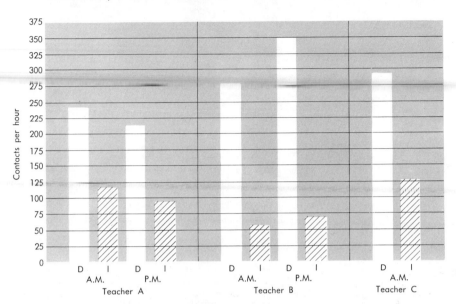

FIG. 1–2. Mean number of dominative and integrative contacts per hour which teachers A, B, and C respectively had with individual children.

tion as to how many children constitute a teacher load. Were the children in school Y receiving twice as much "teaching" as the children in school X? The data show that the children in school Y had almost twice as many individual contacts per hour as did the children in school X. Again the question as to how many contacts are desirable pedagogically and psychologically must remain unanswered. All that can be said here is that in this study measures have been developed that indicate considerable differences in teachers' techniques.

It may be noted in Table 1–3 that in all cases the dominative contacts outnumber the integrative contacts by at least two to one and that in one case the ratio of domination to integration contacts is five to one. The contrast between teachers' dominative contacts and integrative contacts is shown graphically in Fig. 1–2 which gives the respective frequencies per hour for individual teachers.

Five groups of data offered in Table 1–3 have been broken down to show the frequencies of contacts per hour which teachers had with individual children. These data are presented graphically in Figs. 1–3 to 1–7 inclusive. Figs. 1–3 and 1–4 show respectively for teachers A and B the mean number of contacts per hour which they had with each child enrolled in the morning group. A glance at these figures shows that as far as can be indicated by the frequency of the teachers' contacts per hour the individual children in this kindergarten live at school in different environments.

Figure 1–3 shows a range of total contacts of from 4.1 to 39.3 per hour, with the median child receiving 13.2 contacts per hour. The median child thus received about three times as many contacts per hour as the child lowest in rank

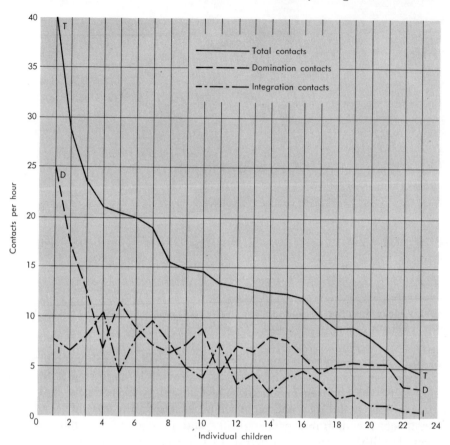

FIG. 1–3. Mean number of contacts per hour which teacher A had with individual children enrolled in the morning session.

and only about one-third the frequency of that of the highest child in rank order. The child at the top of the rank order received almost 50% more contacts than the child who was next in rank.

The frequencies of dominative contacts show a range of 3.2 to 24.9 with the median at 6.5 dominative contacts per hour. The rank orders show generally small differences from child to child from the bottom of the list up to the fifth ranking child. The fourth child in rank, however, is about 50% above the fifth in rank or almost twice the median.

The range of integration frequencies is from 0.7 to 10.7 contacts per hour with the median at 4.5. From Fig. 1–3 it can be seen that the curve for integrative contacts not only extends within a shorter range than the curve for dominative contacts but that, excepting the cases of three individual children, the integration curve lies below the domination curve. For these three children the Domination–Integration ratios become less than one.

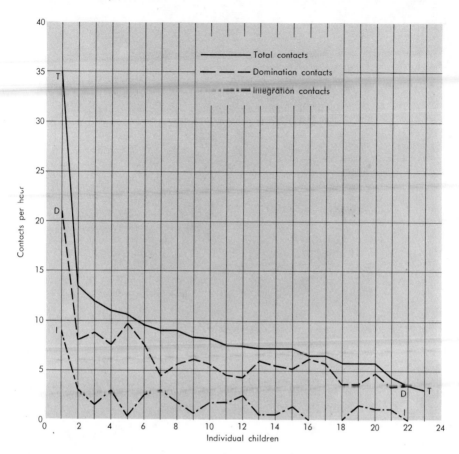

FIG. 1–4. Mean number of contacts per hour which teacher B had with individual children enrolled in the morning session.

The Domination–Integration ratios for the children represented in Fig. 1–3 range from 0.6 to 4.6. It can be noticed that the child with highest D–I ratio is the child who had the lowest total number of contacts per hour with the teacher. In anticipation of further research it may be asked: Is this child to be regarded as "pedagogically self-sufficient" or merely neglected? Or what does it mean to a kindergarten boy whose frequency of total contacts with the teacher is relatively "negligible" to have four out of five of those contacts of a dominative character?

Figure 1–4 shows the contacts per hour which teacher B had with individual children in the morning session. In comparison with the contacts of teacher A in Fig. 1–3 it can be seen that teacher B had much lower frequencies of integrative contacts; with six children she had none. The ranges of dominative, integrative and of total contacts, however, are about the same for teacher B as for teacher A.

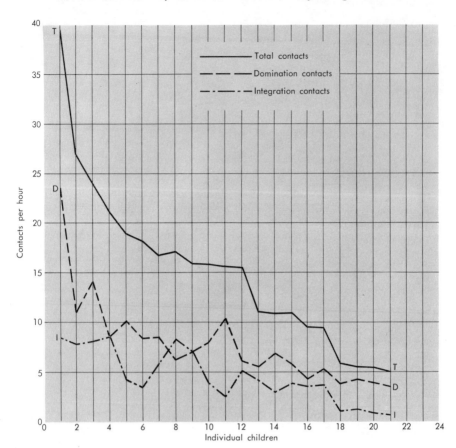

FIG. 1–5. Mean number of contacts per hour which teacher A had with individual children enrolled in the afternoon session.

Figures 1–5 and 1–6 show respectively for teachers A and B the individual contacts per hour which these teachers had with the children enrolled in the afternoon group. Although the children in this group were older the curves show ranges, medians and tendencies toward individual differences similar to the curves for the contacts with the children enrolled in the morning group.

A contrast is shown, however, in Fig. 1–7 which represents graphically the contacts per hour which teacher C had with 11 children. In general, the children with teacher C, numbering approximately half those with teacher A, received mean numbers of contacts per hour not quite double the frequencies of those with teacher A.

The striking contrasts between teacher C and teachers A and B suggest that an extension of the present research techniques to the measurement of the behavior of teachers in a larger number of schoolrooms selected for greater control of known variables would have important theoretical value for the psychology of human relations and practical values for educators and mental hygienists.

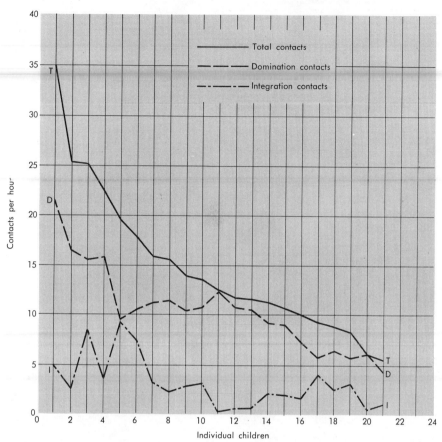

FIG. 1–6. Mean number of contacts per hour which teacher B had with individual children enrolled in the afternoon session.

NUMBER OF TEACHERS' GROUP CONTACTS PER HOUR

The contrasts and comparisons given in Figs. 1–3 to 1–7 inclusive represent the teachers' direct contacts with individual children. In addition to the frequencies represented on those graphs there were many contacts which the teachers had with the children as a group. The frequencies of these group contacts per hour are shown in Table 1–4.

It can be seen in Table 1–4 that teacher B had approximately twice as many group contacts of all kinds, categories 1–24, per hour of observation as did teacher A, both for morning and for afternoon. When the data for total numbers of contacts for teachers A and B are combined, the new mean is not greatly in excess of the mean shown by teacher C.

With group contacts as with individual contacts domination exceeds integration. The range of D–I ratios in Table 1–4 is from 5.4 to 11.4.

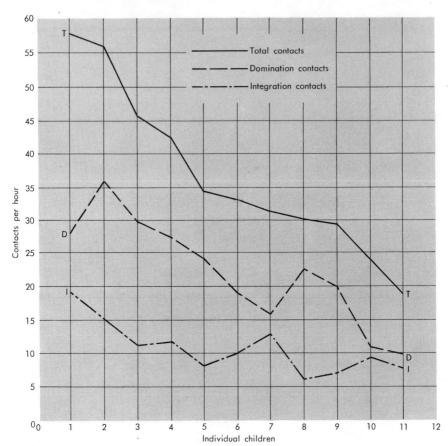

FIG. 1-7. Mean number of contacts which teacher C had with individual children.

SUMMARY

Domination is the behavior of a person who is inflexible, rigid, deterministic, who disregards the desires or judgment of others, who himself in the conflict of differences has the answers. Examples are the use of force, commands, threats, shame, blame, attacks against the personal status of another. Domination is the technique of autocracy or dictatorship; it obstructs the growth processes in others. It is the antithesis of the scientific attitude and the open mind.

The term integrative behavior was chosen to designate behavior leading to a oneness or commonness of purpose among differences. It is the behavior of a flexible growing person who is looking for new meanings, greater understandings in his contacts with others. It is noncoercive; it is the expression of one who attempts to understand others, who is open to new data. It is consistent with the scientific approach, the open mind. It is both an expression of growth in the person using it and a stimulus to growth in others. It does not

Table 1–4

Frequencies per Hour of Teachers' Group Contacts

School	Session	Teacher	Total obs. time (min.)	Categories			
				1–24 Total contacts	1–8 Domination	15–23 Integration	D–I ratio
X	A.M.	A & B	460.5	112.6	80.7	11.5	7.0
		A	362.0	93.0	65.5	10.0	6.6
		B	98.5	184.6	136.5	17.1	8.0
	P.M.	A & B	461.5	106.5	80.4	9.9	8.1
			352.5	84.1	60.4	9.0	6.7
			109.0	178.9	144.8	12.7	11.4
			440.5	105.8	64.4	12.0	5.4

stifle differences, it makes the most of differences; it actually creates new and harmonious differences.

No behavior is entirely integrative; none short of extermination is entirely dominative, but in the interplay of differences specific acts or contacts can be reliably said to be expressions of domination or of integrative behavior.

The purpose of this study was to develop reliable measures for recording in terms of dominative and integrative behavior the contacts which teachers have with kindergarten children.

Three kindergarten groups in two schools taught by three teachers supplied the final data.

Reliability coefficients were established by data from 73 pairs of consecutive and simultaneous records of five minutes each by two independent observers. The observers showed high agreement in defining a contact, in recording the total number of contacts as well as contacts per five-minute period. They were more reliable in observing dominative contacts than integrative contacts.

The number of contacts per hour was computed for contacts with individual children and contacts with the group.

In individual contacts teachers A and C each had twice as many dominative as integrative contacts and teacher B had five times as many dominative as integrative contacts.

In group contacts the ratios were higher, all being over five to one for domination.

Teacher C had less than half as many children as teachers A and B, yet had more individual contacts per hour per child. It cannot be said that these frequencies are "too high," for there are no norms or standards. Questions were raised as to what constitutes a teacher load.

During several hours of observation some children had almost no individual contacts with the teacher; others averaged as high as 55 contacts per hour.

2

PATTERNS OF AGGRESSIVE BEHAVIOR IN EXPERIMENTALLY CREATED "SOCIAL CLIMATES"[2]

KURT LEWIN, RONALD LIPPITT, and RALPH K. WHITE

PROBLEMS AND METHODS

The present report is a preliminary summary of one phase of a series of experimental studies of group life which has as its aim a scientific approach to such questions as the following: What underlies such differing patterns of group behavior as rebellion against authority, persecution of a scapegoat, apathetic submissiveness to authoritarian domination, or attack upon an outgroup? How may differences in subgroup structure, group stratification, and potency of ego-centered and groupcentered goals be utilized as criteria for predicting the social resultants of different group atmospheres? Is not democratic group life more pleasant, but authoritarianism more efficient? These are the sorts of questions to which "opinionated" answers are many and varied today, and to which scientific answers are, on that account, all the more necessary. An experimental approach to the phenomena of group life obviously raises many difficulties of creation and scientific control, but the fruitfulness of the method seems to compensate for the added experimental problems.

In the first experiment Lippitt organized two clubs of 10-year-old children, who engaged in the activity of theatrical mask-making for a period of three months. The same adult leader, changing his philosophy of leadership, led one club in an authoritarian manner and the other club in accordance with democratic techniques, while detailed observations were made by four observers. This study, reported in detail elsewhere (Lippitt, 1940), suggested more hypotheses than answers and led to a second and more extensive series of experiments by White and Lippitt. Four new clubs of 10-year-old boys were organized, on a

[2] From *Journal of Social Psychology* **10**, 1939, 271–299. Reprinted by permission of *Journal of Social Psychology* and the authors.

voluntary basis as before, the variety of club activities was extended, while four different adult leaders participated. To the variables of authoritarian and democratic procedure was added a third, "laissez-faire" or group life without adult participation. Also the behavior of each club was studied in different "social climates." Every six weeks each group had a new leader with a different technique of leadership, each club having three leaders during the course of the five months of the experimental series. The data on aggressive behavior summarized in this paper are drawn from both series of experiments.

Some of the techniques used for the equating of groups have been described previously (Lewin and Lippitt, 1938), but will be summarized here with the improvements in method of the second experiment. Before the clubs were organized the schoolroom group as a whole was studied. Using the sociometric technique developed by Moreno (1934) the interpersonal relations of the children, in terms of rejections, friendships, and leadership, were ascertained. Teacher ratings on relevant items of social behavior (e.g. teasing, showing off, obedience, physical energy) were secured, and observations were made on the playground and in the schoolroom by the investigators. The school records supplied information on intellectual status, physical status, and socioeconomic background. From the larger number of eager volunteers in each room it was then possible to select from each schoolroom two five-member clubs which were carefully equated on patterns of interpersonal relationships, intellectual, physical, and socio-economic status, in addition to personality characteristics. The attempt was not to equate the boys within a particular club, but to ensure the same pattern in each group as a whole.

In spite of the methods described above to control by selection some of the more elusive social variables, it was essential to use a number of experimental controls which would help to make the results more clear-cut. First of all, to check on the "individuality" of the club as a whole, each group was studied in different social atmospheres so that it could be compared with itself. A second question raised by the first experiment was that concerning the personality of the leader as a factor in the creating of social atmospheres. The second experiment, with four leaders, makes possible a comparison of the authoritarianism and democracy of four different leaders, and the "laissez-faire" method of two different leaders. In two cases it is also possible to compare the same atmosphere, created by two different leaders with the same club.

One other type of control seemed very important, the nature of the club activity, and the physical setting. Using the same clubrooms (two clubs met at the same time in adjacent but distinctly separate areas of the same large room) seemed to answer the latter problem, but the question of activity was more complex. The following technique was developed: a list of activities which were of interest to all the children was assembled (e.g., mask-making, mural painting, soap carving, model airplane construction, etc.). Meeting first, in chronological time, the democratic groups used these possibilities as the basis for discussion and voted upon their club activity. The authoritarian leaders were then ready, as their clubs met, to launch the same activity without choice

Table 1–5

Authoritarian	Democratic	Laissez-faire
1. All determination of policy by the leader.	1. All policies a matter of group discussion and decision, encouraged and assisted by the leader.	1. Complete freedom for group or individual decision, without any leader participation.
2. Techniques and activity steps dictated by the authority, one at a time, so that future steps were always uncertain to a large degree.	2. Activity perspective gained during first discussion period. General steps to group goal sketched, and where technical advice was needed the leader suggested two or three alternative procedures from which choice could be made.	2. Various materials supplied by the leader, who made it clear that he would supply information when asked. He took no other part in work discussions.
3. The leader usually dictated the particular work task and work companions of each member.	3. The members were free to work with whomever they chose, and the division of tasks was left up to the group.	3. Complete nonparticipation by leader.
4. The dominator was "personal" in his praise and criticism of the work of each member, but remained aloof from active group participation except when demonstrating. He was friendly or impersonal rather than openly hostile.	4. The leader was "objective" or "fact-minded" in his praise and criticism, and tried to be a regular group member in spirit without doing too much of the work.	4. Very infrequent comments on member activities unless questioned, and no attempt to participate or interfere with the course of events.

by the members. The "laissez-faire" groups were acquainted with the variety of materials which were available, but they were not otherwise influenced in their choice of activity; in their case, consequently, the activity factor could not be completely controlled.

The contrasting methods of the leaders in creating the three types of group atmosphere may be briefly summarized as in Table 1–5.

It should be clear that due to the voluntary nature of the group participation, and the cooperation of the parents and school systems, no radically autocratic methods (e.g. use of threats, instilling fear, etc.) were used. Fairly congenial extra-club relationships were maintained with each member by the leader.

The kinds of data collected during the course of the experiments may be classed roughly as: (a) pre-club data, described above in relation to the problem of equating the groups; (b) observations of behavior in the experimental situation; and (c) extra-club information.

Observations of club behavior consisted of:

a) A quantitative running account of the social interactions of the five children and the leader, in terms of symbols for directive, compliant, and objective (fact-minded) approaches and responses, including a category of purposeful refusal to respond to a social approach.

b) A minute by minute group structure analysis giving a record of: activity sub-groupings, the activity goal of each sub-group was initiated by the leader or spontaneously formed by the children, and ratings on degree of unity of each sub-grouping.

c) An interpretive running account of significant member actions, and changes in dynamics of the group as a whole.

d) Continuous stenographic records of all conversation.

e) An interpretive running account of inter-club relationships.

f) An "impressionistic" write-up by the leader as to what he saw and felt from within the group atmosphere during each meeting.

g) Comments by guest observers.

h) Movie records of several segments of club life.

All of these observations (except f, g, and h) were synchronized at minute intervals so that side by side they furnish a rather complete cross sectional picture of the ongoing life of the group. The major purpose of this experiment in methodology of observation was to record as fully and with as much insight as possible the total behavior of the group, a distinct breakaway from the usual procedure of recording only certain predetermined symptoms of behavior. The second aim was to ascertain whether data collected by this method could be fruitfully analyzed from both a sociological and psychological point of view (Lewin, 1939a).

Extra-club information is of the following types:

a) Interviews with each child by a friendly "non-club" person during each transition period (from one kind of group atmosphere and leader to another) and at the end of the experiment, concerning such items as comparisons of present club leader with previous ones, with the teacher, and with parents; opinions on club activities; how the club could be run better; who were the best and poorest club members; what an ideal club leader would be like, etc.

b) Interviews with the parents by the investigators, concentrating on kinds of discipline used in the home, status of the child in the family group (relations with siblings, etc.), personality ratings on the same scale used by the teachers, discussion of child's attitude toward the club, school, and other group activities.

c) Talks with the teachers concerning the transfer to the schoolroom, of behavior patterns acquired in the club.

d) Administration of a Rorschach test to each club member.

e) Conversations with the children during two summer hikes arranged after the experiment was over.

These data were gathered with a view to correlating the individual pattern of behavior in the club situation with the types of group membership which existed outside the experiment, and with the more or less stable individual personality structure. The individual differences in "social plasticity" seem to be rather striking.

Two other points of experimental technique seem of interest. The first concerns the introduction of observers into the club situation. In Lippitt's first experiment it was found that four observers grouped around a table in a physically separated part of the club room attracted virtually no attention if it was explained at the first meeting that "those are some people interested in learning how a mask-making club goes; they have plenty to do so they won't bother us and we won't bother them." In the second experiment the arrangement was even more advantageous and seemed to make for equally unselfconscious behavior on the part of the clubs. In this set-up the lighting arrangement was such that the observers were grouped behind a low burlap wall in a darkly shaded area, and seemed "not to exist at all" as far as the children and leaders were concerned.

The second point of interest is the development of a number of "group test" situations, which aided greatly in getting at the actual social dynamics of a given group atmosphere. One test used systematically was for the leader to leave the room on business during the course of the club meeting, so that the "social pressure" factor could be analyzed more realistically. Another practice was for the leader to arrive a few minutes late so that the observers could record the individual and "atmospheric" differences in spontaneous work initiation and work perspective. A third fruitful technique was that of having a stranger (a graduate student who played the role of a janitor or electrician) enter the club situation and criticize the group's work efforts. A rather dramatic picture of the results of this type of situation may be seen in Figs. 1–12 and 1–13. Further variations of such experimental manipulations are being utilized in research now in progress.

RESULTS

The analysis of the results from the second experiment is now proceeding in various directions, following two main trends: (a) interpretation of sociological or "group-centered" data; (b) interpretation of psychological or "individual-centered" data. The sociological approach includes such analyses as differences in volume of social interaction related to social atmosphere, nature of club activity, out-group relationship, differences in pattern of interaction related to outgroup and ingroup orientation, atmosphere differences in leader group relationship, effect upon group structure pattern of social atmosphere and types of activity, group differences in language behavior, etc. The psychological approach includes such analyses as relation of home background to pattern of club behavior, range of variation of member behavior in different types of social atmosphere, patterns of individual reaction to atmosphere transitions in relation to case history data, correlation between position in group stratification and pattern of social action, etc. In this paper will be presented only certain data from the partially completed general analysis which are relevant to the dynamics of individual and group aggression.

We might first recall one or two of the most striking results of the first experiment (Lippitt, 1940). As the club meetings progressed the authoritarian club members developed a pattern of aggressive domination toward one another, and their relation to the leader was one of submission or of persistent demands for attention. The interactions in the democratic club were more spontaneous, more fact-minded, and friendly. Relations to the leader were free and on an "equality basis." Comparing the two groups on the one item of overt hostility the authoritarian group was surprisingly more aggressive, the ratio being 40–1. Comparing a constellation of "ego-involved" types of language behavior (e.g., hostile, resistant, demands for attention, hostile criticism, expression of competition) with a group of objective or "nonemotive behaviors," it was found that in the authoritarian group 73% of the analyzed language behavior was of the "ego-involved" type as compared to 31% in the democratic club. Into the objective category went 69% of the behavior of the democratic group as compared to 37% of the language activities of the authoritarian group.

A second type of data related to the dynamics of aggression as it existed in the first experiment may be seen in Fig. 1–8. Twice during the course of the meetings of the authoritarian club the situation shifted from one of mutual aggression between all members to one of concentrated aggression toward one member by the other four. In both cases the lowered status of a scapegoat position was so acutely unpleasant that the member left the group, rationalizing his break from the club by such remarks as, "The doctor says my eyes are so bad I'll have to play outdoors in the sunshine instead of coming to club meetings." Interestingly enough the two members who were singled out for persecution had been rated by the teachers as the two leaders in the group, one of them scoring second in popularity by the sociometric technique, as well as being physically the strongest. After the emergence of both scapegoats, there was a rather brief rise in friendly cooperative behavior between the other members of the group.

In the second experiment (see previous discussion) there were five democratic, five autocratic, and two "laissez-faire" atmospheres. The fact that the leaders were successful in modifying their behavior to correspond to these three philosophies of leadership is clear on the basis of several quantitative in-

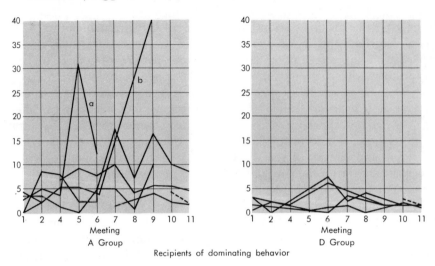

FIG. 1–8. The emergence of scapegoats in an autocratic atmosphere (Lippitt, 1937). The curves (which indicate the amount of aggression directed against each individual) show a much lower general level of dominating behavior in the democratic (D) than in the autocratic (A) group. Twice during the meetings of the authoritarian club the aggression of four members was focused upon the fifth (a and b). In both cases the scapegoat dropped out of the group immediately or soon afterwards.

dices. For instance, the ratio of "directive" to "compliant" behavior on the part of the autocratic leaders was 63 to 1; on the part of the democratic leaders it was 1.1 to 1. The total amount of leader participation was less than half as great in "laissez-faire" as in either autocracy or democracy.

The data on aggression averages in these three atmospheres are summarized in Figs. 1–9, 1–10, and 1–11. All of them indicate average amounts of aggression per 50-minute club meeting. They represent behavior records, as recorded by the interaction observer, and include all social actions, both verbal and physical, which he designated as "hostile" or "joking hostile." Figure 1–9 shows especially the bimodal character of the aggression average in autocracy; four of the five autocracies had an extremely low level of aggression, and the fifth had an extremely high one. For comparison, a sixth bar has been added to represent aggression in Lippitt's 1937 experiment, computed on the same basis. It is obviously comparable with the single case of exceptionally aggressive behavior in the 1938 experiment. For comparison, also, four lines have been added which indicate the aggression level in the two laissez-faire groups, in the four 1938 democracies, and in Lippitt's 1937 democracy. It can be seen that two of the six autocracies are above the entire range of the democracies.

Figures 1–10 and 1–11 show especially the character of the experimental controls. Together, they show how each of four groups was carried through

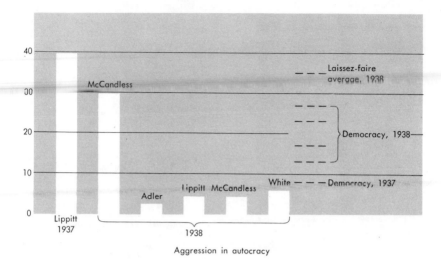

FIG. 1–9. The amount of aggression is either very great or very small compared with aggression in democracy.

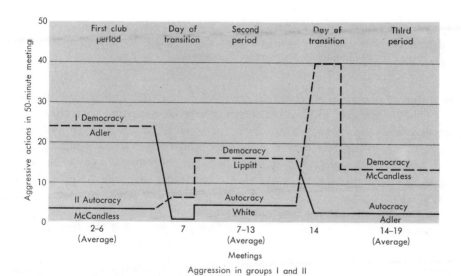

FIG. 1–10. The same group in different atmospheres. In each group, the aggression was at a medium level in democracy and at a very low level in autocracy. Note that the leaders in the third period were the same as in the first, but reversed. Note also the sharp rise of aggression in one group on the day of transition to democracy. Group I shows "release of tension" on the first day of freedom (14) after apathetic autocracy. The name of the leader is indicated below that of the atmosphere.

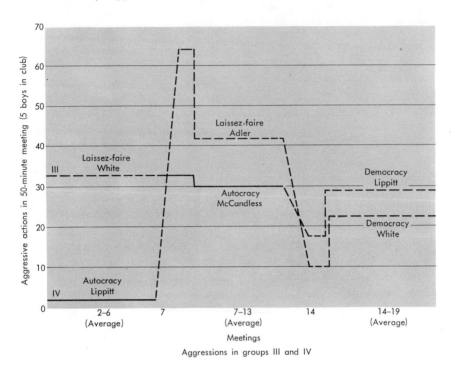

FIG. 1–11. The same group in different atmospheres. Group IV shows changes to the levels typical for each atmosphere. It shows also the "release of tension" on the first day of freedom (7) after apathetic autocracy. Group III seemed resistant to change; it was relatively aggressive even in democracy.

three different periods with three different adult leaders. The relative importance of the deliberately created social atmosphere, as compared with either the personality make-up of the group or the personality of the adult leader, can be estimated from the character of these curves. It is clear that the same group usually changes markedly, and sometimes to an extreme degree when it is changed to a new atmosphere under a different leader. In such transitions the factor of group personnel is held relatively constant, while the factors of leader personality and social atmosphere are varied. In addition, the factor of leader personality was systematically varied, as can be seen if the four curves are compared with each other. Each of the four leaders played the role of a democratic leader at least once; also each played the role of an autocrat at least once; two of them (Adler and White) played in addition the role of bystander in a "laissez-faire" group. One leader (Lippitt) was democratic with two different groups; and one (McCandless) was autocratic with two different groups. Through this systematic variation of both club personnel and leader's personality, the effects of the deliberately created social atmosphere (autocracy, democracy, and laissez-faire) stand out more clearly and more reliably than would otherwise be possible.

In Fig. 1–10, for instance, the two curves both tell the same story; a moderate amount of aggression in democracy and an abnormally small amount in autocracy, regardless of the personality of the leader (note that the roles of Lippitt and McCandless were reversed, with each playing once the role of autocrat and once the role of democratic leader), and regardless of the personnel of the group itself (note that the curves cross once when the atmospheres are reversed, and cross back again when the atmospheres return to what they were at the beginning). In Fig. 1–11, the two laissez-faire atmospheres give very high levels of aggression although different groups and different leaders are involved. The most extreme change of behavior recorded in any group occurred when Group IV was changed from autocracy (in which it had shown the apathetic reaction) to laissez-faire. One of the autocratic groups (Fig. 1–11) reacted apathetically, the other very aggressively. The aggressiveness of Group III may be due to the personalities of the boys, or to the fact that they had just previously "run wild" in laissez-faire.

The average number of aggressive actions per meeting in the different atmospheres was as follows:

Laissez-faire	38
Autocracy (aggressive reaction)	30
Democracy	20
Autocracy (apathetic reaction)	2

Critical ratios for these comparisons have not yet been computed. The data are comparable, however, with Lippitt's 1937 data, in which the critical ratios for the more important indices ranged between 4.5 and 7.5.

In the interpretation of these data it is natural to ask: Why are the results for autocracy so paradoxical? Why is the reaction to autocracy sometimes very aggressive, with much rebellion or persecution of scapegoats, and sometimes very nonaggressive? Are the underlying dynamics in these two cases as different as the surface behavior? The high level of aggression in some autocracies has often been interpreted mainly in terms of tension, which presumably results from frustration of individual goals. Is it, then, an indicaton of non-frustration when the aggression level in some other autocracies is found to be extremely low?

Four lines of evidence in our experiments indicate that this is not the case, and that the low level of aggression in the apathetic autocracies is not due to lack of frustration.

First of all, there are the sudden outbursts of aggression which occurred on the days of transition from a repressed autocratic atmosphere to the much freer atmosphere of democracy or laissez-faire. Two of these are well illustrated in Fig. 1–11. The boys behaved just as if they had previously been in a state of bottled-up tension, which could not show itself overtly as long as the repressive influence of the autocrat was felt, but which burst out unmistakably when that pressure was removed.

A second and very similar type of evidence can be obtained from the records on the days when the leader left the room for 10 or 15 minutes. In the three other atmospheres (laissez-faire, aggressive autocracy, and democracy) the aggression level did not rise when the leader left the room. In the apathetic autocracies, however, the level of aggression rises very rapidly to 10 times its former level. These data should not be overstressed because aggression even then does not rise to a level significantly above that of the other atmospheres. It is so extremely low in the apathetic atmosphere that even multiplication by 10 does not produce what could be called a high level of aggression. (The effect of the leader's absence is shown more significantly in a deterioration of work than in an outburst of aggression.) Nevertheless, the rapid disappearance of apathy when the leader goes out shows clearly that it was due to the repressive influence of the leader rather than to any particular absence of frustration. In this connection it should be added that the autocratic leader never forbade aggression. His "repressive influence" was not a prohibition created by explicit command but a sort of generalized inhibition or restraining force.

In the third place, there are the judgments of observers who found themselves using such terms as "dull," "lifeless," "submissive," "repressed," and "apathetic" in describing the nonaggressive reaction to autocracy. There was little smiling, joking, freedom of movement, freedom of initiating new projects, etc.; talk was largely confined to the immediate activity in progress, and bodily tension was often manifested. Moving pictures tell the same story. The impression created was not one of acute discontent, by any means, and the activities themselves were apparently enjoyable enough so that the net result for most of the boys was more pleasant than unpleasant. Nevertheless, they could not be described as genuinely contented.

The fourth indication and perhaps the most convincing indication of the existence of frustration in these atmospheres is the testimony of the boys themselves. They were individually interviewed, just before each day of transition to a new atmosphere, and again at the end of the whole experiment. The interviewing was done by an adult who had not served as a leader in the boy's own group. On the whole good rapport was achieved, and the boys talked rather freely, comparing the three leaders under whom their club had been conducted. (For them it was a question of comparing leaders they liked or did not like, as they were unaware of the deliberate change in the behavior of the same leader from one atmosphere to another or of the nature of the experiment.) With surprising unanimity the boys agreed in a relative dislike for their autocratic leader regardless of his individual personality. Nineteen of the 20 boys liked their leader in democracy better than their leader in autocracy. The twentieth boy, as it happened, was the son of an army officer (the only one in the group), and consciously put a high value upon strict discipline. As he expressed it, the autocratic leader "was the strictest, and I like that a lot." The other two leaders "let us go ahead and fight, and that isn't good." For the other 19, strictness was not necessarily a virtue, their description of the autocrat being that he was "too strict." Typical comments about the autocrat were: "he didn't let us do what we wanted to do"; "he wouldn't let us go behind the burlap"; "he was all right mostly, sort of dictator-like"; "we just had to do things; he wanted us to get it done in a hurry"; "he made us make masks, and the boys didn't like that"; "the other two guys suggested and we could do it or not, but not with him"; "we didn't have any fun with him; we didn't have any fights." Typical comments about the democratic leader were: "he was a good sport, worked along with us and thinks of things just like we do"; "he never did try to be the boss, but we always had plenty to do"; "just the right combination, nothing I didn't like about him"; "we all liked him; he let us tear down the burlap and everything." These comments were almost uniformly dependent upon the role played by the leader, and were exactly reversed when he played a different role.

As between the leaders in autocracy and "laissez-faire," the preference was for the "laissez-faire" leader in seven cases out of ten. The three boys who preferred the autocrat made such comments about the "laissez-faire" leader as: "he was too easy-going"; "he had too few things for us to do"; "he let us figure things out too much"; in contrast the autocrat "told us what to do, and we had something to do all the time." For the other seven, even disorder was preferable to rigidity: "we could do what we pleased with him"; "he wasn't strict at all."

Another form of aggression was outgroup hostility, as manifested especially in two "wars" between clubs meeting in the same large room at the same time. Both wars seemed to be mainly in a spirit of play. They were much more like snowball fights than serious conflicts. (This is one more reason why in this case one should be cautious in comparing adult political phenomena directly with our data on small groups of children.) Our two small "wars" are interesting in their own right, however, especially since the same general constellation of factors seemed to be operating in both cases.

The curves of rising hostility, computed for five-minute intervals, are shown in Figs. 1–12 and 1–13. From these curves it can be seen that the first "war" started gradually, with a long period of minor bickering and name calling, followed by a much steeper gradient of increasing hostility. The overt hostilities consisted of throwing water, small pieces of clay (which nearly always missed their mark), and sometimes water color paint, flicked from the end of a long paint brush. No one was hurt. The second conflict (Fig. 1–13) began much more suddenly. Name calling began in the first minute after the "hostile stranger" left the room, and almost immediately the boys seemed to remember their previous conflict and to wish a repetition of it. Beginning with verbal aggression such as, "Why don't you learn to talk, you sissies?" they passed within three minutes to throwing small pieces of soap (small pieces of soap statuettes, which they had carved, were lying about), and within five minutes nearly all the boys on both sides were wholeheartedly participating. This difference in steepness of the hostility gradient was perhaps due in part to a higher level of tension or to weaker restraining forces on the

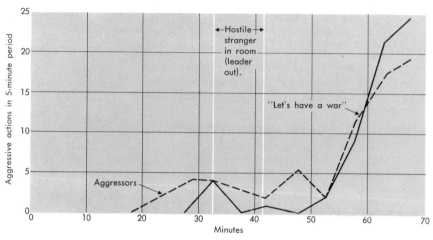

Outgroup aggression, sixth meeting

FIG. 1–12. Conflict between groups after intrusion of hostile stranger. After the stranger left, strong hostility developed between the two groups. Before the major conflict, minor hostilities had already occurred, with one or two members of the *laissez-faire* group playing the role of aggressors. This *laissez-faire* group, White's, is shown with a dotted line; Adler's democracy group is shown by a solid line.

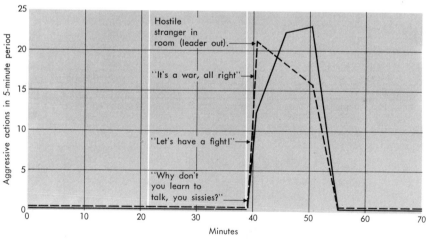

Outgroup aggression, nineteenth meeting

FIG. 1–13. Conflict between groups after intrusion of hostile stranger. The intrusion of a hostile stranger was followed by intergroup conflict (as in Figure 1–12). In this case the hostilities began suddenly, rising within four minutes almost to their maximum level. McCandless' democracy group is represented by a solid line; Lippitt's by a dashed line.

later occasion, but it seemed to be due also to a cognitive difference. On the later occasion the pattern of intergroup conflict had been established; it was, by that time, a part of the boys' "cognitive structure," a clearly defined region which they could enter or not as they chose; and since they had found the first "war" to be very pleasantly exciting, they readily and quickly entered the same region again when the general psychological situation was conducive to conflict. In this connection it may be noted that the second conflict was labelled verbally almost immediately, while the first one was not labelled until it was already well under way. On the first occasion the shout, "Let's have a war!" went up long after the minor hostilities had begun; on the second occasion, one boy shouted, "Let's have a fight," only two minutes after the name calling began, and another one legalized it two minutes later with the words, "It's a war all right."

Certain similarities between the two days of conflict suggest some very tentative hypotheses as to the psychological factors conducive to this sort of conflict. In the first place, both occurred on days when, with the adult leader absent, a hostile stranger had been in the room and had criticized the work which the boys were doing. This had been deliberately planned as a "test situation"; a graduate student, playing the role of a janitor or an electrician, was the hostile stranger. It may be doubtful whether or not the term "substitute hate object" is an appropriate one here; but there was no question in the observers' minds that in both cases the intrusion of the stranger tended to disorganize the regular play activities of the clubs and to build up a tense, restless psychological condition which was conducive to intergroup conflict. In the second place, both conflicts started when no respected adult was present. In the first one the main aggressors were unquestionably the laissez-faire group (see Fig. 1–12). Their leader was physically present at the time, but he was psychologically unimportant. The second conflict began when the leaders on both sides were out of the room, and by the time the leaders returned, it had gathered great momentum. In the third place, both conflicts occurred at a time when there was no absorbing group activity as an alternative. The first one began at a time when the members of the laissez-faire group seemed unusually bored and dissatisfied with their own lack of solid accomplishment. The second one began after the boys had become somewhat bored with their soap carving, and after this individualistic activity had been further disrupted by the criticisms of the stranger.

The free direct expression of aggression by the "wars" following frustration in the *laissez-faire* and democratic situations offers a contrast to several other patterns of expression which were observed in some of the authoritarian situations. These types of behavior might be briefly labelled: (a) a "strike"; (b) rebellious acts; (c) reciprocal aggression among all members; (d) scapegoat attack; (e) release behavior after a decrease in leader pressure; (f) aggression against impersonal "substitute hate objects."

Both the "strike" and symptoms of rebellious action occurred in the aggressive type of autocracy. About the middle of the series of six meetings the club members went to their teacher with a letter of resignation signed by four of them. They asked their teacher to give this to the leader when he came to get them after school. The teacher refused to act as a go-between, suggesting that the boys go to the leader directly, but when he appeared after school, courage seemed to wane and they all went to the meeting as usual. Overt rebellious acts were of the following nature: breaking a rule by carving on the posts in the clubroom (while casting sidelong glances at the leader), deliberately walking behind the burlap walls of the clubroom without permission (mentioned to an interviewer), leaving the club meeting early, and pretending not to hear when spoken to by the leader. The third and fourth kinds of behavior were also typical of aggressive authoritarianism and have been mentioned in describing the first experiment during which two scapegoats emerged. As has been mentioned, changes in amount of aggression while the leader was out, and days of transition to a freer atmosphere were especially good indicators of the existence of unexpressed tension in the apathetic autocracies.

Two very interesting examples of what we have tentatively called "release behavior through an impersonal substitute hate object" are worthy of description. During the eleventh meeting of the first experiment the authoritarian group was given a chance to indicate by secret ballot whether they would like the club to stop or continue for several more meetings. We may go to an observer's record for further comments:

Peculiar actions follow the leader's announcement that because of the vote there will be no more meetings after today. The leader asks RO and J to put the paper on the floor as usual. They put it down and run and jump on it in a wild manner. The group masks are divided among the members and J immediately begins to throw his around violently, pretending to jump on it. He throws it down again and again, laughing. R wants to know if it won't break, then starts to throw his down too. Later J and RO chase each other around the room wildly with streamers of towelling. . . .

Rather clearly the work products of this authoritarian atmosphere seemed to be the objects of aggressive attack rather than the objects of prideful ownership.

During a last meeting of the second experiment a rather similar burst of behavior occurred in one of the democratic groups. The group was highly involved in an activity of making an oil painting on glass. While the leader was out for a short time (by arrangement) a student in the janitor role came in to sweep. From the running accountist's record of the twenty-second minute we find,

He is making dirt fly and sweeping it toward the group. They all begin to cough but don't move from their work. Several minutes later we find the comment, Janitor has almost swept them away, but still no hostile response. The project seems to have a very high valence.

Five minutes later the janitor had gotten them out of their chairs in order to sweep, then

the janitor accidentally knocks a piece of their glass on the floor. They all yell and R makes as if to throw something at him. F says that if the leader were here he would beat up the janitor.

Five minutes later, after a number of comments criticizing the art work of the club, the janitor left. The members dropped their work completely, climbed the rafters and made considerable noise. On the thirty-sixth minute we find,

R comes down from the rafter and begins to complain about the janitor, L joins him and they all complain bitterly and loudly.

Within three minutes the group began to destroy a large wooden sign upon which they had painted the club name. Such comments as this appear in the running account.

F is wielding two hammers at once . . . R is busy pulling out all the nails . . . They are excited . . . F knocks the first hole through it . . . R tries to caution F for a minute, and then gets busy himself . . . their unexpressed aggression toward the janitor is taking a violent outlet . . . they are all very serious and vicious about the destruction of the sign . . . they seem to be getting a great deal of "pure animal pleasure" out of the pillage.

The meeting ended with three or four minutes of pleasant conversation.

INTERPRETIVE COMMENTS

From the many theoretical problems involved we should like to discuss but one; namely, the problem of aggression and apathy. Even here we wish to show the complexity of the problem and its possible attack from a field theoretical point of view rather than to set forth a definite theory.

It is not easy to say what aggression is, that is, if one is not satisfied with mere verbal definition. One important aspect obviously is that one group or an individual within a group turns against another group (or individual). In case these groups are subgroups of one original group, it can be called aggression within a group, otherwise aggression against an outgroup.

Both kinds of aggression occurred in our experiments. All of these aggressions were spontaneous in character. In other words, it was not a situation where a group of people are ordered by a politically dominating power (like the state) to indulge in a certain type of directed activity called war. On the whole the aggression was the outcome of the momentary emotional situation, although in two cases the aggressions had definitely the character of a fight of one group against another group and showed a certain amount of cooperative organization within each group.

It is necessary to mention four points which seem to play a dominant role in the spontaneous aggressions: tension, the space of free movement, rigidity of group structure, and the style of living (culture).

1. Tension

An instance where tension was created by annoying experiences occurred when the group work was criticized by a stranger (janitor). There were two cases where fighting broke out immediately afterwards.

In the autocratic atmosphere the behavior of the leader probably annoyed the children considerably (to judge from the interviews reported above).

In addition, there were six times as many directing approaches to an individual by the leader in autocracy than in democracy (Fig. 1–14). It is probably fair to assume that the bombardment with such frequent ascendant approaches is equivalent to higher pressure and that this pressure created a higher tension.

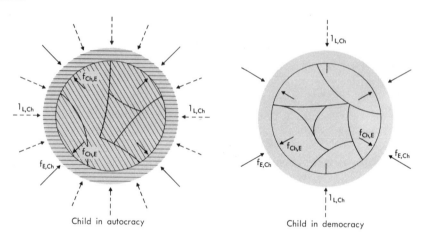

FIG. 1–14. Leader pressure and child tension. In the authoritarian situation the leader makes six times as many directing approaches ($1_{L, Ch}$) to the child member as in the democratic situation. This creates social pressure (equivalent to forces $f_{E, Ch}$ of the environment on the child) and therefore a higher state of tension in the child in the autocratic group; this tension demands some sort of outlet toward the environment (equivalent to forces $f_{CH, E}$).

2. Narrow space of free movement as a source of tension

On the whole, even more important than this single annoying experience was the general atmosphere of the situation. Experiments in individual psychology (Lewin, 1935) seemed to indicate that lack of space of free movement is equivalent to higher pressure; both conditions seem to create tension. This seemed particularly true if an originally larger space was narrowed down (one is reminded here of the physical tension created by decreasing volume, although one should not overstress the analogy).

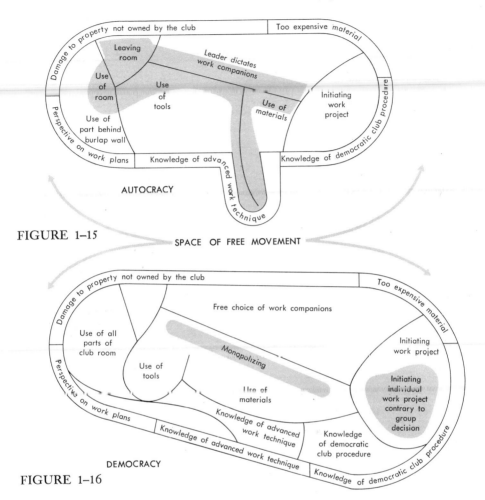

FIGURE 1–15

FIGURE 1–16

FIGS. 1–15 and 1–16. Space of free movement in autocracy and democracy. In the autocratic situation the space of free movement (within the dotted lines) was originally bounded by the limitation in ability and knowledge (peripheral areas) of the members, but was soon limited much further by the social influence of the leader. In democracy the space was increased to the whole figure, excepting that within dotted lines, with the help of the leader.

Our experiments seemed to indicate that a similar relation between the narrow space of free movement and high tension holds also in regard to groups. The space of free movement in autocracy was smaller in relation to the activities permitted and the social status which could be reached (Figs. 1–15 and 1–16). In laissez-faire, contrary to expectations, the space of free movement was not larger but smaller than in democracy, partly because of the lack of time perspective and partly because of the interference of the work of one individual with the activities of his fellows.

3. Aggression as the effect of tension

The annoying occurrences, the pressure applied by the leader, and the lack of space of free movement, are three basic facts which brought up a higher tension. Our experiments indicate that this higher tension might suffice to create aggression. This seems to be of theoretical importance; obviously some aggressive acts can be viewed mainly as a kind of "purposive" action (for instance, to destroy a danger), and one might ask whether or not this component is an essential part in the causation of any aggression. In our experiments, the two wars between the two outgroups can hardly be classified in this way. They seemed to be rather clear cases where aggression was "emotional expression" of an underlying tension.

4. Rigidity of group structure

However, to understand aggression one will have to realize that tension is only one of the factors which determine whether or not an aggressive action will take place. The building up of tension can be said to be equivalent to the creation of a certain type of need which might express itself in aggressive action. Tension sets up the driving force (Lewin, 1938) for the aggression (in the two situations with which we are dealing). However, whether these driving forces actually lead to aggression or to some other behavior, for instance that of leaving the group, depends on additional characteristics of the situation as a whole. One of these seems to be the rigidity of the social position of the person within the group.

Aggression within a group can be viewed as a process by which one part of the group sets itself in opposition to another part of the group, in this way breaking the unity of the group. Of course, this separation is only of a certain degree.

In other words, if M indicates a member or a subgroup and Gr the whole group, an aggression involves a force acting on the subgroup in the direction away from the main group (fm-Gr) or other part of the subgroup. From this it should follow theoretically that if a subgroup can easily locomote in the direction away from the group it will do so in case this force shows any significant strength. In other words, a strong tension and an actual aggression will be built up only in case there exist forces which hinder the subgroup from leaving the group (Fig. 1–17).

Cultural anthropology gives examples which might be interpreted from this angle. The Arapesh (Mead, 1937), for instance, are living in a society where everyone is a member of a great variety of different groups and seems to shift easily from one group to another; it is a society without rigidly fixed social position. The fact that they show extremely little aggression might well be linked with this lack of rigid social structure.

Another example might be seen in the fact that adolescents who have been kept within the family probably show more aggression; in other words, the more rigid the family structure the more difficult it is for them to move from childhood to adulthood.

An additional example is the well-known fact that narrow family ties which serve to make it difficult for husband and wife to leave each other may make aggression between them particularly violent.

In our experiment, autocracy provided a much more rigid social group than democracy. It was particularly difficult for the members of an autocracy to change their social status (Lewin, 1939). On the other hand, in both groups the member did not like to leave the group as a whole because of the interest in the work project and the feeling of responsibility to the adult leader.

On the whole, then, the rigidity of the group will function as a restraining force (Lewin, 1938) against locomotion away from the group, or from the position within the group. Sufficient strength of this restraining force seems to be one of the conditions for the building up of a tension which is sufficiently high to lead to aggression.

It can be seen easily that the barriers limiting the space of free movement may have a similar function. We mentioned above, that a narrow space of free movement seems to be equivalent to pressure, and, in this way, creates tension. At the same time, the barriers prevent locomotion, thus providing the restraining forces necessary for building up higher tension.

It was already mentioned that these restraining forces are particularly strong in our autocratic group (Fig. 1–17).

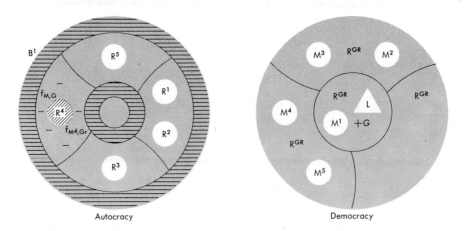

Autocracy   Democracy

FIG. 1–17. Rigidity of group structure as a tension factor. In autocracy where each member of subgroup (M^1, M^2...M^5) has a circumscribed region of activity (R^1, R^2...R^5), and especially where the central regions of group life (polity formation R^P) are inaccessible to most members, rigid barriers (B) to own goals (G) continually frustrate members' efforts. The member's own position in the group structure (R^4) therefore acquires a negative valence, usually creating a force away from group membership $f_{M^4, -Gr}$). But in rigid group structures a restraining barrier (B^1) keeps members or subgroups from leaving until a very high state of tension develops.

5. Style of living (culture)

Whether or not a given amount of tension and given restraining forces will cause a person to become aggressive depends finally upon the particular patterns of action which are customarily used in the culture in which he lives. The different styles of living can be viewed as different ways a given problem is usually solved. A person living in a culture where a show of dominance is "the thing to do" under certain conditions will hardly think of any other way in which the solution of this problem may be approached. Such social patterns are comparable to "habits." Indeed, individual habits as well as cultural patterns have dynamically the character of restraining forces against leaving the paths determined by these patterns. In addition, they determine the cognitive structure which a given situation is likely to have for a given individual.

For the problem of aggression, this cultural pattern, determined by the group in which an individual lives and by his past history, is of great importance. It determines under what conditions aggression will be, for the individual concerned, the "distinguished path" to the goal (Lewin, 1938). It determines how easily a situation will show for him a cognitive structure where aggression appears to be one possible path for his action (Fig. 1–18).

The factors named are sufficient to warn against any "one-factor" theory of aggression. Here, as in regard to any other behavior, it is the specific constellation of the field as a whole that determines whether or not aggression will occur. In every case one has to consider both the driving and the restraining forces and the cognitive structure of the field. Such a field theoretical approach seems to be arduous. On the other hand, only in this way will one be

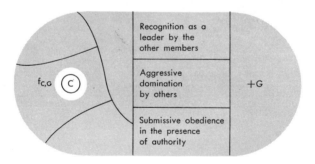

FIG. 1–18. Different styles of living as represented by different distinguished paths (aggressive autocracy). The goal (G) of maximum social status and space of free movement can be reached by one or more of several procedures, depending on actual possibilities and the prevailing mode of behavior in that group. In our "experimentally created cultures," the distinguished path to G was, for a child (C) in aggressive autocracy, that of aggressive domination of other members. In a similar situation the distinguished path for a member of democratic groups seemed to be that of gaining voluntary recognition of the other members as a leader through work and social efforts. In the situation of apathetic authoritarianism the path seemed to be that of submissive obedience to authority, which might win praise from the leader.

able to understand for instance the paradox of behavior that autocracy may lead either to aggression or to apathy. It was stated that aggression is partly to be viewed as an emotional outbreak due to tension and that this tension, in turn, is due to pressure and restraining forces (lack of space of free movement). We have apathy when the pressure and the restraining forces from without are kept stronger than the forces (fch, E in Fig. 1–14) within the person which lead to the emotional expression, and are due to the tension. Whether or not the forces from without or those from within are stronger depends upon the absolute amount of pressure and also on the "willingness" of the person to "accept" the pressure.

The field theoretical approach also provides indications for the circumstances under which one might generalize the results of such experimental group studies. One must be careful of making too hasty generalizations, perhaps especially in the field of political science. The varieties of democracies, autocracies, or "laissez-faire" atmospheres are, of course, very numerous. Besides, there are always individual differences of character and background to consider. On the other hand, it would be wrong to minimize the possibility of generalization. The answer in social psychology and sociology has to be the same as in an experiment in any science. The essence of an experiment is to create a situation which shows a certain pattern. What happens depends by and large upon this pattern and is largely, although not completely, independent of the absolute size of the field. This is one of the reasons why experiments are possible and worthwhile.

The generalization from an experimental situation should, therefore, go always to those life situations which show the same or sufficiently similar general patterns. This statement includes both the rights and the limitations of generalization.

SUMMARY

1. In a first experiment, Lippitt compared one group of five 10-year old children, under autocratic leadership, with a comparable group under democratic leadership. In a second experiment, Lippitt and White studied four comparable clubs of 10-year old boys, each of which passed successively through three club periods in such a way that there were altogether five democratic periods, five autocratic periods, and two "laissez-faire" periods.

2. In the second experiment, the factor of personality differences in the boys was controlled by having each group pass through autocracy and then democracy, or vice versa. The factor of leader's personality was controlled by having each of four leaders play the role of autocrat and the role of democratic leader at least once.

3. Records on each club meeting include stenographic records of conversation, quantitative symbolic records of group structure, quantitative sym-

bolic records of all social interactions, and a continuous interpretive running account. Parents and teachers were interviewed; each boy was given the Rorschach ink blots, a Moreno-type questionnaire, and was interviewed three times. Analysis of casual relationships between these various types of data is still far from complete. As a preliminary report we are giving here a part of the data bearing upon one specific problem, that of aggression.

4. In the first experiment, hostility was 30 times as frequent in the autocratic as in the democratic group. Aggression (including both "hostility" and "joking hostility") was eight times as frequent. Much of this aggression was directed toward two successive scapegoats within the group; none of it was directed toward the autocrat.

5. In the second experiment, one of the five autocracies showed the same aggressive reaction as was found in the first experiment. In the other four autocracies, the boys showed an extremely nonaggressive, "apathetic" pattern of behavior.

6. Four types of evidence indicate that this lack of aggression was probably not caused by lack of frustration, but by the repressive influence of the autocrat: (a) outbursts of aggression on the days of transition to a freer atmosphere; (b) a sharp rise of aggression when the autocrat left the room; (c) other indications of generalized apathy, such as an absence of smiling and joking; and (d) the fact that 19 out of 20 boys liked their democratic leader better than their autocratic leader, and 7 out of 10 also liked their "laissez-faire" leader better.

7. There were two "wars," more or less playful, and without bodily damage, between clubs meeting in the same room at the same time. The first of these began gradually, the second suddenly. Three factors, present in both cases, seemed conducive to group conflict: (a) irritation and tension produced by a hostile stranger, (b) absence of a respected adult, and (c) lack of any absorbing alternative activity.

8. There were two striking instances of aggression against impersonal objects.

9. A general interpretation of the above data on aggression can be made in terms of four underlying factors: tension, restricted space of free movement, rigidity of group structure, and style of living (culture).

3

THE DEVELOPMENT OF A TECHNIQUE FOR THE MEASUREMENT OF SOCIAL–EMOTIONAL CLIMATE IN CLASSROOMS[3]

JOHN WITHALL

RATIONALE. In the study (Withall, 1949) proper a brief overview of current theories of learning from the associationist and field-theorist point of view precedes a statement of the major concepts, gleaned largely from the field-theorists, that guide the study. Certain postulates regarding the motivational factors in personality and regarding learning conditions are proposed. The primary motivational force of human behavior is postulated to be a drive toward self-actualization. This drive is said to be influenced by:

1. Need for self-consistency.

2. Interaction in terms of an internal frame of reference.

3. Self-directive behavior.

4. Achievement of personal significance and private meanings in a social milieu.

It is postulated that learning (changes in behavior) is most likely to occur when experiences are both

1. *meaningful to the learner,* that is, are perceived by the learner as pertinent to his needs and purposes, are consistent with his personality organization, and are associated with self-directive behavior; and

[3] The author is indebted to several members of the faculty of the Department of Education at the University of Chicago for their counsel and constructive criticisms during the carrying out of the study reported here. He is particularly grateful to both Dr. Herbert A. Thelen of the Department of Education and the Department of Psychology and to Dr. Carl R. Rogers of the Department of Psychology, University of Chicago, for their facilitation of the experimenter's efforts to make the study as scientifically sound and as theoretically fruitful as possible. This article is from the *Journal of Experimental Education* 17, 1949, 347–361. Reprinted by permission of *Journal of Experimental Education* and the author.

2. *occur in a nonthreatening situation,* that is the learner is free from a sense of personal threat, interacts with others in a wholesome social milieu, and is helped to evaluate himself on the basis of objective criteria.

Since condition number one is postulated to be dependent on condition number two, some knowledge of the psychological atmosphere represented by number two is necessary. Little objective evidence exists regarding psychological atmospheres either in learning or other situations. It was decided, therefore, to attempt to develop a technique to measure social–emotional climate in the classroom through a categorization of teacher statements. It seems reasonable to assume that the teacher's behavior influences the conditions of learning since she is placed in the classroom by society to manipulate the conditions so as to facilitate learning.

ASSUMPTIONS AND HYPOTHESIS. The basic assumptions of the study are (1) that the social–emotional climate is a group phenomenon; (2) that the teacher's behavior is the most important single factor in creating climate in the classroom, and (3) that the teacher's verbal behavior is a representative sample of her total behavior.

The hypothesis to be tested is that by means of a categorization of teacher statements a valid and reliable index of social–emotional climate can be obtained.

WORK PREVIOUSLY DONE IN AREA OF CLIMATE

Some work has been done in the area of climate, notably by Ronald Lippitt at Iowa University and Harold H. Anderson at Michigan State College.

Lippitt's study

Lippitt's work in social climate is best represented by his doctoral study (1940a). In that study he organized four clubs of five boys each and gave each club successive experiences with an "autocratic" and "democratic" leader during three consecutive six-week periods. Several leaders were used to head each of the clubs. The leaders were required to employ different leadership styles with each successive group. The leadership styles were implemented in accord with certain specific criteria drafted to guide the club leaders. Records of social interaction between group members and leader, stenographic records of conversation in each club, analysis of activity subgroupings, and a running account of psychologically interesting interaction in each group were among data collected by observers of each club session.

The major conclusions of Lippitt's study were:

1. That different leadership styles produced different social climates and resulted in different group and individual behaviors;

2. That conversation categories differentiated leader-behavior techniques more adequately than social-behavior categories;

3. That autocratic leadership elicited either an aggressive rebelliousness towards the leader or an apathetic submission to the leader;

4. That leadership style was the primary factor in producing climatological differences and that club personnel was of secondary importance.

Lippitt's work represents one of the earliest and most significant attempts to observe and control the climate variable in a group situation. His findings regarding the value of categorizing verbal behavior as a means of assessing the quality of group life provides a sound basis for the methodology of this study which utilizes a categorization of teachers' verbal behaviors as its major technique.

Anderson's work

Harold H. Anderson, Joseph E. Brewer and others (1945, 1946) have conducted at Michigan State College investigations into the influence of teachers' classroom personalities on children's behavior, particularly at the primary and elementary school levels. In order to obtain objective measurements of teachers' classroom personalities and concomitant children-behavior, Anderson and Brewer developed 26 teacher-behavior categories and 29 children-behavior categories by which both teacher and pupil verbal and nonverbal behavior might be categorized. Anderson divided teacher behaviors into two main kinds, Integrative Teacher Behavior and Dominative Teacher Behavior. Integrative behavior was that which expanded the children's opportunities for self-directive and cooperative behavior with the teacher and their peers, dominative behavior tended to restrict children's activities and to lead to distracted, aggressive, noncooperative conduct. Anderson demonstrated that children's behaviors were consistent with the kind of personality the teacher displayed in the classroom.

Anderson's studies bring out evidence that is highly pertinent to the hypothesis that the main direction of influence in the classroom is from the teacher to the pupil. He has demonstrated, too, that reliable patterns of teacher and pupil behavior can be obtained in the classroom through categorizations of their overt behaviors.

Development of climate index

The concept of climate or psychological atmosphere has been used by others in the area of psychology and education besides Lippitt and Anderson. Lewin, Prescott and Rogers, for example, have made considerable use of the concept. However, no clear-cut definition of the concept can be cited and for the purpose of more effective communication and clearer understanding of the notion as used here, a definition of the term "social-emotional climate" is offered.

DEFINITION OF SOCIAL–EMOTIONAL CLIMATE. Climate is considered in this study to represent the emotional tone which is a concomitant of interpersonal interaction. It is a general emotional factor which appears to be present in interactions occurring between individuals in face-to-face groups. It seems to have some relationship to the degree of acceptance expressed by members of a group regarding each other's needs or goals. Operationally defined it is considered to influence: (1) the inner private world of each individual; (2) the *esprit de corps* of a group; (3) the sense of meaningfulness of group and individual goals and activities; (4) the objectivity with which a problem is attacked, and (5) the kind and extent of interpersonal interaction in a group.

PROCEDURE FOR IDENTIFYING CATEGORIES. Proceeding from our assumption that climate is largely determined by the teacher's behavior, we undertook an analysis of the teacher's verbal behaviors contained in sound recordings of regular class sessions. A teacher's verbal behavior is assumed to represent adequately her total behavior. Guided by the postulates regarding individual motivation and conditions of learning, teacher statements were analyzed in order to ascertain whether the teacher was utilizing behaviors likely to create the postulated conditions for learning. Individual teacher statements tended to fall into about 25 types of responses, e.g.:

1. Reproof statements made with the apparent intent of halting the pupil's present behavior and modifying future behavior;

2. Questions seeking further information from pupil about problem;

3. Statement offering simple administrative information, e.g., about place of next class meeting;

4. Questions containing reproof and a plea for cooperation;

5. Statement approving pupil's behavior and commending him;

6. Statement urging a particular course of action on the learner; and so on.

These 25 kinds of responses were soon found to overlap and to be not mutually exclusive. They were reduced to 13 and finally to 7 categories. These categories seemed to encompass all the types of statements which teachers utilized in classrooms. The categories are:

1. Learner-supportive statements that have the intent of reassuring or commending the pupil.

2. Acceptance and clarifying statements having an intent to convey to the pupil the feeling that he was understood and help him elucidate his ideas and feelings.

3. Problem-structuring statements or questions which proffer information or raise questions about the problem in an objective manner with intent to facilitate learner's problem-solving.

4. Neutral statements which comprise polite formalities, administrative comments, verbatim repetition of something that has already been said. No intent inferable.

5. Directive or hortative statements with intent to have pupil follow a recommended course of action.

6. Reproving or deprecating remarks intended to deter pupil from continued indulgence in present "unacceptable" behavior.

7. Teacher self-supporting remarks intended to sustain or justify the teacher's position or course of action.

It seemed that more than one continuum was identifiable in the seven categories; for example, a continuum from problem-centeredness to person-centeredness might be discerned, a continuum from objectivity to subjectivity or a continuum from learner-centeredness to teacher-centeredness. The latter continuum was accepted as useful in applying the categories to teachers' verbal behaviors. Categories 1, 2, and 3 were said to be learner-centered and categories 5, 6, and 7 were said to be teacher-centered. The neutral category had no influence on either bloc. Certain conventions were suggested for interpreting patterns of verbal behavior; for instance, if the proportion of statements falling into one or more of the first three categories outweighed the proportion falling into one or more of the last three categories, the teacher was said to be learner-centered. If the proportion were reversed, the teacher was said to be teacher-centered. Similarly, if the proportion of statements falling into catgory 3 outweighed the proportions falling into either categories 1 and 2 combined or categories 5, 6, and 7 combined, then the teacher was said to be more problem-centered than learner or teacher-centered. If the largest proportion fell into the combination of either categories 1 and 2 or categories 5, 6, and 7, then the teacher was said to be more highly learner-centered or more self-centered as the case might be. Once the seven categories had been identified and procedures developed for facilitating their application to data, the next step was to ascertain the objectivity, reliability, and validity of the technique.

DETERMINING THE OBJECTIVITY, RELIABILITY, AND VALIDITY OF THE CLIMATE INDEX

Objective study

The objectivity of the instrument was ascertained by having four trained judges apply the index independently to typescripts 1A, 2A, and 3A comprising 68, 71, and 45 teacher statements respectively. The percentage of agreement of each judge with the researcher was computed. The percentage of agreement was computed by the formula:

$$\text{Percentage of agreement} = \frac{\text{Number of identical statements which researcher and judge place in a given category}}{\text{Number of statements which researcher places in same category}} \times 100$$

The mean percentage of agreement between the judges and researcher on the three typescripts was:

Judge 1	64%
Judge 2	66%
Judge 3	56%
Judge 4	75%

The highest mean percentage of agreement of the four judges with the researcher on the three typescripts was 78% on category 1 and the lowest 53% on category 7. The grand mean percentage of agreement for four judges with the researcher on the three typescripts was 65%.

A further measurement of the index's objectivity was made by computing tetrachoric correlations between the categorization of each of the five judges (the researcher included) on the three typescripts. Two hundred ten r^{tets} were computed to ascertain the degree of association between each of the judges with one another on each category in turn.

The range of correlation and median r^{tet} correlation of five judges was:

Typescript	Range	Md.
1A	−0.09 to 0.95+	0.84
2A	0.20 to 0.95+	0.76
3A	0.36 to 0.95+	0.93

Reliability study

The size of an adequate sample was empirically determined by the classic procedure of adding further data to ascertain at what point further addition caused little or no change in the obtained pattern of statements. Successive blocs of 50 statements from the typescripts of one class session were added to each other and the fluctuation in pattern of statements falling into the seven categories noted (Table 1–6).

Standard errors were computed to ascertain whether the differences between the successive percentages in each category and the mean were significant, that is, were three times the standard error. No significant differences were found except with regard to the percentage of category 3 statements respectively, and for the first 50 statements of category 4. The other 32 differences were not reliable.

It was concluded that 200 statements would offer an adequate sample of a given teacher's statements since the statements processesd represented a class session drawn at random from several class sessions. The class from which the sample was drawn was, as regards size of group, resources, classroom arrangement, et cetera, in no way peculiar or biased.

A further check on the consistency of the index was made by comparing the day to day variations of the pattern of statements of three teachers, A, B, and C.

The chi-square test was used to check the hypothesis that no significant differences occurred from day to day. It was not possible to reject the hypothesis insofar as teachers B and C were concerned. The P's for these samples were 0.14 and 0.42 respectively. In the case of teacher A, however, a P of 0.02 was obtained which suggested that other than chance factors were operative. An "explanation" for this low P might be found in the fact that sample 7 alone contributed more than half the total value of chi-square and was a deviate

Table 1–6

Percentage of Increment or Decrement in the Proportion of Statements Falling into Each of Seven Categories as Additional Blocs of Statements Are Added

	Categories						
	1	2	3	4	5	6	7
	%	%	%	%	%	%	%
First fifty statements	0.0	0.0	0.0	0.0	0.0	0.0	0.0
Fifty added to 50	0.0	0.0	2.0	−7.0	3.0	−1.0	3.0
Fifty added to 100	2.7	0.7	3.3	−3.7	−1.7	−0.3	−1.0
Fifty added to 150	−0.2	−0.7	3.7	−0.8	−2.7	−0.2	0.5
Fifty added to 200	−0.1	0.0	1.0	0.4	−1.0	−0.1	−0.2
Twenty-one added to 250	−1.6	−0.3	1.0	0.0	0.2	0.4	0.3

session in that the teacher, contrary to her usual pattern of behavior, was compelling the class to carry out a project to which they objected bitterly. The whole tone of the class session was greatly at variance with the usual tenor of this teacher's session. If this sample 7 is omitted from the series, the P obtained for the rest is 0.54, which does not allow rejection of the hypothesis and permits us to say the differences are insignificant.

Validation procedures

The validity study has employed four procedures to validate the technique developed.

1. We have used H. H. Anderson's Teacher Behavior Categories (Anderson *et al.*, 1945, pp. 22–26) as a criterion instrument that has been applied to the same data as the climate index.

2. We have related pupil's recorded comments and feelings to the picture of climate in the classroom situation obtained by application of the climate index to the teacher's statements.

3. We have predicted from results obtained on typescripts the ratings that independent judges would make of teacher behaviors in terms of a Teacher-Characteristics Rating Scale.

4. We have related the description of a classroom situation from three frames of reference—a categorizer using objective criteria, judges' ratings of the teacher's verbal behavior in a "live" situation and pupils registering their negative or positive feelings.

USE OF ANDERSON'S TEACHER-BEHAVIOR CATEGORIES. Anderson has developed Teacher-Behavior Categories by which to describe Teacher's Classroom Personalities. The categories distinguish between Integrative and Dominative

Table 1–7

I.D. Ratios and Climate Index Ratios on Typescripts 1A, 2A, and 3A

Typescript	I.D. ratio	Ratio of $\dfrac{\text{learner-centered statements}}{\text{teacher-centered statements}}$
1A	6.3	2.4
2A	1.6	2.2
3A	0.4	0.2

teacher behavior and are the basis for an I.D. ratio (Anderson, *et al.*, 1945, pp. 41–42) which represents the ratio of approving, cooperative, integrative behavior by the teacher. It can be shown that the I.D. ratio in many respects is similar to a proportion of learner-centered to teacher-centered verbal behaviors. I.D. ratios and learner-centered to teacher-centered ratios are comparable since in each instance a ratio greater than 1.00 denotes a greater use of integrative, acceptant and facilitating behaviors over dominative, unacceptant and limiting behaviors by the teacher.

Anderson's categories and the climate index categories were applied to the same data with the results found in Table 1–7.

Analyses by both Anderson's and the climate index criteria appear to concur that a greater proportion of teacher behaviors in the situation represented by typescript 1A and 2A were integrative and acceptant whereas a greater proportion of teacher behaviors in 3A were dominative and rejecting.

PUPILS' EVALUATIONS. The pupils' evaluation of the teacher's methods and of the classroom situation in general is admissible evidence which may sustain or contradict the picture of climate obtained in a given classroom. We have such pupil evaluations regarding teacher A in class W. We also have climate index indications of the major focus of concern of the teacher derived from categorizing typescripts 1A and 2A as well as a mean pattern obtained from 8 random

Table 1–8

Percentage of Teacher A's Statements Falling into Each of Three Areas of Concern

Areas of concern	Typescript 1A %*	Typescript 2A %*	Mean for eight random samples, %*
Sustain herself (categories 5, 6, and 7)	28.0	77.9	37.4
Helping the learner (categories 1 and 2)	44.0	13.3	23.4
Developing the problem (category 3)	22.1	4.4	28.8

* The remaining percentage in each instance is accounted for by the neutral category, number 4.

samples drawn from the same teacher's class sessions. The climate index analysis shows that, on the whole, in order of importance the teacher's concern is first with herself, second with the learner, and third with the problem (Table 1–8).

There is some evidence here which suggests that the teacher tended to place more emphasis on interpersonal relationships than on structuring the objective problem in the learning situation. The concensus of the part of the 25 pupils who filled out evaluation sheets was ambivalent and can be best summarized as follows:

Approving

Teacher was cooperative
Teacher was unprejudiced and impartial
I got new ideas
Teacher helped me

Disapproving

I wasted considerable time
Teacher ought to have guided and controlled class more
I was bored
Teaching method was unsatisfactory

The picture obtained both from the climate index and from the pupils' evaluations tended to concur in depicting a teacher who evidenced more concern with personality factors in the learning situation than with the objective problem elements.

The comparison of these data affords another crude indication that the climate index categorization tends to represent with some accuracy the actual atmosphere obtained in a classroom, at least, as seen through the eyes of the pupils.

TEACHER-CHARACTERISTICS SCALE. Four judges who had not used the climate index and who had no knowledge of the criteria contained in the index were asked to scale typescripts 1A, 2A, and 3A according to two dichotomous lists of teacher behaviors which were labeled "A" and "C" on a nine-point scale. The midpoint was marked "B."

Point "A" was defined by such teacher behaviors as:

1. Raising objective questions about procedures and purposes of learner

2. Evaluating pupil achievement in terms of stated, objective criteria

3. Helping learners to identify a wide choice of problem-solving activities, etc.

Point "C" was defined by such teacher behaviors as:

1. Limiting choices of behavior of the learner

2. Evaluating the learner's achievement on the basis of the teacher's unstated, subjective criteria

3. Setting the pace of problem-solving behaviors for the learner, etc.

Table 1–9

Comparison of Weighted Ratings of Teacher-Characteristics Rating Scale with Climate Index Ratio of Learner-centered to Teacher-centered Statements on Typescripts 1A, 2A, and 3A

Typescripts	Weighted ratings				Ratio of $\dfrac{\text{learner-centered statements}}{\text{teacher-centered statements}}$
	Judge 5	Judge 6	Judge 7	Judge 8	
1A	0.0	1.3	3.0	3.7	2.4
2A	3.0	1.0	0.8	3.0	2.2
3A	−2.5	0.5	−2.0	−3.5	0.2

Ten such behaviors for "A" and "C" were listed. The training given the judges was comparatively brief, a 40-minute session, and then they were asked to apply the scale to typescripts 1A, 2A, and 3A. From the categorization of statements on the basis of the climate index criteria, it was predicted that the judges would place their ratings on the nine-point scale between "A" and "B" for typescripts 1A and 2A, and between "B" and "C" for typescript 3A. The results were that the ratings were as predicted for typescripts 1A and 2A except that on 1A Judge 5 placed his rating exactly at "B" and were as predicted for 3A except that Judge 6 placed his rating on the "positive" side of "B" instead of on the "negative" side as predicted. Positive weights were given to the points from "B" to "A" marked zero and "A" marked plus 4; negative weights were given the steps from "B" to "C" being weighted minus 4. The resultant weighted ratings are represented in Table 1–9.

DESCRIPTION OF CLASS SITUATION FROM THREE FRAMES OF REFERENCE. A further validation procedure involved the relating of data describing an experimental classroom situation from three frames of reference:

1. The objective frame of a categorizer using the criteria of the climate index

2. The frame of observers rating teacher-statements *in situ* with the aid of illustrative teacher behaviors on a dichotomous scale

3. The frame of the pupils in the classroom

The experimental session was 45 minutes long. In the first part of the period, the teacher sought by means of his verbalizations to create a learner-centered climate and in the last part of the period a teacher-centered climate.

The data that are reported here refer to session Number 2 of Group "X" comprising ten pupils. In the categorization of teacher statements by means of the climate index, it was found that of the 83 statements in the learner-centered part of the session:

> 48.2% were learner-centered
> 12.0% were teacher-centered
> 39.8% were neutral

Of the 33 neutral statements comprising 39.8% neutral statements, 21 were simple verbalizations of pupils' names.

Of the 119 statements in the teacher-centered part of the session:

> 31.9% were learner-centered
> 55.5% were teacher-centered
> 12.6% were neutral

Of the 15 neutral statements comprising the 12.6%, four were simple verbalizations of pupils' names.

There is an obvious difference between the learner-centered and teacher-centered parts of the class session as regards the percentages of teacher-centered statements. The difference, however, between the proportions of learner-centered statements is not large quantitatively but differs considerably qualitatively. For example, the percentage of category 1 remarks is nil and the bulk of the learner-centered statements falls into category 2 during the learner-centered portion of the lesson, whereas in the teacher-centered half of the lesson 24.4% of the total 31.9% of learner-centered statements fall into category 1. These category 1 statements, described as learner-supportive, were mostly superficially commendatory remarks such as "Right!", "Good!", and "Very good!"

The categorizations by means of the climate index show that there was a preponderance of learner-centered remarks over teacher-centered remarks in the first portion of the session and a preponderance of teacher-centered over learner-centered remarks in the second portion of the session.

During the class session proper, four judges who were trained therapists rated the teacher's statements in terms of illustrative criteria drawn from the Teacher-Characteristics Rating Scale. One end of the scale was designated "A," the opposite end "C" and the midpoint "B." If a judge rated a statement as falling between "A" and "B," it was interpreted as being learner-centered; if he rated between "B" and "C," it was considered to be teacher-centered; if he rated it at "B," it was interpreted as a neutral statement.

In the learner-centered part of the session the mean percentages of the four judges' ratings of teacher statements are found in Table 1–10, and in the teacher-centered portion of the session the mean percentages of the four judges' ratings are found in Table 1–11.

The data arrived at from an objective categorization of statements by means of the climate index and that obtained from four judges' ratings of statements *in situ* are in general agreement.

For the experimental class periods each of the ten pupils of Group "X" was supplied with two push buttons; one labeled plus and the other minus. They were requested, (1) to push the plus button whenever they felt "good" at what the teacher said whether the remark was directed at them or not, and (2) to push the minus button whenever they felt badly at what the teacher said. An orientation session was held with the group prior to the experiment proper to get them acquainted with the equipment and procedure but no training was

Table 1–10

Mean Percentages of Judges' Ratings of Teacher Statements Used during Learner-centered Part of Session

Mean %	Kind of statement	Range of four judges' percentages
63.8	Learner-centered	45.0* to 77.7
18.6	Neutral	10.0 to 22.3
17.6	Teacher-centered	0.0 to 45.0*

* Judge 4 was responsible for the 45% item in both instances. He explained afterwards that his bias had been to scale objective questions which sought information as probing-directive statements; the other judges interpreted them as problem-structuring and therefore as learner-centered comments.

Table 1–11

Mean Percentages of Judges' Ratings of Teacher Statements Used during Teacher-centered Part of Session

Mean %	Kind of statement	Range of four judges' percentages
2.9	Learner-centered	1.5 to 5.7
6.9	Neutral	1.5 to 12.8
90.2	Teacher-centered	81.5 to 97.0

Table 1–12

Comparison of Number and Percentage of Positive and Negative "Feeling" Reactions of Pupils Recorded during the Learner-centered and Teacher-centered Parts of a Class Session

"Feelings"	Learner-centered portion of session		Teacher-centered portion of session	
	Number of reactions	%	Number of reactions	%
Positive	54	54.0	72	30.2
Negative	46	46.0	166	69.8
Total	100	100.0	238	100.0

given them regarding the kinds of statements which were to evoke their negative responses or positive responses.

It was the prediction of the researcher that more positive than negative reactions from the pupils would be registered in the learner-centered portion of the session, and more negative than positive reactions in the teacher-centered part of the session. The recorded pupil reactions are found in Table 1–12.

The positive reactions slightly predominated during the learner-centered part of the class session and the negative reactions predominated during the teacher-centered part of the class.

These data derived from three frames of reference: (1) a categorizer using climate index criteria, (2) the observers' ratings of statements *in situ*, and (3) the pupils' "feeling" reactions, on the whole, tend to concur in depicting the first part of the session as probably more learner- and problem-oriented, with a greater possibility of objective attitudes by the teacher and pupils to the learning situation, and the latter part of the lesson as more teacher centered and more conducive to a subjective[4] orientation by the teacher and pupils to the learning situation.

By the procedures outlined in the preceding pages, the climate index was shown to have objectivity, reliability and validity.

Application of climate index to excerpts from five different classes

To test the applicability of the index categories to regular classroom sessions, samples were drawn from the sound recordings of five regular classes held in the laboratory classroom. These classes included a seventh-grade mathematics class, two eighth-grade social science classes, an eighth-grade art class, and a ninth-grade Latin class. The classes met regularly in the classroom three or four times a week and were conducted by the regular class teacher in her usual manner.

SAMPLING. Eight random samples, each seven minutes in length, were drawn from the recorded class sessions of the art, mathematics, and Latin class. In addition, one full class session was taken from each of the three aforementioned classes as well as from the two social science classes. A total of 23 seven-minute excerpts (one sample from the Latin class was unusable) and five full class sessions were available from classes at the secondary school level. These excerpts from the sound records of the several class sessions were typed and the seven categories applied to the teacher statements contained in the protocols.

Patterns of statements for each of the four teachers were obtained and an attempt was made, largely for illustrative purposes, to interpret these patterns. A mean pattern of distribution of statements among the seven categories was obtained for each of teachers A, B, and C from the several excerpts from their respective classes. A pattern of statements for teacher D in classes W and Z, respectively, was also obtained from two full class sessions of the social science classes (Table 1–13).

COMMENT REGARDING TEACHERS' PATTERNS OF STATEMENTS. Teacher B appears to use a larger proportion of learner-centered statements (categories 1, 2, and 3) than the other three. Teachers A, C, and D_z seem to use a somewhat similar proportion of teacher-centered remarks; teacher B uses a low proportion of

---

[4] Greater concern with one's self and one's status in the group than with the objective problem.

Table 1–13

Percentage of Statements Located in Each of the Climate Index Categories for Teachers A, B, C, and D

	Teacher				
	A	B	C	D_w	D_z
Category	Mean %	Mean %	Mean %	Mean %	Mean %
1	18.2	20.3	8.6	2.5	4.7
2	5.2	7.8	2.8	0.0	0.9
3	28.8	39.7	30.7	53.0	41.1
Total	52.2	67.8	42.1	55.5	46.7
4	10.4	22.2	20.2	21.4	16.8
5	14.8	6.8	23.9	13.7	20.6
6	9.1	1.6	8.9	6.8	10.3
7	13.5	1.6	4.9	2.6	5.6
Total	37.4	10.0	37.7	23.1	36.5
Grand total	100.0	100.0	100.0	100.0	100.0
	N = 497	N = 408	N = 525	N = 117	N = 107

teacher-centered remarks (categories 5, 6, and 7). Teacher D in both sessions uses a slightly larger proportion of problem-structuring remarks (category 3) than the other three teachers and teacher A uses the lowest percentage of such comments. Teacher B uses the largest proportion of category 1 statements and of category 2 remarks. In the teacher-centered area, teacher D_z and teacher C use the largest proportion of directive (category 5) statements, and teacher B the lowest proportion of such statements. Teacher B uses the lowest proportion of reproving (category 6) remarks and of self-supportive (category 7) statements.

A POSSIBLE INTERPRETATION OF B'S PATTERN OF STATEMENTS. Teacher B would appear to be an individual who would offer verbal support and encouragement to the pupils (category 1) and would attempt, to a lesser extent, to convey to them her understanding of them and of their point of view. She possibly tries to keep the objective problem clearly defined and attempts to keep it the central object of attention and concern (category 3). She appears to utilize a small proportion of hortative statements (category 5). Her negative evaluations of pupil-behavior appear to be minimal (category 6). She appears to feel slight need for indulging in self-supportive and defensive comments. Here is a teacher, we might infer, whose methodology for facilitating learning is (1) to keep the learners well oriented to the objective problem, and (2) to maintain a helpful and understanding attitude towards them. At the same time, she would seem to be able to keep her own needs well in the background.

Table 1–14

Percentages of Professor E's Statements Falling into
Each of the Seven Categories

Category	Seminar 1 (N = 102) %	Seminar 2 (N = 84) %
1	2.0	3.6
2	4.9	8.3
3	70.6	59.5
Total	77.5	71.4
4	8.8	11.9
5	5.9	1.2
6	0.0	0.0
7	7.8	15.5
Total	13.7	16.7
Grand total	100.0	100.0

Application of climate index to a higher level of instruction

To test the applicability of the climate index categories to a level of instruction beyond the secondary school level, typescripts derived from recorded sessions of a graduate seminar and from a counselor-training program were processed.

PATTERN OF STATEMENTS DERIVED FROM A CATEGORIZATION OF PROFESSOR E'S VERBAL BEHAVIOR. The protocols containing Professor E's verbalizations are based on two 2-hour seminar meetings of graduate students. These were two consecutive sessions that were recorded and upon which the typescripts were based (Table 1–14).

COMMENTS ON PROFESSOR E'S PATTERN OF STATEMENTS. A high degree of problem orientation is evidenced in these two class situations by the large proportion of problem-structuring comments (category 3). Positive evaluations (category 1) are minimal and negative evaluations (category 6) are nonexistent. Some verbal expression of acceptance of the students' ideas and feelings is in evidence on the basis of the percentages falling into category 2. The proportion of hortative statements (category 5) is not large. However, some evidence of a need to sustain himself and to be concerned about his status appears from the comparatively large (in relation to the rest of the pattern) proportion of category 7 statements in both sessions.

PATTERN OF STATEMENTS DERIVED FROM CATEGORIZATION OF INSTRUCTOR F'S VERBAL BEHAVIOR. The protocols of Instructor F's sessions were based on three 1½-hour sessions. They were random selections from a group of eight available typescripts. The paucity of statements by the instructor, 150 in all for the entire three sessions, is both striking and interesting (Table 1–15).

Table 1–15

Percentage of Instructor F's Statements Falling into Each of the Seven Categories

Category	Session 1 (N = 36) %	Session 2 (N = 62) %	Session 3 (N = 52) %
1	0.0	8.0	0.0
2	63.9	58.1	69.2
3	22.2	21.0	15.4
Total	86.1	87.1	84.6
4	0.0	11.3	15.4
5	2.7	0.0	0.0
6	5.6	1.6	0.0
7	5.6	0.0	0.0
Total	13.9	1.6	0.0
Grand total	100.0	100.0	100.0

COMMENTS REGARDING INSTRUCTOR F'S PATTERN OF STATEMENTS. Instructor F uses a large proportion of clarifying and acceptant statements (category 2) in all three sessions. Encouraging and reassuring statements (category 1) are at a very minimum. Slightly less than one-fifth of his remarks are problem-structuring comments. Directive, reproving, and self-supportive statements are rarely used and are nearly all confined to session 1; the fact that the bulk of F's self-concerned statements fell into session 1 may be "explained" by the fact that it was the first meeting of the class. The whole pattern of F's verbal behavior is explicable largely in terms of his adherence to the principles of client-centered psychotherapy. Counselors of that persuasion place great emphasis on the creation of permissive and acceptant atmosphere by the use of clarifying and acceptant statements and other appropriate procedures. Instructor F clearly transferred his counseling orientation into the classroom situation.

It would appear from the analysis of both Professor E's and Instructor F's statements that the climate index categories are applicable to a higher level of instruction than the secondary school level.

SUMMARY, CONCLUSIONS, AND IMPLICATIONS

Summary

A technique has been developed for assessing the social–emotional climate in a classroom by categorizing teacher statements contained in typescripts made from sound records of class sessions. The technique has been shown to have objectivity, reliability, and validity.

Conclusions

1. Climate can be assessed and described.

2. Several individuals can be trained to use the criteria of the climate index and achieve an adequate measure of agreement among one another in categorizing statements in typescripts.

3. A valid measure of social–emotional climate of groups is obtainable through a categorization of teacher statements.

4. Within the limits of behavioral and personality variations the climate index gives us a consistent pattern of verbal behavior for a given teacher from day to day.

5. Different patterns of verbal behavior used by several teachers can be identified.

6. Statements categorized by the climate index as likely to produce "positive" feelings tend to be similarly categorized by impartial observers and tend to be reacted to with "positive" feelings by the individuals to whom they are addressed.

7. Statements categorized according to the climate index as likely to produce "negative" feelings tend to be similarly categorized by impartial observers and tend to be reacted to with "negative" feelings by the individuals to whom they are addressed.

Some revision of the climate index seems in order as a result of insights arising out of its application to several typescripts and to "live" classroom situations. These improvements should include:

1. Clarification of category 1 in order to distinguish between objective and subjective positive evaluation of pupil behavior; the former may be genuinely learner-supportive; the latter doesn't appear to perform that function; clarification of category 5.

2. More rigid definition of statements to be placed in category 4 which should contain perhaps only verbatim repetitions, polite formalities and administrative comments.

3. Differentiation between types of problem-structuring statements.

4. Considering the possibility of subdividing five of the seven categories (not 4 and 7) into "A" and "B" areas. The "A" area would represent little or no element of self-concern on the part of the teacher; the "B" area would represent a considerable element of self-concern and result in tingeing the statement with some affect.

Implications for further research

Some questions that arise out of this study are:

1. What is the relationship between climate and the quality of the learning that occurs in a classroom?

2. To what extent is the climate in a given classroom a function of the personality of the teacher?

3. To what extent do peer-group relationships influence the classroom climate?

4. Of what value is the climate index to teachers in analyzing their own teaching methods?

5. How applicable is the climate index to the "live" classroom situation?

The study described above represents an attempt to develop a technique for the measurement of social–emotional climate to the end that, ultimately, fuller understanding and control may be achieved of one of the factors hypothesized to influence learning.

4

THEORY AND DESIGN
OF A STUDY
OF TEACHER–PUPIL INTERACTION[5]

MORRIS L. COGAN

This paper sets forth the general background and the theoretical framework of an exploratory research in teaching–learning processes. The study itself is an investigation into the relationship between certain classroom behaviors of teachers and the productive behaviors of their pupils. Although a few references to the conclusions arising from the research will be found in the present article, the analysis and interpretation of the data are presented in more complete detail in companion articles appearing in another journal (Cogan, 1958).

SOME PROBLEMS OF MEASUREMENT

General background

The enigma of the measurement of teacher competence arises again and again in the discussions of educators, like an uneasy ghost stubbornly revisiting the seminar table, and again and again such discussions trail off into acrimony or futility in the face of the controversy aroused by value judgments inhering the question, "What is the good teacher?" The answer to that question is outside the purview of the research here described. Nevertheless, it is the writer's hope that the findings may serve as a portion of the evidence upon which the ultimate value judgments may be the more soundly based.

If, for the purposes of research, a sort of *cordon sanitaire* is set up around the judgmental and intuitive areas in the appraisal of teacher competence, the investigator is brought face to face with other problems that demand resolu-

---

[5] This article is adapted from the author's doctoral dissertation. "The Relation of the Behavior of Teachers to the Productive Behavior of Their Pupils," at the Harvard Graduate School of Education. This article is from *The Harvard Educational Review* 26, 1956, 315–342. Reprinted by permission of *The Harvard Educational Review* and the author.

tion. For present purposes those problems are found at the level of observable behavior and the central concern of this study may be expressed as a question: "What are the relationships between the behaviors of the teacher and the behaviors of his pupils?" It is evident that until such antecedent–consequent relationships become predictable, the effectiveness of teachers cannot be rigorously evaluated. Only relatively incomplete or unsatisfactory answers to the question have thus far been found in the literature.

The present attempt to measure the impact of the teacher's behaviors upon the work of his students is in a very direct sense an attempt to evaluate the effectiveness of the teacher. It is therefore closely related to the large body of research on teacher competence.

Many of the concepts and methodologics thus far formulated for the investigation of competence have been adjudged unsatisfactory. In commenting on the data-gathering devices used in a large and representative sample of studies dealing with the measurement and prediction of teaching efficiency, A. S. Barr makes the following observations:

> The reliabilities of these various devices seem to be relatively high; their validities relatively unknown. The evidence is chiefly of a correlational character and must not be accepted at face value. . . . The data are many times inconsistent. The inconsistencies are probably more apparent than real. With so many different samples, data-gathering devices, criteria, and purposes, a large amount of consistency should not be expected. (Barr, 1948, p. 216)

Among the crucial problems in the measurement of competence are the criteria and the predictors to be used. Five major classifications of such variables have been noted: (1) practice teaching marks or ratings; (2) in-service ratings; (3) college grades or scholarship; (4) the consensus of persons competent to judge and in a position to observe; and (5) measures of pupil growth and achievement. There is also a miscellaneous group of studies, more or less descriptive in character (Barr, 1948, p. 204.

It is apparent that each of these variables may have its advantages and disadvantages. One in particular, however, possesses certain strong attractions for the investigator interested in behavior; the use of pupil growth and achievement as the criterion measure of the teacher's competence. As G. L. Betts has remarked, "Perhaps the most direct method for evaluating the functional effectiveness of a teacher is to measure the changes wrought in pupils under her instruction" (Betts, 1935, p. 87). Such a consequent measure possesses a kind of logical inevitability that is difficult to challenge. If the teacher's task is to change the behavior of his pupils, then the measurement of those changes might well provide one of the measurements of his competence, on the principle that evaluation should be in terms of objectives.

In contrast, the more commonly used criteria, the in-service ratings of the teacher and the opinions of experts as to the teacher's competence, both suffer from a major deficiency: they are measurements taken at a point several steps removed from the criterion generally accepted as valid i.e., pupil change. The reason for this deficiency becomes evident as soon as one considers the attenuations that are almost inescapable when the experts' ratings of the teacher's effectiveness have only an inferential or intuitive relationship to pupil change, and when one takes into account the likelihood of extreme variations in the bases of the experts' evaluations. The criteria upon which such evaluations might be based are not standardized, and many of the most successful efforts to achieve reliability of ratings seem not to convey an equal conviction of validity. The reliability thus achieved gives the impression that a self-validating cycle has been completed. The apparently securely based structure of measurement sags alarmingly under the impact of a question as to the relationship of these reliable measures to the logically defensible consequents: pupil change and pupil behavior.

Therefore, for the purposes of research, two seemingly inconsistent assumptions have been made by the writer. The first is that pupil change is the most appropriate criterion of teacher competence. The second is that another criterion, to be operationally defined below, is at present a valid and productive concept in the measurement of the teacher's effectiveness. The reasons for relinquishing pupil change as the criterion in this study should be clarified.

At first glance, the use of pupil change as the dependent measure of teaching competence is an attractive idea. It seems simple, logically defensible, and apparently amenable to investigation. The challenge was picked up by L. E. Rostker, whose position is that "since a teacher is engaged to teach and modify the behavior of her pupils, the degree to which changes are produced in her pupils is a reflection of the ability of the teacher (Rostker, 1945, p. 6). Rostker himself, however, injects a very necessary caution in the use of this criterion, with this warning:

It cannot, however, be over-emphasized that the measurable pupil changes attained in (his own) study are limited by the type of tests applied to the pupils. The use of pupil changes as the criterion of teaching ability depends upon the tests applied to the pupils and whatever implications are to be drawn must be limited by the tests employed. (Rostker, 1945, p. 7)

In addition, there is a great possibility that a pupil's achievement in the departmentalized grades may be influenced by several teachers rather than by one. This danger has led Rostker and most other researchers using the pupil-gain criterion to confine their efforts to elementary or nondepartmentalized secondary schools.

The fact seems to be, as noted by W. A. McCall (1952) and A. T. Jersild (Jersild, *et al.*, 1941) among others, that at least three important problems still remain unsolved in the measurement of pupil change: (1) lack of adequate subject-matter tests in most areas of achievement; (2) lack of precise instruments capable of measuring changes in social and learning skills and in attitudes; and (3) the difficulty of isolating changes due to a single teacher in a departmentalized school. S. Domas, in his *Report of an Exploratory Study of Teacher Competence*, writes, "The present status of measurement techniques and the impossibility of eliminating factors in pupil growth not attributable to the teacher being evaluated combined to make this (pupil-change) approach impracticable at this time." (Domas, 1950, p. 4) Some of the difficulties surrounding the use of this criterion may be pointed up by comparing a few of the conclusions of Rostker's study with those of the second study in the same series, by J. F. Rolfe (1945, pp. 73–74).

L. E. ROSTKER

The intelligence of the teacher is the highest single factor conditioning teaching ability and remains so even when in combination with other teacher measures.

Personality, as here defined and measured, shows no significant relationship to teaching ability. (Rostker, 1945, pp. 50–51)

J. F. ROLFE

Intelligence as measured by the American Council Psychological examination seems not to be related to teaching efficiency ($r = -0.10$).

Personality as here defined and measured seems to possess a positive relationship to good teaching ($r = 0.35; r = 0.30$). (Rolfe, 1945, pp. 73–74)

It would seem, then, that in some respects the measurement of competence in terms of pupil change has reached an impasse of the sort that is fairly common in the social sciences at their present stage of precision: available instruments and techniques have not kept pace with theoretical and conceptual developments.

The development of new measures

Many investigators seem to have viewed competence as a single variable and to have rated it as such. The rather attenuated predictive value of their work arises perhaps in part from the fact that they have depended upon the judgment of expert raters to provide the criterion of competence, in spite of the fact that critical incidents influencing the raters' judgments may occur in many areas of teaching activity. For example, a teacher may be found deficient in the classroom, or in his relations with colleagues. He may be *persona non grata* in the community because of nonconformity with local mores. Almost any behavior or trait, when maximized, may lead to a blanket judgment of competence or incompetence. It is interesting to note, in connection with some of the more rigorous researches in which pupil gain has been the criterion, that although Rolfe (1945, p. 73) found positive correlations ($r = 0.36$ to $r = 0.43$) between pupil gain and teaching efficiency as determined by experienced and competent supervisors using rating scales, neither Rostker (1945, p. 50) nor La Duke (1945, pp. 75–100) nor McCall (1952) found any significant degree of agreement between pupil gain and the competence ratings given by principals, supervisors, superintendents, or supervising teachers.

This is not surprising when one takes into account the variety of the frames of reference used by raters in their judgments of competence. Barr has found seven major bases for judgments of competence in 209 scales devised to rate teachers: (1) classroom management; (2) instructional skill; (3) personal fitness for teaching; (4) scholarship and professional preparation; (5) effort toward improvement; (6) interest in work, pupils, patrons, subjects taught, etc.; and (7) ability to cooperate with others (Barr, 1947, p. 212). All of these are, of course, relevant. It is their amenability to measurement and, more important, the frame of reference in which such measurements are made that must be questioned. The former difficulty is one of the realities within which social science researchers must work. The latter, however, is called into question in this paper. The writer's position is that one of the valid frames of reference for the measurement of the teacher's competence is the perception of the pupil, as well as the perception of experts, supervisors, principals, etc.

This paper, therefore, will not seek to define competence in the terms of the seven classifications presented above. It will, rather, carefully define smaller dimensions, limiting itself to an analysis of some outcomes of specific teacher behaviors in classroom interaction with pupils. Such smaller variables, taken together, may ultimately provide a more rigorous and productive definition of competence.

The assumption underlying many of the previous researches may be stated as follows: When student-teaching ratings, consensus of observers, college grades, or in-service ratings stand as the criteria of performance, significant positive relationship may be assumed to exist between these ratings and pupil change; therefore pupil change is not measured. Such an assumption appears to bear more relationship to pious wish than to axiom, and is subject to question on several counts. There seems to be good reason to believe that the gap between the criteria employed and the realities of pupil change is too great and too crucial to be bridged by an assumption so open to challenge.

On the other hand, when the criterion of pupil change has been employed, the conceptual scheme seems eminently satisfactory, but the endeavor itself founders in technical and instrumental difficulties. It is, therefore, perhaps desirable to attempt new approaches to the problem.

One such attempt may be found in the present treatment, which seeks to avoid the limitations of both methodologies. The crux of the design of this study is that although it avoids the use of pupil change, it substitutes criterion variables that intervene just prior to pupil change: the amount of required and self-initiated school work performed by pupils in response to teacher stimuli. Although this concept will be discussed below in greater detail, it is in essence an assumption that the gap between such work and actual pupil growth and development is relatively small and can be adequately bridged by logical and empirical demonstrations. It is hoped that such an assumption may be viewed as perhaps a more parsimonious statement than the assumptions previously discussed.

The weakness of the present approach springs from the fact that the criterion of pupil change is not utilized, although the writer believes this to be the appropriate measure. Its strength resides in the hope that pupil performance of required and self-initiated work may be more positively identified and more precisely measured than its consequent-pupil change.

THEORY OF THE RESEARCH

Statement of the problem

This study is primarily an attempt to ascertain the relationships that may exist between certain specific behaviors of classroom teachers in departmentalized schools and the work of their pupils. The major datum is conceived to be the perceptions and judgments of the pupils, since they can report on their own behavior and are well informed on the classroom behavior of the teacher. The analysis deals with the differential effects of specific teacher behaviors termed "Preclusive," "Inclusive," and "Conjunctive." The consequents are defined as measures of pupil performance of required and self-initiated work related to classroom experiences.

Teacher–pupil interaction

Although the writer has in this study relinquished the direct measurement of pupil change and achievement, an attempt has been made to approach that criterion as closely as possible. The following discussion seeks to demonstrate the rationale of the present methodology.

The process by which the classroom behaviors of the teacher are linked to pupil change may perhaps logically be schematized as follows:

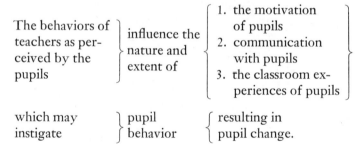

If this diagram is accepted as representing a reasonably accurate though unidirectional symbolization of the processes by which teacher behaviors are related to pupil change, then it may be observed that the variable of pupil behavior is proximate to pupil change (or gain, or achievement). Pupil behaviors are therefore selected as the consequent variable. The rationale underlying this choice is that the manner in which pupils perceive the teacher's behavior leads to certain predictable behavior of the pupils, which in turn may lead to change. The hypotheses soon to be examined are based on this reasoning.

The theoretical position as to the impact of the teacher upon pupil activities has received some verification, especially through the work of Harold H.

Anderson, who has investigated the effects of teachers' dominative and integrative contacts on children's classroom behavior. He writes:

> The high frequencies of integrative behavior of one teacher were associated with high frequencies of socially integrative behavior in the children, and with high frequencies in expression of spontaneity and initiative.
>
> The data in this study lend confirmation to the assumptions regarding a dynamic and measurable relationship between classroom behavior and teachers and children. (Anderson and Brewer, 1946, p. 87)

And further strong corroboration may be found in the work of Jersild (Jersild *et al.*, 1941) and Lewin (1939).

Pupil behaviors

The pupil behaviors considered to be both measurable and closely linked with pupil change have been categorized as (1) the pupil's performance of required school work, and (2) his performance of self-initiated work instigated by classroom experiences. Both kinds of activity, as perceived and reported by the pupil, have been termed "productive." The criterion measures in this study thus become the scores of the coded responses to the questions, "When this teacher gives a required assignment, how often do you do it?" and, "Because of what goes on in the classroom, what things do you do of your own free will and how often do you do them?" This may be interpreted as the limited definition of the teacher's competence.

The specific questions asked of the pupils concerning the two kinds of productive work may be found in Part I and Part II of the "Pupil Survey."[6] An effort was made to phrase the items in the idiom of secondary school pupils. Some of the pupils' activities were drawn from the writer's experience as a teacher in the public schools; others were adapted from compilations[7] of typical classroom acts. A few examples of the items scored for pupil productivity are presented below. A six-point frequency scale accompanied each item.

Required Work (from Pupil Survey, Part One):

(item 4) Make or study graphs.
(item 5) Give a report or a talk.
(item 15) Do drill exercises.
(item 17) Make a notebook.
(item 25) Memorize rules.

---

[6] The "Pupil Survey" is presented in full in the dissertation.
[7] The following publications offer fairly lengthy lists of school activities: W. H. Burton, *The Guidance of Learning Activities* (N.Y.: D. Appleton-Century Co., 1944) pp. 132, 438–439. G. M. Whipple, "What Pupils Do In An Activity," Course of Study Bulletin, No 162 (Los Angeles City Schools, n.d.).

Self-Initiated Work (from Pupil Survey, Part Two):

(item   1)   In this subject I read for pleasure.
(item   2)   I volunteer to answer in class.
(item 10)   I do extra problems or examples.
(item 11)   I do extra drawings, cartoons.
(item 14)   I give extra reports.

It may be remarked that the teachers were also asked to rate each pupil's performance of required and self-initiated work, and that the teachers' reports tended to corroborate the pupils' estimates, indicating that under certain conditions the experimenter may place substantial reliance upon the reports of pupils.

It becomes apparent that the activities of the pupils are considered to be of major consequence in the theoretical structure of this research. The importance attributed to required and self-initiated work stems largely from the philosophical formulations of John Dewey and from the psychological theories of Neal Miller and John Dollard.

The heart of the Deweyan philosophy of education is the concept that "there is an intimate and necessary relation between the processes of actual experience and education" (Dewey, 1938, p. 7). In still more unmistakable terms Dewey reiterates the idea: "I assume that amid all uncertainties there is one permanent frame of reference: namely, the organic connection between education and personal experience" (Dewey, 1938, p. 12). The present study does not of course assume, any more than did Dewey, that the performance of *any* required or self-initiated activity constitutes an educative experience. Nor is there an assumption of equation between activity and learning. The position taken here is only that there must be performance, or work, or activity, before most school learning occurs. No stand is taken concerning the value accruing to the pupil from such activities. This study does not propose to deal with the outcomes of school work, nor with their quality, nor with the values of outcomes. The emphasis upon the productive work of the pupils is in a sense the conclusion to the premises that "Experience itself primarily consists of the active relations subsisting between a human being and his natural and social surroundings . . . (and it is the business of the school) to transport (youth) from an environment of relatively chance activities (accidental in the relation they bear to insight and thought) into one of the activities selected with reference to guidance of learning." (Dewey, 1916, p. 319) The items on required and self-initiated work seem to meet the criterion of "activities selected with reference to guidance of learning."

A psychological basis for the preoccupation of this study with the designated behaviors of pupils is drawn from the learning theory of Miller and Dollard. That theory "may be expressed . . . by saying that in order to learn one must want something, notice something, do something, and get something." (Miller and Dollard, 1941, p. 2) These factors of drive, cue, response, and reward are all prerequisites to most classroom learning. It is the link of "response" that is singled out for special attention as the consequent measure in the theory of this study. Without belaboring the obvious, it is enough to note that the psychologists have echoed the philosopher's meaning. They conclude that if the organism does not behave, it does not learn (Miller and Dollard, 1941, p. 21).

Thus the theoretical basis for the reliance of this study upon the pupils' required and self-initiated work rests upon two demonstrations: (1) that such work is a necessary pre-condition for most school learning, and (2) that such work is proximate to pupil change. This study fully recognizes that the pupil's performance of required and self-initiated work is not totally determined by the teacher. The subjects in this investigation are eighth grade children. Their school behavior is, of course, to some extent determined before they arrive in the classroom. The reasoning is, however, that the behavior of the teacher is an important factor, among others, in the school-related work of his pupils. The criterion measures are considered to be to some appreciable extent related to the teacher's ability to arouse interest, to secure the involvement of his pupils, to motivate them. In a word, such work by the pupils is a partial reflection of the ability of the teacher to motivate, and the measurement of this work may provide a measurement of the teacher's ability. It might therefore be called an index of the teacher's competence in terms of his ability to motivate his pupils.

Teacher behaviors

The teacher behaviors germane to the theoretical framework of this study constitute the independent events of the hypotheses. The theory of the effects of certain kinds of actions upon the pupils' work is derived largely from the social learning concepts of Miller and Dollard.

In the course of the interaction between teacher and pupils, the teacher's acts take on the qualities of cues for the pupils, and the teachers themselves acquire the ability to arouse secondary or learned drives. Thus, because of previous experiences with the teacher, the pupils learn to see him as a cue for different drives: (1) anxiety, to which an appropriate response is avoidance of some sort; and (2) something which might be called "liking" or "respect," for which an appropriate response is approach.

A second segment may now be put into the theoretical structure dealing with the teacher behaviors. Dollard and Miller have demonstrated the processes of avoidance of a feared stimulus and approach to a liked stimulus (1950, p. 352). These concepts underlie a hypothesis of this study, which states that the teacher who becomes a cue for strong anxiety will motivate his pupils to a low performance of self-initiated work. The hypothesis is based on the evidence that an organism tends to use the most expeditious means of avoiding an anxiety-laden stimulus. In paraphrase for the context of this study, the pupils will tend to satisfy, as economically as possible, the minimum demands of certain teachers by doing the required work. They will not, on the other hand, tend to perform very much self-initiated work, since this is the symbolic equivalent of remaining longer than is absolutely necessary in proximity to an unpleasant situation.

Dollard and Miller make it quite clear that most of the experimental evidence for their assumptions is based on relatively simple situations, in which approach and avoidance are operationally defined as actual locomotion of the subject toward or away from the stimulus object. The question of the relevance of such findings to the much more complex situation of the classroom is a major problem as yet unanswered. In a very limited sense, this research is an attempt to secure some evidence as to whether the conclusions derived from the simple experimental situation may be generalized to the interactions of the classroom. Dollard and Miller are of the opinion that such generalization is indeed possible:

> If we extend our analysis from primary stimulus generalization, based on the innate similarity of cues, to secondary generalization, based on learned equivalence of cues, we would expect gradients of approach and avoidance to exist in culturally defined sequences . . . Both a theoretical analysis and such experimental evidence as is available lead us to expect our assumptions to apply in any situation in which the subject can be said to be coming nearer to a goal in space, time, or some dimension of qualitative or culturally defined similarity of cues. All the clinical evidence that we are aware of also strongly suggests the same conclusion. (Dollard and Miller, 1951, p. 354)

It is suggested that the teacher behaviors operationally defined in the "Pupil Survey" tend to cause teachers to become stimuli for either avoidance or approach responses by the pupils. The exposition of the processes of avoidance and approach thus becomes a fundamental substructure of the theory from which the hypotheses of this study are derived.

The chain of interaction between teacher and pupils is arbitrarily considered to start with the behaviors of teachers, and it seems highly desirable to attempt to derive insights about those behaviors from an integrated psychological theory of personality. The attempt to do this has not been entirely successful, and the approach to the problem has therefore been eclectic. If any synthesis is achieved, it is perhaps in the smaller dimensions of the theoretical frame of this study, not in the realm of any systematic anatomy of the personality of the teacher.

The principal indebtedness of this work is to the concepts developed by Henry A. Murray (1938). Some of the teachers' behaviors are also derived from less explicit attempts to express a unified theory of personality, and others have been drawn from ideas implicit in writings directed to other ends. The criteria guiding the eclectic process were: (1) satisfactory logical, experimental, and empirical demonstrations of the utility of the concepts; (2) relevance of the behaviors to the teacher-pupil situation; and (3) the amenability of the formulations to translation into behaviors that might be identifiable and ratable by the children in the sample.

Murray and his colleagues have postulated a system of needs as basic personality variables. Their descriptions of these needs and of certain accompanying behavioral manifestations proved to be a rich source of characteristic

behaviors which could be translated into the classroom situation. The complete
statement of Murray's position is made in *Explorations in Personality* (1938).
The concept considered to be of greater importance is the definition of "need."
The word refers to a logical construct conceived to form the link between
stimulus and action. Need is both the occurrence of a "readiness to respond in
a certain way under given conditions," and "a noun which stands for the fact
that a certain trend is apt to recur" (1938, p. 61). Thus, "need" signifies a
relatively stable trait of personality.

In a chapter on "The Variables of Personality," Murray lists the major
needs and expands each by setting down a glossary of related nouns, verbs, and
adjectives (1938, pp. 142–242). There is, in addition, a list of items used in a
questionnaire administered to his subjects and devised to furnish the experimenter with a general picture of the behavioral trends of the subjects. Since
people are complex, the inventory of needs is lengthy. It must be remarked
here that all the variables listed by Murray are essential to his purpose, which
is the preparation of detailed psychographs of his subjects. All the variables
would also seem to be essential to the present analysis, in which the totality of
the teacher's personality is a factor in classroom events. Nevertheless, only a
very narrow band of Murray's total spectrum of variables was employed. This
selection was dictated by what the writer conceived to be the requirements of
the study.

Thus, for example, *need Sec* and *need Sentience* were passed over as perhaps
of secondary importance in the present analysis of the classroom behavior of
the teacher. Nevertheless, it is inevitable that such omissions should contribute,
along with other limitations of the research, to some attenuation in the predictive value of this work. Furthermore, not all of the selected variables and their
concomitant behaviors are used with Murray's orientation. His purposes, as
a psychologist attempting to construct a model, led him to concentrate upon
the cluster of variables that characterized the individual. The writer's purposes,
on the other hand, led him to concentrate upon those variables which it was
hypothesized would impinge most radically upon the interpersonal systems
operating in the classroom. Thus Murray's *need Dominance* is certainly characteristic of the highly preclusive teachers as defined here. One of the objecti-
fications of *need Dominance* is actions tending to get others to cooperate. Yet,
for obvious reasons, such acts are subsumed in this study under the "Inclusive"
rubric.

The following variables were selected as being of primary relevance to the
kinds of teacher behaviors that tend to structure the climate of the classroom
(*n* = *need* in Murray's symbols).

n Dominance

To control one's human environment. To influence or direct the behavior of O's by
suggestion, persuasion, or command. To dissuade, restrain, or prohibit. To induce
an O to act in a way which accords with one's sentiments and needs. To get O's to
cooperate. To convince an O of the "rightness" of one's opinion.

n Aggression

To overcome opposition forcefully. To fight. To revenge an injury. To attack, injure or kill an O. To oppose forcefully or punish an O. To belittle, censure, curse or ridicule maliciously an O. To deprecate and slander. (The end that is sought is the expulsion of the painful humiliation of the O.)

n Affiliation

To draw near and enjoyably cooperate or reciprocate with an allied O: an O who resembles the S or who likes the S. To please and win the affection of a cathected O. To adhere and remain loyal to a friend.

n Rejection

To separate oneself from a negatively cathected O. To exclude, abandon, expel, or remain indifferent to an inferior O. To snub or jilt an O.

n Nurturance

To give sympathy and gratify the needs of a helpless O: an infant or any O that is weak, disabled, tired, inexperienced, infirm, defeated, humiliated, lonely, dejected, sick, mentally confused. To assist an O in danger. To feed, help, support, console, protect, comfort, nurse, heal.

n Order

Some persons function in a coherent, coordinated and integrated fashion; others are confused, uncoordinated, and disorganized. (Murray, 1938, pp. 152–203)

This last need (*n Order*) is scored by Murray as the ratio of Conjunctivity to Disjunctivity. One of these terms has been adapted for the purposes of this study. Written as "conjunctive," this rubric designates one of the three independent variables of this research. The variable is discussed more fully below. It should be remarked at the very outset, however, that in the present application the conjunctive category includes many behaviors which Professor Murray would not categorize in the same manner.

The needs described above constitute a conceptualization at a level of personality determinants not directly observable. Measurement of needs therefore becomes measurement of indicants, a class of observable phenomena which constitute a second, less fundamental phase of conceptualization. It is at this second, more descriptive level that a major requirement of this body was identified. It became necessary to draw up an inventory of teachers' behaviors springing from their needs and relevant to, and observable in, the classroom.

One of the most productive sources of such behaviors was found in the work of Harold H. Anderson. During the course of extended observations of teachers, Anderson and his colleagues rated their subjects on several scales. One of these he has termed "socially integrative behavior," which is used in a context that makes his operational definitions directly applicable to the development of this research. Socially integrative behavior is the term applied to "responses characterized by flexibility, to behavior which attempts to bring out differences in others and to find common purposes among differences (Anderson, 1943, p. 461). Anderson has also listed examples of "dominative" behavior (1939, p. 123). Dominative and socially integrative contacts express in action the nature of the teacher–pupil and pupil–pupil relationships in the classroom. For the purposes of this analysis, both terms are applied only to the description of the teacher's behavior.

Integrative contacts are operationally defined as those in which the teacher:

1. Seeks to explore and arouse the interests of the child.

2. Accepts the child as he is. "The child is in the situation; he has given some indication of interest or desire. . . . This type of contact is that indicating the closest rapprochement of child and teacher." (Anderson, *et al.*, 1946, p. 26)

Some of the more specific indicants of integrative behavior are occasions on which the teacher:

1. Extends invitation (as opposed to use of order or pressure).

2. Helps child to advance or redefine a problem.

3. Offers approval.

4. Admits own responsibility, ignorance, or incapacity (Anderson, *et al.*, p. 25).

Dominative techniques are termed by Anderson "an attempt at atomistic living; the desires, purposes, standards, values, judgment, welfare of others do not count . . ." (Anderson, 1939a, p. 123) In other terms, dominative contacts are those in which the teacher acts in a somewhat rigid, even compulsive manner. He tries to make others act in accordance with his own relatively unalterable designs or values. He attacks the personal integration of his pupils, employing shame, force, commands, and threats. He is unwilling to permit the pupils' goals or desires or purposes to contribute to the determination of orientation or class goals (Anderson, 1939a).

In sum, the pupils may perceive the teacher as a person who makes them central or peripheral to the classroom decisions. They may feel that their goals, their abilities, their needs, their "feelings" are taken into account or largely ignored. The teacher behaviors tending to keep the pupils central to the objectives of teaching and to the social interactions of the classroom are termed "inclusive." Those teacher behaviors tending to give the pupils a position on the periphery of these objectives and social interactions are called "preclusive." It is necessary to note that in the theory of this study, "inclusive" and "preclusive" designate two separate variables; they are not halves of a single continuum, in spite of the fact that the two terms happen to have the same stem. (Although it is not anticipated that teachers will array themselves as "pure forms" of either "inclusive" or "preclusive" behavior, it is convenient to have names for each category. But the problem of finding or inventing appropriate designations is beset with pitfalls. Neutral terms seem antiseptic, pseudo-scientific: Type A and Type B? or Teacher-centric and Pupil-centric? The first seems denotatively inadequate, too easily confused and too easily forgotten; the second is cumbersome in its adjectival forms and forbidding in its substantive forms: teacher-centrism? teacher-centricity? On the other hand, the terms already current are inapplicable because of their very definition in the special context of some other writer's work. Besides, such terms are often a little too far from being neutral; witness, for example, authoritarian, laissez-faire, democratic, integrative, and dominative. Thus, since the hard choice must be made between neologism, adaptation, and inappropriate borrowing, this writer has adapted two familiar words to his own strange uses. And so, "inclusive" and "preclusive" behaviors!)

It is possible now to set down a portion of the organization of the independent variables:

I. Preclusive	II. Inclusive
A. Dominative	A. Integrative
B. Aggressive	B. Affiliative
C. Rejectant	C. Nurturant

The items for these categories are found in the "Pupil Survey," Part III, numbers 1 through 49. Three examples are given here:

Aggressive (item 39): This teacher slaps us or handles us roughly.
1—Never. 2—Almost never. 3—Few times. 4—Sometimes. 5—Often.

Rejectant (item 44): This teacher says that certain pupils ought not to be in this class.
1—Almost never. 2—Few times. 3—Sometimes. 4—Often. 5—Very Often.

Integrative (item 33): When we start new work, this teacher helps us to see why this work is important to all of us.
1—Almost never. 2—Few times. 3—Sometimes. 4—Often. 5—Very Often.

It may be said that the preclusive and inclusive variables, operationally defined as items in the survey instruments, are used to characterize the teacher's interpersonal relationships with his pupils. They are factors in the classroom climate created by the social processes inhering in the teaching–learning situation in most American public schools. Explicitly, some of the hypotheses of this study state that when the pupils perceive a teacher as preclusive, their perception of the amount of self-initiated work they perform will be negatively related to that preclusiveness; it will be positively related to the teacher's inclusiveness.

The third independent variable has been called "conjunctive." It should be repeated at this point that although this expression derives from Murray's concepts and terminology, it is here used to describe actions that may be very different from those he envisioned. In the theory of this research, conjunctive behaviors comprise certain interpersonally "neutral" behaviors of the teacher, in contrast to the variables more centrally involved in the interpersonal relations in the classroom. For example, items scored as conjunctive are concerned with the teacher's ability to communicate with his pupils; his classroom management; his command of, and creativeness in dealing with, his subject matter; the level of his demands upon his pupils. These behaviors, very much less affect-laden than those of the inclusive and preclusive actions, are nevertheless considered to be a major factor in the teaching–learning process. They structure, through organization, system, and a sense of orderly progress, whatever interpersonal relations the teacher may establish with his pupils.

Specific items coded as conjunctive may be found in the "Pupil Survey," Part III, numbers 50 through 74. Three examples are:

Level of demand (item 57): This teacher requires pupils to do work that is correct and in good order.
1—Almost never. 2—Few times. 3—Sometimes. 4—Many times. 5—Almost always.

Ability to communicate (item 54): This teacher explains things so I can understand them.
1—Almost never. 2—Few times. 3—Sometimes. 4—Many times. 5—Almost always.

Classroom management (item 73): This teacher keeps her (his) classroom clean and neat.
1—Almost never. 2—Few times. 3—Sometimes. 4—Many times. 5—Almost always.

Some discussion of "level of demand" may be in order. This phrase refers to the standards of work and conduct that the teacher establishes for his pupils, both explicitly and tacitly. Items designed to appraise this behavior deal with the teacher's criteria for the neatness of pupils' work, their comportment in class, their accuracy and punctuality in the performance of school assignments. This demand factor plus others such as the teacher's classroom management, his skill in dealing with his subject matter, and his ability to communicate make up the disjunctive–conjunctive variable.

Other sources of items

A major preoccupation of the early stages in the preparation of the instruments devised for the study was the attempt to build up a large inventory of behavioral items to describe the teacher. In this connection, reference was made to the work of R. N. Cattell. In *Description and Measurement of Personality,* Cattell has worked out what he terms a sort of "Basic English for the description of personality" (1946, p. 217). He proceeds by first listing the trait terms to be found in the dictionary and in technical psychological descriptions. By ingenious manipulation involving successive reductions and subsummations, the list is shortened to 171 traits grouped into 12 primary source traits of personality (Cattell, 1946, pp. 313–317). All of these inventories were canvassed by the writer for descriptions which might have a direct kinship to events considered important in the processes of the classroom. Cattell's adjectival designations were then translated into appropriate teacher behaviors. This list of descriptive terms thus served to amplify those already at hand from the work of Murray and Anderson. Some of these adjectives are listed below under the rubrics used in this research:

I. Preclusive

antisocial	dour	self-centered
surly	hostile	self-assertive
spiteful	impatient	aloof

II. Inclusive

outgoing	cheerful	self-effacing
good-natured	trustful	self-submissive
friendly	patient	responsive

III. Conjunctive–disjunctive

unimaginative	habit-bound	thoughtful
indolent	intelligent	imaginative
changeable	conscientious	

Through an inspection of the need systems and the descriptive indicants utilized thus far, it becomes clear that one of the major clusters of teacher behaviors germane to this investigation is concerned with dominative–autocratic and integrative–democratic behavior. It is from the experimental and conceptual writings of Kurt Lewin, Ronald Lippitt, and Ralph White (1939) that many of the preclusive and inclusive items of the instrument used here were directly derived.

In a series of studies these researchers observed groups of boys engaged in club work under three styles of leadership: autocratic, laissez-faire, and democratic. Among the criteria for individual and group acceptance of club goals was the extent of the boys' spontaneous work performed in the absence of the leader. The following results were observed when the leader was absent: (1) in the clubs under autocracy the percent of time spent in serious work dropped from 74 to 29, a dramatic decrease; (2) in the clubs under democracy the percent of time spent in serious work dropped only from 50 to 46 (Lippitt and White, 1943, p. 504). The relationship thus quantitatively demonstrated corroborates a conclusion of Lippitt in another study: "More creative and constructive work products emerged from the higher unity of the democratic life with its greater amount of objectivity and cooperativeness of interpersonal relationships" (1940, p. 190). It is of course recognized that the analogy between the group goals and processes of the clubs and the more individualized goals and processes of the classroom is far from perfect. The most that is suggested here is that the experimental findings lend some support to the theoretical framework linking teacher behavior and pupil productivity.

One of the richest sources of the particulars of teacher behavior was found in a table describing the methods used by club leaders to create the three types of group atmosphere in the experiment of Lewin, Lippitt, and White (1939). The relationships existing between the descriptions reproduced below and the variables of the present research may be observed by referring to the items in Part III of the "Pupil Survey." Many behaviors termed Authoritarian and Democratic will be found as preclusive and inclusive items respectively.

The Authoritarian Leader:

1. Determines all policy.

2. Dictates techniques and the steps of an activity one at a time, so that future steps are always uncertain to a degree.

3. Dictates particular work tasks and work companions.

4. Is "personal" in his criticism and praise of the work of each member, but remains aloof from active group participation except when demonstrating. He is friendly or impersonal rather than openly hostile.

The Democratic Leader:

1. Makes policy decisions a matter of group discussion, encouraged and assisted by the leader.

2. Gives a perspective of the activity early. He sketches in the general steps to the group goal and where technical advice is needed, he suggests two or three procedures from which the children may make choices.

3. Permits the children to choose their work companions and to divide up the work.

4. Is "objective" or "fact-minded" in his praise and criticism, and tries to be a regular member of the group without doing too much of the work.

Before going on to considerations of the hypotheses and the design of the study, it seems advisable to summarize some of the developments up to this point. It has been noted that this research departs from the trait- and pupil-change studies of teacher competence. Nevertheless, the present work owes a great deal to the trait researches for an enormous amount of pioneer and exploratory efforts, and to the pupil-change researches for their sophistication and scientific rigor.

Several facets of this study should be mentioned. The first is the insistent use of specific teacher behaviors as predictors. A second aspect of the research is that it seeks to recognize and take into account the interactive, social nature of classroom events in terms of relatively simple behaviors and behavior sequences.

The problem has been stated as an attempt to measure the impact of teacher behaviors upon pupil work. In an effort to provide a manageable and coherent frame of reference, this research has tried to avoid an atomistic approach to teacher traits. It has also relinquished the pupil-gain criterion in favor of the pupil-behavior criterion. The independent variables have been described as the preclusive, inclusive, conjunctive behaviors of teachers. The fundamental patterns of needs characterizing such teacher actions have been selected from Murray's theory of personality. The differentials in pupil performance hypothesized to spring from the different kinds of antecedents have been related to the demonstrations of Miller and Dollard concerning the processes of avoidance and approach. Both the amplification of the underlying theory and the sources of the specific items on the teacher's behavior have been indicated. And finally, an effort has been made to present the development of the reasoning which has led to the construction of a frame of reference in which the independent terms comprehend three variables of teacher behaviors: (1) those that tend to make the pupils the focus of classroom experiences, (2) those that tend to keep the pupils on the periphery of classroom experiences, and (3) those that are indicants of relevant interpersonally neutral behaviors of the teacher.

THE DESIGN OF THE STUDY

The hypotheses

The independent measures have been described in terms of three major configurations of teacher behavior. The criterion variables are two categories of pupil productivity: amounts of required and of self-initiated work. With the variables stated in terms of the perceptions of pupils, the hypotheses as to the relationships among these variables are:

1. Preclusive behaviors of teachers are negatively related to the amount of self-initiated work performed by the pupils.

2. Preclusive behaviors of teachers are negatively related to the amount of required work performed by the pupils.

3. Conjunctive behaviors of teachers are positively related to the amount of required work performed by the pupils.

4. Conjunctive behaviors of teachers are positively related to the amount of self-initiated work performed by the pupils, although this relationship is weaker than that of conjunctive behaviors to required work.

5. Inclusive behaviors of teachers are positively related to the amount of self-initiated work performed by the pupils.

6. Inclusive behaviors of teachers are positively related to the amount of required work performed by the pupils, although this relationship is weaker than that of inclusive behaviors to self-initiated work.

The pupils' perceptions as data

From an examination of the hypotheses, it may be seen that they are set in the framework of pupils' perceptions. As a necessary consequence, the pupils' reports of their teachers' behaviors and of their own productivity constitute the major body of data. These data have been collected by means of a group-administered questionnaire, called the "Pupil Survey." It may be profitable to scrutinize some of the problems connected with this kind of subjective reporting.

In a discussion of the reliance that may be placed upon data derived from interviews, H. A. Murray has made some observations that serve as both a severe arraignment and as a defense of the questionnaire:

> There are many reasons why subjects' memories and introspections are usually incomplete or unreliable. Children perceive inaccurately, are very little conscious of their inner states and retain fallacious recollections of occurrences. Many adults are hardly better. Their impressions of past events are hazy and have undergone distortion. Many important things have been unconsciously repressed. Insight is lacking. Consequently, even when a subject wants to give a clear portrait of his early life or contemporary feelings he is unable to do so. Over and above this are his needs for privacy, for the concealment of inferiority, his desire for prestige. Thus, he may consciously inhibit some of his sentiments, rationalize or be a hypocrite about others, or only emphasize what a temporary whim dictates. . . . With most of our subjects there was ground for confidence and perhaps because we trusted their intentions they were disposed to truthfulness. (Murray, 1938, p. 15)

It would appear that many of these same strictures should be kept in mind in the use of the questionnaire that constitutes the major instrument of this study. A substantial effort was made, therefore, to avoid the difficulties described by Murray. During both the pretest and final administration of the questionnaire, the pupils gave strong evidence of desire to be accurate, to provide exactly the information the researchers wanted. In the comments secured from 117 pretest subjects in two communities, there was only one indication of pressures that might have tended to make the responses inaccurate. This single instance arose when one pupil noted the presence of one of his teachers in the room while the survey was being administered. A determined effort was made, therefore, during the final administrations of the survey, to exclude all but research personnel from rooms in which data were being collected. The effort was successful on all but one occasion, when a teacher simply refused to leave and remained at his desk, engaged in some work of his own.

It is worthy of note that in their comments on the experimental administration of the survey, many pupils expressed great confidence in the "test" and appeared to put complete reliance in the guarantees of anonymity and of statistical treatment of their answers. It should also be noted that the nature of the items dealing with pupil work and teacher behavior posed no serious threat to the pupils' security. The questions certainly did not plumb the personal depths that Murray's investigations did.

There is, however, still another question to be examined: Can pupils of secondary school age identify and adequately report the behavior of an adult? Kurt Lewin states that children as young as three or four not only perceive complicated social interactions, but they also frequently "see through" superficialities and surface actions. He goes on to add that children may even be more sensitive than adults to certain social inter-relations in their experience

(Lewin, 1943, p. 120). To this evidence may be added the fact that the pupils were asked to report on relatively simple, specific behaviors, and that they had had repeated opportunities to observe their teachers over substantial periods of time, since the surveys were administered about three weeks before the close of school for the summer vacations.

J. Piaget has spent a long lifetime observing children. In *The Child's Conception of the World* (1929) he makes a very penetrating analysis of the problems involved in securing data from children. The Swiss psychologist discusses three techniques: tests (questionnaires), "pure" observation, and clinical method. Although his own preference is for the data collected by the third method, it is profitable to examine his comments on the use of the questionnaire (Piaget, 1929, pp. 2–4).

If the items of a questionnaire are posed in a manner such that the question and the conditions under which it is asked remain the same, and if the answer to each question is related to a qualitative and quantitative standard of comparison, then, says Piaget, such a technique may have important advantages in the diagnosis of individual children and in the collection of data useful in general psychology. Since a great effort was made to standardize the administration of the "Pupil Survey" and to satisfy the criteria of rigorous standards for the coding of responses, the instrument may perhaps be said to give promise of some utility.

It is recognized, however, that the crucial dilemma of what Piaget considers the essential failure of the questionnaire has yet to be resolved for the use of such an instrument in this study. In essence, Piaget points out the danger that the wording of an item may falsify or risk falsifying the genuine inclination of the subject's answer; i.e., a question may crystalize in the mind of the child an answer heretofore unformulated, which is then stated in terms of the question rather than in pristine form. Piaget's demonstration of this point is powerful and convincing. He concludes that for his purposes the only solution to the difficulty is to give up all idea of using a fixed questionnaire.

It would seem desirable to explain the present use of such an instrument after so trenchant a criticism. It is both necessary and easy to point out differences between the objectives and problems of the two studies. Piaget was concerned with the unknown complexities of concept formation in the child, whereas the present paper deals with phenomena nearer to the perimeter of the child's life experiences, and thus with the relatively easy reporting of overt behaviors. But it may also be possible to meet Piaget's objections in his own terms. In adopting the method of "pure observation" as a substitute for the questionnaire, he develops a procedure at once ingenious and relevant to present purposes. The technique consists simply in observing and recording the *spontaneous* questions of children. An analysis of such data reveals the daily concerns of children as they express them. After this, the relevant questions may be couched in the idiom of the children themselves. Therefore, the form and content of the items thus developed will correspond closely to the original query as it arises spontaneously from the subjects (Piaget, 1929, pp. 4–7). The logic of such an approach seems to be rather clear.

The writer considers that the items used in his survey do to an appreciable degree satisfactorily meet Piaget's own test of derivation from observation. They have, perhaps, been developed through a process closely resembling Piaget's own; i.e., they are an outgrowth of more than fifteen years of professional observation, guidance, and teaching of children of the age of those in the population of this study. In sum, the writer has attempted to use the concepts, vocabulary, and idiom of his subjects in framing the items.

Finally, it may be enlightening to examine the findings of some of the researchers who have already used pupil reports as data for their own investigations. The number of such studies is quite small. Domas and Tiedeman (1950a), having annotated a total of 672 studies of teacher competence, list only seven in which the reliability of the pupils' judgments was reported. Relationships of this measure to other variables were mentioned in only 20 articles.

Cook and Leeds (1947) attempted to measure the emotionalized attitudes of pupils toward teachers and constructed a "Pupils' Rating Scale" for the purpose. The reliability of the instrument approaches 0.90 (1947, p. 406). These writers conclude that children in the intermediate grades furnish ratings that are both reliable and valid. They also find a significant relationship existing between students' ratings and those of principals and experts (1947, p. 409).

Lins employed the device of asking pupils to rank the different teachers by whom they were being taught. Of all the variables he used, only the pupils' evaluation was significantly correlated with the various ratings of a standardized teacher-rating instrument (1946, p. 33).

An analysis made by Flanagan shows that pupils' ratings of the general knowledge possessed by the teacher and of his clarity in presenting ideas were significantly correlated with the scores made by the teacher on the common examinations and on the English Expression Test of the National Teachers Examinations, respectively (1941, p. 64).

On the basis of the preceding discussion, the writer concludes that the framework of pupils' perception constitutes an adequate, even productive, basis for the collection of the kinds of data utilized in this study.

The sample

The research is based upon data collected from administrators, teachers, and 987 eighth-grade pupils in five public junior high schools in two New England communities. All the schools offer departmentalized instruction in the eighth grade. The sample includes 18 teachers of English, 11 teachers of arithmetic, and four of science, a total of 33 teachers.

The pupil sample at the eighth grade level was chosen in order to minimize the selective factor of school dropouts, which begins to operate strongly in the more advanced grades. The U.S. Bureau of Census reports that, of the total population of age 10 to 13 years, 98.5% are in attendance at school. For ages 14 and 15 years, the figure drops to 94.8%. For ages 16 and 17 years, only 71.3% are still in attendance at school (1952). It would appear likely, then, that a sample drawn from the eighth grade might well be more representative of the total population of secondary school age than one drawn from higher grades. It even seems possible that a fairly large percentage of the dropouts above the age of compulsory school attendance might include many pupils who are adversely affected by preclusive and disjunctive behaviors of teachers. The writer concludes, therefore, that the sample drawn from the eighth grade more clearly reflects the impact of teacher behavior upon pupil productivity than if the sample were older and more subject to attrition of voluntary dropouts.

The choice of departmentalized schools was dictated mainly by the interests of the writer. There has been relatively little research of this kind done in such schools, and an approach to the question of isolating the influence of a single teacher among the many with whom secondary pupils customarily work seemed to offer an interesting problem.

Some results of the analysis

The data secured from the scoring of the "Pupil Survey" were analyzed from two different points of view. The first is called the "perception" analysis. As the name suggests, this is an examination of the relationships between the individual pupil's perception of his teacher's behavior and the amounts of work reported by the pupil. In this phase of the work the basic data are the raw scores of each pupil on each of the variables.

The following summary indicates the general trends of the conclusions of this first analysis:

1. A pupil's ratings for each of the two teachers on whom he reported tended to differ rather sharply. This is taken to mean that the instrument provided items by which the individual pupil could make consistent differentiations between the behavior of different teachers.

2. There is only inconclusive evidence that within the framework of the pupil's perceptions the teacher's preclusive behaviors are negatively related to the pupil's scores on required and self-initiated work.

3. There is strong evidence to show that in the individual pupils' perceptions the teacher's conjunctive and inclusive behaviors are each positively related to the pupils' scores in required work and in self-initiated work. The inclusive variable appears to be most closely related to the dependent variables. (Corroborative evidence for these findings appears when r's are computed for all the pupils as one sample and for all the pupils in each community separately.)

The second analysis, termed the "trait" analysis, deals with the average scores of the teachers and seeks to determine whether there are trait differences among teachers on the scales of the survey, i.e., whether the teachers can be characterized in terms of the pupils' observations, and whether these traits are related to average productivity scores of the pupils. (In this discussion the word "group" will denote all the pupils in the sample who take the same subject of instruction with the same teacher.) The following conclusions seem to be warranted in the trait analysis:

1. The reliability coefficients for group assessments are quite substantial, and there is some reason to conclude that the five scales furnish reliable measurements of the teacher traits and of pupil productivity. That is, whereas an individual pupil tended to perceive different teachers differently, the group seemed to be in substantial agreement about the behaviors of the same teacher and about the amount of work done for that teacher.

2. Simple analysis of variance indicates that the scores serve to discriminate among teachers, i.e., the pupils report differing levels of the three kinds of teacher behavior and differing amounts of required and self-initiated work for different teachers.

3. Results very similar to those reported directly above are found when the analysis of variance is computed by schools and by communities. However, from an ingenious application of analysis of variance to hierarchical classifications, devised by Professor John B. Carroll of the Harvard Graduate School of Education, it is possible to say that the consistent and genuine differences observed are those among teachers; the significance noted among the schools and communities is, with two exceptions, no more than would be expected in view of the differences among teachers.

4. The significant differences among teachers are also observed for the sub classes of teachers in each of the three subject areas (English, mathematics, science).

5. When covariance adjustment is made, it is observed that the groups differ in the amounts of required and self-initiated work they report, over and above what would be expected because of the teachers' inclusiveness. These results are not unanticipated, since the theory of the research does not assume that these differences are determined solely or in their greatest part by the groups' perceptions of the teachers' inclusiveness.

6. The trait of inclusiveness, for all teachers and for the teachers in each community, is positively related to average required work scores and to average self-initiated work scores.

It may be said, then, that the method used in this research appears to be productive. The results are marked by strength and consistency, and the reliance upon the observations of pupils was certainly justified. However, it seems clear in retrospect that the conjunctive variable has severe shortcomings. This general category is too broad to be informative; it lacks unity and precision. It is the writer's present opinion that the four factors subsumed under this title each constitute a separate variable that would be important in the analysis of a teacher's classroom behavior. On the other hand, the inclusive variable proved to be very valuable, as did the pupils' productivity scores. The self-initiated work score especially offers exciting new possibilities, since it seems to represent one of the major, but rarely measured, objectives of much modern instructional theory and practice. On sum, there may be some reason to hope that the measures of teacher behaviors and of pupil productivity may be of value in the development of measures of teacher competence and perhaps in the formulation of a more adequate theory of the teaching–learning process.

5

PHASES IN GROUP PROBLEM-SOLVING[8]

ROBERT F. BALES and FRED L. STRODTBECK

The idea that groups go through certain stages or phases in the process of solving problems, or that problem-solving would somehow be more effective if some prescribed order were followed, has been current in the literature for some time (Dewey, 1910; Elliott, 1928; Lasker, 1949). However, the distinction between predicting an empirical order of phases under given conditions and prescribing an ideal order in terms of value judgments has not in all cases been clearly drawn. Furthermore, it has not always been recognized that different types of conditions or problems may result empirically in different sorts of phase movement. The persistence of these confusions has probably been related to the fact that until recently empirical methods which would give operational substance to the ideas have been lacking.

This paper presents a method of testing for the empirical existence of differentiated phases in group process and some evidence that under certain particular conditions a certain type of phase movement does tend to appear. The type of phase movement described is *not* held to be universal in an empirical sense. Whether it appears empirically depends upon a large number of conditions. Whether this type of phase movement is "optimum" under certain conditions in terms of value standards is a different problem and is not discussed in this paper.

By phases in the hypothesis presented below, we mean qualitatively different subperiods within a total continuous period of interaction in which a group proceeds from initiation to completion of a problem involving group decision.

A PHASE HYPOTHESIS FOR FULL-FLEDGED PROBLEMS

The present phase hypothesis is restricted to instances in which groups work toward the goal of a group decision on a full-fledged problem. Briefly stated, the phase hypothesis is the proposition that under these conditions groups tend

[8] From *The Journal of Abnormal and Social Psychology* **46**, 1951, 485–495. Reprinted by permission of the American Psychological Association and the authors.

to move in their interaction from a relative emphasis upon problems of *orientation*, to problems of *evaluation*, and subsequently to problems of *control*, and that concurrent with these transitions, the relative frequencies of both *negative reactions* and *positive reactions* tend to increase. The terms in the statement of the hypothesis have as their operational referents the acts which are briefly defined in Fig. 1–19. There are 12 categories on the observation list. The present hypothesis is stated in terms of five groups of these categories, identified by the brackets on the left and right of the list. Categories 6 and 7 are grouped as dealing with problems of orientation; 5 and 8 deal with problems of evaluation; 4 and 9, with problems of control; 10, 11, and 12, with negative reactions; and 1, 2, and 3, with positive reactions. This is a relatively crude grouping, and it seems likely that further experience will enable us to state the hypothesis in a way which treats each category separately.

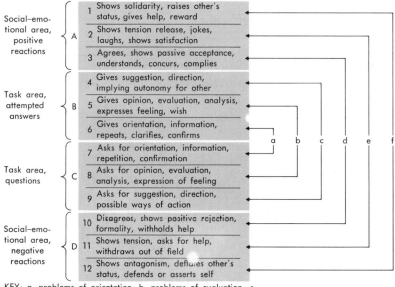

KEY: a, problems of orientation; b, problems of evaluation; c, problems of control; d, problems of decision; e, problems of tension-management; f, problems of integration

FIG. 1–19. Interaction process categories defined and grouped by types.

This particular phase hypothesis is expected to hold only under *certain conditions*, which we try to identify and state below. In general, we believe that the rates of activity we observe in each of the categories, and the way these rates move, over time, vary with changes in the conditions under which the interaction takes place. A major distinction can be drawn between those conditions which may be regarded as constituted prior to the period of observation, and those which arise and change during the actual period of observation.

Under prior conditions we tend to think of three broad classes of variables: (a) the personalities of the individual members in their idiosyncratic aspects; (b) those characteristics the members have in common, as a part of their parent culture, as well as of the subculture of the particular group under observation; and (c) the organization of the group, that is, the expectations the members have established concerning their social relationships with each other and their different positions in this total constellation of expectations.

In addition to these prior conditions, we recognize (d) a series of conditions arising from the nature of the problems faced during the specific period of observation, which change as the group interaction moves through time.

Obviously, we are not able to specify the content of these four classes of conditions with the degree of refinement we should like, but as a first approximation we sketch the following requirements as the conditions under which the present phase hypothesis is expected to hold. Whenever the group or the problem does not meet the requirements, the particular phase movement described above is not expected to appear.

We have no experimental evidence as to the effects of variations in personality composition of the group on phase movement. Our data are all obtained from groups of persons assumed to be "normal." There are more or less obvious reasons for supposing that the hypothesis should not be expected to apply to groups involving persons of subnormal intelligence or seriously disturbed personalities.

We assume the participants will be adult, or near-adult, members of our own culture. This gives us some expectation that they will speak English, have some formal education, etc. As to the particular subculture of the groups, if the group has met before, it seems possible that such features as special procedural customs and training in group discussion methods might directly affect the phase movement. Hence, it may be that certain groups could deliberately evolve procedures to circumvent the expected movement, or to follow it in spite of conditions which would otherwise prevent it. Obviously, it is necessary to exclude cases of this type.

We require a group in which there is some minimum pressure to maintain its solidarity so that joint decisions will have some binding power over the members after the sequence observed, and so that the presence of disagreement, tension, and antagonism will be negatively valued. The status differences among members of the group should not be so great as to deny each member the right to participate and influence the choice of the ultimate decision. It appears likely that serious status struggles within the group may modify the phase movement, although this has not yet been explored. The group size may vary from two to twenty, or may be even larger, perhaps, if there is the possibility of face-to-face interaction among the participants over a common problem.

As to the duration of the period of observation itself, we require the selection for analysis of a single complete "topical cycle of operations," from the recognition of a topical problem to its disposition by the group. We do not mean this requirement to exclude periods in which a group considers several topics involved in a single major decision, but we do require that, when topical problems are considered serially as items on an agenda, the period of discussion on each topic be analyzed separately. Thus, an entire meeting in some cases may be an appropriate period for analysis; in other cases, discussion of a single agenda item may be appropriate. (In addition, we exclude groups not concerned with a fairly specific problem of group planning and decision. For example, we exclude groups in which the aim or main emphasis is on expressive personal interaction, such as therapeutic interviews, play groups, meetings of friends at a cocktail party, and the like.)

Finally, we require a task in which it may be assumed that the functional problems of *orientation, evaluation,* and *control* are each to a major degree unsolved at the beginning of observation and are solved in some degree during the period of observation. More specifically:

With regard to *orientation,* members of the group must have some degree of ignorance and uncertainty about the relevant facts, but individually possess facts relevant to decision. A clear example of a group which meets this requirement is a diagnostic council, where the members have seen the patient separately and have made different tests relevant to a decision as to what to do with the patient.

With regard to problems of *evaluation,* we require that the problem not be what is sometimes called an "open and shut" case. We need to be able to assume that the members possess somewhat different values or interests and that the problem is such that it involves several different values and interests as criteria by which the facts of the situation and the proposed course of action are to be judged.

With regard to problems of *control* (of the members over one another and over the common environment) we require that there be both pressure for a group decision and the expectation of further joint action. It is also assumed that there are a number of possible alternatives with different, and perhaps uncertain, degrees of potential frustration or satisfaction associated with various choices.

When problems lack or greatly minimize any of these three characteristics, we speak of them as being *truncated.* When the three characteristics are present, we speak of the problem as being *full-fledged.* We do not expect the particular phase hypothesis stated above to hold for truncated problems. Presumably, it may be possible to formulate other phase hypotheses which will describe the phase movement for particular kinds of truncated problems.

The above conditions may seem formidable at first glance, but it is our opinion that they are met in group conferences, committees, and the like with sufficient frequency to insure the practical importance of investigating situations of this type.

In order to test the hypothesis empirically, it is necessary to specify the length of a phase. In the absence of any compelling rationale, we have adopted a simple convention: After the observations have been recorded on a moving tape (Bales and Gerbrands, 1948), we divide into thirds the cycle of opera-

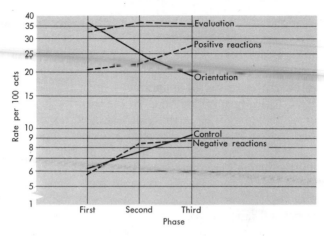

FIG. 1–20. Relative frequency of acts by type and phase, based upon 22 sessions.

tions which constitutes the total period to be analyzed, producing the *first*, *middle*, and *final* phases. The total period is divided so that each phase includes one-third of the acts of the total set. (This is approximately equivalent to a time division into thirds, though not quite, since we have observed that there is some tendency for the interaction to speed up toward the latter part of topical cycles.) Since we have no basis for predicting the absolute number of acts by type for each phase, we implement the hypothesis by designating the phase in which we expect the number of acts of a particular type to be high, intermediate, or low when rank-ordered.

We have drawn Fig. 1–20 on the basis of the summary data for all group sessions examined in the present study in order to illustrate something of the magnitude of the variation which may be expected. It should be emphasized that, when we say there is a shift in relative emphasis from problems of orientation in the first phase, to problems of evaluation in the second phase, to problems of control in the third phase, we do not mean that the absolute magnitude for the selected activity is greater than all others in that phase; we mean, rather, that the rate of the selected activity is at its own high point in the designated phase. (It should be noted that the cases upon which Fig. 1–20 is based include a number in which the conditions for the hypothesis are not fully met, and yet the phase movement of the aggregate is of the type we specify will hold for individual cases only under full-fledged conditions. This apparent paradox will be discussed later.)

RATIONALE FOR THE HYPOTHESIS

For an interacting group, the solution of problems of orientation is assumed to bear an enabling relation to the solution of problems of evaluation and control and, in this sense, to be functionally prerequisite to their solution. That is, an individual may be cognitively oriented to a situation and speak of it to others in cognitive terms without committing himself overtly either to evaluation of it, or an attempt to control it; but speaking to the other in evaluative terms implies previous orientation, and the attempt to control the situation by joint action implies both previous orientation and evaluation. Something like this sequence of process may be characteristic of individual human problem-solving on the nonovert level. Historically speaking, most of the theories about steps or stages in group problem-solving seem to be more or less direct extrapolations of steps or stages assumed to exist in individual mental processes. The present rationale is based directly on conditions present in the overt process of social interaction between individuals through an appreciable lapse of time, and it may be compatible with any number of theories regarding the mental processes of individual problem-solving.

In the most general rationale of the whole set of categories (see Fig. 1–19), 3 and 10 are thought of as dealing with problems of *decision;* 2 and 11, with problems of *tension management;* and 1 and 12, with problems of *integration* or *reintegration* of the group. For the present phase hypothesis, these categories have been grouped, not according to the type of functional problem with which they deal, but according to their implication, positive or negative, for the solution of these types of problems. These problems we call social–emotional problems, to distinguish them from those which are more directly task-connected (see Fig. 1–19, brackets on left).

It is our assumption that efforts to solve problems of orientation, evaluation, and control (that is, attempts to accomplish the task) tend to lead to differentiation of the roles of the participants, both as to the functions they perform and their gross amounts of participation. Both types of differentiation tend to carry status implications which may threaten or disturb the existing order or balance of status relations among members and thus impair the basic solidarity of the group.

This impairment, we assume, tends to grow more marked as the group passes from emphasis on problems of orientation to problems of evaluation, and still more acute as it passes on to its heaviest emphasis on problems of control. This assumption seems to be a more generalized way of stating the findings of certain other studies. For example, Lippitt (1940) found negative reactions to autocratic control or leadership in boys' clubs under certain conditions, and Rogers and his associates (1942) tend to find a minimization of negative reactions on the part of clients when the counselor confines himself to nondirective (or, in our categories, orienting) types of activity. Thus, the present assumption may be regarded as a generalization of this connection between degree of control and negative reactions, and as applying to different points in the process of the same group, not simply to differences between groups.

Thus, as we conceive the process, a series of changes in the social–emotional relationships of the members tend to be set in motion by pressures arising initially from the demands of the external problem or outer situation. As they grow more acute, these social–emotional problems, as well as the task problems, tend to be expressed or dealt with in overt interaction. These, in brief, are the theoretical reasons for expecting that with our crude division of the cycle of operations into three phases, rates in Categories 10, 11, and 12 will be lowest in the initial period and highest in the final period, moving concomitantly with the emphasis on problems of control.

However, at the extreme end of the final period, assuming that the members' attempts at control over the outer situation and over each other are successful and a final decision is reached, we expect the rates in Categories 1, 2, and 3 also to rise to their peak. In other words, the group tends to confirm its agreement and to release in diffuse ways the tensions built up in its prior task-efforts, repairing the damage done to its state of consensus and social integration. We note joking and laughter so frequently at the ends of meetings that they might almost be taken as a signal that the group has completed what it considers to be a task effort, and is ready for disbandment or a new problem. This last-minute activity completes the hypothetical cycle of operations both for the task problems and social–emotional problems. The apparent incongruity of predicting a peak for both negative and positive reactions in the third phase is thus explained. Negative and positive reactions tend to be successive emphases within the crudely defined third phase.

TESTING THE PHASE HYPOTHESIS

To test the phase hypothesis, we have considered *all* the protocols available in our files which had been scored in a form appropriate for this investigation. The number is small, only 22 cases. Some of these cases represent several hours of sustained interaction by one group, while others represent the discussion of single topics taken from longer sessions. The groups involved were originally observed for a number of different purposes. Some were experimentally formed groups with assigned tasks. Some were operating groups that allowed us to sit in and observe. We have given a brief description of the task considered by each of these groups in Table 1–16.

The writers have judged each of the 22 cases separately and have agreed that 8 of the 22 satisfactorily fulfill the conditions outlined in earlier paragraphs. The distinction between cases which meet and cases which fail to meet the conditions can be illustrated by discussion of a few concrete ones.

Cases 8, 10, 11, and 15 were chess problem-solving groups in which the participants were well oriented to the factual aspects of the problem before beginning interaction. Chess problems are almost uniquely "full information" problems, and the participants were skilled chess players. The profile of scores generated in these sessions was uniformly below the expected limit on giving information and orientation, according to empirical norms we have published elsewhere (Bales, 1950a). On this basis, the writers classified this problem as being *truncated;* it was assumed not to have the necessary requirement for orientation.

An interesting and partially parallel instance is Case 1. Here, again, a chess problem which the group solves cooperatively is involved, but the participants

Table 1–16

Transpositions Required to Establish the Order Predicted by the Phase Hypothesis for 22 Sets of Observations

Case No.	Fulfills conditions	Description of group and task	No. of transpositions required
1	Yes	Five-man chess novice group planning first move of seven-move problem	0*
2	Yes	Three-man group on 1st group projective story	1*
3	Yes	Eight-man academic group planning thesis	2*
4	Yes	Four-man chess club evaluating past performance and planning future performance	2*
5	Yes	Seven-man college group in discussion skills planning own operations	2*
6	Yes	Four-man steering committee planning arrangements for Christmas party	3*
7	Yes	Four-man chess club evaluating past performance and planning future operation	4
8	No	4-man chess club solving 2-move problem	4
9	No	3-man group on 3rd group projective story	4
10	No	4-man chess club solving 2-move problem	5
11	No	4-man chess club solving 2-move problem	5
12	No	3-man group on 4th group projective story	5
13	Yes	7-man college group on discussion skills	5
14	No	3-man chess club constructing chess problem	6
15	No	4-man chess club solving 2-move problem	6
16	No	3-man group on 5th group projective story	6
17	No	3-man group on 2nd group projective story	6
18	No	3-man role-playing group deciding between two fictional alternative purchases	6
19	No	8-man academic discussion group on theory	7
20	No	3-man chess club constructing a chess problem	8
21	No	3-man chess club constructing a chess problem	10
22	No	5-man chess novice group planning second move of 7-move problem	11

* Significant at or beyond the 0.05 level.

are novices who have just been instructed for one hour in the rules of the game. They have their instruction manuals with them and they are still uncertain about the identity of the pieces and the best mode of attack. The phase sequence of their interaction up to their decision as to their first move is in complete accord with the hypothesis. In the planning of their second move, however, they were able to draw upon their earlier discussion in which they had discussed future moves as well, and the problem was truncated for them in terms of the reduced emphasis on orientation, just as it had been for the previous chess group described above.

A similar sequence of topical cycles which seemed to involve successively less orientation is seen in Cases 2, 9, 12, 16, and 17. In these cases the same group made up stories to the five cards of the Guetzkow and Henry Group Projection Sketches (1949). The interaction only up to the point of completion of the first card (Case 2) was markedly in the expected phase order.

In Cases 14, 20, and 21, members of a chess club were confronted with the task of *constructing* an original chess problem, starting from an empty board. They were fully oriented to the task at the beginning of the sequence, since they were quite familiar with chess problems. They began with suggestions in order to determine initial placements of pieces on the board, and they became more concerned with problems of orientation as more pieces were added to the board and the complications thus increased. Two of these three sequences were the direct reverse of the phase order expected under full-fledged conditions on problems of orientation and control. It may be that certain types of creative problems typically produce this type of approach, and that a different sort of phase hypothesis could be evolved for such tasks. An increasing complexity of orientation needed as the task evolves might be a factor in limiting the number of persons who may work together successfully on creative problems.

To test the conformity between the observed orderings and the orderings predicted by our original theoretical analysis, we have employed a model based upon the occurrence of the maxima and minima in the predicted phase rather than a model in which absolute magnitudes were considered. Table 1–17 presents the hypothesis in a form appropriate for this type of test. Table 1–17 may be compared with Fig. 1–20 to clarify its meaning.

The following hypothetical example, which involves only one type of act, illustrates this method of analysis.

Phases in which acts of orientation are:

	High	Intermediate	Low
Predicted:	First	Middle	Final
Observed:			
Example I	First	Middle	Final
Example II	Middle	First	Final
Example III	Final	Middle	First

In Example I, the observed values match exactly with the prediction; that is, the high, intermediate, and low values occur in the periods in which they were predicted to occur. In Examples II and III there are departures from the prediction. The main point of this discussion of the model is the justification of the method adopted to evaluate the degree of departure. We believe that it is inappropriate to consider the goodness of fit in terms of the number of instances in which the predicted values match the observed values. In terms of matches alone, there is no distinction between II and III; in each example one element

Table 1–17

Expected Phase in Which Frequencies of Acts by Type Will Be High, Intermediate, and Low under Conditions of the Full-Fledged Problem

Type of act	High	Intermediate	Low
Orientation	First	Middle	Final
Evaluation	Middle	Final	First
Control	Final	Middle	First
Negative	Final	Middle	First
Positive	Final	Middle	First

corresponds with the predicted placement. This is not a satisfactory description, however, since one feels that there is a more serious departure from expectation if the predicted high is interchanged with the predicted low, as in III, than if the predicted high is interchanged with the predicted median, as in II. Fortunately, if we count not the number of matches but the number of *transpositions* of adjacent values required to establish the predicted order, we may take account of the distinction between II and III.

To illustrate the counting of transpositions, Example II can be modified to fit the predicted order by exchanging the middle and first element, whereas for Example III there are three transpositions required: first with middle, first with final, and middle with final. A statistical evaluation of the difference between the predicted and observed orders can be made on the basis of the number of transpositions required. It can be demonstrated[9] that if there are three or fewer transpositions, the null hypothesis may be rejected at the 0.05 level.

By reference to Table 1–16, it may be noted that six of the eight sessions which were judged to have fulfilled the stated necessary conditions were also significant in the sense that they would require only the three transpositions or less required to reject the null hypothesis of random distribution at the .05 level. Two sessions which we judged to meet the conditions were not significantly different from random expectations.

It is thus apparent that cases which meet the conditions do deviate significantly from random expectations, and that cases which do not meet the conditions do not deviate significantly. In short, one or more alternative phase hypotheses, accompanied by corresponding specification of conditions, are required before we can duplicate the relatively accurate predictions of the occurrence of maxima and minima which we have made for the eight individual cases in question.

---

[9] The statistic employed is essentially a repeated application of Kendall's rank correlation coefficient tau. Persons wishing to perform computations for orderings of other sizes can obtain the appropriate coefficients of the powers of x to be inserted in the formula from Kendall (1943, pp. 388–437).

DISCUSSION OF RESULTS

The 14 cases which failed to meet the conditions also failed to conform to the phase movement predicted for full-fledged conditions. Nevertheless, when all of the acts of the 22 cases are summed together by type of act and phase, the values for each type of act have maxima and minima which correspond exactly with the particular phase movement under discussion. These data are presented in Table 1–18 and earlier, graphically, in Fig. 1–20. How is this paradoxical finding to be interpreted?

It may be that we simply have a sample of cases in which compensating differences happen to exist, and that new aggregates of cases would fail to show the pattern. On the other hand, it may be that certain conditions are operating which tend to be similar from case to case, in spite of particular differences. There are certain conditions which seem to be more or less inherent in the nature of the process of interaction or communication itself. If this were not so, it would be difficult to produce a set of categories of the sort used in the present observations, which we believe to be very general and applicable in formal terms at least, to any interaction.

Table 1–18

Acts by Type and Phase, Total for 22 Cases

Type of act	Phase			Total
	First	Middle	Final	
Orientation	1,668	1,170	916	3,574
Evaluation	1,550	1,792	1,656	4,998
Control	285	364	429	1,078
Negative	275	374	408	1,057
Positive	984	1,058	1,361	3,403
Total*	4,762	4,758	4,770	14,290

* The Totals in phases are not quite equal, due to the fact that no systematic technique was employed to distribute the extra acts when the total acts of a session were not divisible by three.

We suggest that parts of the interaction process itself tend to affect other parts in such a way that, at the time of any given act, the acts which have gone before, or which have not yet occurred but are expected to come, constitute a set of "internal" conditions which operate in addition to whatever "external" conditions there may be of the sorts specified in the statement of the hypothesis. We know that in the more microscopic act-to-act sequences this is the case. Questions tend to be followed by attempted answers, and these in turn tend to be followed by positive or negative reactions or more questions (Bales, 1950, pp. 129–131). These are "internal tendencies" of the process itself on a microscopic time span. It may be that similar internal tendencies operate on the more molar level of longer chains of sequences leading to group decision.

It can now be pointed out that the rationale of the phase hypothesis presented earlier is essentially an argument based on an assumption that there are internal tendencies of interaction considered as a system distributed between persons and through time. If one started with the assumption that interaction does constitute a social system and that it will tend to exhibit certain systematic properties on that account, how would he go about demonstrating this empirically? The critical logical difficulty would seem to be that the system he is trying to investigate never operates apart from external conditions which are expected to influence the behavior which actually occurs. The effects of the external conditions are always compounded with, or confounded with, the effects of the internal conditions.

One approach, perhaps, is to attempt to observe the system operating in a set of conditions complete enough and balanced in such a way as to call out the full range of internal tendencies or possibilities of the interaction process, so that the empirical observations might display in most articulate form the effects of the internal conditions. Here it may be pointed out that the description of the set of conditions we have called the full-fledged problem is essentially an attempt to specify a set of external conditions which might meet this methodological requirement so far as the problem the group is working on is concerned.

The other approach which suggests itself is an attempt to randomize in some fashion the kinds of external conditions involved, and to deal with large aggregates of cases. If there are internal tendencies characteristic of interaction as a systematic process or social system, the similarity of these tendencies from case to case, in spite of the differences due to external conditions, would be expected to exert a constant "biasing" effect away from randomness. In aggregates of cases, then, where the external conditions of individual cases are varied enough to average out, one would expect the effects of the internal-system tendencies to become apparent.

In short, the present reasoning suggests that there are two ways of detecting the presence and nature of rather general internal tendencies, if, indeed, they exist: first, by letting them operate under *full-fledged* rather than *truncated* external conditions, and second, by averaging out various kinds of truncation and accentuation by adding many widely varied cases together.

If later research indicates the general methodological position taken here to be tenable, the problems of experimentally investigating how particular types of external conditions influence the course of interaction are greatly simplified. It may be that empirically average phase tendencies like those presented in Table 1–18 can be taken as sufficiently representative of the effects of parts of the process on other parts, i.e., the social system effects. In experimental designs, then, where a full-fledged problem is used as the basic testing situation, deviations from the empirical norm might be used as evidences of the effects of known or experimentally introduced conditions. For example, the experimental introduction of persistent difficulties of communication or orientation might upset the phase sequence expected on the basis of the internal tendencies of the interaction system alone.

Conversely, in using the method for clinical analysis or training of particular groups, groups might be set up under full-fledged conditions, and the deviations from the empirical norm used as diagnostic indicators of otherwise unknown characteristics of the group or the members. For example, the appearance of a high rate of negative reactions in the first phase of a standard full-fledged problem might indicate the presence of hostilities not arising out of the present interaction itself, but existing as a prior condition.

SUMMARY

A set of categories for the firsthand observation of group process has been presented. A set of conditions has been described which we believe to be characteristic of many staff conferences, committees, and similar groups dealing with problems of analysis and planning with the goal of group decision. We have presented a hypothesis which states that under these specified conditions the process tends to move through time from a relative emphasis upon problems of *orientation,* to problems of *evaluation,* and subsequently to problems of *control;* and that concurrent with these transitions, the relative frequencies of both *negative reactions* and *positive reactions* tend to increase.

It has been shown that all 22 sessions available to the experimenters from prior observations, when considered as an aggregate, show a significant departure from a random distribution of acts between phases. It has been shown further that the observed significance is attributable to the inclusion of cases which meet the specified conditions. Individual cases which do not meet the conditions do not show a significant departure from a random distribution of phase movements.

However, when all of the acts of the 22 cases are summed together by type of act and phase, the values for each type of act have maxima and minima which correspond exactly with the particular phase movement postulated for individual cases under the specified full-fledged conditions. This finding may be accidental. The suggestion is offered, however, that in addition to the external conditions specified, the interaction process should be considered as a system, with internal tendencies which make each part of the process a condition to other parts. These "internal" conditions are assumed to be similar to some degree from case to case and to exert a constant "biasing" effect. This biasing effect becomes apparent either in individual cases under full-fledged external conditions or in aggregates of cases in which differences in external conditions average out.

It is suggested that if the phase movement described here does represent the effect of conditions internal to the process itself, it may be used with some advantage as a base-line for the detection of discrepancies or accentuations due to known or experimentally introduced external conditions or, conversely, as diagnostic indicators of the presence of otherwise unknown conditions.

Finally, the general method of testing for the existence of any given phase pattern seems to open the way for an experimental attack on problems of determining the effects of various patterns of process under various conditions, effects on the motivation and satisfaction of participants and on their performance of the group task.

TEACHER INFLUENCE
IN THE CLASSROOM[10]

NED A. FLANDERS

Most of the research reviewed in this article makes use of observational techniques to assess the spontaneous behavior of the teacher. The analysis of spontaneous teacher behavior involves the development and standardization of a system of categories that an observer can use to note the frequency of qualitatively different acts. Systematic observation produces a frequency distribution within discrete categories that can be drawn as a histogram profile covering short or long periods of observation. Profiles from long periods of observation ignore variability of teacher influence that is easily seen if profiles of the same teacher over short time periods are compared.

The ultimate goal of the study of teacher influence in the classroom is to achieve understanding of teacher–pupil interaction, and, in particular, to specify conditions in which learning is maximized. The research on classroom climate that is reviewed in the next section contributes to a general understanding of teacher influence over long time periods, but it ignores short-term influence patterns of the teacher and changes in classroom conditions that occur as a result of learning.

RESEARCH ON CLASSROOM CLIMATE

The words *classroom climate* refer to generalized attitudes toward the teacher and the class that the pupils share in common in spite of individual differences. The development of these attitudes is an outgrowth of classroom social interaction. As a result of participating in classroom activities, pupils soon develop shared expectations about how the teacher will act, what kind of a person he is, and how they like their class. These expectations color all aspects of classroom behavior, creating a social atmosphere or climate that appears to be fairly

[10] This previously unpublished paper is published here with the permission of the author.

stable, once established. Thus the word *climate*[11] is merely a shorthand reference to those qualities that consistently predominate in most teacher–pupil
contacts and contacts between pupils in the presence or absence of the teacher.

The earliest systematic studies of spontaneous pupil and teacher behavior
that relate directly to classroom climate are those of H. H. Anderson and his
colleagues Helen and Joseph Brewer, and Mary Frances Reed (1939, 1945,
1946), and are based on the observation of "dominative" and "integrative"
contacts. It is essential to understand the qualitative differences between an
integrative and a dominative social contact because most of the research on
classroom climate makes similar behavioral distinctions.

A preliminary study showed that it was possible to devise reliable measures of
the behavior of young children. Behavior was recorded as "contacts" and divided
into two groups of categories. If a child snatched a toy, struck a playmate, or com-
manded him, or if he attempted to force him in some way, such contacts were included under the term "domination." By such behavior he ignored the rights of the
companion; he tended to reduce the free interplay of differences and to lead toward
resistance or conformity in responding or adapting to another.

Other contacts were recorded which tended to increase the interplay of differences. Offering a companion a choice or soliciting an expression of his desires
were gestures of flexibility and adaptation. These tended in the direction of discov-
ering common purposes among differences. Such contacts were grouped under the
term "socially integrative behavior" (Anderson *et al.*, 1946, p. 12).

The findings of Anderson *et al.* are based on the study of preschool, primary, and elementary school classrooms involving several different teachers and
extending over several years. Taken altogether, their imaginative research has
produced a series of internally consistent and significant findings. First, the
dominative and integrative contacts of the teacher set a pattern of behavior
that spreads throughout the classroom; the behavior of the teacher, more than
that of any other individual, sets the climate of the class. The rule is that when
either type of contact predominates, domination incites further domination,
and integration stimulates further integration. It is the teacher's tendency that
spreads among pupils even when the teacher is no longer in the room. Furthermore, the pattern a teacher develops in one year is likely to persist in his
classroom the following year with completely different pupils. Second, when
a teacher's integrative contacts increase, pupils show an increase in spontaneity
and initiative, voluntary social contributions, and acts of problem-solving.
Third, when a teacher's dominative contacts increase, the pupils are more easily

---

[11] Climate is assessed either by analysis of teacher–pupil interaction and inference of
underlying attitudes, or by the use of a pupil attitude inventory and prediction of
the quality of classroom interaction. Its precise meaning, when commonly used, is
seldom clear, just as its synonyms "morale," "rapport," and "emotional tone" are
also ambiguous. To have any meaning at all, the word must always be qualified by
an adjective, and it is in the choice of adjectives that researchers reduce their scientific integrity by losing their objectivity; e.g., Lippitt and White's choice of "authoritarian" and "democratic" to describe climate.

distracted from schoolwork, and show greater compliance to, as well as rejection of, teacher domination.

A year or so after Anderson started his work, Lippitt and White (1943), working with Kurt Lewin, carried out laboratory experiments to analyze the effects of adult leaders' influence on boys' groups. The laboratory approach used had certain advantages (or disadvantages, depending on your point of view) in studying the effects of the adult leader's behavior. First, the contrasting patterns of leader behavior were purified and made more consistent as a result of training and role playing. Second, differences in the underlying personalities and appearances of the adult leaders were minimized through role rotation. Third, since there were only five boys to a group, the effect of the pattern of leader behavior was greater than it would have been in a classroom. Roughly speaking, the pattern Lippitt and White named "authoritarian leadership" consisted of dominative contacts, "democratic leadership" consisted of integrative contacts, and "laissez-faire leadership" consisted of irregular and infrequent integrative contacts with an element of indifference to the total group that is seldom found in a classroom and was not present in the studies of Anderson *et al.*

Most of the conclusions of the study by Lippitt and White confirm or extend the general conclusions of Anderson *et al.* with some semantic modification but very little change, if any, in behavioral meaning. From the point of view of classroom teaching, one interesting extension was the conceptualization of "dependence on the leader" by Lippitt and White. This is a state of affairs in which group members are unable to proceed without directions from the leader. Anderson *et al.* used the category "conforming to teacher domination," and thus noted its occurrence, but in the more concentrated social climates of the laboratory experiments it was clearly seen that extensive compliance occurs when there is a generalized condition of dependence.

As a result of these two basic and independent studies that produced mutually supportive results, the notion of social climate was established. Additional research revealed minor variations of the central theme already established. Withall (1949) showed that a simple classification of the teacher's verbal statements into seven categories produced an index of teacher behavior almost identical to the integrative–dominative (I–D) ratio of Anderson *et al.* Flanders (1951) created laboratory situations in which contrasting patterns of teacher behavior were exposed to one pupil at a time. A sustained dominative pattern was consistently disliked by pupils, reduced their ability to recall, later on, the material studied, and produced disruptive anxiety as indicated by galvanic skin response and changes in the heartbeat rates. Pupil reactions to integrative contacts showed these trends reversed. Perkins (1951), using Withall's technique, studied groups of teachers organized to study the topic of child growth and development. He found that greater learning about child growth and development occurred when group discussion was free to focus on that topic; groups with an integrative type of leader were able to do this more frequently than were groups led by a dominative type of leader. In a large cross-sectional study that did not use observation of spontaneous teacher behavior, Cogan (1956) administered a single paper-and-pencil instrument containing three scales to 987 eighth-grade students in 33 classrooms. On one scale, student perceptions of the teacher were assessed; on another scale, students reported how often they did required schoolwork; on the last scale, students reported how often they did extra, nonrequired schoolwork. Cogan's first scale assessed traits one would associate with the behavior patterns observed in the research already cited, although it was developed in terms of Murray's list of major personality needs (1938). The items of one pattern were grouped as "dominative," "aggressive," and "rejectant"; these correspond to Anderson's dominative and integrative patterns. Cogan found that students reported doing more assigned and extra schoolwork when they perceived the teacher's behavior as falling into the integrative pattern rather than the dominative pattern.

Altogether, these research projects support the statements about classroom climate that appear in the first paragraph of this section. The two teacher behavior patterns that create the contrasting classroom climates have been well established.

The integrative pattern[12]	The dominative pattern[12]
a) Accepts, clarifies, and supports the ideas and feelings of pupils.	a) Expresses or lectures about own ideas or knowledge.
b) Praises and encourages.	b) Gives directions or orders.
c) Asks questions to stimulate pupil participation in decision making.	c) Criticizes or deprecates pupil behavior with intent to change it.
d) Asks questions to orient pupils to schoolwork.	d) Justifies his own position or authority.

Associated attitudes of teacher (suggested by Cogan)		Associated attitudes of teacher (suggested by Cogan)	
Outgoing	Patient	Antisocial	Impatient
Good-natured	Self-effacing	Surly	Self-assertive
Friendly	Self-submissive	Spiteful	Self-centered
Cheerful	Responsive	Dour	Aloof
Trustful		Hostile	

These research results should be interpreted with caution. They do not suggest that there is a single pattern of teacher behavior that should be continually maintained in the classroom. Anyone with teaching experience recognizes that there are situations in which an integrative teacher behavior pattern

---

[12] Most of the researchers cited have their own favorite words to describe essentially the same behavior patterns. Anderson *et al.:* "dominative vs. integrative"; Lippitt and White: "authoritarian vs. democratic vs. laissez-faire"; Withall, Flanders, Perkins: "teacher-centered vs. student-centered"; and Cogan: "preclusive vs. inclusive." For the sake of simplicity, Anderson's terms have been used in the first section of this paper; the concepts of "direct influence" and "indirect influence" will be introduced later.

is less appropriate than a dominative pattern; furthermore, it is possible that identical acts by the teacher may in one situation be perceived by pupils as dominative and in another situation as integrative. These research results do show that, over a period of time, more integrative than dominative teacher pupil contacts will establish desirable pupil attitudes and superior patterns of work. The work of Anderson *et al.* and Cogan presents evidence that a desirable climate results in more learning, although additional evidence is needed to confirm the conclusion.

THE IMPLICATION OF RESEARCH ON CLASSROOM CLIMATE FOR A THEORY OF INSTRUCTION

Research on classroom climate is incomplete because it does not contribute to the question, "Why and when should a teacher react in either a dominative or integrative manner?" An adequate theory of instruction should specify the effects of integrative or dominative contacts for different types of situations that occur frequently in the classroom. In other words, there is a need for a dynamic explanation of how short-term patterns of teacher influence affect momentary situations so that the flexibility of the teacher's behavior is taken into account.

One clue that supports the notion that teachers probably are flexible in exerting dominative and integrative influences over short periods of time appears in the work of Mitzel and Rabinowitz (1953), who used Withall's technique to assess the classroom climate of four teachers. Their observation data were organized to permit an analysis of variance between teachers, visits, and observers. Since the median length of an observer's visit was about 20 minutes, the finding of statistically significant, wide variability among visits to the same teacher suggests that teachers adapt their influence to the immediate situation. There may be several reasons for the flexibility of teacher influence.

Teachers may adapt their influence to fit different phases of problem-solving that probably occur in the classroom. Bales and Strodtbeck (1951) have found that, in group problem-solving discussion, the quality of verbal interaction changes as the discussion progresses through phases of orientation, evaluation, and control.

Teachers may also adapt their influence to fit the needs of the individual pupil in contacts with single pupils. In two different studies involving college-age students, Wispe (1951) and Smith (1955) have shown that psychologically different types of students, identified by personality tests, have different reactions to the same teacher-behavior patterns. This was equally true of the two contrasting patterns used in each study, and, while the patterns were by no means identical to Anderson's dominative–integrative contrast, they were in many ways similar. Gage *et al.* (1956), in a study of elementary school children, found that pupils' perceptions of the same teacher were different according to whether the pupil could be classified as tending to seek "affective" or "cognitive" responses from a teacher.

Even though research on climate tends to ignore flexibility of teacher influence and is restricted to generalized, broad patterns of teacher behavior, it does
make a fundamental contribution to a theory of instruction. This contribution
consists of identifying general patterns of the teacher's influence that produce
predictable pupil responses. Thus it establishes cause-and-effect principles that
are true in the long run. However, the task of investigating flexibility of
influence remains uninvestigated.

TENTATIVE HYPOTHESES OF TEACHER INFLUENCE

The purpose of this section is to develop hypotheses of teacher influence that
are consistent with generalizations about classroom climate but which account
for flexibility of teacher influence. Most of the hypotheses are not yet supported by research evidence. If future experimentation provides evidence in
support of the hypotheses, they may contribute to a theory of instruction.[13]

In the classroom, teacher–pupil relationships are essentially superior-
subordinate in quality. The responsibility for classroom activities is the
teacher's, and both the teacher and the pupils expect the teacher to take charge,
to initiate, and to control the learning activities. The freedom to direct or not
to direct the activities of others is initially given only to the teacher; whatever
freedom pupils have in this respect results from the actions of the teacher. No
pupil can consistently ignore the authority of the teacher, and it is most difficult
and sometimes impossible for a pupil to escape from the teacher's control. In
the discussion that follows, the word *dependence* refers to these essential qualities of a superior–subordinate relationship. The presence of dependence has
already been noted in the work of Anderson and of Lippitt and White.

The opposite of dependence is *independence*, and since various degrees
of dependence or independence exist, they must be distinguished in the discussion that follows. *High dependence* refers to a condition in which pupils voluntarily seek additional ways of complying with the authority of the teacher.
This condition has aptly been described by Lewin (1935, p. 132) as, "at every
point within his (the pupil's) sphere of action he is internally controlled by the
wishes of the adult (teacher)." He adds, later, that a pupil might even anticipate these wishes. *Medium dependence* refers to the average classroom condition in which teacher direction is essential to initiate and guide activities but the
pupils do not voluntarily solicit it. When it occurs they comply. *Low dependence* refers to a condition in which pupils react to teacher directions if they
occur, but their present activities, usually teacher initiated, can be carried on
without continued teacher direction. In the face of difficulties pupils prefer the
teacher's help. *Independence* refers to a condition in which the pupils perceive
their activities to be "self-directed" (even though the teacher may have helped

---

[13] For an initial consideration of a "theory of instruction" the author is indebted to
Professor Herbert A. Thelen, University of Chicago. See "Toward a Theory of
Instruction" (entire issue), *J. educ. Res.*, Oct., 1951.

create the perception) and they do not expect directions from the teacher. In the face of difficulties pupils prefer to at least try their own solutions before seeking the teacher's help. If teacher direction is given, pupils feel free to evaluate it in terms of the requirements of the learning activities.

Underlying the entire discussion that follows is the basic assumption that the learning potential of pupils is inversely related to their level of dependence within reasonable and practical limits of classroom organization. In a condition of high dependence a pupil is too concerned with his relationship to the teacher to be completely objective about the learning task. "Objectivity cannot arise in a constraint situation; it arises only in a situation of freedom." (Lewin, 1935, p. 178) No doubt there are philosophical values at issue here, but it is psychologically sound and logically self-evident to point out that the learning experience is distorted to the extent that the dependence present in the learning situation is not present in the situation in which the learning is applied. No pupil is ever completely independent of the teacher's authority, nor is anyone completely independent in society, but there are certain types of desirable educational objectives that can be achieved only in a situation involving the degrees of independence defined in the preceding paragraph. It is equally true that there are some limited objectives that can best be achieved in a condition of medium dependence, also defined above.

Conditions of dependence or independence are created by the teacher's choice of influence. One can conceive of *direct influence* and *indirect influence* which, under appropriate circumstances, determine the degree of dependence. These two kinds of influence can be defined, in terms of verbal behavior, as follows:

Direct influence consists of stating the teacher's own opinion or ideas, directing the pupil's action, criticizing his behavior, or justifying the teacher's authority or use of that authority.

Indirect influence consists of soliciting the opinions or ideas of the pupils, applying or enlarging on those opinions or ideas, praising or encouraging the participation of pupils, or clarifying and accepting their feelings.

It will be shown in later articles that the teacher's direct and indirect influence can be reliably assessed by observation in spontaneous classroom situations and that the dependence of pupils can also be assessed by observation or paper-and-pencil techniques.

If the flexibility of teacher influence is to be understood, a theory of teacher influence should explain why direct influence may increase or maintain dependence in one situation, and increase or maintain independence in another. The cues used consciously or unconsciously by a teacher to guide his choice of influence may arise from a *Gestalt* so complex as to defy conceptualization. In order to be parsimonious, the theory about to be conceptualized will employ the fewest number of variables that seem necessary to predict and understand the teacher's choice of influence.

One aspect of the classroom situation that should make a difference in the pupil's reaction to teacher influence is his perception of the learning goal and the methods of reaching that goal. One can conceive of a situation in which the goal and the methods of reaching the goal are clear to the pupil and another situation in which these are unclear. Certainly, when a student knows what he is doing, his reactions to teacher influence will not be the same as when he isn't sure of what he is doing. In order to distinguish between these two situations in the discussion that follows, references will be made to *clear goals* and *unclear goals*.

Another aspect of the goal in a learning situation is whether or not the goal is perceived by the student as desirable or undesirable. The attraction of a goal determines motivation[14] and this attribute of a goal has been designated by Lewin (1935, p. 77) as *positive valence* or *negative valence*. In the discussion that follows, a positive valence is assigned to goals that satisfy the interests of pupils *and* require goal activities that match their abilities. A negative valence is assigned to goals that fail to satisfy the interests of pupils and/or require activities that do not match their abilities.

By logical convention, an unclear goal has an unknown or neutral valence.

It should now be clear that the theory about to be developed will suggest that direct and indirect influence will have a different but predictable effect in situations in which (a) the goal is unclear, (b) the goal is clear with a positive valence, and (c) the goal is clear with a negative valence. The operational differences between these three situations, necessary for experimentation, are that (a) the pupils do not know what goal will develop, (b) the pupils know what the goal is, know what steps they will take to reach the goal, see necessary actions as matching their ability, and are very interested and satisfied to be working toward that goal, and (c) the pupils know what the goal is, what steps are necessary to reach the goal, may or may not see necessary actions as matching their ability, and are very uninterested and dissatisfied to be working toward that goal.

Situations in which goals are unclear

Suppose one makes the following assumptions:

Assumption A: There exists a drive in both the teacher and the pupils to establish a learning goal in the classroom and work toward that goal.

Assumption B: When the goal is unclear, the behavior of pupils participating in identifying and clarifying a goal is determined by the real or imagined restraints of the teacher's control.

This is to say that most pupils expect to work on "schoolwork" in the classroom; that in order to get started, they expect the teacher to initiate activities that will clarify a learning goal and spell out the steps required to reach the goal. In short, in a classroom with unclear goals, there exists a state of medium dependency.

---

[14] Whether one refers to motivation as a "drive toward" or an "attraction to" a goal is irrelevant to the present discussion.

H 1.00 Indirect influence increases independence, when goals are unclear, by reducing the real or imagined restraints[15] of the teacher's control. ("H" will refer to "hypothesis"; "SH" to "sub-hypothesis.")

> *SH 1.10* When restraints are at the barest minimum needed to coordinate class activity, pupils will have the maximum opportunity to express their interests in the goals suggested and to compare their abilities with the activities required.
>
> *SH 1.20* Pupils who tend to be uncomfortable with minimum teacher restraints will need considerable support and encouragement, as part of the teacher's indirect influence, in order to continue to express their interests and to compare their abilities.

These hypotheses suggest that, when goals are unclear, the effect of indirect influence is to stimulate the expression of the pupils' interest, curiosity, and appreciation of several possible learning goals, and to evaluate these goals in terms of the methods required to reach them. To be realistic, the goal requirements should be within range of the abilities of the pupils. During this activity the teacher takes an active part by asking questions, praising and encouraging pupil participation, and expressing his own opinions primarily in terms of pupil ideas. In practice, the more mature judgment of the teacher is expressed by what he chooses to praise and the particular ideas he chooses to question or develop.

H 2.00 Direct influence increases dependence, when goals are unclear, by maintaining or increasing the restraints of the teacher's control.

> *SH 2.10* With high dependence or increasing medium dependence, direct influence results in overt compliance.
>
> *SH 2.11* If the goals subsequently prove interesting and match the pupils' ability, the overt compliance will occur with inner acceptance.
>
> *SH 2.12* If goals subsequently prove uninteresting or do not match the pupils' ability, the overt compliance will occur with inner resistance.
>
> *SH 2.13* Either type of compliance maintains the restraints of the teacher's control and pupils will be more dependent throughout the entire process of reaching the goal, compared to goals identified with direct influence.
>
> *SH 2.20* Pupils who are more comfortable in a dependent teacher relationship will actively solicit the teacher's direct influence when goals are unclear.

---

[15] "Restraints" is a word originally used by Lewin to refer to barriers. Here it refers to barriers the teacher sets to pupil behavior or that pupils imagine that the teacher sets. Included would be prohibitions, admonitions and imposed directions. The author recognizes that every teacher must set "minimum restraints," but he believes that if they are set reasonably, pupils will perceive a degree of freedom that permits disciplined self-direction. Technically, restraints refer to forces which exist in the pupil's social environment (life space).

These hypotheses suggest that the effect of direct influence, when goals are unclear, is to increase, or at least maintain, the existing dependence of pupils on the teacher's control. Under these circumstances, direct influence restricts the alternative reactions of pupils to overt compliance. Festinger (Sherif and Wilson, 1953, pp. 232–256) has suggested that public compliance to group pressures can occur with private acceptance or without private acceptance; with a slight change in words, his analysis is adapted here as a reasonable outcome of direct influence. The notion that either type of compliance maintains a dependent relationship is, perhaps, most questionable in the case of overt compliance with inner acceptance. However, it can be argued that compliance is not so much a matter of working on an interesting or uninteresting goal as it is a perception of the pupil that he must work on that goal only if he is to receive the approval of the teacher, who holds ultimate authority. The consequences of this perception will be discussed later.

Both SH 1.20 and SH 2.20 are tentative extensions of the work of Wispe, Smith, and Gage, whose studies of individual pupil reactions to various types of teacher influence have already been mentioned.

The hypotheses stated are presumed to hold whenever goals are unclear either for individual pupils or for the class as a whole, whether this occurs at the beginning, at the middle, or near the end of a particular learning cycle. Goals are most likely to be unclear for the total class during the initial phases of a learning cycle. However, it is a common experience to be working toward what appears to be a clear goal only to find, after some progress, that the original picture of the goal has become unrealistic. Barriers to progress lower goal clarity by changing the steps required to reach the goal. The incidence of unclear goal perceptions among pupils may be far more frequent at the beginning of a school year when pupils, teacher, subject, and methods are less understood. In general, unclear goals become clear with the passage of time, either suddenly or gradually, so long as efforts to reach the goal are maintained. Since perceptions of the goal are subject to individual differences, and some goals are more difficult to understand than others, a teacher must assume that there is a range of goal perceptions in a class at any given moment.

The development of positive or negative valence occurs simultaneously with the clarification of goals and methods of reaching goals. As soon as a pupil imagines a relationship between his interests and abilities and the nature of a goal, positive or negative valence is anticipated. Many pupils bring into the classroom a generalized anticipation of goal valence based on past experience, the previous class, or their attitudes toward the teacher. Indirect influence is particularly useful for clarifying such feelings and relating them to the present goal activities.

In the next two sections consideration is given to situations in which the goal and the goal activities are sufficiently clear for pupils to have definite positive or negative reactions toward the goal. But before these situations are discussed, it is necessary to examine more closely the meaning of dependence and independence when goals are clear.

As a goal becomes clear with a positive valence, a force toward the goal develops, action becomes rewarding, and the resultant pupil behavior is usually classified as "self-motivated." As a goal becomes clear with a negative valence, a force away from the goal develops, action becomes unrewarding, and if the resultant pupil behavior is oriented toward the goal, it is usually the result of a force created by the teacher through the use of reward or punishment. In this latter situation, medium or high dependence exists and pupils comply with forces that stem from the teacher's authority. In the case of a clear, positive goal, dependence exists to the extent that the pupil reacts, either consciously or unconsciously, to forces that stem from the teacher's authority. This latter case is most clearly illustrated by the pupil who senses that his present enjoyment in working on a rewarding task is a "gift," or is permitted by the teacher. He expresses his dependence by appreciating the teacher as well as the nature of the task. In a practical problem-solving sense, his objectivity is distorted, since his decisions include judgments of what the teacher will approve or disapprove, as well as the more objective requirements of the problem. His behavior is the resultant of both the restraining forces set by the teacher and the force that results from the positive goal valence.

Situations in which the goal is clear with a positive valence

With a clear, positive goal there is a strong force toward the goal which will be stable as long as the action satisfies the pupil's interests and his ability permits him to proceed. If the restraining forces set by the teacher are small compared with the valence force, the pupil's behavior will be relatively independent. If the restraining forces approach significance compared with the valence force, the dependence of the pupil will increase. The proportional balance of these two sets of forces depends on the use of direct or indirect influence when the goals are initially clarified and upon subsequent influence that the teacher provides.

H 3.00 When the initial positive valence of a goal is clarified with indirect influence, the effect of subsequent direct or indirect influence on the existing independence is insignificant.

> SH 3.10 The tendency of subsequent direct influence to increase dependence, and indirect influence to decrease it, is greater when the influence is initiated by the teacher, compared with being solicited by pupils.

> SH 3.20 Independent progress toward a clear, positive goal reenforces the valence and provides pupils with objective criteria with which to evaluate teacher influence.

These hypotheses emphasize the primary goal orientation of an independent pupil moving successfully toward a clear, positive goal. Teacher influence solicited by pupils is likely to have a goal orientation and, as such, will not affect independence. Influence initiated by the teacher is unlikely to affect independence unless the pupil fails to see a relationship between such influence

and the goal; e.g., when the teacher attempts to change to a completely different goal. Under these conditions, which include a maximum of independent
goal orientation and a minimum of teacher restraints, barriers to progress are
more likely to appear as an intellectual challenge. With proper teacher stimulation and direct challenge there will be an opportunity to enrich the problem-
solving experience by stretching the goal requirements to the limit of pupil
ability without loss of positive valence.

In the case of a clear goal with a positive valence that was developed with
direct influence, the restraining forces set by the teacher would be of sufficient
magnitude to affect the pupil's behavior. However, successful progress toward
a positive goal may modify the original dependence. This modification is probably due to the development of the valence force, and not to a decrease in the
restraining forces; on this point, however, different interpretations are certainly
possible. Lewin (1935, p. 169) would suggest that the decrease in restraining
forces would be more likely to occur with younger children, provided that
the goal activities are truly rewarding. With older children, the realization
that the original direct influence was, in a sense, unjustified would increase the
pupil's awareness of the restraining forces. Although the dynamics of this
situation are not yet clear, the author is disposed to suggest the following
hypotheses, primarily because dependence is easier to create during initial
stages than it is to diminish in later stages.

H 4.00 When the initial positive valence of a goal is clarified with direct influence, subsequent direct influence maintains or increases existing dependence,
and subsequent indirect influence decreases existing dependence only slightly,
if at all.

    SH 4.10 If a goal that is initiated with direct influence develops a positive
    valence, the existing dependence of the pupils is reenforced by the reward-
    ing experience.

    SH 4.20 Direct influence during initial clarification of positive goals, fol-
    lowed by indirect influence, maintains existing dependence if pupils become
    aware of the inconsistency in the teacher's influence.

These hypotheses suggest, in effect, that once dependence is established,
under conditions of H 2.00, it is not likely to decrease even if the learning goal
develops a positive valence.

Situations in which the goal is clear with a negative valence

In this situation the actions of both the teacher and pupils are limited. The
teacher usually attempts to maintain the restricted learning possibilities by
exerting direct influence through either reward or punishment. The only other
alternative is to attempt to change the valence of the goal. This second alternative will be considered first.

    Dislike of a goal or the activities required to reach a goal depends on the
total perceptual field of the pupil. He may think the task too difficult, too

tedious, of no future value, or he may simply dislike the teacher. The reorganization of the pupil's perceptual field is best facilitated by indirect influence that clarifies and supports the pupils' diagnosis of his own difficulties. Successfully carried out, the process is very similar to initiating a new goal. A resourceful teacher recognizes that it is the pupil's perception that must be changed, that only he can change it, and that the change can often occur with only minor alterations in the nature of the goal or goal activities. In fact, the same task, imbedded in a different perceptual organization, may take on a completely different valence. (Lewin, 1935, p. 168)

H 5.00 A shift from negative to positive goal valence is most likely to occur in response to indirect influence by the teacher.

The analysis of situations involving reward and punishment has already been carried out by Lewin (1935, pp. 114–170) and an analysis of compliant behavior has been published by Festinger (Sherif and Wilson, 1953, pp. 232–256). In both references there are many principles which apply directly to the classroom and are related to direct influence, compliance, and dependence. In nearly every classroom, reward or punishment is never used alone; instead, the two are used in combination. The essence of direct influence with the threat of punishment or possibility of reward is the creation of a conflict situation which restricts the pupil's freedom and narrows the alternative actions of the pupil to one or two that the teacher desires. The maintenance of these restrictions requires alert and active surveillance of pupil behavior by the teacher because there are usually a few pupils who are willing and able to test the limits of their freedom in imaginative and unusual ways. With negative goal valence, if the threat of punishment is relaxed or if rewards are unfulfilled, action toward the goal decreases or stops. Thus, high dependence is maintained at all times.

SUMMARY AND CONCLUSIONS

The major purpose in reviewing research on classroom climate and in developing hypotheses about the effects on direct and indirect teacher influence is to explain variability of teacher influence. In considering, first, situations in which goals are unclear, and, second, situations in which goals are clear, different effects of the same teacher behavior were hypothesized. Other articles in this series will be concerned with testing these hypotheses in either field studies or laboratory experiments.

A general assumption underlying the discussion is that in the control of classroom learning, there are times when direct influence is most appropriate and other times when indirect influence is most appropriate. At first glance, this assumption may appear to conflict with the findings of research on classroom climate. However, a careful study of the data collected indicates that in all types of classroom situations, both direct and indirect influence occurred. A widespread misinterpretation of research on classroom climate has been that direct influence should be avoided in the classroom. H 3.00 suggests that there will be no change in dependence when direct influence is exerted during periods when goals are clear. In fact, direct influence related to a clear goal may provide opportunities to challenge the ideas and conclusions of the pupil and to enrich the learning process.

The contrast between the predictions of H 1.00 and H 2.00 and those of H 3.00, provides a tentative explanation of why direct or indirect influence may have different outcomes in different situations.

Many factors have been ignored in this initial statement of teacher influence. Some data have already been collected (and will be reported in later articles) suggesting that younger pupils, ages five through seven, do not react to direct influence in the same way as older pupils. If this trend is supported, some modification of H 1.00 and H 2.00 will be required that takes into account the age of the pupils. Data from the classrooms of older pupils also suggest that certain kinds of learning activities can be introduced into classrooms with what appears to be almost instantaneous goal clarity. If this is true, such activities may be unrelated to H 1.00 and H 2.00. Data from high school classes suggest that certain topics such as mathematics and science are normally associated with a higher proportion of direct influence, although, at the moment, this should be considered as no more than a commentary on current school practice.

No effort has been made in the present article to indicate how patterns of direct influence can be modified by using group activities in the classroom. It may be that the teacher who uses group methods can control dependence by making appropriate shifts in the classroom group organization. Finally, there are certain obvious relationships between the hypotheses of teacher influence, principles of counseling, and the trainer's role in group therapy that have not been developed.

chapter two

INTERACTION ANALYSIS:
PROCEDURES AND RESEARCH
ON TEACHING PATTERNS

CHAPTER OVERVIEW

Teaching is more than talking, but visits to a randomly selected number of classrooms will confirm the fact that the predominant instructional behavior of the teacher is talk. Indeed, almost 70% of classroom instructional time is spent in talk by either the teacher or students. This chapter deals with a technique for recording and analyzing the spontaneous classroom verbal behavior of teachers and students, and the use of this technique in research on classroom climate and its effects on students.

When a teacher talks he may present information, praise or criticize students, give directions, ask questions, or accept and help clarify student ideas and feelings. When students talk they may respond with specific information to narrow questions, or they may respond with or initiate ideas or questions of their own. It is a classification of teacher and student talk such as this which constitutes the categories for the system of interaction analysis.

An analysis of the classroom verbal behavior of teachers and students should, however, do more than provide data to describe the type or classification of talk that is used. For such an analysis to be optimally useful, it should yield data regarding the relative frequency of various types of talk, and in addition should make possible a cause-and-effect analysis of classroom verbal behavior.

In the first paper in this chapter, Edmund Amidon and Ned Flanders describe such a system, the system of interaction analysis. The paper deals not only with a category system for classifying spontaneous classroom verbal behavior, but in addition explains how the system allows observers and teachers to explain, summarize, analyze, and draw inferences about teaching from data gathered by means of the systems.

Two modifications of the basic interaction analysis system are presented in the second and third papers in this chapter. In the second paper, Edmund Amidon and Elizabeth Hunter describe the Verbal Interaction Category System which, while it employs many of the categories and procedures used in the basic system of interaction analysis, includes additional student and teacher categories. Further, the categories of this system are organized around the functions of initiation and reponse rather than the concept of direct and indirect influence. The Observational System for the Analysis of Classroom Instruction was developed by John Hough and is presented in the third paper. This system, while preserving the categorization, matrix analysis and indirect–direct characteristics of Flanders' original system, is designed to measure certain teaching behaviors and classroom activities that are consistent with principles of instruction derived from learning theory.

For an observational system to be useful to researchers and teachers, it must not only yield useful data but it must also be reliable and easily learned. In the fourth paper in this chapter, Ned Flanders describes some successfully practiced techniques for training reliable classroom observers, and presents a procedure for estimating interobserver reliability.

The fifth paper in this chapter is a descriptive study of the verbal behavior patterns used by a selected sample of elementary school classrooms. This paper by Norma Furst and Edmund Amidon helps the reader gain an understanding of the various levels of description that are possible through the use of interaction analysis. In addition, elementary school teachers will be interested in the variation in the verbal behavior patterns that were typical of elementary teachers at various grade levels in Furst's sample.

Casual observation indicates that the percentage of classroom time spent in teacher talk, student talk and silence will vary from one classroom to another. Similarly, the percentage of time that any one teacher spends in using a particular verbal behavior such as giving information, questioning, or giving directions will also vary from day to day. Yet, if one were to observe a teacher during a number of typical lessons, one could describe the teacher as having a predominantly direct, indirect or flexible teaching style. Theory and research presented in the first chapter would lead one to believe that the teaching styles and patterns of verbal behavior that teachers use create a social–emotional climate in their classrooms that has a direct effect on the attitudes and behavior of their students. One might question, however, whether a relationship between teacher verbal behavior and teaching effectiveness really does exist. The answer to this question, of course, depends upon the definition of and the criteria used for defining effective teaching. Typically, effective teaching has been defined on the basis of two types of criteria which may be described as external and internal. The term external refers to judgments of teaching effectiveness made by persons not directly involved in the classroom. Typical external criteria are those used by principals and supervisors as they rate teachers. The term internal criteria refers to behaviors, reactions and perceptions of persons directly involved in the classroom situation. Pupil ratings of teachers and pupil achievement are two such criteria.

The extent to which principals and supervisors are aware of and able to identify effective teaching has been widely and hotly discussed. The ability of principals to accurately characterize the teaching of members of their faculty has often been questioned. The sixth paper in this chapter, by C. V. Robbins, presents evidence that principals can, with some accuracy, characterize the teaching style of members of their faculty. Robbins' work represents an important step in the validation of the external criteria often used in studies of teacher effectiveness.

If the theory presented in Chapter One has any correspondence with reality, and if principals and supervisors can characterize accurately the teaching patterns of their faculty, then one might expect that the verbal behavior patterns of teachers, rated by their supervisors as being "superior" would differ from the behavior patterns of an average group of teachers. In addition, one might predict from theory that the verbal behavior of "superior" teachers would be less direct than that of average teachers. Data presented by Edmund Amidon and Michael Giammatteo in the seventh paper in this chapter support the theory.

The eighth article, by Roger Pankratz, reports a study of teacher effectiveness that uses both external and internal criteria. The research by Pankratz further supports the theory presented in Chapter One. Physics teachers in his study identified as above average on three criterion measures (principal rating, student rating and a test designed to predict teaching effectiveness) differed in their use of verbal teaching behavior from a population of physics teachers rated as "below average" on the same variables. The behavior of the "above average" physics teachers could have been predicted from the theory presented in Chapter One.

Three papers based on research projects that have used only internal criteria of teaching effectiveness complete Chapter Two. In the ninth paper in this chapter, Edmund Amidon and Ned Flanders report a study which used the achievement of junior high school students in mathematics as the criterion measure of teacher effectiveness. The results of this study are consistent with theory. A unique characteristic of this study was the inclusion of two additional variables: a dimension of individual differences of students as measured by a test of dependent proneness and a curriculum variable of clear and unclear instructional goals.

In the tenth paper in this chapter Ned Flanders reports the results of a series of studies designed to test hypotheses which were presented in the final paper in Chapter One. The results of this research clearly support hypotheses that students of teachers who use a teaching style that is both indirect and flexible have more positive attitudes toward school and their teacher and achieve more than students of teachers who use a more direct teaching style.

The final paper in this chapter, by Robert Soar, reports the findings from a study of the relationship of the verbal behavior of elementary school teachers to the reading achievement of their students. The data reported by Soar only in part support hypotheses generated from theory. The results presented in this paper serve as a reminder to teachers and teacher educators that classroom verbal behavior as measured by interaction analysis provides data on only a portion of the variables which constitute effective teaching.

In summary, papers included in this chapter present evidence to support the contention that classroom climate can be objectively and reliably measured and that such climate is related to teaching effectiveness.

INTERACTION
ANALYSIS
AS A FEEDBACK SYSTEM[16]

EDMUND AMIDON and NED FLANDERS

The social forces at work in the classroom are so complex that it looks on the surface as if any attempt to analyze them would be extremely difficult. The teacher's interaction with children, which is a portion of the total social process, seems almost as difficult to identify. Nevertheless, teacher–pupil contacts have been classified into specifically defined behavioral acts by various researchers who have studied teacher behavior.

The Flanders system is concerned with verbal behavior only, primarily because It can be observed with higher reliability than can nonverbal behavior. The assumption is made that the verbal behavior of an individual is an adequate sample of his total behavior.

DESCRIPTION OF CATEGORIES

In the Flanders system of interaction analysis all teacher statements are classified first as either indirect or direct. This classification gives central attention to the amount of freedom the teacher grants to the student. In a given situation, therefore, a teacher has a choice. He can be direct, that is, minimizing the freedom of the student to respond, or he can be indirect, maximizing the freedom of the student to respond. His choice, conscious or unconscious, depends upon many factors, among which are his perceptions of the situations and the goals of the particular learning situation.

In order to make total behavior or total interaction in the classroom meaningful, the Flanders system also provides for the categorizing of student talk. A third major section, that of silence or confusion, is included in order to

---

[16] Extracted from Edmund Amidon and Ned Flanders, *The Role of the Teacher in the Classroom*. Minneapolis: Paul S. Amidon and Associates, Inc., 1963. Reprinted by permission of Paul S. Amidon and Associates, and the authors.

account for the time spent in behavior other than that which can be classified as either teacher or student talk. All statements that occur in the classroom, then, are categorized in one of three major sections: (a) teacher talk, (b) student talk, and a separate category, (c) silence or confusion, used to handle anything else that is not teacher or student talk.

The larger sections of teacher and student verbal behavior are subdivided in order to make the total pattern of teacher–pupil interaction more meaningful. The two subdivisions for teacher verbal behavior; indirect and direct teacher talk, are further divided into smaller categories. Indirect influence consists of four observation categories: (1) accepting feeling, (2) praising or encouraging, (3) accepting ideas, and (4) asking questions. Direct influence is divided into three categories: (5) lecturing, (6) giving directions, and (7) criticizing or justifying authority. Student talk is divided into only two categories: (8) responding to teacher, and (9) initiating talk. All categories are mutually exclusive, yet totally inclusive of all verbal interaction occurring in the classroom.

Indirect teacher behavior

CATEGORY 1, ACCEPTANCE OF FEELING. The teacher accepts feelings when he says he understands how the children feel, that they have the right to have these feelings, and that he will not punish the children for their feelings. These kinds of statements often communicate to children both acceptance and clarification of the feeling.

Also included in this category are statements that recall past feeling, refer to enjoyable or uncomfortable feelings that are present, or predict happy or sad events that will occur in the future.

In our society people often react to expressions of negative feelings by offering negative feelings in return. Acceptance of these emotions in the classroom is quite rare; probably because teachers find it difficult to accept negative emotional behavior. However, it may be just as difficult for them to accept positive feelings. Feelings expressed by students may also be ignored by the teacher if he considers the classroom to be a place where people are concerned primarily with ideas rather than feelings.

CATEGORY 2, PRAISE OR ENCOURAGEMENT. Included in this category are jokes that release tension, but not those that threaten students or are made at the expense of individual students. Often praise is a single word: "good," "fine," or "right." Sometimes the teacher simply says, "I like what you are doing." Encouragement is slightly different and includes statements such as, "Continue." "Go ahead with what you are saying." "Uh, huh; go on; tell us more about your idea."

CATEGORY 3, ACCEPTING IDEAS. This category is quite similar to category 1; however, it includes only acceptance of student ideas, not acceptance of expressed emotion. When a student makes a suggestion, the teacher may paraphrase the student's statement, restate the idea more simply, or summarize what the student has said. The teacher may also say, "Well, that's an interesting point of view. I see what you mean." Statements belonging in category 3 are particularly difficult to recognize; often the teacher will shift from using the student's idea to stating the teacher's own idea.

Statements belonging in category 3 can be identified by asking the question, "Is the idea that the teacher is now stating the student's or is it the teacher's?" If it is the student's idea, then this category is used; if it is the teacher's another category must be employed.

CATEGORY 4, ASKING QUESTIONS. This category includes only questions to which the teacher expects an answer from the pupils. If a teacher asks a question and then follows it immediately with a statement of opinion, or if he begins lecturing, obviously the question was not meant to be answered. A rhetorical question is not categorized as a question. An example of another kind of question that should not be classified in category 4 is the following: "What in the world do you think you are doing out of your seat, John?" With proper intonation the question is designed to get John back in his seat; if such is the case, it must be categorized as criticism of the student's behavior (category 7).

Questions that are meant to be answered are of several kinds. There are questions that are direct in the sense that there is a right and wrong answer. The question, "What are 2 and 2?" is a question that limits the freedom of the student to some extent. Although he can refuse to answer, give the wrong answer, or make a statement of another kind, in general, this kind of question focuses the student's answer more than does a question such as, "What do you think we ought to do now?" Questions, then, can be very broad and give the student a great deal of freedom in answering. All questions, however broad or narrow, which require answers and are not commands or criticism, fall into category 4.

Direct teacher behavior

CATEGORY 5, LECTURE. Lecture is the form of verbal interaction that is used to give information, facts, opinions, or ideas to children. The presentation of material may be used to introduce, review, or focus the attention of the class on an important topic. Usually information in the form of lecture is given in fairly extended time periods, but it may be interspersed with children's comments, questions, and encouraging praise.

Whenever the teacher is explaining, discussing, giving opinion, or giving facts or information, category 5 is used. Rhetorical questions are also included in this category. Category 5 is the one most frequently used in classroom observation.

CATEGORY 6, GIVING DIRECTIONS. The decision about whether or not to classify the statement as a direction or command must be based on the degree of freedom that the student has in response to teacher direction. When the teacher says, "Will all of you stand up and stretch?" he is obviously giving a direction. If he says, "John, go to the board and write your name," he is giving a direction or command. When he says, "John, I want you to tell me what you have done with your reader," he is still giving a direction.

CATEGORY 7, CRITICIZING OR JUSTIFYING AUTHORITY. A statement of criticism is one that is designed to change student behavior from nonacceptable to acceptable. The teacher is saying, in effect, "I don't like what you are doing. Do something else." Another group of statements included in this category are those that might be called statements of defense or self-justification. These statements are particularly difficult to detect when a teacher appears to be explaining a lesson or the reasons for doing a lesson to the class. If the teacher is explaining himself or his authority, defending himself against the student, or justifying himself, the statement falls in this category. Other kinds of statements that fall in this category are those of extreme self-reference or those in which the teacher is constantly asking the children to do something as a special favor to the teacher.

Categories 1 through 4, those of indirect teacher influence, and categories 5 through 7, those of direct teacher influence, have been described. They are all categories of teacher talk. Whenever the teacher is talking, the statements must be categorized in one of the first seven categories. If the observer decides that with a given statement the teacher is restricting the freedom of the children, the statement is tallied in categories 5, 6, or 7. If, on the other hand, the observer decides that the teacher is expanding freedom of children, the category used is either 1, 2, 3, or 4.

There are three additional categories for use in classroom interaction:

Student behavior

CATEGORY 8, STUDENT TALK: RESPONSE. This category is used when the teacher has initiated the contact or has solicited student statements, when the student answers a question asked by the teacher, or when he responds verbally to a direction the teacher has given. Anything that the student says that is clearly in response to initiation by the teacher belongs in category 8.

CATEGORY 9, STUDENT TALK: INITIATION. In general, if the student raises his hand to make a statement or to ask a question when he has not been prompted to do so by the teacher, the appropriate category is 9.

Distinguishing between Categories 8 and 9 is often difficult. Predicting the general kind of answer that the student will give in response to a question from the teacher is important in making this distinction. If the answer is one that is of a type predicted by the observer (as well as the teacher and class), then the statement comes under Category 8. When in response to a teacher-question the student gives an answer different from that which is expected for that particular question, then the statement is categorized as a 9.

Other behavior

CATEGORY 10, SILENCE OR CONFUSION. This category includes anything else not included in the other categories. Periods of confusion in communication, when it is difficult to determine who is talking, are classified in this category.

A summary of these categories, with brief definitions for use of the observer, can be found in Fig. 2–1.

Teacher talk	Indirect influence	1. *Accepts feeling:* accepts and clarifies the feeling tone of the students in a nonthreatening manner. Feelings may be positive or negative. Predicting and recalling feelings are included. 2. *Praises or encourages:* praises or encourages student action or behavior. Jokes that release tension, not at the expense of another individual, nodding head or saying "uh huh?" or "go on" are included. 3. *Accepts or uses ideas of student:* clarifying, building, or developing ideas or suggestions by a student. As teacher brings more of his own ideas into play, shift to category five. 4. *Asks questions:* asking a question about content or procedure with the intent that a student answer.
	Direct influence	5. *Lectures:* giving facts or opinions about content or procedure; expressing his own idea; asking rhetorical questions. 6. *Gives directions:* directions, commands, or orders with which a student is expected to comply. 7. *Criticizes or justifies authority:* statements, intended to change student behavior from nonacceptable to acceptable pattern; bawling someone out; stating why the teacher is doing what he is doing, extreme self-reference.
Student talk		8. *Student talk-response:* talk by students in response to teacher. Teacher initiates the contact or solicits student statement. 9. *Student talk-initiation:* talk by students, which they initiate. If "calling on" student is only to indicate who may talk next, observer must decide whether student wanted to talk. If he did, use this category.
		10. *Silence or confusion:* pauses, short periods of silence, and periods of confusion in which communication cannot be understood by the observer.

FIG. 2–1. Summary of categories for interaction analysis.

PROCEDURE FOR CATEGORIZING TEACHER–PUPIL INTERACTION

The Flanders system of interaction analysis was originally used as a research tool and continues to serve this function. As such, it is employed by a trained observer in order to collect reliable data regarding classroom behavior as a part of a research project.

The system is also useful as an in-service training device for teachers. It may be employed by a teacher either as he observes someone else teach or as he categorizes a tape recording of his own classroom behavior. In either case the method is the same.

Every three seconds the observer writes down the category number of the interaction he has just observed. He records these numbers in sequence in a column. He will write approximately 20 numbers per minute; thus, at the end of a period of time, he will have several long columns of numbers. The observer preserves this sequence of numbers that he has recorded. It is important to keep the tempo as steady as possible, but it is even more crucial to be accurate. He may also wish to write down marginal notes from time to time, which can be used to explain what has been happening in the classroom.

No matter whether he is using a live classroom or a tape recording for his observations, it is best for the observer to spend five to ten minutes getting oriented to the situation before he actually begins to categorize. He then has a feeling for the total atmosphere in which the teacher and pupils are working. After he has begun to get the feeling of the classroom interaction, he begins to record the interaction.

The observer stops classifying whenever the classroom activity is changed so that observing is inappropriate as, for instance, when there are various groups working around the classroom, or when children are working on workbooks or doing silent reading. He will usually draw a line under the recorded numbers, make a note of the new activity, and resume categorizing when the total class discussion continues. At all times the observer notes the kind of class activity he is observing. The reading group in the elementary school is obviously different from an informal discussion period, a review of subject matter, a period of supervised seat work, teacher-directed discussion, introduction of new material, or evaluation of a completed unit. Such diverse activities may be expected to show different types of teacher–pupil interaction even when guided by the same teacher. A shift to new activity should also be noted.

Ground rules

Because of the complexity of the problems involved in categorization, several ground rules have been established. These rules of observation aid in developing consistency in trying to categorize teacher behavior. They have been useful in working in classrooms with all subject areas and at all grade levels.

Rule 1: When not certain in which of two or more categories a statement belongs, choose the category that is numerically farthest from category 5. This is true except when one of the two categories in doubt is category 10, which is never chosen if there is an alternate category under consideration. Because those categories farthest from the center (5) of the category system occur less frequently, the observer maximizes information by choosing the less frequently occurring category (except 10) when there is a choice. For example, if the observer is not sure whether it is a 2 or 3, he chooses 2. If in doubt between a 5 and a 7, he chooses a 7, etc.

Rule 2: If the primary tone of the teacher's behavior has been consistently direct or consistently indirect, do not shift into the opposite classification unless a clear indication of shift is given by the teacher. The trained observer is in the best position to judge whether or not the teacher is restricting or expanding the freedom of action of class members. If the observer feels that the teacher's pattern of behavior is generally one of expanding the freedom of students to act, a slightly more direct statement in a very indirect pattern may tend to look, in contrast, like a more direct statement than it actually is. On the other hand, he must remain alert to shift as the teacher shifts momentarily to one of the more direct categories. Conversely, if the observer feels that the teacher has been consistently restrictive in his behavior, he is particularly careful in his use of the indirect categories.

In observing this rule the observer is reacting to the general tone of the teacher's influence, either direct or indirect, and does not use the opposing categories unless it is clear that the teacher has shifted from this more general pattern. He must, of course, be certain that the teacher has established a direct or indirect pattern before he categorizes consistently in either of the two areas. Clearly he must also be ready to change when the teacher obviously moves all the way along the system; that is, to 1 or 2 from 6 or 7, or when the teacher moves all the way to a 6 or 7 from a 2 or a 3. This rule is often called the rule of the biased unbiased observer; that is, the observer is operating in a climate of general direct or indirect influence, and although he is ready to move to the opposite set of categories, he must feel that the teacher has definitely moved to the opposite type of influence before he is willing to grant a change in interaction pattern.

Rule 3: The observer must not be overly concerned with his own biases or with the teacher's intent. Rather, he must ask himself the question, "What does this behavior mean to the pupils as far as restriction or expansion of their freedom is concerned?" If, when the teacher attempts to be clever, pupils see his statements as criticism of a pupil, the observer uses category 7, rather than category 2. If the teacher in being sarcastic says how good the children are, again category 7 is used. If a statement intended as a question has the effect of restricting students' freedom so that it becomes a direction, then it must be classified as a direction. The effect of a statement on the pupils, then, not the teacher's intent, is the crucial criterion for categorizing a statement.

This rule has particular value when applied to the problem of helping teachers to gain insight into their own behavior. In trying to categorize their own tapes teachers comment, "But I meant . . . ," or "I was really trying to get the pupils to talk more," or "I think that I wanted them to answer that question," or "I was trying to praise them," or "I meant to use that child's idea." All these protests indicate that the teacher is thinking about his intent rather than the effect of his behavior on the class members.

The meaning and value of this category system for an individual teacher come from the attention it gives to the effect of teacher behavior on the freedom of the class. Use of this criterion requires a great deal of training, particularly when a teacher is categorizing a tape of his own teaching. He must learn to be nondefensive about categorizing the behavior, recognizing that there is absolutely no evaluation or good–bad orientation implied in the category system. The question is simply, "What category best describes this particular bit of interaction?"

Rule 4: If more than one category occurs during the three-second interval, then all categories used in that interval are recorded; therefore, record each change in category. If no change occurs within three seconds, repeat that category number. This rule is concerned with the situation in which statements from two categories occur during a three-second period. Generally an observer writes down a category number every three seconds. The pace of recording is evenly maintained so that only one category number is written during this period.

However, if there is a change in categories during this interval, the observer records the change. Within the three-second interval, for example, the teacher may ask a question, the child answers, and the teacher praises the child. The observer records all three of the categories. The fourth rule, therefore, is that a category number is recorded every three seconds unless the teacher changes categories within the three-second interval. If he changes categories, or if more than one category occurs during the three-second interval, then all categories used in the time period are recorded.

Rule 5: If a silence is longer than three seconds, it is recorded as a 10. (This rule is listed because observers tend to ignore short periods of silence.) The 10 is also used when two or more people are talking at once and when there is slight confusion in the classroom so that the observer cannot identify a single speaker. Breaks in the interaction in the form of silence or confusion are classified in category 10.

The importance of preserving the sequence when categorizing teacher statements was emphasized earlier in this paper. In this way the sequence of events in a classroom can be preserved for analysis. It is not enough to say that a teacher uses lecture 50% of the time or that he criticizes 5% of the time. When does he use this lecture or this criticism? With what other kinds of statements are they combined?

Recording data in a matrix

There is a method of recording the sequence of events in the classroom in such a way that certain facts become readily apparent. This method consists of entering the sequence of numbers into a 10-row by 10-column table, which is called a matrix (see Table 2–1). The generalized sequence of the teacher–pupil interaction can be examined readily in this matrix. The following example shows how an observer would classify what happens in a classroom and how the observations are recorded in the matrix. The example is a fifth-grade teacher who is beginning a social studies lesson. The observer has been sitting in the classroom for several minutes and has begun to get some idea of the general climate before he begins to record. The teacher says to the class, "Boys and girls, please open your social studies books to page 5." (Observer classified this as a 6, followed by a 10, because of the period of silence and confusion as the children try to find the page.) The teacher says, "Jimmy, we are all waiting for you. Will you please turn your book to page 5?" (Observer records a 7 and a 6.) "I know now," continues the teacher, "that some of us had a little difficulty with, and were a little disturbed by, the study of this chapter yesterday; I think that today we are going to find it more exciting and interesting." (Observer records two 1's; reacting to feeling.) "Now, has anyone had a chance to think about what we discussed yesterday?" (Observer records a 4 for a question.) A student answers, "I thought about it, and it seems to me that the reason we are in so much trouble in southeast Asia is that we haven't really had a chance to learn to understand the ways of the people who live there." (Observer records three 8's.)

The teacher responds by saying, "Good, I am glad that you suggested that, John. Now let me see if I understand your idea completely. You have suggested that if we had known the people better in southeast Asia, we might not be in the trouble we are in today." (This is classified as a 2, followed by two 3's.)

The observer has now classified the following sequence of numbers in this fashion:

```
              10
                 ) 1st pair
              6
2nd pair (
              10
                 ) 3rd pair
              7
  4th pair (
              6
              1
              1
              4
              9
              9
              9
              2
              3
              3
              10
```

(The use of a 10 at the beginning and end of the sequence is explained in the discussion that follows.)

Tabulations are now made in the matrix to represent pairs of numbers. Notice in the listing above that the numbers have been marked off in pairs. The first pair is 10-6; the second pair is 6-10; etc. The particular cell in which tabulation of the pair of numbers is made is determined by using the first number in the pair to indicate the row and the second number in the pair for the column. Thus, 10-6 would be shown by a tally in the cell formed by Row 10 and Column 6. The second pair, 6-10, would be shown in the cell formed by Row 6 and Column 10. The third pair, 10-7, is entered into the cell, Row 10 and Column 7. Notice that each pair of numbers overlaps with the

Table 2–1

Sample Interaction Matrix

Second

		1	2	3	4	5	6	7	8	9	10	Total
	1	1			1							
	2			1								
	3			1							1	
First	4								1			
	5											
	6	1									1	
	7						1					
	8		1						11			
	9											
	10						1	1				
	Total	2	1	2	1	0	2	1	3	0	2	14

previous pair, and each number, except the first and the last, is used twice. It is for this reason that a 10 is entered as the first number and the last in the record. This number is chosen as it is convenient to assume that each record began and ended with silence. This procedure also permits the total of each column to equal the total of the corresponding row.

It is convenient to check the tabulations in the matrix for accuracy by noting that there should be one less tally in the matrix than there were numbers entered in the original record (N-1).

In this case we started with 15 numbers and the total number of tallies in the matrix is 14. This tabulation is shown in Table 2–1.

Ordinarily a separate matrix is made for each specific lesson or major activity. If the observer is categorizing 40 minutes of arithmetic and 20 minutes of social studies, he makes one matrix for the arithmetic and another for the social studies lesson. If a secondary teacher has a 30-minute discussion period followed by a 20-minute period of more structured lecture in another area, then the observer usually makes two separate matrices. Matrices are more meaningful when they represent a single type of activity or work.

Using the matrix to determine general aspects of classroom interaction

After the observer tabulates a matrix, he then has the job of developing a description of the classroom interaction. He has several ways of describing the interaction but begins by reporting the different kinds of statements in terms of

Table 2–2

A Typical Illustration

Second

		1	2	3	4	5	6	7	8	9	10	Total
	1	2	1									
	2		5		2							
	3			8		2						
	4		1		18				1			
First	5					53	2					
	6						3		1	1		
	7							3			2	
	8			2				2	26			
	9	1							1	10		
	10								1	1	1	
	Total	3	7	10	20	55	5	5	30	12	3	150
	Column %	2	4½	6½	13½	36½	3½	3½	20	8	2	

Teacher talk	Student talk
Columns 1–7 = 105	Columns 8–9 = 42
105 ÷ 150 = 70%	42 ÷ 150 = 28%

Indirect (1–4)–Direct (5–7) = ID ratio

40 ÷ 65 = 0.62

Indirect (1–3)–Direct (6–7) = Revised ID ratio

20 ÷ 10 = 2.0

percentages. The first step is computing the percentage of tallies in each of the columns. This is done by dividing each of the column totals, 1 through 10, by the total number of tallies in the matrix. This computation gives the proportion of the total interaction in the observed classroom situation found in each category. A similar procedure is used to determine the percentage of total teacher talk that falls in each category. This is done by dividing the total of each category, 1 through 7, by the sum of these seven categories. For example, in Table 2–2, the teacher had 105 tallies in columns 1–7. If 10 of these tallies are in column 3, then 10 is divided by 105 and we find that the amount of teacher talk that falls in category 3 is approximately 9½% of the total amount of teacher talk. The pattern of interaction which the teacher has used with the class is now evident.

The total percentage of teacher talk, of prime importance in interpreting the matrix, is found by dividing the total number of tallies in columns 1 through 7 by the total number of tallies in the matrix. There are 150 tallies in the matrix, 105 of which are in columns 1–7. This teacher talked 70% of the total time of the observation. To find the percentage of student talk, the total number of tallies in columns 8 and 9 is divided by the total number of tallies in the matrix. Assuming that columns 8 and 9 contained 42 tallies, the students talked 28% of the time. A total of three tallies in Column 10, when divided by 150, shows that 2% of the time was spent in silence or confusion.

Next the observer focuses on the relative number of indirect and direct teacher statements. The total number of tallies in Columns 1, 2, 3, and 4 is divided by the total number of tallies in Columns 5, 6, and 7 to find the ID Ratio or the ratio of indirect to direct teacher statements. An ID Ratio of 1.0 means that for every indirect statement there was one direct statement; an ID ratio of 2.0 means that for every two indirect statements there was only one direct statement, etc.

A Revised ID Ratio is employed in order to find out the kind of emphasis given to motivation and control in a particular classroom. The number of tallies in columns 1, 2, and 3 is divided by the number of tallies in columns 6 and 7 to find this revised ratio. Categories 1, 2, 3, 6, and 7 are more concerned with motivation and control in the classroom and less concerned with the actual presentation of subject matter. This ratio eliminates the effects of categories 4 and 5, asking questions and lecturing, and gives evidence about whether the teacher is direct or indirect in his approach to motivation and control.

Using the matrix to determine specific aspects of classroom interaction

The matrix provides the observer with a convenient device for analysis of the summarized teacher–pupil interaction data. By studying the matrix the observer will be able to identify those cells in which he has heavy build-ups of tallies as well as the cells in which there are no tallies.

Tables 2–3 through 2–9 describe the interaction more specifically in terms of certain areas of the matrix. Table 2–3 indicates the area called the "content cross," because tallies in this area represent teacher statements consisting primarily of lecture; statements of opinion, ideas and information; and teacher questions about information and content that he has presented. A heavy concentration of tallies in this area indicates an emphasis on the content.

Table 2–4 represents the emphasis that the teacher gives to using student ideas extending and amplifying student statements, and accepting and enlarging upon student feelings. It also includes stages of transition from one of these areas to the other. High frequencies of tallies in the cells indicated in Table 2–4 indicate the use of extended indirect influence by the teacher.

Table 2–5 indicates the cells representing the teacher's emphasis on criticism, giving lengthy direction, or moving from one of these types of influence to the other. In general, tabulations in this area suggest extended direct influence on the part of the teacher and a heavy focus on the teacher's use of authority. One

Table 2–3

The "Content Cross"

Second

	1	2	3	4	5	6	7	8	9	10
1				▨	▨					
2				▨	▨					
3				▨	▨					
4	▨	▨	▨	▨	▨	▨	▨	▨	▨	▨
5	▨	▨	▨	▨	▨	▨	▨	▨	▨	▨
6				▨	▨					
7				▨	▨					
8				▨	▨					
9				▨	▨					
10				▨	▨					
Total				▨	▨					

First (label for rows)

Table 2–4

Extended Indirect Influence

Second

	1	2	3	4	5	6	7	8	9	10
1	▨	▨	▨							
2	▨	A	▨							
3	▨	▨	▨							
4										
5										
6										
7										
8										
9										
10										
Total										

First (label for rows)

Table 2–5

Extended Direct Influence

Second

	1	2	3	4	5	6	7	8	9	10
1										
2										
3										
4										
5										
6						B				
7										
8										
9										
10										
Total										

(First)

Table 2–6

Teacher Response to Student Comments

Second

	1	2	3	4	5	6	7	8	9	10
1										
2										
3										
4										
5										
6										
7										
8		A			B					
9										
10										
Total										

(First)

Table 2–7

Student Talk Following Teacher Talk

		Second									
		1	2	3	4	5	6	7	8	9	10
	1										
	2										
	3										
	4								A		
First	5										
	6										
	7										
	8										
	9								B		
	10										
	Total										

pattern often observed shows a teacher giving direction that is then followed. Criticism ensues, and the teacher repeats the direction or gives a new direction. If it is not followed, the teacher again criticizes. This cycle of behavior, shown in the pattern 6-6, 6-7, 7-6, 7-7, often indicates discipline problems or problems of student rejection of teacher influence. High frequencies in the 6-6 cell alone do not necessarily reflect on discipline.

An important aspect of the classroom is the way the teacher responds to student comment. Area A, Table 2–6, represents the indirect responses to student comment. Area B represents the direct responses to student comment. A comparison of the relative number of tallies in these two areas indicates the pattern of behavior used by the teacher in response to students at the moment that a student stops talking.

Table 2–7 refers to student talk. Examination of the tabulations that fall into Area A, Table 2–7, can indicate the kinds of teacher statements that tend to stimulate student talk. They help to answer the question, "How do students in this classroom become involved in classroom interaction?" Area B, Table 2–7, represents student talk of two types: prolonged talk by one student and sustained talk by several students. In both cases the talk is not interrupted by teacher talk.

Column 10, represented in Table 2–8, shows particularly the kind of teacher or student talk that is followed by silence or confusion.

Table 2–8

Silence or Confusion

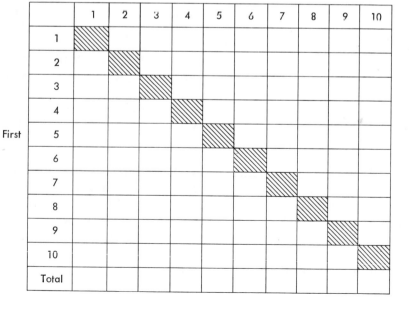

Second

	1	2	3	4	5	6	7	8	9	10
1										
2										
3										
4										
5										
6										
7										
8										
9										
10										
Total										

First

Table 2–9

Steady-State Cells

Second

	1	2	3	4	5	6	7	8	9	10
1										
2										
3										
4										
5										
6										
7										
8										
9										
10										
Total										

First

Table 2–9 shows cells that are referred to as the "steady-state cells." They lie along the diagonal of the matrix. Only when the behavior remains in a single category for longer than three seconds will there be tallies in these cells. If, for example, there is a tally in the 1 1 cell, it means that the teacher was accepting or clarifying student emotion during a period of more than three seconds. Note particularly that these cells along the diagonal are the only cells in the entire matrix that identify continuous talk in a single category; *all other cells are transitional cells* representing movement from one category to another. A build-up in any one of these cells, except 10-10, indicates that one specific kind of communication is being used for extended periods. Either the teacher is, or the students are, taking time to expand on the ideas being presented. Heavy loading in diagonal categories 1-7 indicates that the teacher is being deliberate in communication, taking time to extend his ideas or those of the students. Above average or heavy loading in the 8 and 9 diagonal cells indicates that individual students are being permitted to expand their own ideas.

Interpreting matrix data

In developing an intensive description about a particular matrix, it is well to remember that only the individual teacher can make the final decisions about what behavior is "good" or "bad," "undesirable" or "desirable." There are certain predictions, however, that can be made about the effects of certain kinds and combinations of behavior in the classroom. In this section the matrix will be systematically analyzed in order to discuss consequences that can be expected for particular kinds of cell totals and cell build-ups.

Interpretations in this section are made on the basis of analysis of matrices that were built in the research program by Flanders while at the University of Minnesota, as well as those that were collected by Amidon and his associates at Temple University.

Teachers referred to here as "direct" are those who were identified in the research and in the laboratory as using considerably more than the average amount of direct influence. The indirect teachers are those who used much more than the average of "indirect" influence. The average percentages given are based on matrices of junior high school teachers because this is the only level at which large numbers of teachers have been observed. Subsequent examination of matrices of elementary teachers or high school teachers has revealed no major differences between those teachers and teachers at the junior high school levels. *Average percentages reflect current practice, not the best or most desired practices.* For example, a naturally indirect teacher with special training is likely to become even more indirect than is indicated in the paragraphs that follow.

Statements belonging in category 1 are used very rarely in any teaching style, the average time appearing to be less than 0.5% of the total time. Little difference in the use of category 1 is found between direct and indirect teachers. Indirect teachers may use up to 0.5% while direct teachers usually use less than 0.1%. Not much use, then, is made of clarifying emotion of students in the classroom. This category is maintained because of the significance of such behavior when it does occur.

Direct and indirect teachers seem to use practically the same number of statements fitting into category 2. The average amount of praise used is about 2% of the total time of the classroom interaction. It is somewhat surprising to many teachers to learn that the direct teacher uses as much praise as the indirect teacher. The 2-2 cell, showing extended praise, is particularly significant as it is used almost twice as much by the indirect as by the direct teacher.

The greatest difference between teachers who are identified as direct and those who are indirect is in their use of category 3, acceptance or clarification of ideas. Only about 2% of the tallies of direct teachers fall in category 3, but about 9% of indirect teacher statements fall in this category. Although some difference can be accounted for by subject matter area, fewer differences seem to be due to subject matter areas than to type of teacher. Teachers who use the 3-3 cell are not only accepting and using student ideas but also enlarging upon these ideas by using them to show children the relationships between their own ideas and the content in the classroom. The use of category 3, particularly the further extension of student ideas, which is shown in the 3-3 cell, often distinguishes between two types of teachers; the one who is alert to and utilizing the relationship between a student's idea (whether right or wrong) and classroom content, and the teacher who is apparently unaware of or does not care to utilize this relationship.

Category 4 and Category 5, although one indicates indirect and the other direct influence, will be discussed together since they seem to be closely related by their use in the classroom. The percentage of teacher talk that is questioning, falling in category 4, usually varies from 8% to 15%. Category 5 statements, or lecture, constitute 25% to 50% of the total verbal behavior of teachers. There seems to be very little difference between direct and indirect teachers in the use of categories 4 and 5. Questions appear to constitute about 8% of the interaction for direct teachers and 11% of the pattern of indirect teachers. No consistent differences appear to exist between the direct and indirect teachers in the amount of lecture used in the classroom.

In their use of category 6, direct and indirect teachers are often found to differ significantly, with the direct teacher using about 8% and the indirect teacher only 4% of the total interaction time in giving directions.

A look at category 7, too, helps in discriminating between direct and indirect teachers because the two types differ in the amount of time they spend in criticism and self-justification. The direct teacher employs criticism about 5% of the time, and the indirect teacher less than 1% of the time. Nor do the two kinds of teachers use category 7 statements in the same way. Most of the criticism used by the direct teacher is extended criticism, which shows up in cell 7-7. The direct teacher also uses criticism after lecture, direction, and student talk. This use of criticism shows up in the 5-7, 6-7, 8-7, and 9-7 cells.

The indirect teacher, who rarely uses the 6-7 and 7-6 cells, tends to distribute his use of criticism more evenly among the other cells of the matrix than does the direct teacher.

The significant difference between the direct and indirect teacher in relation to category 8 is not in the amount of student talk it represents but rather in the way in which the teachers induce pupil participation. In the matrix of the direct teacher, about 50% of category 8 tallies occur in the 4-8 cell, which implies answers to teacher questions. In the matrix of the indirect teacher the total in the 4-8 cell is closer to 30% of the total in category 8. A larger percentage of student talk in the 8-8 cell occurs in the matrix of the indirect teacher than in that of the direct teacher.

The differences are also significant in category 9. Although there is very little difference in total percentages of category 9 statements appearing in matrices of direct and indirect teachers, sustained student talk, shown in the 9-9 cell, occurs frequently in the matrix of the indirect teacher and infrequently in the matrix of the direct teacher. Students in the classroom of the indirect teacher, according to this information, express themselves more freely.

Category 10, which shows the total amount of silence or confusion in the classroom, is more heavily loaded in the matrix of the direct than in that of the indirect teacher.

Other facts revealed in the matrix

A careful examination of columns 4 and 5 and rows 4 and 5 will enable the observer to identify for study several cells that are important primarily because of the function of categories 4 and 5 in the presentation of subject matter. Variation in the amount of time spent in categories 4 and 5 is due largely to the subject area that is taught. This seems to be more true in the case of these categories than in the case of any other category or pair of categories. The teacher who is teaching mathematics, science, or another relatively structured subject lectures more than he questions pupils. The social studies teacher uses more questions and less lecture. The common pattern in an arithmetic or mathematics class is for the teacher to use lecture 50% of the time and questions between 5 and 10% of the time. In a social studies class the teacher is likely to lecture about 30% of the time and use 10 to 15% of the time for questions.

When a teacher uses extensive lecture, is he taking time to find out whether or not he is communicating as he wants to communicate with the class? A question–answer pattern, or a pattern of question and clarification by the teacher of student ideas may indicate that the teacher is taking time to relate the responses of children to the material or to determine how effectively he is communicating his ideas. Conversely, a pattern of extended lecture with few questions, or one of only direct questions with specific answers required, may indicate limited attempts on the part of the teacher to find out how well he is communicating or to find out whether or not there is a clear relationship between student ideas and the content being discussed.

The kind of question and answer pattern that is in use is indicated by examining rows 4 and 8 and columns 4 and 8. Note first the 4-8 cell that contains tallies indicating teacher questions followed immediately by student response. A heavily loaded 4-8 cell indicates that the teacher has asked many direct questions, that is, questions that limit the range of a student response. If the 8-4 cell is also heavily loaded, with few tallies appearing in other row 8 cells, then it is probable that the teacher is following the student's answer to one question with another question.

The use of a modified question-answer pattern can be shown by heavy buildups in the 4-8, 8-2, 8-3, 2-4 and 3-4 cells. This pattern is indicative of a teacher who asks a question and then encourages or accepts student ideas before asking a second question.

Still another modified question-answer pattern centers around the 4-10 cell. Frequent use of this 4-10 combination reflects periods of silence following teacher questions. What follows this silence that occurs after the teacher question? When the verbal action that follows is student response, indicated by heavily loaded 10-8 or 10-9 cells, then the teacher has perhaps asked thought-provoking questions and allowed time for pupils to think before answering. If, however, there is heavy loading in the 10-4 cell rather than in the 10-9 and 10-8 cells, then the teacher has either restated his original question or has phrased a new one before allowing students to answer.

A teacher using a pattern in which the 4-5 and 4-6 cells are heavily loaded may not be allowing pupils to answer questions he has asked. Either he is directing them to answer, or he is extending lecture after his questions, perhaps to explain them further.

Frequent use of the 5-4 cell means that the teacher is interjecting questions throughout his lecturing. When the 5-4 cell is heavily loaded, it is probably important to check the 4-8 and 4-9 cells, as well as the 8 and 9 rows to find out more about how the teacher uses questions during the lecture.

Frequent use of the 5-7 cell, indicating lecture broken by criticism, suggests the teacher is attempting to maintain order and control while he is lecturing.

Considerable use of the 5-5 cell with little use of other cells in the 5 row means that the teacher uses periods of concentrated lecture unbroken by teacher questions or pupil contributions.

SUMMARY

This paper has dealt with the process of gathering and interpreting data about spontaneous verbal interaction in the classroom. Once gathered, the data are useful for purposes of research or for giving feedback to teachers regarding their verbal teaching behavior.

VERBAL INTERACTION IN THE CLASSROOM:[17] THE VERBAL INTERACTION CATEGORY SYSTEM

EDMUND AMIDON AND ELIZABETH HUNTER

Researchers in the field of education have only recently begun to study the interactive behavior of teachers and pupils in the classroom. One of the primary concerns of these researchers has been the determination of the relationship between the behavior of the teacher and such outcomes as pupil attitude and achievement. A variety of systems designed to analyze pupil–teacher interaction in the classroom have been developed by Withall (1949), Anderson (1939), Smith (1960), Aschner (1959), Hughes *et al.* (1959a), Medley and Mitzel (1958), and Amidon and Flanders (1963) among others.

One of the best known systems for examining verbal interactive classroom behavior was developed by Flanders (Amidon and Flanders, 1963) in the 1950's. The system to be discussed in this article, the Verbal Interaction Category System (VICS), is based on the Flanders system, but has been further developed in an attempt to overcome some of the limitations of that as well as other systems.

THE VERBAL INTERACTION CATEGORY SYSTEM

The Verbal Interaction Category System (VICS) contains five major categories for analyzing classroom verbal behavior. They are: (1) Teacher-initiated talk, (2) Teacher response, (3) Pupil response, (4) Pupil-initiated talk, (5) Other. (See Fig. 2–2.)

The system requires that persons planning to use it to study verbal behavior in the classroom begin by memorizing the categories. Once these are

[17] This paper was prepared specially for this book.

CATEGORIES

Teacher-initiated talk	1. Presents information or opinion 2. Gives directions 3. Asks narrow question 4. Asks broad question
Teacher response	5. Accepts a) Ideas b) behavior c) feeling 6. Rejects a) ideas b) behavior c) feeling
Pupil response	7. Responds to teacher a) predictably b) unpredictably 8. Responds to another pupil
Pupil-initiated talk	9. Initiates talk to teacher 10. Initiates talk to another pupil
	11. Silence
Other	Z. Confusion (Z may be used alone when confusion drowns out verbal behavior, or may be used alongside another category to indicate interfering disruption while someone is talking: 1 Z 1 Z 3 Z 7a Z)

(Numbers may be placed to the right of and slightly above the category numbers to indicate change in pupils who are participating: 4

$7b^1$

3

$7a^2$

1

2

9^3

1

4

$7b^2$

$7b^4$

FIG. 2–2. Categories in the Verbal Interaction Category System.

learned so that response is automatic, tapes of various teaching situations are used for practicing the tallying of categories. A category is tallied every time the behavior changes and every three seconds in any behavior that lasts longer than three seconds. These tallies are written in a column, preserving their sequence, at the rate of approximately twenty tallies per minute. These numbers can then be entered into a matrix which represents summary information clearly and succinctly about the type, sequence, and amount of verbal behavior which has been recorded.

THE VICS CATEGORIES

TEACHER-INITIATED TALK. Teacher-initiated talk is divided into four categories:

1. *Presents information or opinion:* When the teacher is presenting facts or opinions to the class, either in the form of short statements or in the form of an extended lecture, category 1 is used. Generally this category is used when the teacher is presenting content. Explanation, discussion, and rhetorical questions are included here.

2. *Gives direction:* Whenever the teacher tells the students to take some specific action, category 2 is used. Examples of this category are: "Open your books to page five," "Take your seats," and "Please add the following numbers." Directions may be given in question form, such as, "Will everyone turn around?" or "Can you come here a moment, Jane?"

3. *Asks narrow question:* If the general nature of the response can be predicted, category 3 is tallied. Drill questions and questions requiring one word or yes-or-no answers fall into this category. "How much is three and three?" "What is the capital of France?" "Is that correct?" "What happened next in the story?" "What are the principal exports of Brazil?" are examples of narrow or predictable response questions.

4. *Asks broad question:* Questions which are relatively open-ended fall into category 4. When the teacher asks questions which are thought-provoking or require expressions of opinion or feeling, this category is used. The broad or unpredictable-response question is more apt to elicit a rather long response, while the narrow or predictable-response question is more apt to bring forth a short reply. Examples of broad questions are: "Can you tell me some things you know about number three?" "Why do you think Paris came to be the capital of France?" "What are some other things the author might have written next in this story?" "What are some of the ways in which geography and history have probably influenced Brazilian production and exports?"

TEACHER-RESPONSE TALK. Teacher-response talk is divided into two major categories; acceptance and rejection:

Acceptance

5a. *Accepts ideas:* When the teacher accepts, reflects, clarifies, encourages, or praises an idea of a pupil, category 5a is used. If the teacher summarizes the ideas of a pupil or of several pupils, or comments on the ideas without rejecting them, this category is indicated. Saying, "Good," "Yes," and so forth, are examples of category 5a.

5b. *Accepts behavior:* Responses to pupil behavior which are accepting and encouraging of that behavior fall into category 5b. Such statements as, "I like the way the boys and girls in this group are behaving," "Billy really knows how to use books properly," and "We can be proud of the way we handled ourselves on our trip," are all examples of 5b.

5c. *Accepts feeling:* When the teacher responds to pupil feelings in an accepting manner, or merely reflects their feelings, this category is used. "I know that it's a warm day and many of us would rather be outside," "Of course you feel disappointed because there isn't any assembly program today," "I'd be happy, too, if that happened to me," and "No wonder you feel sad," are examples of category 5c.

6a. *Rejects ideas:* When the teacher rejects, criticizes, ignores, or discourages pupil ideas, category 6a is used. "No," "Can someone else tell us the right answer?" "That's not right," "Where did you ever get *that* idea!" "Is that what I asked you to discuss?" are examples of category 6a. Note that some of them are stated in question form, but would be taken by pupils as criticism.

6b. *Rejects behavior:* Teacher comments that are designed to discourage or criticize pupil behavior fall into category 6b. "I said to sit down!" "We shouldn't have our books open now," "Where do you think you are?" are all expressions of rejection of behavior. The tone of voice and the resultant effect are what differentiate these from the categories of giving direction and asking questions.

6c. *Rejects feeling:* When teachers respond to pupil expression of feelings by ignoring, discouraging, or rejecting the child, category 6c is noted. "Aren't you ashamed of yourself for crying?" "Just because there's no assembly today doesn't mean we need to sit and mope," "There's no need to bring our personal feelings up," are examples of this category.

PUPIL-RESPONSE TALK. Student-response talk is divided into two major categories; response to teacher and response to another pupil:

Response to teacher

7a. *Responds to teacher predictably:* This ordinarily follows category 3, a narrow question from the teacher, and tends to be a relatively short reply. Category 7a also frequently follows category 2, a direction; as for example, when the teacher says, "David read the first line on page six."

7b. *Responds to teacher unpredictably:* This category usually follows the asking of a broad question by the teacher. However, a pupil may give an unpredictable response to a question which is tallied as category 3, a narrow question. For instance, when a teacher asks, "What was the cause of this conflict?" a pupil may reply, "It seems to me that there wasn't any one cause—I think there were many factors at work."

Response to another pupil

8. *Responds to another pupil:* Whenever one pupil responds to the question or ideas of another, category 8 is used. When there is conversation between pupils, replies are noted in this category.

PUPIL-INITIATED RESPONSE. Student-initiated response is divided into two major categories; initiation to teacher and initiation to pupil:

Initiation to teacher

9. *Talks to teacher:* If a pupil initiates a conversation with the teacher, then category 9 is used. "Will we have art today?" "I don't understand how to do this problem." "Here's a clipping I brought in for our social studies project," "Would you repeat that last part again?" are all examples of category 9.

Initiation to pupil

10. *Talks to another pupil:* Any conversation which one pupil initiates with another falls into this category.

OTHER. This is the last major category of the system and contains two sub-categories:

11. *Silence:* When there are long pauses or short periods of silence, category 11 is tallied. For long periods of silence, as when the class is engaged in seat work or silent reading, the observer simply notes this in the margin and stops tallying.

Z. *Confusion:* When there is considerable noise and disruption of planned activities, this category is used. Z may also be placed alongside another category to indicate some accompanying confusion while the teacher and some pupils continue with the scheduled activities (See Honigman, 1964).

SOME DIFFERENCES BETWEEN THE FLANDERS SYSTEM AND THE VERBAL INTERACTION CATEGORY SYSTEM

Perhaps the primary difference between the Flanders system and the system discussed here is that the dimension of teacher behavior pointed up in the Flanders system is directness as opposed to indirectness. Does the teacher use more direct or indirect influence in his teaching? Although the point is made that no value is implied, there is argument about whether direct or indirect behavior is more desirable. Direct teacher influence as opposed to indirect is not a dimension of the VICS. The teacher categories are looked at rather in terms of initiation and response.

The Flanders system does not provide a method for differentiating the type of teacher question. There is only one category, "Asks questions." The VICS, on the other hand, allows for the division of teacher questions into "narrow," which bring forth predictable responses, and "broad," which elicit unpredictable responses.

A third difference between these two systems is in the area of pupil talk. The VICS adds the dimension of predictable or unpredictable response. The Flanders system has one category to indicate silence or confusion, while the VICS separates these two. In addition, the VICS encourages the recorder to use the confusion category simultaneously with other categories when the interaction in the classroom can still be followed but when some disruption of order is occurring.

Table 2–10

Area in the Matrix of the VICS

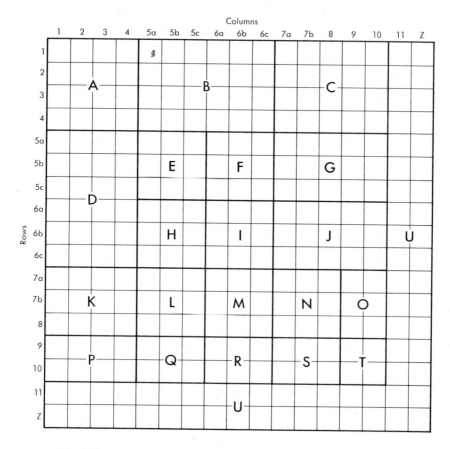

A fifth difference between the two systems is the manner in which teacher response to pupil behavior is noted. The Flanders system has three categories for reacting positively to pupils, but only one for reacting negatively. The VICS has three for each, accepting or rejecting pupils' *ideas, behavior*, or *feeling*. The Flanders system indicates the teacher's acceptance of feeling, behavior, and ideas, but rejection or criticism is not further defined.

The VICS has seventeen categories rather than the Flanders ten, and thus is more unwieldy and harder to learn and use. However, previous experience by Withall (1949) and Bales (1950) indicates that seventeen categories (of which eight are really subheadings) is not a difficult number for trained recorders to use.

The authors believe that the Verbal Interaction Category System provides a usable tool for teachers and teachers in training, as well as for supervisors of teachers. The categories are clearly understandable, and thus easy to recognize and tally. The feedback provided to the teacher about the nature of interaction in his classroom is invaluable, since objective feedback is not ordinarily available. With a matrix, used by both the VICS and the Flanders system, an objective picture of the pattern of verbal behavior in the classroom is provided.

Once the tallies are entered on the matrix, the interaction pattern of the classroom can be interpreted by studying that matrix. Different parts of the matrix indicate different kinds of classroom interaction, as will be seen from Table 2–10 and the following discussion.

Areas within the matrix in the VICS

AREA A. This is the area of prolonged teacher initiation, and includes presenting information or opinion, giving directions, and asking questions. The major characteristic of this area is that the teacher is speaking for a relatively long period. This is not an area which shows interaction between pupil and teacher.

AREA B. The cells in this area indicate teacher-initiated statements followed by teacher-response statements, either accepting or rejecting.

AREA C. This group of cells includes all student talk which follows teacher-initiated talk.

AREA D. Area D indicates teacher-response statements followed by teacher-initiated statements.

AREA E. This area indicates prolonged accepting behavior on the part of the teacher. This includes extended acceptance of ideas, behavior, and feelings, as well as transitions from one of these verbal patterns to another.

AREA F. These cells indicate teacher-accepting behavior followed by teacher-rejecting behavior.

AREA G. This area shows accepting teacher statements followed by any student statements.

AREA H. Area H indicates teacher-rejecting behavior followed by teacher-accepting behavior.

AREA I. These cells indicate extended rejecting behavior on the part of the teacher. Rejection of ideas, behavior, and feelings are indicated here, as well as transition from one of these behaviors to another.

AREA J. These cells show all student statements which follow teacher-rejecting statements.

AREA K. This area indicates student-response behavior followed by teacher-initiated behavior.

AREA L. This group of cells show student response followed by teacher acceptance.

AREA M. Area M shows teacher rejection of student responses.

AREA N. These cells show extended student response to either the teacher or another pupil.

AREA O. Area O indicates student-response statements followed by student-initiated statements.

AREA P. These cells indicate student-initiated behavior followed by teacher-initiated behavior.

AREA Q. This area shows student-initiated talk followed by teacher acceptance.

AREA R. Area R indicates teacher rejection of student initiated talk.

AREA S. These cells indicate student-initiated statements followed by student-response statements.

AREA T. This area indicates extended student-initiated talk to either the teacher or another pupil.

AREA U: Area U indicates silence or confusion. If the tallies are in row or column 11 they indicate silence, and if they are in row or column Z, they indicate confusion. Tallies in columns 11 or Z represent silence or confusion following teacher or student talk, while tallies in rows 11 or Z represent silence or confusion before student or teacher talk.

The matrix indicates the amount, the sequence, and the pattern of verbal behavior in the classroom according to the categories of the VICS. One can determine, for example, how much direction the teacher gave, or to what extent he accepted or rejected the pupils. One can also determine from the matrix what kind of behavior followed each preceding behavior. And one can determine recurring patterns in the classroom.

The matrix can indicate, for example, whether or not teacher questions are followed by periods of silence during which students may be thinking about their responses. If a teacher allows pupils time to think before they answer, then the silence category will be followed by a pupil-response category, rather than by another teacher category. This is just one example of the wide spectrum of classroom interactive behavior which can be determined from the matrix.

THE IMPLICATION AND POTENTIAL OF THE
VERBAL INTERACTION CATEGORY SYSTEM FOR TEACHER EDUCATION

The VICS has particular utility in the field of teacher education. It is a system that can be used to help teachers and student teachers focus upon their behavior in the classroom in an objective manner. By recording their teaching activities on tape, or by having another person trained in the use of the system categorize the verbal behavior in their classrooms, teachers and student teachers can obtain a record of their classroom conversation for analysis. College supervisors of student teaching and cooperating teachers will find that a knowledge of the system is particularly helpful in their work with student teachers.

Use of a system such as this one helps to stimulate teachers and future teachers to develop an attitude of inquiry toward the entire field of teaching behavior. When teachers are provided with a system of objective feedback, they become conscious of the importance of verbal patterns of which they were not previously aware.

In addition to its direct use in the classroom with children, the VICS might be used in student-teaching seminars or other college classes to categorize the verbal behavior of participants in role-playing situations. For instance, student teachers may practice the acceptance of pupil feeling followed by the rejection of pupil ideas, or they might try asking questions that require unpredictable responses from pupils. The role-playing might consist of setting up situations in which the teacher rejects pupils' ideas, behaviors, or feelings, followed by a reenactment of those situations with the teacher changing to more accepting behavior. Other students can categorize the teaching behavior and tapes can be made for further listening and analysis.

It will be seen that the Verbal Interaction Category System for analyzing verbal behavior in the classroom offers teachers, future teachers, and supervisors a tool that can provide objective data about teaching behavior. Objective feedback is a necessary component of teacher growth and change, and educators must continue the process of developing and working with effective feedback systems.

AN OBSERVATIONAL SYSTEM
FOR THE ANALYSIS
OF CLASSROOM INSTRUCTION[18]

JOHN B. HOUGH

The Observational System for Instructional Analysis is a 16-category system that has been developed to test instructional hypotheses generated from learning theory. The 16 categories of the system have been grouped into four major subdivisions: (1) teacher indirect verbal behavior, (2) teacher direct verbal behavior, (3) student verbal behavior, (4) silence or nonfunctional verbal behavior. A conscious attempt has been made to organize the sixteen categories of the Observational System for Instructional Analysis so as to parallel the four-part organization and category sequence of Flanders' system of interaction analysis (1965a). It was hoped that by so doing, positive transfer would be facilitated for those persons who wish to learn to use both systems. Because the Observational System for Instructional Analysis preserves the social–emotional dimensions of Flanders' system, researchers using either this system or Flanders' system will be able to draw certain types of common conclusions from investigations of classroom verbal behavior done by other researchers.

Certain types of analyses of verbal behavior not possible with the Flanders system have been made possible by the Observational System for Instructional Analysis. This has been accomplished through minor revisions of some of Flanders' categories and by the creation of new categories.

The major contribution of this system lies in its potential for testing instructional hypotheses derived from learning theory. For example, if separate categories are provided for corrective feedback and for criticism or rejection of student behavior or ideas, the effects of corrective feedback on student learning may be distinguished from the effects of aversive stimulation. When three categories are created for productive conditions of silence [(a) directed practice or activity, (b) silence for contemplation, and (c) demonstration], one of the more important dimensions of behavior associated with insightful learning may be studied more exactly. Provision of separate categories for productive silence as compared with nonfunctional behavior (Flanders' silence

---

[18] This paper was prepared specially for this book.

and confusion; category 10) permits a clear distinction to be made between those behaviors designed to facilitate learning and those which are nonproductive, or at least have no great promise of being productive. In the area of student verbal behavior, two types of student-declarative responses have been categorized. These two types of responses have been called elicited responses and emitted responses. Elicited responses are distinguished from emitted responses on the basis of prior conditioning and the predictability of the response. Such a distinction makes possible the study of the differential effects of several types of reinforcement given by a teacher following responses which have been previously conditioned (and thus are elicited by teacher questions or commands) as compared with responses which have not been previously associated with a specific stimulus (and thus are emitted). For example, the effect on student learning of various types of teacher reinforcing behavior (such as teacher reward, praise, and corrective feedback) following emitted and elicited responses may be compared with teacher acceptance and clarification as a reinforcing mechanism. In addition to elicited and emitted responses, both of which are declarative, the Observational System for Instructional Analysis contains a category for student questions and a companion category for teacher answers to student questions. Addition of these two categories allows the function of teacher information-giving to be analyzed in terms of whether it is initiated by the teacher or by student questions.

It is therefore characteristic of this system that the categories have been developed so as to focus on observable behaviors that are commonly associated with principles of learning drawn from learning theory. The testing of hypotheses regarding the effects of instructional behavior on student learning (hypotheses generated from learning theory) seems to be the major contribution of this system.

Listed below are the sixteen categories of the Observational System for Instructional Analysis:

INDIRECT TEACHER VERBAL INFLUENCE

1. AFFECTIVE CLARIFICATION AND ACCEPTANCE: Includes the acceptance, clarification and recognition of students' emotional states. Statements which deal in a nonevaluative way with student emotions and feelings, i.e., fear, anger, anxiety, happiness, pleasure, etc., are included in this category. Such statements may recall or predict student feelings or may be a reaction to current emotional states of students. Statements of encouragement which do not praise or reward or do not deny expressed student feelings are also included in this category.

2. PRAISE AND REWARD: Includes statements with a positive value orientation directed at student behavior. Statements praising or rewarding current behavior as well as statements of praise or reward for previous or predicted future behavior are included in this category. Also included are statements which indicate teacher agreement with student behavior and thus by implication express teacher feelings regarding the value of the behavior.

3. COGNITIVE AND SKILL CLARIFICATION AND ACCEPTANCE: Includes statements that show acceptance of, or are designed to clarify, student ideas or performance, but are nonevaluative. Statements that repeat or paraphrase what a student has said or that are designed to help the student think through what he has said or done are included in this category. Also included are such statements as "um hum," "go on," and "OK," when such statements are not said with an inflection that connotes praise or do not represent habitual teacher behavior.

4. TEACHER QUESTIONS: Includes questions to which answers are expected, but do not serve the function of other categories. Such questions may be about content or procedure or may ask for student opinion regarding content or procedure.

5. RESPONSE TO QUESTIONS: Includes direct answers to student questions. Such answers may give information or opinion but must be responses that answer or are directed toward answering student questions.

TEACHER DIRECT INFLUENCE

6. INITIATES INFORMATION OR OPINION: Includes all statements regarding content or process that give information or opinion. Also included in this category are rhetorical questions.

7. CORRECTIVE FEEDBACK: Includes statements that are designed to indicate the incorrectness or inappropriateness of behavior so that the student sees that his behavior is incorrect or inappropriate. Such teacher statements are restricted to cognitive or skill areas in which behavior can be considered correct or appropriate by definition, by generally accepted convention, or by being empirically validated as fact.

8. REQUESTS AND COMMANDS: Includes directions, requests and commands to which compliance is expected. Also included are questions preceded by a student's name after a question has been asked which the student has not indicated a readiness to answer.

9. CRITICISM AND REJECTION: Includes statements that criticize or reject student ideas or behavior without reference to clearly identifiable authority (i.e., definition, common convention, or empirically validatable fact). Also included in this category are sarcasm and rejection or denial of student feelings.

STUDENT VERBAL BEHAVIOR

10. ELICITED RESPONSES: Includes conforming responses to narrow questions, commands, and requests, and all responses which are highly predictable as a function of their having been previously associated with a specific stimulus or class of stimuli. Also included are incorrect responses to narrow questions,

commands, or requests, such statements as "I don't know," and unison responses either verbal or nonverbal.

11. EMITTED RESPONSES: Includes responses to broad questions or requests which have not been previously associated with specific stimuli or a class of stimuli. Also included are statements of opinion, feeling, and judgment.

12. STUDENT QUESTIONS: Includes comments which ask for information, procedure, or opinions of the teacher or another student.

SILENCE

13. DIRECTED PRACTICE OR ACTIVITY: Includes all nonverbal behavior requested or suggested by the teacher. Working problems, silent reading, etc., are included in this category. This category is also used to separate student-to-student interaction.

14. SILENCE AND CONTEMPLATION: Includes all instances of silence during which students are not overtly working on problems, reading, etc. Silence following questions and periods of silence interspersed with teacher or student talk are also included in this category, as are periods of silence intended for purposes of thinking.

15. DEMONSTRATION: Includes periods of silence when chalkboard, felt board, pictures, filmstrips, motion pictures, etc., are being used to present information or when a nonverbal demonstration is being conducted by the teacher.

NONFUNCTIONAL BEHAVIOR

16. CONFUSION AND IRRELEVANT BEHAVIOR: Includes all occasions when more than one person is talking and neither person can be understood (excepting unison responses), or when the noise level in the class is so high that the person speaking cannot be understood. Also included in this category are confused behavior in response to a command or direction, irrelevant comments that have no relation to the purpose of the classroom, and nonfunctional periods of silence such as when the teacher answers and talks on the classroom telephone.

In an attempt to further facilitate transfer between the learning of the Flanders system of interaction analysis and the Observational System for Instructional Analysis the ground rules to be observed during observation have been retained from the Flanders system (Amidon and Flanders, 1963).

These ground rules are stated below for purposes of clarification:

Rule number one: States that numbers representing the various categories are recorded by an observer at three-second intervals. When more than one category occurs within a three-second interval all such categories are recorded.

In recording the classroom interaction, the observer records the numbers corresponding to the categories in columns of figures, twenty to a column.

Teacher _____ Date _____

Situation _____

16	6	6	10	4	6	8	13	13	3	11	4	14	11	6
6	6	6	3	14	6	8	13	12	3	11	14	10	11	6
6	4	6	2	14	6	8	13	12	4	13	14	10	11	6
6	4	6	4	14	6	8	13	12	4	11	2	7	3	6
6	4	6	4	4	4	8	13	12	11	11	2	8	3	6
6	10	6	4	4	4	12	13	3	11	11	11	14	3	6
6	10	12	4	4	4	12	13	3	10	11	11	14	6	6
6	2	12	10	10	14	12	13	3	10	3	11	14	6	6
6	4	12	10	10	10	12	13	8	10	3	3	14	6	6
6	4	5	10	7	10	5	12	8	3	3	3	14	6	6
6	4	5	2	7	7	5	12	8	3	6	8	11	6	16
6	4	5	4	4	7	5	5	13	4	6	8	11	6	
6	10	5	4	10	7	5	5	13	4	6	4	3	6	
6	10	5	10	10	7	8	5	13	4	6	4	3	6	
6	10	4	10	10	10	8	13	13	11	6	4	11	6	
6	10	4	10	2	10	8	13	4	11	1	4	11	6	
6	2	4	3	6	10	8	13	10	11	1	14	11	6	
6	3	14	2	6	2	16	13	10	11	2	14	13	6	
6	3	10	4	6	2	16	13	10	3	2	14	11	6	
6	6	10	4	6	8	16	13	3	3	4	14	11	6	

FIGURE 2–3.

In this way, approximately one column will be used each minute, thus giving the observer an automatic feedback mechanism by which to check his timing of one observation every three seconds.

Rule number two: States that student talk which is followed by student talk is indicated by inserting the number 13 in the column of numbers at the point at which the first student stops talking and the second one begins.

Rule number three: States that when two or more categories seem equally appropriate, and/or when a discrimination cannot be made between two or more categories, the observer should use the category numerically furthest from category 6.

Rule number four: States that if the primary pattern of influence used by the teacher has been either direct or indirect, the observer should not shift to categories in the opposite area unless there is a clear indication of such a shift. This rule supersedes rule number three.

Rule number five: States that the observer does not try to second-guess the intent of the teacher, but rather records the categories of behavior as he perceives their effect on the students.

When the Observational System for Instructional Analysis is used, observations are plotted into the matrix in the same fashion in which they are

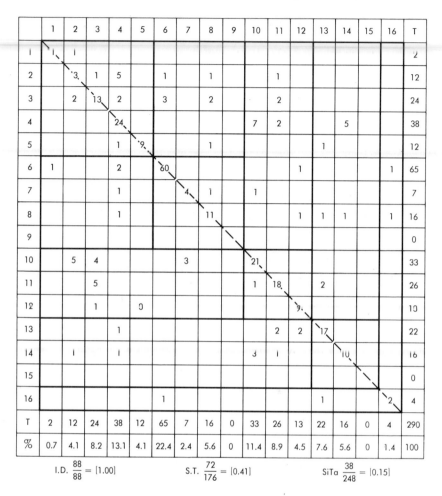

FIGURE 2–4.

plotted into the matrix used with the Flanders System. Category numbers are paired in such a way that any number, with the exception of the first and last numbers, always appears in two pairs, first as the second number of a pair and then as the first number of a pair. The first number of any pair refers to the row in the matrix into which it will be plotted, and the second number refers to the column. Tabulation always arbitrarily starts and ends with the number 16. In this way the column and row tallies of the matrix always balance if the plotting of the matrix has been accurate. Figures 2–3 and 2–4 show the tabulation for a short guided discovery lesson, and the matrix built from this tabulation. The first tally mark put into the matrix was put in the 16-6 cell, the second tally mark was put in the 6-6 cell and so on until all of the pairs of numbers had been used. The last tally mark was put into the 6-16 cell.

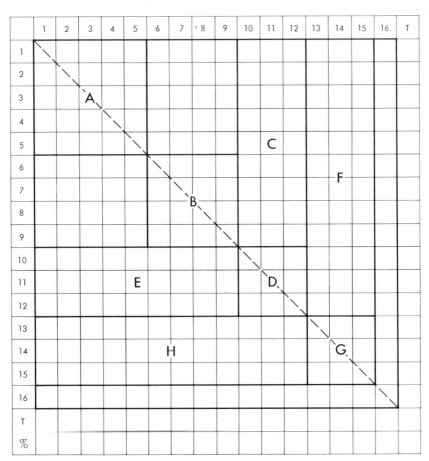

FIGURE 2–5.

When the matrix is plotted, columns and rows are totaled and the percentage for each category is computed. To analyze teacher use of direct and indirect verbal behavior, for example, one would compute the I/D ratio by dividing the sum of the indirect column totals (columns 1 through 5) by the sum of the direct column totals (columns 6 through 9). Similar analyses of verbal patterns may be obtained by computing the ratio of student talk to teacher talk (the S/T ratio) or the ratio of talk to silence (the Si/Ta ratio).

The completed matrix may be analyzed to show patterns of interaction in the classroom. Such an analysis is aided by identifying areas of the matrix which contain common elements. Listed below are the descriptions of areas of the matrix shown in Fig. 2–5.

Area A: Contains all instances of extended indirect influence. For example, when a teacher uses extended praise or extended acceptance, tally marks will be plotted into this area, as will instances of transition from one indirect category to another, e.g., shifts from answering student question to praise.

Area B: Contains all instances of extended direct influence. For example, when a teacher uses extended lecture or extended directions, tally marks will be plotted in this area, as will instances of transition from one direct category to another, e.g., shifts from lecture to criticism of student behavior.

Area C: Contains all instances of student talk following teacher talk. All cells in area C are transition cells; that is, they indicate the beginning of student talk following teacher talk. For example, when a student responds to a teacher's question, the beginning of such a response would be entered in this area, as would student responses to directions or corrective feedback.

Area D: Contains all instances of extended student talk. For example, when a student continues to talk for an extended period of time, tally marks will be plotted in this area, as will all instances of transition from one student-talk category to another, e.g., shifts from an emitted response to asking the teacher a question.

Area E: Contains all instances of teacher talk following student talk. All cells in area E are transition cells; that is, they indicate the beginning of teacher talk following student talk. For example, if a teacher praised a student's answer, the information would be entered in this area, as it would in the case of teacher criticism or acceptance of student responses.

Area F: Contains all instances of silence following either teacher or student talk. All cells in area F are transition cells; that is, they indicate the beginning of periods of silence following talk.

Area G: Contains all instances of extended silence. For example, if a teacher tells the class to think about something for a few minutes, their silence would be indicated in Area G.

Area H: Contains all instances of teacher or student talk following silence. For example, a teacher has asked a question which has been followed by silence. He repeats the question, and the initiation of the second question, following the silence, is plotted in Area H.

When one is interpreting the patterns of interaction shown on a matrix, it is helpful to remember that cells intersected by the dotted line are cells that indicate extended use of the same category, e.g., long questions, long answers to questions, etc. All other cells are transition cells; that is, they indicate the beginning or ending of a particular teacher or student behavior.

The Observational System for Instructional Analysis is a system of classroom observation that has been built to more precisely describe the classroom behaviors that are associated with the facilitation of learning as they are implicitly described in commonly accepted principles of learning and instruction. In order to facilitate transfer of learning from one system to another, this system has been consciously created to parallel, where possible, the Flanders system of interaction analysis.

4

THE PROBLEMS
OF OBSERVER TRAINING
AND RELIABILITY[19]

NED A. FLANDERS

The problem of observer training is twofold: first, converting men into machines, and second, keeping them in that condition while they are observing. The ideal observer team is a group of like-minded individuals who will respond consistently with the same category number when presented with the same communication events. The problem is twofold because once training has produced an acceptable level of reliability, it can still deteriorate due to the unending variety of judgments that arise and require consistent treatment. Apparently no system of training can anticipate all of the judgments that an observer will be required to make. Since most observer teams must maintain their reliability over periods of time that may be as long as three to nine months, new judgments must be discussed so that all observers treat them consistently.

Individuals differ in their ability to become reliable observers. We have found that successful teaching experience, particularly in the elementary field, is a strong recommendation. Others who have become successful observers at Minnesota have had counseling experience, a broad background in social psychology, or experience as observers in some other system of interaction analysis.

TRAINING PROCEDURES

After memorizing the categories, training begins with tape recordings of classroom interaction. It is desirable to have a variety of training tapes that provide unusual examples of indirect or direct influence patterns and to have an

[19] This paper originally appeared in "Interaction Analysis in the Classroom: A Manual for Observers," 1960 (mimeographed). Reprinted by permission of the author.

exact category distribution for each tape. Observer trainees seem to learn faster, working with tapes, in teams of two or more. They can start and stop the playback to discuss each classification; an experienced observer on hand is helpful and frequent but short straight runs without interruption should be carried out to develop a consistent tempo.

Six to ten hours of preliminary training with tapes is necessary before moving into "live" classrooms.

During the preliminary training it becomes apparent that classroom observation involves judgments that are not as objective, automatic, and "black-and-white" as the trainees originally thought. They soon learn that reliable observation requires consideration of the total social situation being observed in order to understand the individual acts being classified. Trainees also discover the need for ground rules in order to be consistent when choices occur. Some of these ground rules will now be discussed.

First, when there is a choice of two or more acts in a three-second time period, always record the act represented by the category most distant numerically from category five, with the exception of category ten. This rule can be restated: always maximize information by choosing the least frequently occurring category (except 10), when there is a choice.

Second, the trained observer is in the best position to judge whether the teacher is, in general, restricting or expanding the freedom of action of the students; if he feels that the pattern at the moment is restrictive, he is cautious in the use of direct categories; but he remains alert to a shift in momentary patterns by remaining alert to the total social situation.

At first, this ground rule seems to be an invitation to biased observation, yet there is a theory of the "unbiased, biased observer." The observer is biased in the sense that his categorization must be consistent with his general assessment of the teacher's intent for a given sequence of action. He is unbiased in that he remains open to all evidence that the general intent of the teacher may be changing.

During preliminary training, the problem of distinguishing shifts from 5 to 3 and 3 to 5 usually arises. When this problem is recognized, it is appropriate to introduce the second ground rule and discuss how it may be inconsistent with the first ground rule. For example, a teacher does, in fact, repeat what a student has just said, but this appears to be merely a verbal habit and not evidence of a true acceptance and development of the students' ideas. In this situation, how does one use categories 5 and 3? The answer is never fixed or final, but the observer must learn to be skeptical of verbal habits which are often unreliable cues compared with the total time the teacher talks, the nature of the learning activities, and other more general evidence.

Another problem will arise concerning the use of category two. A teacher may have a verbal habit of responding to nearly all student statements with "right" or "good" which must be distinguished from true praise. True praise must get through to the student and must provide reward and encouragement; this cannot be accomplished by a verbal habit alone.

After preliminary training with tape recordings, the trainees start first-hand classroom experience. During this second phase of training the presence of an experienced trainer is essential. A soundproof observation booth is helpful so that the observers can stop and can discuss their observations whenever they wish. If no booth is available, a tape recording that the observation team can go over as soon as possible may serve as an alternative.

Direct classroom observation provides "presence" that is essential to distinguishing between categories 8 and 9. A host of problems arise at this point. For example, the teacher asks a question, ten hands go up volunteering an answer. If the teacher calls on a student whose hand is not raised, his contribution is clearly an 8. But if the teacher calls on a student whose hand is raised, is this also an 8? Suppose a student's answer has no content relation, or very little, with the teacher's question. How does this affect the use of categories 8 and 9? Suppose the student answers the teacher's questions and then goes on to develop another line of thought, how is this to be classified?

We have found it impossible to establish a simple ground rule such as: if the hand is up it is always a nine. In some instances of teacher-dominated high-speed drill in which the freedom of action of the student is obviously restricted, the teacher's questions are more like sixes than fours, and the student responses are clearly eights in spite of hand raising. Often when the teacher is lecturing, questions are merely used to check up on the student's understanding of what the teacher has said and again, in spite of the hand raising, the classification of eight seems more appropriate than nine. The best rule about categories 8 and 9 is to have a clear answer to the question, "How is the student showing his initiative?", before assigning a nine. When the observer can answer this question and explain (to himself) the method used by the student to show his initiative, then the total number of nine tallies decreases and they become a better index of student freedom of action.

Another ground rule about student talk applies during spontaneous student-to-student communication, usually shown as a series of nines. We have found it useful to insert a 10 in the sequence of nines to indicate when one student stopped and another began. These tens must be slipped in as an extra observation whether or not the talk of different students is naturally separated by a three-second pause.

In some lecture situations a teacher uses a question as criticism, which raises a question about the use of categories four and seven. For example, the teacher sees Jane whispering to Mary and promptly asks Jane a question. (Jane frequently says, "I'm sorry, I didn't hear you.") When it is clear to the observer that both the teacher and Jane recognize the intent of criticism, the teacher's statement is properly classified as 7.

No matter how extensive the training, creative teachers will present sequences of behavior that raise new problems of categorization. After five years of experience, for example, the writer was stumped by a teacher who spontaneously started to role-play a student in the library using the general catalog.

The teacher wanted to summarize a lesson in how to use the library for reference purposes. Her actions were both humorous and informative. She asked a student what topic he expected to look up, during the class's impending first library visit, and pretended to thumb through a series of cards, reading imaginary topics, some of which were very funny. "Oh dear!" she said, "There is nothing on crocodiles. What shall I do now?" "Try reptiles," said a brighter student. As the little dramatization developed, the class learned how to cross-reference. After discussing the incident with the observer team, we decided that the teacher's primary intent was to develop a problem in terms of the students' experience, that the teacher was working with an anticipated student problem, and that the humor encouraged both present and future participation. The decision was to classify most of the role playing in category three with the humorous parts in category two.

Consistent observation by a team requires group training, discussion of common ground rules, each observer's understanding of his own unique biases, and regular meetings after training to discuss unusual categorization problems. The next section explains an information statistic that can be used to estimate reliability.

ESTIMATING RELIABILITY

A method of estimating reliability should be as simple and quick to calculate as possible. Bales (1950, p. 104) proposes an adaptation of Chi-square, which was found to be less appropriate for our purposes than was Scott's (1955) coefficient. Scott's method is unaffected by low frequencies, can be adapted to per cent figures, can be estimated more rapidly in the field, and is more sensitive at higher levels of reliability.

Scott calls his coefficient "pi" and it is determined by the two formulae below.

$$\pi = \frac{P_o - P_e}{1 - P_e}$$

P_o is the proportion of agreement, and P_e is the proportion of agreement expected by chance which is found by squaring the proportion of tallies in each category and summing these over all categories.

$$P_e = \sum_{i=1}^{k} P_i^2$$

In formula two there are k categories and P_i is the proportion of tallies falling into each category. π, in formula one, can be expressed in words as the amount that two observers exceeded chance agreement divided by the amount that perfect agreement exceeds chance.

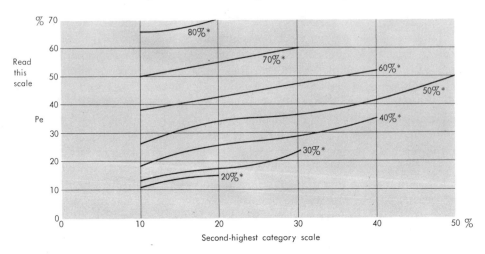

FIGURE 2–6.

In estimating reliability during training, problems of tempo or the speed of tallying are less important than the proportional distribution within the categories. Sooner or later in the training cycle observers settle down to the required tempo of 20 to 25 tallies per minute. Effective training, however, requires immediate feedback regarding category discriminations, so we chose to modify Scott's method by converting tallies into per cent figures and developing a graphical method for estimating P_e from the size of the two largest categories. The resulting shortcut method can be quickly estimated in the field by the use of a pocket slide rule.

The procedure we now use is as follows:

Step One: the original tallies are recorded as "hash marks" for quick summing on a sheet containing ten columns, one for each category.

Step Two: add column totals, divide each by the grand total, and multiply by 100 to convert to per cent.

Step Three: while one observer finds the total per cent disagreement by subtracting the per cent figures corresponding to each category, summed over all categories, the other observer estimates P_e by entering Fig. 2–6 with the largest and second largest categories as determined by either distribution or averaged from both.

Step Four: P_o is determined by subtracting the total per cent disagreement from 100.

Step Five: π is found by entering Fig. 2–7 with P_o and P_e.

The tallies of two trainees after about ten hours of training are shown in Table 2–11, columns two and three. The proportion of tallies in each category is expressed as a per cent in four and five. The differences between columns four and five are shown in column six and the sum of this column is the per cent disagreement. Column seven, consisting of the average per cent falling

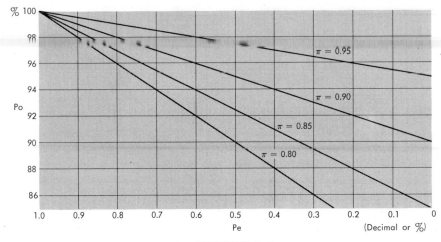

FIGURE 2–7.

in each category squared, is not normally calculated by observer trainees, but it is included here as the most accurate estimate of P_e, in this case $P_e = 23.7$ and is shown as the sum of column seven. This number can be compared with two estimates of P_e that the observer trainees would obtain by using Fig. 2–6.

First, if Trainee A entered Fig. 2–6 with his two highest categories, 41% and 21%, he would estimate P_e as 25+%. Second, if Trainee B made the same estimate with his highest, 38% and 23%, his estimate would be 24%.

Table 2–11
Calculating Reliability by Scott's Method, Using Per Cent*

Category	Observer A	Observer B	% A	% B	% Diff.	(Ave. %)²
(1)	(2)	(3)	(4)	(5)	(6)	(7)
1	12	9	3.3	2.1	1.2	0.072
2	3	4	0.8	0.9	0.1	0.008
3	24	34	6.5	8.1	1.6	0.403
4	25	25	6.8	5.9	0.9	0.530
5	76	97	20.7	23.1	2.4	4.840
6	3	7	0.8	1.8	1.0	0.017
7	3	4	0.8	0.9	0.1	0.007
8	151	160	41.2	38.0	3.2	15.500
9	51	59	13.9	14.1	0.3	1.960
10	19	22	5.4	5.2	0.2	0.280
Totals	367	421	100.2	100.1	11.0	23.617

* The figures in columns 4, 5, & 7 were found by using a pocket slide rule.

Table 2-12

Errors for Two Observers During a Four-Month Period

Row	Date of observation	Category*									Total	π
		1	2	3	4	5	6	7	8 & 9	10		
1	January 6	1/1	6/30	1/33	11/105	26/816	6/28	3/15	12/154	6/30	72/1,212	0.88
2	January 12	1/1	4/40	4/36	1/187	50/884	1/13	1/3	3/361	9/76	74/1,601	0.92
3	April 2	4/8	3/11	6/67	3/107	4/516	0/12	1/5	2/367	5/23	29/1,116	0.96
4	April 10**	0/0	0/10	4/26	5/291	86/906	24/294	26/82	24/566	12/42	181/2,217	0.88
5	May 1	0/0	3/13	0/18	7/243	33/1209	5/283	3/13	7/405	5/62	63/2,246	0.96
6	May 29	1/1	2/21	8/8	33/273	11/727	12/62	0/2	3/1168	9/81	79/2,343	0.94
7	Total Errors/Tallies	7/11	18/125	24/188	60/1206	210/5058	48/692	34/120	51/3021	46/314	498/10,735	
8	% Error	63.7	14.4	12.8	5.0	4.1	6.9	28.3	1.7	14.6	4.66	
9	% Category	0.10	1.17	1.75	11.24	47.20	6.45	1.12	28.17	2.82		
10	Category Limits	±0.03	±0.09	±0.11	±0.23	±0.97	±0.22	±0.16	±0.24	±0.21		

* Categories 8 and 9 were not separated in 1956; all student talk appeared in one category.
** Reliability check "live" vs. tape recording.

Below are three calculations of π using these three estimates of P_e.

$$\pi = \frac{P_o - P_e}{100 - P_e} = \frac{(100 - 11) - 23.6}{100 - 23.6}$$

$$\frac{65.4}{76.4} = 0.855 \quad \begin{array}{l} P_e \text{ estimated} \\ \text{from Column 7.} \end{array}$$

$$\pi = \frac{P_o - P_e}{100 - P_e} = \frac{(100 - 11) - 25}{100 - 25}$$

$$\frac{64}{75} = 0.853 \quad \begin{array}{l} P_e \text{ estimated} \\ \text{by Trainee A.} \end{array}$$

$$\pi = \frac{P_o - P_e}{100 - P_e} = \frac{(100 - 11) - 24}{100 - 24}$$

$$\frac{65}{76} = 0.854 \quad \begin{array}{l} P_e \text{ estimated} \\ \text{by Trainee B.} \end{array}$$

These three estimates are quite close and show that a graphical-slide rule method of estimation is quite adequate for training purposes.

Scott's reliability coefficient as we use it, is quite arbitrary. It is legitimate to ask about the approximate error involved when observers maintain a coefficient of 0.85 or higher. One way to illustrate all errors[20] is shown in Table 2-12.

In rows one through seven the errors are shown separately for each category in the numerator and the total judgments are shown in the denominator. Row eight shows the per cent error of the fraction just above in row seven. The per cent of total judgments falling in each category is shown in row nine, based on the grand total, 10,735. Row ten is a crude estimate of the limits of error for each category.

The limits are estimated as follows: for category one, two-thirds (approximately 63.7%) of 0.10 (row nine) is 0.06, which can be expressed as ±0.03; for category two, 14.4% of 1.17 is approximately 0.18, which can be expressed as ±0.09, and so on.

An inspection of row eight indicates that error decreases with increasing frequency of a category. The especially high error of category seven is caused by the poor performance on April 10th when one observer used a tape recording without the benefit of seeing the original interaction. Table 2-12 gives ample evidence that this system of interaction analysis is far from a precision instrument, but when the combined error limits of any two categories is small compared with the difference between the two categories, it is proper to proceed with statistical tests of significance.

---

[20] There are many different types of error: (a) omission; (b) heard it, but misclassified it; (c) failed to record it—dropped pencil; etc.

A continuous estimate of observer error could be obtained if two observers were always present at each observation. Such duplication is costly in both time and money; with proper training and control, observer teams can maintain reliability with weekly discussions and bi-monthly reliability check. A Scott coefficient of 0.85 or higher is a reasonable level of performance.

5

TEACHER–PUPIL INTERACTION PATTERNS IN THE ELEMENTARY SCHOOL[21]

NORMA FURST and EDMUND AMIDON

At the present time there is a lack of data which describe objectively the way in which teachers carry out their roles in the elementary classroom. Although Flanders and his students at the University of Minnesota have engaged in extensive observations of the junior high school classrooms, they have collected little systematic data in the elementary schools (Amidon and Flanders, 1961; Flanders, 1960). The Flanders interaction analysis provides a research tool which can be used for inferential research (Amidon and Flanders, 1963). A detailed description of the system of interaction analysis may be found starting at the beginning of this chapter.

The purpose of this study was to determine the kinds of teacher–pupil interaction patterns which are present in elementary school classrooms. Specifically, answers to two questions were sought:

1. What differences in interaction patterns, if any, exist among the six grade levels?

2. What differences in interaction patterns, if any, exist among subject areas of reading, social studies, and arithmetic in the elementary grades?

PROCEDURE

SELECTION OF CLASSROOMS. Schools for the study were selected from three socioeconomic levels. Approximately one-third of the observations were made in low socioeconomic areas in a large metropolitan school system, one-third in suburban schools adjacent to the city, and one-third in middle socioeconomic areas in the city. One hundred sixty separate classroom observations were

---

[21] Paper read at Schoolmen's Week, University of Pennsylvania, October 1962. Reprinted by permission of the authors.

made between late January, 1962, and May 15, 1962. A minimum of 25 class-rooms was observed at each grade level with a minimum of five observations in each of the subject areas of arithmetic, social studies, and reading at each grade level. The observer sat in each classroom for the duration of the lesson, from 30 minutes in some first grade subject areas to over 45 minutes in the intermediate grades.

OBSERVER TRAINING. Training of the observer took place at the Temple University Group Dynamics Center. After learning to recognize the categories and record the associate numbers in a column, tape recordings of actual class-room sessions were used to practice categorizing. When the reliability of the observer, as determined by the Scott coefficient, was at 0.99 for intra-observer consistency, the observer who collected the data for this study made a trial observation in a classroom simultaneously with another trained observer. Their reliability coefficient proved to be 0.90. In April 1962, another reliability check was made, and this time the observer and a third trained observer recorded coefficients of 0.87 and 0.92 in two different classroom observational periods.

RESULTS: GENERAL GRADE AND SUBJECT COMPARISONS

Data collected through the use of interaction analysis can be looked at from several different points of view. The total number of indirect tallies can be compared with the number of direct tallies recorded in an observation. Teacher talk can be compared to student talk and the number of tallies in each specific category can be noted and compared with one another.

The matrix provides an opportunity to analyze even more specifically the amount of time certain patterns of teacher influence occur. The matrix may be studied to determine which cells are heavy with tallies and which ones are empty.

THE RELATIONSHIP OF INDIRECT TO DIRECT INFLUENCE. The first important over-all statistical description is the I/D ratio which is the total number of indirect teacher statements divided by the total number of direct teacher statements. In grades one and two the I/D ratio for all subject areas is between 1 and 1.4, indicating that the teacher uses more indirect statements than direct statements. The I/D ratio for arithmetic and reading in the third and fourth grades varies between 0.6 and 0.9, indicating more direct influence than indirect influence. Social studies I/D's for these grade levels are 1.2 and 1.32 respectively, or slightly more indirect. In the fifth and sixth grades, the I/D's are down to 0.60 and 1.0 respectively. This is indicative of more direct than indirect influence at these grade levels.

The revised i/d ratio represents only those categories of teacher talk which are concerned with motivation and control (acceptance of feeling, acceptance of ideas, praise, giving direction, and criticism), and excludes the categories concerned with content (question and lecture). Whereas in the first four grades the revised i/d is lower than the I/D ratios, in fifth and sixth grades it is higher.

TEACHER TALK. Of the total interaction in first grade, teacher talk comprises 50%. Some decrease is evident in second grade where only 45% of the total talk is the teacher's. A slight increase to 47% occurs in the third with a continued rise to 52% in the fourth grade. In both fifth and sixth grades teacher talk comprises 49% of the total interaction.

PERCENTAGE OF STUDENT TALK. Student talk makes up 34% to 39% of the total interaction in the first and second grades, dropping to between 33% and 36% in the third and fourth grades. It drops still further to between 27% and 30% in the fifth and sixth grades.

PERCENTAGE OF SILENCE. Silence in first and second grades represents 15% of the total lesson. In third grade it increases to 17%, and in fourth grade it is again 15%. A definite rise is noted in the fifth and sixth grades where silence increases to 20% and then to 25%.

PERCENTAGES IN SPECIFIC CATEGORY TOTALS. Praise, representing 5% to 6% of the total interaction in first and second grades, decreases to 3% and 4% in third and fourth grades and increases in fifth and sixth grades to 4% and 5% respectively.

Acceptance of student ideas, representing about 4% in first grade, drops to slightly more than 2% in second grade and to slightly less than 2% in third grade. It rises to 3.5% in fourth, fifth, and sixth grades.

Teacher questions represent 18% of the total lesson time in first, 16% in second, and 15.5% in third grade. In fourth grade it increases to 17%, dropping again to 13% in fifth and to even slightly less than 13% in sixth grade.

Teacher lecture representing 9% of the total lesson time in first grade increases with each grade level. Thus, it becomes 10% in second grade, 14% in third and fourth grades, and 21% in fifth and sixth grades.

The amount of time spent in direction giving, on the other hand, decreases fairly consistently from first to sixth grade with some notable exceptions. The first-grade teacher uses the most time in direction giving. Although the second-grade teacher uses much less time for this purpose, the third-grade teacher uses more than does the second and nearly as much as does the first-grade teacher. In two subject areas, reading and arithmetic, the third-grade teacher uses direction giving as much as, or more than, the first-grade teacher. The only consistent differences in the relative amount of directions given in different subject areas are in third and fifth grades where teachers give fewer directions in social studies than in other areas.

Very little time is spent in criticism in any of the grades. There is an apparent decrease from first to sixth grade with the first-grade teacher using the most criticism (3%) and the sixth-grade teacher using the least (2%).

MOST-USED CELLS IN THE MATRIX. In first grade the cell indicating a teacher question followed by a student response (4-8) is the cell with the greatest number of tallies. The second largest cell (8-8) is the one showing student response following student response. Both of these cells tend to be large in all subject areas in first grade.

In second grade 8-8 is the largest single cell in all subject areas with the 4-8 and 10-10 cells (continuous silence or confusion) next.

The two heaviest cells in use in third grade as a whole are 8-8 and 10-10. However, in social studies the cell indicating student initiated response followed by student initiated response (9-9) is heaviest.

In fourth grade the largest cells are 4-8 and 8-8 although in reading and arithmetic, teacher lecture followed by teacher lecture (5-5) is nearly as large as these other two. The subjects of arithmetic and reading in fifth grade utilize the 10-10 cells most, and then the 5-5 cell. In social studies 5-5 is the largest cell with 10-10 and 8-8 following. An examination of the matrix in sixth grade shows 5-5 to be the largest cell in reading and social studies and 10-10 the largest in arithmetic.

AREA OF EXTENDED INDIRECT INFLUENCE. In first grade the area which indicates extended indirect influence represents slightly over 2%; in second grade, 2%; in third grade, 1%; in fourth grade, slightly over 1%; and rises in sixth grade to 2%.

AREA OF EXTENDED DIRECT INFLUENCE. In first and second grades the area indicating direct influence is 3%. By third grade it has increased to 5%. It then decreases to 3.5% in fourth grade and to 2% in fifth and sixth grades.

RESPONSE TO STUDENT COMMUNICATION. The first-grade teacher responds to student talk with praise about 5% of the total time and with a question about 4% of the time. In second grade, praise comprises 2% of the teacher's responses and questions still about 4%. The teacher in third grade responds with questions 4% of the time; lecturing, about 2%; accepting ideas, about 1%; and praising, 1% of the time.

The fourth-grade teacher questions 5%, praises 2%, lectures 2%, and accepts ideas 2% of the time. In fifth grade, questions are used 3%, praise 3%, lecture 1.5%, and acceptance of ideas 2% of the time. Similarly, questions are used in sixth grade 3%, praise 2%, and acceptance of ideas 2% of the time in response to student talk.

RESULTS: SUMMARY OF SUBJECT MATTER COMPARISON

I/D RATIO. The I/D ratio and revised i/d ratio are both highest in social studies in the first four grades. In the fifth and sixth grades the I/D's for the three subject areas are about the same.

PERCENTAGE OF TEACHER TALK. First- and second-grade teachers talk more in social studies than in any other subjects; whereas in third, fourth, and fifth grades, teachers talk more in arithmetic. In sixth grade, teacher talk is highest in social studies.

PERCENTAGE OF STUDENT TALK. Although in first and second grades, student talk is lowest in social studies, in third, fourth, and fifth grades it is highest in social studies and lowest in arithmetic. In sixth grade students talk most in reading and least in arithmetic.

PERCENTAGE IN INDIVIDUAL CATEGORIES. Teachers in all elementary grades use more praise in social studies than in other subjects. The difference in amount of praise used is greatest in first and third grades where the teachers use much more praise in social studies than in either of the other two subject areas.

The third-grade teacher uses criticism and directions only one-third as much in social studies as in reading and arithmetic. In other grades there are few differences among subjects in the use of directions and criticism.

Social studies is the area of the most teacher questioning at the first grade level; whereas little difference among areas in questions asked by the teacher is noted in second and third grades. The fourth-grade teacher questions more in arithmetic and social studies than in reading, the fifth-grade teacher questions more in arithmetic and reading than in social studies, and the sixth-grade teacher questions more in social studies than in the other two areas.

Lecture is used by teachers in grades one and two, primarily in social studies and in grade three, primarily in arithmetic and social studies. Grade four social studies lessons, however, contain only half the number of questions found in the other two subject areas. The amount of lecture in fifth and sixth grades is approximately the same for all subject areas.

EXTENDED INDIRECT INFLUENCE. Extended indirect influence is generally greater in social studies than in the other two subject matter areas. Reading and arithmetic contain nearly equal amounts of this type of influence.

EXTENDED DIRECT INFLUENCE. The use of extended direct influence is greater in arithmetic than in either reading or social studies and is least frequently observed in social studies.

TRENDS

Certain trends which become apparent as grade levels are compared with respect to the directness or indirectness of the teacher are worthy of close examination. On the surface teachers in general appear to be more indirect in the early grades, becoming more direct in fifth and sixth grades. A closer look reveals a partial explanation. The first-grade teacher asks many more questions than do teachers at any other grade level, whereas the sixth-grade teacher uses more lecture than does any other teacher. Interestingly enough, in terms of influence which excludes content, the fifth- and sixth-grade teachers show more indirect patterns than do teachers in the first four grades.

A similar direction in trends is indicated by the amount of teacher talk and student talk. Teacher talk, high in the first grade, decreases in the second grade. Although it increases in third and fourth grades, it is slightly less again in fifth and sixth grades. Student talk is highest in first and second grades, decreases slightly in third and fourth grades, and is lowest in fifth and sixth grades.

How can teacher and student talk both be so great in first grade? An explanation lies in the use of silence in the classroom. In first and second grades, silence is lowest; it increases in third and fourth grades, becoming highest in sixth grade where 25% of the observations were recorded in the silence category.

Comparison of subject matter areas with respect to both types of teacher behavior, direct or indirect, and amount of pupil and teacher talk focuses on some interesting trends. In general, teachers are more direct in the areas of arithmetic and reading, less direct in the area of social studies. The trend is not so clear with respect to teacher talk in these same areas. In first, fifth, and sixth grades, teachers talk more in social studies than in arithmetic and reading; whereas in second, third, and fourth grades, more teacher talk is recorded in arithmetic than in the other two areas. Analysis of this type of teacher talk indicates that the greater amount of teacher talk in social studies is primarily due to an emphasis on questioning; whereas teacher talk in third, fourth, and fifth grades in arithmetic is largely lecture. Differences in methodology between subject areas, then, appear to be the cause of this trend.

A look at some of the specific categories of teacher talk affords an indication of some trends worth noting. The almost total lack of use of category one is a striking example of one such trend. In no grade or subject area does the number of tallies in this category reach 1% of the total. In only three situations observed, a second-grade social studies lesson, a third-grade social studies lesson, and a sixth-grade reading lesson, did the total in this category reach even one half of 1%. It is interesting to note that these three cases involved teachers who admitted to a conscious awareness and a philosophy which stressed acceptance of feelings as basic to the teaching–learning process.

A somewhat surprising trend is observable in the amount of praise used at various grade levels. Praise is most used in first and second grades. It decreases to its lowest point in third and rises again in fifth and sixth grades. Comparing subject matter areas reveals that the greatest amount of praise used is in social studies and the least praise is in reading and arithmetic. In grades one, two, and three, however, teachers use the least amount of praise in reading; whereas in fourth, fifth, and sixth grades they use the least amount of praise in arithmetic.

The pattern apparent in the use of acceptance of student ideas is similar to that of praise. It is highest in first grade, decreases slightly in second grade, reaches its lowest point in third grade, then increases in fourth, fifth, and sixth grades. The statements involving acceptance of ideas are found most frequently in social studies and least frequently in arithmetic.

As might be expected, use of lecture, lowest in first grade, gradually increases throughout elementary school. With the exception of third and fourth grades the teacher lectures most in social studies. In these two grades the teacher lectures most in arithmetic.

The use of questions indicates a trend from first to sixth grade which is the reverse of that indicated by lecture. The first-grade teacher uses more time in questioning than does any other teacher. Teacher questioning gradually decreases until at sixth grade the teacher is using the least amount. This trend is continuous, except that the fourth grade teacher uses more time in questioning than the teacher at any other grade level except first. First-, second-, and third-grade teachers use more questions in social studies than in the other two areas. No trend is indicated in fourth, fifth, and sixth grades.

Regardless of grade level, more extended indirect influence is observed in social studies than in the other two subject areas.

Use of extended direct influence in the elementary school indicates a trend which is the reverse of that of extended indirect influence. First- and second-grade teachers use the least amount of this type of influence, and third-grade teachers the most. A decrease in fourth, fifth, and sixth grades brings the amount of extended direct influence down nearly to its low in first grade. Subject matter appears to exert little influence in the amount of extended direct influence used.

Teachers at the primary grade level respond to student talk most often by use of praise or question. The first grade teacher responds most often with a question; he also often responds with praise. From third grade on teacher responses vary more to include not only praise and questioning, but also lecture and criticism. No consistent differences are apparent among subject matter areas.

CONCLUSIONS

Several possible conclusions may be drawn from the results of the study:

1. Teachers at different grade levels hold varying assumptions about the teaching–learning process. Apparently, primary grade teachers feel that children at that level can learn best via the question–answer technique and that lecturing or giving information is far less appropriate. On the other hand, intermediate-grade teachers apparently conceive of lecture as most conducive to learning.

2. The role of student participation in teaching is another area of diversity of opinion. Again, it is the teachers in the early primary grades that behave as though pupil participation were important, for they encourage and reinforce more student talk than do teachers at other levels. The least amount of student-to-student talk, however, is in the third grade. The reason for an increase in the upper grades in the amount of student-initiated talk may be that

teachers feel that children at these levels have much to contribute and hence encourage more student-initiated talk than do the teachers in the primary grades.

3. Apparently, teachers in the primary grades feel that encouragement, acceptance, and praise are important techniques to use with their children. Teachers in the upper elementary grades, in comparison, seem to feel that less of this is necessary with their pupils and that more information and ideas need to be communicated.

4. Upper-grade teachers apparently feel that it is important for the pupils to spend a large proportion of class time in independent work. Although the largest category in the upper grades is lecture, a close second is category 10, silence. Most of this time was spent in seatwork. An exception to this occurred in social studies where little category 10 time was seatwork.

5. Both early primary and intermediate grade teachers show by their teaching methods that they consider extended indirect influence to be important. It is in the third grade where little of this kind of teacher behavior occurs. In general, first- and sixth-grade teachers seem to be the most persistent of all elementary teachers in the use of extended indirect influence.

6. Teachers seem to feel either that it is more important or that it is easier to be indirect in social studies than in reading and arithmetic. Even though they are more indirect in this area than in the others, the first-, fifth-, and sixth-grade teachers, nevertheless, do more talking during social studies. They apparently consider teacher talk more effective than student independent activities in social studies.

7. Perhaps the most interesting conclusion is concerned with what appears to be happening in third grade, for example: (1) amount of teacher talk begins to increase, becoming greater than in first and second grades, (2) amount of praise is lowest, (3) acceptance of student ideas is lowest, (4) amount of time spent in giving directions increases, (5) use of extended indirect influence is lowest, (6) extended direct influence is highest, (7) teachers begin to use ways of responding to student talk other than praising and questioning, and (8) amount of student-initiated response is lowest.

QUESTIONS RAISED BY THIS STUDY

The study raises a number of questions which seem worthy of further research such as:

1. Why do the first- and sixth-grade teachers show a similar pattern in praise and flexibility in the extended indirect influence area?

2. Why are the other grade teachers, especially in third grade, so sparing in the amount of praise given?

3. Does the fact that the third-grade child initiates less verbal interaction in reading and arithmetic reflect the lack of praise by the teacher and also the amount of direct influence used?

4. How much do the teacher manuals and teacher editions of textbooks, especially in reading, influence the teacher's approach to the teaching process and is this influence reflected in her verbal behavior?

6

THE PRINCIPAL
AND HIS KNOWLEDGE
OF TEACHER BEHAVIOR[22]

C. V. ROBBINS

One of the most important responsibilities of the school principal is to improve instruction in the classroom. It seems reasonable to assume that, in order to carry out this responsibility, the principal must have an adequate knowledge of what is happening in every classroom in his school. While such knowledge may not be a guarantee of an improved program of instruction, it certainly might be considered a necessary prerequisite. Much of the research reported elsewhere in this volume has examined the importance of the classroom verbal behavior of the teacher and the pupils; the study reported here deals with the amount of knowledge that the principal had of such teacher behavior.

The purpose of this study was to assess the knowledge that a group of elementary school principals had of the classroom verbal behavior of certain teachers in their schools. The principals' description of the behavior of their teachers was compared with information gathered by an observer in teachers' classrooms and with information supplied by the pupils themselves. The principals were grouped according to their ability or inability to describe patterns of behavior similar to those revealed by the other sources, and the characteristics of the groups were compared. In making this comparison, the following questions were investigated:

1. What is the relationship between the principal's knowledge of the teachers' classroom behavior and the information gathered by a classroom observer?

2. What is the relationship between the principal's knowledge of the teachers' classroom behavior and the information supplied by the pupils in the classroom?

3. What are the characteristics of those principals who have a more accurate conception of their teachers' behavior compared with the principals who have a less accurate conception?

---

[22] This paper was prepared specially for this book.

BACKGROUND OF THE STUDY

This study developed as part of an action research project of the Philadelphia Suburban School Study Council Group E. The study was limited to elementary school principals and teachers of the fourth, fifth, and sixth grades. There were several reasons for this limitation. (1) Because of the time involved in gathering the observational data, not more than 12 principals could be included in the study. (2) Inclusion of principals at the secondary level would have introduced an extraneous variable, the influence of which would have been difficult to assess. (3) The reading ability of the students involved had to be sufficient to assure meaningful responses to the pupil questionnaire.

Thirty-two elementary principals were available as possible subjects. Of these, 12 were selected as a stratified random sample. The stratification was made on the basis of three variables: years of experience of the principal, number of teachers supervised, and sex of the principal. This information was obtained concerning each of the 32 possible subjects. Principals were selected by random method until 12 principals from nine different school districts had been chosen as having the desired characteristics. Of the 12 subjects, six were classified as experienced and six were classified as inexperienced on the basis of their number of years as principals. Each of these two groups contained three principals from large schools and three from small schools. Four of the principals selected were females, one in each of the experience and school-size categories. Table 2–13 contains a description of the 12 principals selected. The selection of the six teachers in each of the 12 schools presented less of a

Table 2–13

Characteristics of the Sample Group of Principals

Principal	Number of teachers supervised	Size of school category	Years of experience as principal	Experience category	Sex
A	23	Large	0	Inexperienced	M
B	40	Large	6	Experienced	F
C	21	Small	1	Inexperienced	M
D	20	Small	11	Experienced	M
E	27	Large	4	Inexperienced	M
F	20	Small	5	Experienced	F
G	46	Large	5	Experienced	M
H	42	Large	6	Experienced	M
I	13	Small	5	Experienced	M
J	22	Small	4	Inexperienced	F
K	16	Small	0	Inexperienced	F
L	32	Large	0	Inexperienced	M

problem. In some of the small schools, all teachers in the fourth, fifth, and sixth grades had to be included in order to supply the desired number per school. In the larger schools, the teachers were randomly selected from those three grades.

GATHERING THE DATA

The author was the primary observer for the present study, and used the Flanders system of interaction analysis[23] as the observational tool to gather data concerning the six teachers in each of the 12 schools. Observational visits were conducted during October, November, December, and January of the 1963–64 school year, and, since each of the 72 teachers was observed at least twice, there were 144 such visits. The observer reported to a school at approximately 8:30 a.m. and discussed the schedule with the principal. The entire day was devoted to the six observations, which permitted a visit of 45 to 60 minutes in each classroom. The procedure called for the observer to sit in the classroom in a position to see and hear the teachers and the pupils. After a few minutes spent in observing the feeling or tone of the classroom, the observer began to record the categories of verbal behavior. Then, sometime during the day, conferences were held with the teachers to explain further the nature of the study and to answer questions.

It was necessary to revisit 13 of the classrooms in six different schools. Eleven of these revisits were caused by scheduling problems; either the teacher had been absent on previous visits or there had not been enough time to see all six teachers in the building. Two observations had to be repeated due to the inappropriateness of the activity in the classroom at the time of the first visit. An activity was deemed inappropriate when the observation yielded less than 200 behavior tallies, and was usually an instance of silent work or the use of an audio-visual aid. After the observations had been completed, matrices were constructed combining the two observations for each teacher, and I/D ratios were calculated which permitted the comparison of every teacher on an indirect–direct behavior scale.

The second source of information about the classroom behavior of teachers was their pupils. Since over 1900 pupils would be asked to describe their teachers' behavior, a questionnaire was developed to get the necessary information. In his study of students' knowledge concerning teacher influence, J. P. Anderson (1960) used a 20-item multiple-choice questionnaire to measure patterns of teacher behavior. He constructed this questionnaire with reference to Flanders' categories and developed a number of statements characterizing either direct or indirect patterns of teacher influence. As the following examples indicate, four possible completions were developed for each of the 20 items. Two of these were intended to be associated with direct teacher behavior and two

---

[23] See first article in this chapter.

with indirect teacher behavior. Here are two of the items from Anderson's questionnaire:

5. When we talk about our own experiences our teacher usually:
    a) Thinks they are very interesting.
    b) Listens carefully to everyone.
    c) Thinks some of the things we do are silly.
    d) Doesn't seem to be very interested.

9. Our teacher's reactions to our ideas seem to be:
    a) That they are worth developing.
    b) They are good.
    c) They are sometimes not so good.
    d) They are not very useful.

    In his study, Anderson arranged for experimental teachers to play either direct or indirect roles. The pupils were successful in using his questionnaire to identify each type of teacher. The Anderson instrument appeared to be ideal in that it offered a tested method of obtaining pupil estimates of pertinent behavior of teachers. In addition, it was keyed to the first source of information, the Flanders system of interaction analysis. This instrument had to be revised in order to make it suitable for use in the grades participating in the present study. Several trial runs and a readability test resulted in a revision of the questionnaire which was used. Fourteen of the items had synonyms substituted for the more difficult words. Thus the final questionnaire was suitably adjusted to the fourth-grade reading level.

    The final step was to submit the revised questionnaire to Dr. Anderson and ask him to score each of the choices as direct or indirect. The author also identified each of the items in a like manner. After the questionnaire for pupils had been approved for use in the school districts involved, it was applied in sample classrooms. Then the author visited each of the 72 classrooms in the 12 schools. He explained to the pupils that although he had visited the classroom twice to "see how good teachers in some good schools teach," he now needed the pupils' help. The students, he explained, had been in the classroom much more than he had, and they could help a study being made in many schools by carefully answering the questionnaire. The directions were then read and the students proceeded to select their choices. No names were placed on the answer sheets since it was believed that the children would be more willing to supply accurate answers if they were guaranteed anonymity.

    The responses of pupils to the 14 questions about teacher behavior were tallied on the master sheet for each teacher. A count was made of the total number of open and closed responses ascribed to each teacher, and from these data an open–closed ratio was calculated by dividing the number of open responses by the number of closed responses. For instance, a teacher with 30 students would receive a total of 420 responses. If 176 of these were items classified as open or indirect behaviors, and 224 as closed or direct behaviors, the teachers' O/C ratio on the Our-Class questionnaire would be 176/244, or 0.71.

The larger this O/C number, of course, the greater the relative number of open or indirect type responses which had been selected by the pupils. After each of these ratios had been calculated for all the teachers, another measure of teacher behavior had been achieved. The previous measure had been derived from information provided by an observer in the classroom. Now the six teachers in each school could be ranked according to an I/D ratio provided by their students and a similar ratio provided by an observer.

GATHERING DATA FROM THE PRINCIPALS

The final step in gathering data for this study consisted of a one-day workshop for the 12 principals participating, held in an elementary school of one of the districts. The purpose of the workshop was to gather from the principals their estimate of their teachers' behavior. A second purpose was to provide the principal with some feedback about the procedures and preliminary findings of the study. An important advantage of the workshop was that it permitted all the principals involved to respond to the questionnaires, and at the same time prevented communication between principals from affecting the results. After the principals responded to a data form which recorded certain background information about each of them, they were asked to fill in a series of instruments designed to measure their knowledge of the verbal behavior of teachers. The first such instrument was entitled "The Principal's Perception Test" and consisted of a series of nonlinear scales intended to measure their knowledge of teacher behavior. For instance, some of the scales used were:

3. How often does this teacher accept or use the ideas of students during discussion in the classroom?

1	2	3	4	5	6	7	8	9	10

seldom   once in   a great
or never   awhile   deal of
                                                     the time

5. How often does this teacher praise or encourage student action or behavior?

1	2	3	4	5	6	7	8	9	10

seldom   once in   a great
or never   awhile   deal of
                                                     the time

6. How often does this teacher give directions, commands, or orders with which a student is expected to comply?

1	2	3	4	5	6	7	8	9	10

seldom   once in   a great
or never   awhile   deal of
                                                     the time

Each principal was given six sets of this test, one for each of the teachers studied in the school. The principals were asked to read each statement and to circle the number on the scale which best described the teacher in question. The scales were constructed with the lower numbers representing the more direct behaviors, and the sum of the numbers circled gave a behavior score for the purpose of comparing teachers. Thus the behavior scores derived for each of the six teachers made it possible to rank them from most to least direct, according to the opinion of their principal. The second instrument was very comparable in purpose to the first. It consisted of a sheet describing direct and indirect behaviors in a very simple ranking chart such as that shown in Table 2–14. This chart requested that the principals rank their teachers from most direct to most indirect.

Table 2–14

I/D Ranking of Teachers by the Principal

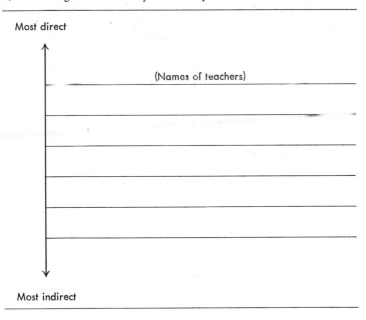

The final item submitted to the principals was the "Our-Class" questionnaire. Each of the principals was given a copy of the questionnaire with six answer sheets and was asked to reply for each of the six teachers. Since this instrument was identical with the one used by the pupils, it was possible to compare results directly. After the principals had ranked their teachers via the "Principal's Perception Test," the rankings were compared with the corresponding rankings of the observers. Table 2–15 presents such rankings by two principals. It may be seen that principal I and the observer were in substantial agreement over the indirect and direct behaviors of the teachers in his school. The rank difference correlation of 0.77 was significant at the 0.10 level. Prin-

Table 2–15

Indirect/Direct Behavior Patterns of Teachers According to the Principal's Perception Test Compared with Observers' Ranking

Teachers				Teachers	
Ranked by Principal I	Ranked by Observer			Ranked by Principal L	Ranked by Observer
I-152	I-152	Direct		L-167	L-169
I-150	I-153	↑		L-168	L-171
I-153	I-150			L-169	L-170
I-151	I-149			L-170	L-172
I-149	I-154	↓		L-171	L-167
I-154	I-151	Indirect		L-172	L-168
	$r_d = 0.77$				$r_d = 0.43$

cipal L, on the other hand, did not agree at all with the observer's rankings of teachers. These two principals exhibited the range of agreement–disagreement between the observer and the principals. The I/D ranking charts completed by the principals were compared with the observer's ranking, and a comparison was made between the principals' and children's scores on the "Our-Class" questionnaire.

Table 2–16 summarizes the rankings of the 12 principals on the three instruments used, compared with the observer in two cases and with the children in the other cases. A mean score was computed for principals for the purpose of ranking the principals from 1 to 12 on the basis of their agreement or disagreement with the other sources of information.

Table 2–16

Twelve Principals Ranked According to Their Mean Scores on Three Tests of Awareness of Teacher Behavior

1	2	3	4	5	6
Principal	I/D ranking chart r_d	Principal perception test r_d	Our class r_d	Mean score r_d	Rank
J	0.83	0.71	0.64	0.73	1
D	0.60	0.66	0.69	0.65	2
I	0.77	0.77	0.34	0.63	3
G	0.49	0.49	0.83	0.60	4
B	0.71	0.54	0.43	0.56	5
F	0.20	0.20	0.82	0.41	6
K	−0.03	0.20	0.94	0.37	7
C	0.31	0.34	0.43	0.36	8
H	−0.24	0.19	0.94	0.30	9
E	−0.43	0.24	−0.10	−0.10	10
A	−0.60	−0.37	0.60	−0.12	11
L	−0.83	−0.43	0.19	−0.36	12

PRINCIPAL CHARACTERISTICS

When the 12 principals in the sample had been ranked according to their aware-ness of teacher behavior, it was possible to view this ranking either in rela-tion to certain characteristics of the principals or in relation to certain elements of the situation. In all, the relationships of 13 such factors were investigated. Three of the 13 factors were significant at the 0.05 level; the average I/D ratio of the teachers, the years of administrative experience of the principal, and the mean percentage of time the observed teachers devoted to teacher talk. The principals' years of experience in education was significantly related to their awareness at the 0.10 level of confidence. The other factors were not considered significantly related. It is particularly noteworthy that one of the factors that showed no significant relationship was that of school size. Other research has indicated that this is an important consideration, but the results of the present study were not in agreement.

CONCLUSION

The major conclusions of this study may be presented in terms of three ques-tions stated as part of the purpose of the study. The first question concerned the relationship between the principal's knowledge of the teachers' classroom behavior and the knowledge of that behavior gained by the observer. Evidence gathered as part of the study revealed that the principals and the observers agreed on teacher behavior to a limited degree. This conclusion is based on a comparison of the principals' and observers' rankings of the six teachers in each school on an indirect–direct rating scale. While only a few rank correlations reached conventional levels of significance, almost all showed a positive trend. Examination of the rankings reveals that the correlations were generally lowered by the fact that there were usually one or two teachers about whom the observer and the principal could not agree. On the other hand, there was general agreement on the most direct and most indirect teachers.

The second question concerned the amount of agreement between prin-cipals and pupils concerning teacher behavior. The principals and the pupils agreed on teacher behavior to a greater extent than did the principals and the observer. When pupil–principal rankings of teacher behavior were compared, only one correlation was negative, and four of the 12 were significantly re-lated at the 0.10 level. It is interesting to note that the observer and the pupils did not show a consistently high percentage of agreement on the rankings of teacher behavior. The cause of this is not easily determined, but there is a pos-sibility that they did not concern themselves with identical behaviors. While this does not affect the usefulness of determining the principal's knowledge of behaviors compared with two other sources of information, it does indicate that the relationship of the Anderson instrument to indirect–direct behaviors as seen by the observer was not sufficient to qualify it as the most appropriate instrument for the present study.

The third question asked as part of the purpose of the study concerned those characteristics of the principal and of the school situation that seem to be related to the principals' awareness of teacher behavior. Factors which were significantly related were the years of administrative experience of principal and the years of experience in education. The information received supported the findings of Clarke, who also reported that experienced principals know their subordinates better (1961). Both studies would thus lend support to the general practice of structuring salary schedules of principals on the basis of their experience, at least if we assume that knowledge of teacher behavior is necessary for effective supervision. The present study did not reveal a significant relationship between the number of teachers supervised (size of school) and the principal's awareness of teacher behavior. It might be generally assumed that the principals of small schools have the better knowledge of teacher behavior. The present study did not support this assumption. Similarly, neither the number of college courses in supervision nor the number or type of the degrees held by the principal was found to be a significant variable. This finding supports that of Hemphill, who found that the number of years of academic preparation does not seem to affect administrative performance (Hemphill *et al.*, 1962, p. 341). The other characteristics investigated were the sex of the principal, the average number of years he had known his teachers, and the number of reported minutes spent per month in classroom supervision. None was found to be significantly related to awareness. The finding of no difference for male and female principals holds implications for the prevailing practice of granting male principals preference in higher promotion, at least as far as knowledge of teacher behavior is concerned. Hemphill also found no significant differences in administrative performance among male and female administrators (Hemphill *et al.*, 1962, p. 341).

Certain aspects of the school situation were also investigated as variables in relation to the principals' awareness of teacher behavior. The availability of an elementary supervisor, the opinion of the teachers concerning their principals, or the opinion of the pupils concerning their principals were not found to be significantly related. Interestingly, factors that correlated highly were the average I/D ratios of the teachers, and the average percentage of time devoted to teacher talk. In other words, the principal was most accurately aware of teacher behavior in the situations in which the most indirect, least talkative teachers were to be found. This is perhaps one of the most interesting findings of the present study. While the causes for this finding must remain in the area of speculation, several hypotheses might be put forward. Perhaps the principals who are most aware of teacher behavior tend to select or to influence their teachers to be more indirect in their control behaviors in the classroom. Another possible reason might be that the better school districts attract both the teachers who are more indirect and the principals who are more aware of teacher behavior.

One further point should be made concerning these conclusions. They are limited, of course, to the population from which the sample principals were drawn; the elementary principals of the 12 school districts of the Philadelphia Suburban School Study Council Group E. This population is readily comparable, however, to many other districts and groups of principals in the United States, hence the conclusions are worthy of consideration.

A secondary purpose of this study was to devise and test a procedure which could be used by any school district or supervisor to get information about teacher behavior. It is the opinion of the author that the instruments and procedures of this study could be readily adapted to use in a program that will improve supervision. Effective supervision must be based on adequate knowledge of the situation. This study provides systematic methods for acquiring and testing such knowledge.

7

THE VERBAL BEHAVIOR
OF SUPERIOR
ELEMENTARY TEACHERS[24]

EDMUND AMIDON AND MICHAEL GIAMMATTEO

In an attempt to determine whether or not there are verbal behavior patterns which are characteristic of superior teachers, the authors conducted a study involving 153 elementary school teachers from 11 suburban districts in Pennsylvania. Administrators and supervisors were asked to identify superior teachers in their districts, and the top three teachers from those identified in each district were observed as superior or "master" teachers, giving a sample of 33 teachers in this group. One hundred twenty teachers were then selected at random from the 11 districts to provide the average group.

All 153 teachers were then observed by a trained observer who used the Flanders system of interaction analysis. The observer categorized the verbal behavior of teachers and students during language-arts periods by writing down the appropriate number from the Flanders system at three-second intervals. The language-arts periods varied in length from 30 to 45 minutes. No class was observed prior to or after any special event, and no substitute, special, or visiting teachers were observed. A profile of the verbal patterns of the superior teachers was prepared, and data on the 120 other teachers were compiled by grade and reported as normative data. The interaction patterns of the randomly selected group and the superior group were compared, and teachers were compared for frequency of each category in the Flanders system, as well as for total verbal patterns, indirect and direct.

RESULTS

The comparison of the normative group with the superior group gave the following results:

Acceptance of feeling was used about three times as much by those teachers identified as superior. However, both the normative group and the superior group used this category extremely infrequently.

---

[24] This paper was prepared specially for this book.

Statements of praise and encouragement were used about equally by both groups, but the superior teachers used more praise after student-initiated ideas. They also gave reasons for praise more often than the normative group.

Acceptance and use of student ideas as a category was used over twice as much by the superior teachers, and this category was used over three and one-half times as often by superior teachers in response to student-initiated talk. The average teachers tended to ask narrow questions which called for pre-dictable responses ("What is two times two?"). The superior teachers used questions as a means for controlling noise and clarifying ideas about twice as often as did the normative group.

Lecture in a continuous fashion was used more by the average group of teachers, but total lecture time accounted for about 40% of teacher talk for both groups. The superior teachers were interrupted more frequently by questions during their lectures than were the average teachers.

Direction-giving was used twice as much by the regular teachers, and their directions were more apt to elicit silent responses from students.

Criticism was used about twice as much by the average group of teachers as a technique for controlling student noise, but both groups used criticism sparingly. Direction-giving followed by criticism, which usually indicates dis-cipline problems, appeared about twice as frequently in the verbal patterns of the normative group of teachers.

Student Patterns were markedly different in the two groups. There were twice as many student-initiated statements in the classes taught by the superior teachers. Students participated over 52% of the time in the classes of the su-perior teachers, and about 40% of the time in the average classes.

Silence or confusion appeared as a category more than twice as often in classes taught by the normative group of teachers.

SUMMARY

One hundred fifty-three elementary school teachers were observed during language-arts classes in an attempt to determine whether or not there is a difference in the verbal behavior of superior teachers from that of average teachers. The 33 superior teachers were identified as such by their supervisors and administrators, and the other 120 teachers were selected at random from eleven different school districts. The Flanders system of interaction analysis was the observation instrument used.

The results indicate that the verbal behavior patterns of superior teachers do differ substantially from those of average teachers. The superior teachers talked approximately 40% of their total class time, while the normative group talked approximately 52% of the time. The superior teachers were more ac-cepting of student-initiated ideas, tended to encourage these ideas more, and also made more of an effort to build on these ideas than did the average group of teachers. The superior teachers dominated their classrooms less, used in-direct verbal behavior more, and used direction-giving and criticism less than the normative group of teachers. The superior teachers asked questions which were broader in nature than the normative group, and their lectures were interrupted more by questions from the students. There was about 12% more student participation in the classes of the superior teachers.

IMPLICATIONS

Taken by themselves, the results of this study might indicate only that administrators and supervisors tend to favor the kind of teaching behavior attributed here to superior teachers. However, a large scale study conducted by Flanders, in which he relates pupil achievement to teacher verbal behavior patterns, lends support to the findings of this study.

Flanders found in his study that the teachers of high-achieving classes accepted, clarified, and used student ideas significantly more; criticized significantly less; and encouraged significantly more student-initiated talk than did teachers of low-achieving classes.

As a result of his research, Flanders developed what he refers to as "the rule of two-thirds." This rule states that in the average classroom someone is talking two-thirds of the time; two-thirds of that time the person talking is the teacher; and two-thirds of the time the teacher talks, he is using direct influence (lecture, direction-giving, criticism). However, the rule of two-thirds was modified for teachers of the high-achieving children and teachers of the low-achieving children. The first part of the rule, that two thirds of the time someone is talking, held for both groups, but the teachers of the low-achieving groups talked about 80% of this time, while teachers of the high-achieving groups talked about 55% of this time. In the low-achieving groups, teachers used direct influence about 80% of the time, while the teachers of the high-achieving groups used direct influence about 50% of the time.

The results of the present study, as well as the results of the Flanders study, would seem to indicate that verbal behavior patterns of superior teachers can be identified, and that these patterns do differ markedly from the verbal behavior patterns of other teachers.

8

VERBAL INTERACTION PATTERNS IN THE CLASSROOMS OF SELECTED PHYSICS TEACHERS[25]

ROGER PANKRATZ

During the past half-century, the role of the science teacher in the classroom has undergone a marked change. In the early 1900's the teacher's ability to impart knowledge *per se* was considered to be of utmost importance. During the past 30 years, however, the role of the teacher as a director of learning activities has been emphasized to a greater degree, and more attention has been given to those teaching abilities that help students to think and act like scientists. Studies by Davis (1952), Farmer (1964), and Spore (1963) indicated that there was general agreement among educators, and more specifically among science educators, that verbal skills in conducting stimulating class discussions, verbal skills in handling students' questions, and verbal skills in the development of critical thought, scientific attitudes, and problem-solving abilities are important to successful science teaching.

The identification of the particular verbal behavior patterns most fruitful in the development of these teaching skills is a problem area in which more investigation is needed.

Previous research has indicated that different verbal behavior patterns are present in the classrooms of different types of teachers. Two studies by Flanders (1965a, pp. 49–65) showed that classes of elementary teachers that scored high on fondness of the teacher, motivation, fair rewards and punishments, lack of anxiety, and independence used more indirect influence than classes of teachers that scored low, who used comparatively little indirect influence. A third study by Flanders (1965a, pp. 66–110) indicated that teachers of seventh-grade social studies and eighth-grade mathematics who used more indirect verbal patterns stimulated higher achievement than did teachers whose patterns of verbal behavior in the classroom were more direct.

---

[25] This paper was prepared specially for this book.

Amidon and Giammatteo (1965) reported the kinds of verbal behaviors that distinguished superior-rated elementary teachers from average teachers. The results of their study indicated that the verbal behavior patterns of superior teachers can be identified and that they differ markedly from those of other teachers.

THE PROBLEM

The study was designed to reveal the differences in verbal behavior patterns present in the classrooms of two samples of twelfth-grade physics teachers. One sample ranked extremely high, the other extremely low, on a composite of three factors assumed important to teaching success:

1. The principal's perception of the teacher's success in teacher–pupil relationships and personal adjustment.

2. The student's perceptions of the teacher's all-around teaching ability.

3. The ability of the teacher to react to classroom situations in accord with educational theory.

Measuring instruments

Teacher–pupil relationships and personal adjustments were measured by the *Teacher Rating Scale*. Part A of this instrument was developed by Williamson (1956) from a scale used by Leeds to assess teacher–pupil relationships. Part B was designed by Williamson to reveal the personal adjustment problems of the teacher (1956, pp. 43, 46, 122).

The student's perception of the teacher was measured by the *Student-Opinion Questionnaire*. This instrument was developed by Roy C. Bryan and Otto Yntema (1939) to give teachers a better understanding of students and the effects of their teaching on the students.

The teacher's response to classroom situations was measured by the *Teaching Situation Reaction Test* (often referred to as TSRT). This instrument was developed by Hough and Duncan to measure and predict aspects of teaching potential not associated with the subject field competence of the teacher (1965, pp. 1–14).

Verbal classroom behaviors which occurred in the classrooms of the subjects were measured by a trained observer using the *Observational System for the Analysis of Classroom Instruction* developed by Hough (1966). This system is a sixteen-category modification of the Flanders system of interaction analysis. The modifications of the Flanders system that were used in this study include the following: (a) a sub-classification of Flanders' category 5 to distinguish between teacher-initiated lecture and teacher answer to student questions, (b) a subclassification of Flanders' category 7 to distinguish between corrective feedback and personalized criticism and sarcasm, (c) a subclassification of Flanders' category 9 to distinguish between student questions and declarative emitted

Category number		Description of verbal behavior
	1	*Accepts feeling:* Accepts and clarifies the feeling tone of students in a non-threatening manner. Feelings may be positive or negative. Predicting and recalling feelings are also included.
	2	*Praises or encourages:* Praises or encourages student action or behavior. Jokes that release tension not at the expense of another individual, nodding head or saying "uh-huh" or "go on" are included.
	3	*Accepts or uses ideas of student:* Clarifying, building on, developing and accepting ideas of students.
	4	*Asks questions:* Asking a question about content or procedure with the intent that the student should answer.
Teacher talk	5	*Answers student questions:* Direct answers to questions regarding content or procedure asked by students.
	6	*Lectures:* Giving facts or opinions about content or procedures; expressing his own ideas; asking rhetorical questions.
	7	*Corrective feedback:* Telling a student that his answer is wrong when the incorrectness of the answer can be established by other than opinion, i.e., empirical validation, definition or custom.
	8	*Gives directions:* Directions, commands or orders to which a student is expected to comply.
	9	*Criticizes or justifies authority:* Statements intended to change student behavior from a nonacceptable to an acceptable pattern; bawling out someone; stating why the teacher is doing what he is doing so as to achieve or maintain control; rejecting or criticizing a student's opinion or judgment.
	10	*Student talk—response:* Talk by students in response to requests or narrow teacher questions. The teacher initiates the contact or solicits student's statement.
Student talk	11	*Student talk—emitted:* Talk by students in response to broad teacher questions which require judgment or opinion. Student declarative statements emitted but not called for by teacher questions.
	12	*Student questions:* Questions concerning content or procedures that are directed to the teacher.
	13	*Directed practice or activity:* Nonverbal behavior requested or suggested by the teacher. This category is also used to separate student-to-student response.
Silence	14	*Silence and contemplation:* Silence following questions, periods of silence interspersed with teacher talk or student talk and periods of silence intended for the purpose of thinking.
	15	*Demonstration:* Silence during periods when visual materials are being shown or when nonverbal demonstration is being conducted by the teacher.
Nonfunctional	16	*Confusion and irrelevant behavior:* Periods when the noise level is such that the person speaking cannot be understood or periods of silence that have no relation to the purposes of the classroom.

$$\text{Indirect-direct ratio} = \frac{\text{categories 1, 2, 3, 4, 5}}{\text{categories 6, 7, 8, 9}}$$

$$\text{Revised indirect-direct ratio} = \frac{\text{categories 1, 2, 3}}{\text{categories 7, 8, 9}}$$

$$\text{Direct-student talk ratio} = \frac{\text{categories 6, 7, 8, 9}}{\text{categories 10, 11, 12}}$$

FIG. 2–8. Summary of the sixteen categories of verbal behavior used in this study.

responses, and (d) a subclassification of Flanders' category 10 to distinguish between teacher-directed activity, teacher demonstration, silence intended for purposes of thinking, and confusion or irrelevant behavior. A summary of the category system used in this study is given in Fig. 2–8.*

Hypotheses

Six hypotheses were tested to determine the differences in verbal classroom behavior of the two samples of physics teachers.

On comparing those teachers who ranked high on the three evaluation instruments with those who ranked low, it was hypothesized that there would be a significant difference in regard to the following:

1. The percentage of classroom time spent in each of the 16 categories of classroom behavior.

2. The indirect–direct ratio.

3. The revised indirect–direct ratio.

4. The direct–student talk ratio.[26]

5. The ratio of sustained classroom verbal behavior to transitional behavior.

6. The total interaction pattern for all 16 categories.

PROCEDURE

A population of 30 physics teachers from 30 separate high schools in the Columbus and Dayton, Ohio, areas were evaluated by (a) the *Teacher Rating Scale*, completed by the principal of the teacher, (b) the *Student-Opinion Questionnaire*, completed by the students in one class of each teacher, and (c) the *Teaching Situation Reaction Test*, completed by the teacher himself. To be included in the original population, each teacher and administrator was required to give his individual consent to participate in the study. The excellent cooperation that was obtained from all who participated was attributed to the large number of personal contacts that the researcher made with the teachers and principals.

The five highest and five lowest ranking teachers according to the three evaluative instruments comprised the high and low samples and were selected for direct classroom observation. Each of the five teachers in the high and low samples was visited during six class periods by the researcher, a trained observer, who observed, classified, and recorded the ongoing verbal behavior in the class-

---

* The categories of verbal behavior used in this system are basically those used by Flanders in his ten-category system of interaction analysis. Categories 5, 7, 12, 13, 14, and 15 represent additions to Flanders' category system.
[26] Ratios 2, 3, and 4 are defined in Fig. 2–8.

room. Using the *Observational System for the Analysis of Classroom Instruction,* the researcher classified and recorded verbal classroom behavior during each three-second period into one of the sixteen categories described in Fig. 2–8.

From previous studies by Flanders and others it was clear that the data gathered by means of interaction analysis are only as valid as the reliability of the observer. Prior to gathering data the researcher checked his reliability against three tape-recorded classroom sessions that contained all sixteen categories. Each of the tapes had been standardized by Hough, who developed the observational system used in this study. Observer reliability was computed by a formula suggested by Scott (Flanders, 1965a, pp. 25–27). Coefficients of 0.84, 0.85, and 0.81 were obtained by the researcher for the three tape recordings.

To minimize observer bias during classroom visitation, the scoring of the evaluation instruments and the selection of the two samples of teachers was carried out by individuals other than the researcher. The researcher had no knowledge of the individual ranking of teachers until after all data had been gathered.

All observational data were tabulated and converted to matrix form according to the method used in Flanders' system of interaction analysis (Flanders, 1965a, pp. 33–44). The t-test was used to compare the percentages of time the high and low samples of teachers spent in each of the sixteen categories. The t-test was also employed to compare the ratios in hypotheses 2, 3, 4, and 5 for the two samples of teachers. The Darwin chi-square test (1959) was used to compare the total interaction pattern for the two groups of teachers.

RESULTS

A composite matrix showing the average percentage of total tallies for the high sample of teachers is presented in Table 2–17. In like manner, Table 2–18 shows the master matrix for the low sample. The total of each column indicates the average percentage of tallies recorded for that category and is a measure of the percentage of time teachers use a particular category. Tallies in cells 1-1, 2-2, 3-3, etc. indicate the number of times a category of behavior is sustained for a period longer than three seconds. All other cells indicate transitional behavior, that is, the number of times the verbal discourse changes from one category to another. The tallies in cell 4-8, for example, represent the number of times a category 4 was followed by category 8.

Figure 2–9 illustrates graphically how the patterns of influence compare for the teachers in the high and low samples with respect to the percentage of verbal responses in the sixteen categories. In cases where the percentage of tallies was relatively small, several categories of similar behavior were combined.

In analyzing a matrix it is instructive to consider the total tallies in eight general areas of the matrix. These areas are identified in Fig. 2–10 and are described briefly as follows (Hough, 1966, pp. 7–8):

Table 2–17

Composite Matrix of the Five Teachers in the High Sample*

Category	1	2	3	4	5	6	7	8	9	10	11	12	13	14	15	16
1	0.04	0.00	0.00	0.01	0.00	0.02	0.00	0.00	0.00	0.01	0.01	0.00	0.00	0.01	0.00	0.00
2	0.00	0.12	0.06	0.06	0.01	0.15	0.00	0.04	0.00	0.04	0.03	0.03	0.00	0.02	0.00	0.01
3	0.01	0.11	3.34	0.82	0.17	1.69	0.03	0.08	0.00	0.21	0.38	0.24	0.00	0.10	0.12	0.01
4	0.00	0.02	0.02	2.00	0.01	0.44	0.00	0.27	0.00	2.62	0.33	0.14	0.00	0.34	0.02	0.00
5	0.02	0.02	0.06	0.32	12.04	0.42	0.00	0.03	0.00	0.01	0.39	1.03	0.02	0.11	0.08	0.03
6	0.02	0.13	0.07	2.14	0.09	44.65	0.00	0.32	0.00	0.08	0.37	0.54	0.03	0.21	0.53	0.07
7	0.00	0.00	0.02	0.02	0.00	0.10	0.01	0.00	0.00	0.06	0.01	0.00	0.00	0.01	0.00	0.00
8	0.00	0.01	0.00	0.07	0.01	0.24	0.00	0.34	0.00	0.29	0.07	0.02	0.10	0.06	0.01	0.03
9	0.00	0.00	0.00	0.01	0.00	0.00	0.00	0.00	0.00	0.00	0.00	0.00	0.00	0.00	0.00	0.00
10	0.00	0.06	2.55	0.25	0.03	0.22	0.16	0.06	0.00	2.10	0.05	0.02	0.00	0.05	0.02	0.00
11	0.01	0.07	0.89	0.14	0.04	0.24	0.03	0.02	0.00	0.01	3.97	0.27	0.07	0.02	0.03	0.00
12	0.00	0.01	0.18	0.06	0.00	0.05	0.00	0.01	0.00	0.00	0.05	2.22	0.00	0.03	0.02	0.00
13	0.00	0.00	0.00	0.03	0.00	0.04	0.00	0.03	0.00	0.01	0.08	0.04	0.49	0.00	0.00	0.00
14	0.01	0.02	0.05	0.14	0.08	0.34	0.00	0.05	0.00	0.15	0.05	0.04	0.00	0.35	0.03	0.00
15	0.00	0.00	0.04	0.12	0.07	0.54	0.00	0.01	0.00	0.00	0.03	0.05	0.00	0.00	1.24	0.00
16	0.00	0.00	0.00	0.02	0.00	0.12	0.00	0.01	0.00	0.00	0.01	0.00	0.00	0.00	0.00	0.01
Total	0.11	0.57	7.28	6.21	14.55	49.26	0.23	1.27	0.00	5.59	5.83	4.64	0.71	1.31	2.10	0.18**

* N = 22,973 tallies. All numbers in the matrix represent percentage of N.
** The actual percentage of tallies recorded for nonfunctional behavior is 0.05. This difference is caused by recording a "16" at the beginning and ending of each observation.

Table 2-18

Composite Matrix of the Five Teachers in the Low Sample*

Category	1	2	3	4	5	6	7	8	9	10	11	12	13	14	15	16
1	0.00	0.00	0.00	0.00	0.00	0.00	0.00	0.00	0.00	0.00	0.01	0.00	0.00	0.00	0.00	0.00
2	0.00	0.01	0.00	0.01	0.00	0.06	0.00	0.00	0.00	0.01	0.02	0.00	0.00	0.00	0.00	0.00
3	0.00	0.02	0.54	0.77	0.02	1.17	0.00	0.20	0.00	0.21	0.23	0.13	0.02	0.06	0.03	0.01
4	0.00	0.00	0.02	1.80	0.01	0.64	0.00	0.55	0.01	3.18	0.20	0.10	0.01	0.69	0.01	0.02
5	0.00	0.00	0.00	0.21	2.25	0.36	0.00	0.12	0.01	0.03	0.21	0.50	0.09	0.09	0.02	0.04
6	0.00	0.02	0.03	2.41	0.02	41.68	0.00	0.95	0.03	0.19	0.73	0.69	0.13	0.44	0.36	0.22
7	0.00	0.00	0.94	0.02	0.00	0.08	0.00	0.01	0.00	0.10	0.01	0.00	0.00	0.01	0.00	0.00
8	0.00	0.00	0.02	0.09	0.00	0.54	0.00	1.33	0.02	1.50	0.20	0.13	0.36	0.27	0.05	0.05
9	0.00	0.00	0.00	0.03	0.00	0.06	0.00	0.02	0.05	0.04	0.91	0.00	0.00	0.00	0.01	0.00
10	0.00	0.02	2.20	1.03	0.02	0.95	0.20	0.58	0.94	4.37	0.21	0.09	0.13	0.17	0.17	0.04
11	0.01	0.04	0.47	0.26	0.04	0.71	0.03	0.15	0.02	0.03	4.45	0.21	0.49	0.07	0.03	0.06
12	0.00	0.00	0.05	0.12	1.56	0.06	0.02	0.05	0.01	0.02	0.17	1.41	0.01	0.02	0.01	0.00
13	0.00	0.01	0.00	0.04	0.00	0.23	0.00	0.21	0.01	0.10	0.46	0.15	3.49	0.00	0.03	0.02
14	0.00	0.00	0.01	0.36	0.02	0.71	0.01	0.24	0.01	0.35	0.05	0.05	0.02	1.19	0.02	0.00
15	0.00	0.00	0.00	0.08	0.01	0.35	0.00	0.08	0.00	0.07	0.06	0.04	0.01	0.02	1.88	0.00
16	0.00	0.00	0.01	0.03	0.00	0.28	0.01	0.04	0.02	0.02	0.06	0.01	0.01	0.00	0.00	0.55
Total	0.01	0.12	3.27	7.26	3.95	47.88	0.27	4.53	1.14	10.22	7.98	3.51	4.77	3.03	2.62	0.99**

* N = 20,307 tallies. All numbers in the matrix represent percentage of N.
** The actual percentage of tallies recorded for nonfunctional behavior is 0.88. This difference is caused by recording a "16" at the beginning and ending of each observation.

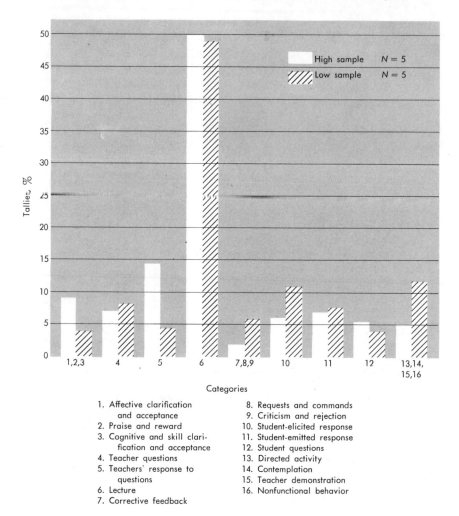

Categories

1. Affective clarification and acceptance
2. Praise and reward
3. Cognitive and skill clarification and acceptance
4. Teacher questions
5. Teachers' response to questions
6. Lecture
7. Corrective feedback
8. Requests and commands
9. Criticism and rejection
10. Student-elicited response
11. Student-emitted response
12. Student questions
13. Directed activity
14. Contemplation
15. Teacher demonstration
16. Nonfunctional behavior

FIG. 2–9. Influence patterns of the high and low samples of teachers with respect to the percentage of tallies in the sixteen categories.

Area A contains all instances of extended indirect influence. For example, when a teacher uses extended praise or extended acceptance, tally marks will be plotted in this area, as will instances of transition from one indirect category to another.

Area B contains all instances of extended direct influence. For example, when a teacher uses extended lecture or extended direction, tally marks will be plotted in this area, as will instances of transition from one direct category to another.

Area C contains all instances of student talk following teacher talk. All cells in area C are transition cells; that is, they indicate the beginning of student talk following teacher talk.

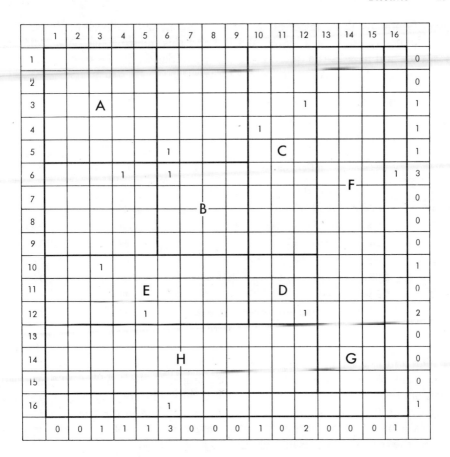

FIG. 2–10. Regions of the matrix of the observational system for the analysis of classroom instruction.

Area D contains all instances of extended student talk. For example, when a student continues to talk for an extended period of time, tally marks will be plotted in this area, as will all instances of transition from one student-talk category to another.

Area E contains all instances of teacher talk following student talk. All cells in Area E are transition cells, that is they indicate the beginning of teacher talk following student talk.

Area F contains all instances of silence following either teacher or student talk. All cells in Area F are transition cells, that is they indicate the beginning of periods of silence following talk.

Area G contains all instances of extended silence. For example, if a teacher tells the class to think about something for a few minutes, their silence would be indicated in Area G.

Area H contains all instances of teacher or student talk following silence. For example, if a teacher has asked a question and this question has been followed by silence and he asks the question again, the initiation of the second question, following the silence, would be plotted in Area H.

Table 2–19

Percentages of Tallies in Areas A–H for the High and Low Samples of Teachers

Area	Description	High sample %	Low sample %
A	Extended indirect influence	19.26	5.66
B	Extended direct influence	45.67	44.78
C	Student talk following teacher talk	6.91	8.43
D	Extended student talk	8.69	10.96
E	Teacher talk following student talk	7.09	8.65
F	Silence following teacher or student talk	2.02	3.59
G	Extended silence	2.11	6.66
H	Teacher or student talk following silence	1.82	3.73

A comparison of the percentage of tallies in each of the Areas A–H, for the high and low sample, is presented in Table 2–19. The percentage of tallies in the areas of extended verbal influence indicates the amount of sustained classroom behavior in a broader sense than is shown by looking only at a single category. In the same manner the percentage of tallies in the transitional areas presents a broad view of transitional behavior that is not achieved by considering the transitional cells in each category separately.

Tests of the hypotheses

Hypothesis number one, that there would be a difference in the amount of time spent in each of the sixteen categories by the teachers in the high and low samples, was supported for the following:

Category 2. Praise and reward
Category 3. Cognitive and skill clarification and acceptance
Category 8. Requests and commands
Category 9. Criticism and rejection
Category 16. Confusion and irrelevant behavior

The data presented in Table 2–20 show that for the above categories the t-values for the difference between the means of the high and low samples exceeded the 2.31 needed for a significance level of 0.05. The corresponding t-values for all other categories failed to reach an acceptable level of significance. The range and mean percentage scores for the five teachers in the low sample are also listed in Table 2–20 for each of the sixteen categories.

Table 2–20

A Comparison of the High and Low Samples on the Percentage of Tallies in Each of the 16 Categories

Category	Sample	% Range	Mean	t-value	Level of significance
1	High	0– 0.25	0.11	2.27	0.10
	Low	0– 0.07	0.01		
2	High	0.18– 0.97	0.59	2.65	0.05
	Low	0.00– 0.39	0.13		
3	High	5.30–11.17	7.31	2.93	0.05
	Low	0.86– 5.17	3.40		
4	High	1.35– 8.37	6.21	0.48	
	Low	3.03–12.53	7.25		
5	High	3.15–38.86	14.56	1.67*	
	Low	0.83– 7.25	3.95		
6	High	30.77–67.07	49.28	0.12	
	Low	29.20–78.09	47.90		
7	High	0.11– 0.47	0.24	0.11	
	Low	0.08– 0.63	0.28		
8	High	0.33– 2.28	1.26	2.98	0.05
	Low	2.89– 7.86	4.54		
9	High	0– 0.06	0.01	2.35	0.05
	Low	0– 0.49	0.25		
10	High	0.93–11.65	5.60	1.36	
	Low	3.24–20.82	10.22		
11	High	0.72–12.09	5.84	0.40	
	Low	0.78–13.99	7.08		
12	High	1.55–12.62	4.64	0.62	
	Low	0.27– 4.99	3.52		
13	High	0.02– 2.11	0.73	1.34	
	Low	1.10–16.73	4.76		
14	High	0.43– 2.77	1.32	2.18	0.10
	Low	1.21– 4.69	3.04		
15	High	0.81– 3.24	2.11	0.43	
	Low	0.32– 6.78	2.64		
16	High	0– 0.10	0.05	3.81	0.01
	Low	0.59– 1.56	0.88		

* See analysis and discussion of category 5.

Hypothesis number two, that a difference would exist between the high and low samples of physics teachers in regard to the Indirect–Direct ratio (the ratio of categories 1–5 to categories 6–9), was not supported by a test of the difference of means for the two groups.

Table 2–21

A Comparison of the High and Low Samples of Teachers on i/d Ratios

	Teacher number	i/d ratio	Mean	t
High sample	540	11.96		
	580	8.52		
	650	5.08	6.24	
	700	5.34		3.85
	710	3.22		Significant
Low sample	570	0.91		at the 0.01
	780	0.29		level
	760	1.53	0.78	
	800	0.86		
	550	0.29		

Hypothesis number three, that there would be a difference between the high and low samples of teachers for the ratio of categories 1–3 to categories 7–9 (i/d ratio or the revised indirect–direct ratio) was clearly supported. Table 2–21 contains the data which show that the difference between the two groups was significant beyond the 0.01 level, $t = 3.85$. According to these data the i/d ratio for the high sample is about nine times that of the low sample.

Hypothesis number four, that there would be a difference between the high sample and the low sample for the ratio of direct influence to student talk (D/ST ratio, the ratio of categories 6–9 to 10–12), was not supported by the data. An examination of the data indicated that the difference for the two groups of teachers on this item is small.

Hypothesis number five, that the ratio of the percentage of tallies in the steady-state cells (cells 1-1, 2-2, 3-3, etc. representing a sustained pattern) to the total percentage in the transitional cells (all cells other than the steady-state cells) for each category would be different for the high and low samples of teachers, was supported for categories 3 and 5. The data indicate that the t-values for the ratios of categories 3 and 5 are 3.8 and 4.3 respectively. These values are both significant at the 0.01 level. The t-values for the ratios of all other categories did not reach an acceptable level of significance. Teachers in the high sample used significantly more extended clarification and extended answers to student questions.

Hypothesis number six, that the total interaction pattern for the high sample would be different from the total interaction pattern of the low sample of teachers, was conclusively supported. A Darwin chi-square test was calculated as a test of significance, using the total numbers of tallies from the original matrices of the high and low samples (Flanders, 1965a, pp. 31–33). The Darwin χ^2 was converted to a standard score ($z = 7.77$) which was beyond the value 2.58 needed for a 0.01 level of significance. The probability that the difference between the high and low composite matrices could have occurred by chance was considerably less than 0.01.

Analysis and discussion

A more detailed analysis of the results is made by considering the percentage of tallies in individual cells and groups of cells. It is essential to refer to the composite matrices in Tables 2–17 and 2–18 for this discussion.

Category 1 (acceptance, clarification, and recognition of students' emotional states) is shown in the first column and row. Of all the 16 categories used, this category was used the least. Although an estimate of the error in this category was relatively high, only one teacher in the low sample used category 1, whereas four of the five teachers in the high sample gave verbal responses in this category. The fact that constructive reactions to the feelings or emotional status of pupils existed in the classroom may be indicative of a particular type of classroom climate.

Category 2 (teacher praise and reward) is shown in the second column and row. This category was used four and one-half times as often by teachers in the high sample as it was by teachers in the low sample. A closer examination of category 2 suggests two trends. First, the higher frequency of tallies in the 2-2 cell by the high sample indicates that once a teacher in this group initiated praise, he was more likely to persist in this type of behavior. Secondly, the higher frequency of tallies in the 6-2 cell by the high sample probably means more humor was introduced during lecture by this group of teachers.

Category 3 (clarifying and making use of students' ideas) is shown in the third column and row. This category was used more than twice as often by the high sample of physics teachers as by the low sample. The frequency of tallies recorded for the high sample in the 3-3 cell (steady-state) was more than six times that of the low group, indicating a more lengthy development of student ideas by the former. Cells 5-3 and 3-5 (from answering students' questions to using students' ideas and vice versa) also show higher frequencies in favor of the high sample. This suggests that this group used students' ideas to answer their questions more often than did the teachers in the low sample.

Category 4 (teachers' questions) was used almost as frequently by one group as by the other. A closer examination of category 4 shows a general trend for teachers in the low sample to ask more narrow, short-answer questions and for the high sample to ask more broad questions encouraging student-emitted responses. This trend was not consistent for all teachers in the two samples. The most striking difference in category 4 appeared in cell 10-4 (from student-elicited response to another question by the teacher). The relative frequencies of tallies in this cell are four to one in favor of the low group. These data support the observation of the researcher that teachers in the low sample frequently used the cyclic pattern of question–answer–question–answer in their classrooms.

Category 5 (response to students' questions) occurred three and one-half times as often in the classrooms of the high sample as in those of the low sample. Due to a large variance in the high sample, this difference was not significant; nevertheless, a trend existed for the high group to spend more time

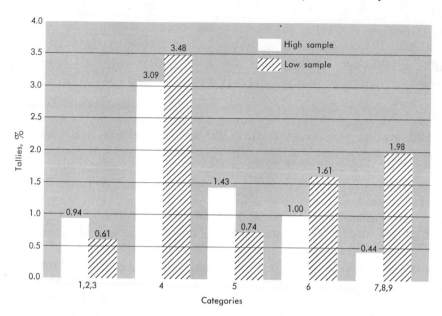

FIG. 2–11. Teacher talk which solicits student response.

answering students' questions, and it was most pronounced in the 5-5 cell (steady-state). This suggests that teachers in the high sample offered longer answers to students' questions. An estimate of the average number of three-second periods each teacher used to answer students' questions was obtained by dividing the total percentage in category 5 by the percentage of tallies in cell 12-5 (transition from students' questions to teachers' answers). This gave an approximate ratio of the total number of three-second periods during which the teacher answered questions to the number of questions asked by students. An examination of these ratios shows that the teachers in the high sample on the average spent more than twenty seconds per question supplying answers to students, whereas the teachers in the low sample used less than ten seconds per question for this purpose.

Category 6 (lecturing) appeared in nearly equal percentage for both groups. A more detailed look at the distribution of tallies in row 6 and column 6 shows a marked difference in several cells. In cell 6-8 (from lecture to requests or commands) the low sample had three times as many tallies as the high group. This suggests more frequent use of directions and questions stated in the form of commands during lecture by the teachers in the low sample. The 6-16 cell and the 16-6 cell (from lecture to nonfunctional behavior and vice versa) have ratios of 3 to 1 and 2 to 1 respectively in favor of the low group, suggesting that this group had more frequent nonfunctional interruptions during lecture.

Categories 7, 8, and 9 (corrective feedback, directions, and commands and criticism) were used more than three times as often by the low sample as by the

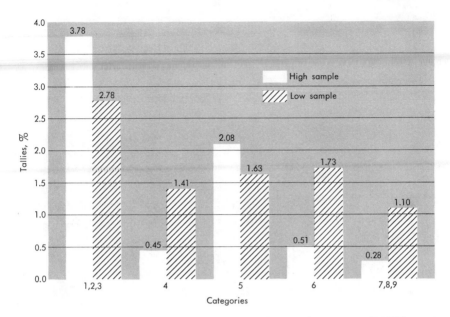

FIG. 2-12. Response of teachers when students stop talking.

high group. This difference was most evident in cells 8-8 (steady-state) and 8-10 (from teachers' request to silence). These results indicate a behavior pattern common to teachers in the low sample and apparent in the observation of these teachers' classrooms. Teachers in the low sample frequently stated their questions in the form of a command. If the student answered (8-10 pattern) the cycle was often repeated. Quite often, however, the student failed to answer and silence prevailed (8-14 pattern). When this occurred, the verbal discourse in the classroom often appeared to take the form of an interrogation session with the climate becoming somewhat tense. The more frequent use of criticism would also seem consistent with the more direct approach used by the teachers in the low group.

A contrast of the type of influence more frequently employed by each of the two samples of teachers can be seen in Figs. 2–11 and 2–12, which show the kind of teacher talk that precedes and follows student talk. The data illustrated in Fig. 2–11 were obtained by adding the tallies in the respective rows of Area C, Fig. 2–10. Fig. 2–12 was obtained by totaling the tallies in the respective columns of Area E, Fig. 2–10. It is evident from these two histograms (Figs. 2–11 and 2–12) that, compared with the low sample, the high group used the indirect influence of categories 1, 2, 3, and 5 more frequently *before* and *after* students' comments, whereas the low group used the direct influence of categories 7, 8, and 9 more frequently.

Category 10 (student-elicited response) on the average appeared about twice as often in the classrooms of the low sample as in those of the high sample. However, the difference of means for the two groups was not significant

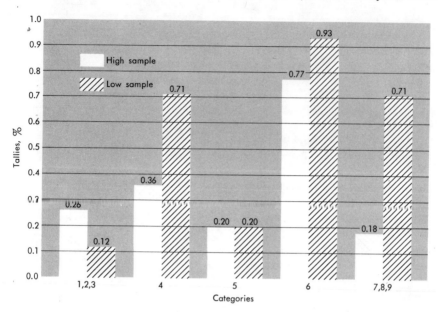

FIG. 2–13. Teacher talk preceding silence.

at the 0.05 level since the overall trend was not consistent for all teachers. There was a much higher proportion of tallies for the low sample in the 10-4 cell (4-to-1 ratio), the 10-6 cell (4-to-1 ratio), and the 10-8 cell (10-to-1 ratio), which would appear to be symptomatic of the conditioned response repeatedly solicited by the teachers in the low group.

Category 11 (student-emitted response) occurred 5.8% of the time for the high sample and 7.1% for the low sample. Although this trend does *not* seem to be consistent with some of the other findings of this study, classroom observation suggests the following explanation. Quite often two or three students in the classrooms of the low sample who appeared to be quite knowledgeable in physics dominated the class time by relating their own personal experiences or arguing among themselves. Very frequently the remainder of the class became disinterested because no direction was given by the teacher in the discussion. The situation described above resulted in a large number of tallies in category 11 and occurred less frequently in the classes of the high group. This hypothesis is supported by the 6-to-1 ratio of tallies in cells 11-13 and 13-11 in favor of the low samples. It should be recalled that a category 13 was recorded to indicate a transition from one student's response to another student's response without teacher talk.

Category 12 (students' questions) occurred slightly more often in the classrooms of the high sample than in classrooms of the low group, as evidenced by the number of tallies in the 12-5 cell (from students' questions to teachers' answers). Classroom observation suggests that the type of question rather than the number of questions is a critical factor separating the two samples of teachers.

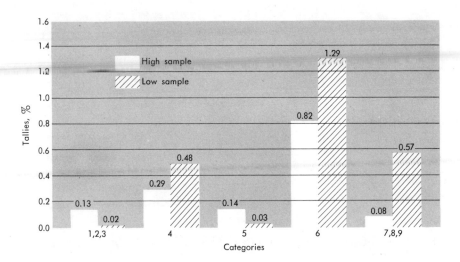

FIG. 2–14. How teachers respond following silence.

Categories 13, 14, and 15 (silence) occurred more than twice as often in the classrooms of the low sample than in those of the high sample, and probably for different reasons. Figures 2–13 and 2–14 are histograms indicating the kind of teacher talk that precedes and follows silence. Figure 2–13 was obtained by adding the tallies in the respective rows of Area F, Fig. 2–10. Figure 2–14 was obtained by adding the tallies in the respective columns of Area H, Fig. 2–10. Figures 2–13 and 2–14 are strikingly similar. In addition to that fact, however, they show that, both in the preceding and following silence, the high sample used the indirect influence of categories 1, 2, and 3 more frequently and the low sample used the direct influence of categories 6, 7, 8, and 9 plus teachers' questions, category 4. This could mean that silence has a different purpose for teachers with different influence patterns.

Category 16 (nonfunctional behavior) was present on the average in the amounts of 0.05% of the time for the high sample and 0.88% for the low sample. This difference occurred mainly in cells 6-16 (from lecture to nonfunctional behavior) and 16-16 (sustained nonfunctional behavior) and 16-6 (from nonfunctional behavior to lecture). This suggests that more frequent interruptions of irrelevant behavior during lecture caused by students interrupting the teacher occurred in the classes of the low sample.

Comparison with other studies

The results of the present study are clearly supported by the research of Flanders (1965a) and of Amidon and Giammatteo (1965), in which the influence patterns of two groups of teachers were compared. Although each age group may have used different amounts of any one category, the relative extent to which each of the two groups in the above studies used any one category of verbal behavior shows a consistent pattern regardless of age level or

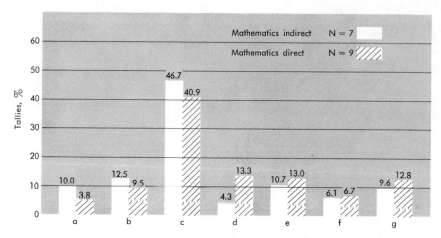

FIG. 2–15. Influence patterns of direct and indirect mathematics teachers.

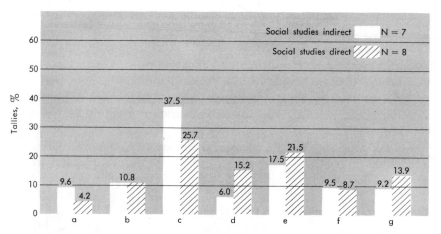

FIG. 2–16. Influence patterns of direct and indirect social studies teachers.

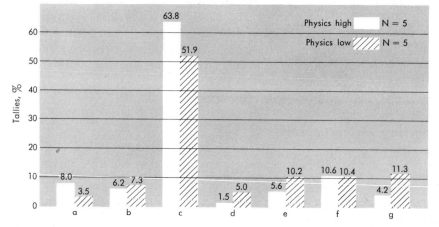

FIG. 2–17. Influence patterns of high and low physics teachers.

academic discipline. This observation is supported by Figs. 2–15, 2–16, and 2–17, which present histograms of the influence patterns of eighth-grade mathematics teachers (Flanders, 1965a), and twelfth-grade physics teachers (present study), respectively. It should be recalled that indirect teachers also were the teachers of high-achieving classes in mathematics and social studies, and that classes of direct teachers in these two disciplines achieved less. The categories of verbal behavior shown in the three histograms are as follows:

a) Indirect influence with respect to student orientation
b) Teachers' questions
c) Lecture and information
d) Direct influence with respect to student orientation
e) Student-elicited response
f) Student-emitted response
g) Silence

The data from the three histograms in Figs. 2–15, 2–16 and 2–17 show that the physics teachers used a greater percentage of lecture, category (c), in their classes than did either social studies or mathematics teachers, and in general, a smaller percentage in all other categories. The relative percentages (the percentage of the indirect or high group as compared to the direct or low group) are somewhat similar for the teachers in all three disciplines. This similarity is especially true in category (a) (indirect influence with respect to student orientation), category (d) (direct influence with respect to student orientation), and category (g) (silence).

SUMMARY AND CONCLUSIONS

The verbal behavior patterns in the classrooms of the two groups of twelfth-grade physics teachers were investigated. One group ranked extremely high on a composite of three factors: the principals' perception of the teachers' personal adjustment and teacher–pupil relationship, the students' perceptions of the teachers' all-around teaching ability, and the teachers' ability to respond to teaching situations in accord with educational theory. The other group ranked extremely low on these same three factors. *The Observational System for the Analysis of Classroom Instruction,* a 16-category modification of Flanders' system of interaction analysis, was used to measure the verbal behavior through direct classroom observation.

The following conclusions were drawn from the data analyzed in this investigation:

1. The teachers' use of certain categories of verbal behavior was significantly different for the two groups at the 0.05 level. Teachers in the high sample used significantly more praise and reward and more cognitive and skill clarification and acceptance than teachers in the low sample. Teachers in the high sample used significantly fewer requests and commands, less criticism and rejection,

and experienced less confusion and irrelevant behavior in their classrooms than did teachers in the low sample.

2. Indirect influence (constructive reaction to students' feelings, praise and reward, and use of students' ideas) as compared with direct influence (corrective feedback, directions, commands, and criticism) was employed by the high sample significantly more often (0.01 level) and in a more sustained manner than by the low sample of teachers. This comparison, known as the i/d ratio, was more than eight times higher for the high sample than for the low sample.

3. The sustained use of students' ideas and the length of teachers' answers to students' questions was significantly greater (0.01 level) for the high sample than for the low sample.

4. Between the high sample and the low sample, the total interaction pattern as determined by the Darwin χ^2 test was significantly different at the 0.01 level.

5. Although questions occurred about as frequently in one group as in the other, there was evidence that the teachers in the two samples asked different kinds of questions and stated them in different forms.

6. Each of the two samples of physics teachers in this study used approximately half of their time in the classroom giving instruction via lecture.

7. Influence patterns that solicited students' responses, as well as the influence patterns following students' responses, differed for the two samples of physics teachers.

8. For both groups, influence patterns preceding silence revealed a striking similarity to the teacher-influence patterns following silence. The high sample used more indirect influence patterns, whereas the low sample emphasized direct influence patterns to a greater degree.

A SPECIAL NOTE REGARDING CATEGORIES 5, 12, AND 14

By subdividing some of the categories in Flanders' system of interaction analysis, the *Observational System for the Analysis of Classroom Instruction* adds a number of new categories into which verbal behavior can be classified. Three of these categories proved very helpful in pointing out differences between the two groups of physics teachers and merit special comment. Students' questions (category 12) and teachers' answers to students' questions (category 5) both occurred somewhat more frequently in the classes of the high group. The real difference, however, became apparent in the analysis of individual cells within these categories. This revealed a very marked difference in the length of answers to students' questions and suggested that the type of answers given to students by each of the two groups of teachers may be different.

Contemplation (category 14) proved to be another fruitful modification of the ten category system. Although somewhat of a misnomer, this category was helpful in identifying the silence after teachers' questions that often caused an unfavorable climate in the classrooms of the low group. Distinguishing category 14 from other silence was also helpful in showing what effects teachers' questions, stated in different forms, have on students.

9

THE EFFECTS OF DIRECT AND INDIRECT TEACHER INFLUENCE ON DEPENDENT-PRONE STUDENTS LEARNING GEOMETRY[27]

EDMUND AMIDON and NED A. FLANDERS

Whether or not a particular type of student can learn when he is exposed to a particular style of teaching has interested a number of researchers. Smith (1955) and Wispe (1951) have both shown that when students are classified by the use of personality test data, they respond differently to highly organized versus loosely organized classroom activities in a college remedial reading course (Smith, 1955) and to college lecturing versus group discussion techniques (Wispe, 1951) in freshman sociology. The present project was concerned with dependent-prone eighth-grade students who were exposed to consistently direct versus indirect styles of teaching while learning geometry.

Asch (1951), Kagen and Mussen (1956), and Livson and Mussen (1957) have studied the reactions of dependent-prone persons in various kinds of experimental situations. They concluded that dependent-prone individuals are more likely to comply with authority figures and conform to group pressures than the less dependent-prone. Their results suggest that a dependent-prone student might become overly concerned with following the suggestions and directions of a teacher and more dependent on support and encouragement. The present project was designed to find out if these concerns inhibit or enhance the learning of geometry at the age level represented in the eighth grade.

PROCEDURE

This study employed a laboratory design in order to exercise experimental control of spontaneous behavior. First, the behavior of the teacher was controlled by training a teacher as a role player. His statements were classified

[27] From *J. educ. Psychol.* **52**, 1961, 286–291. Reprinted by permission of the American Psychological Association and the authors.

by an observer to demonstrate that desired differences were great enough for students to notice. Second, those students who scored high on a dependence-proneness test, developed by Flanders, Anderson, and Amidon (1960) were selected for the experimental population. Third, control of learning was accomplished by using pre- and post-tests of geometry achievement. And fourth, in half of the experimental groups the basic content material, presented in a tape recording, was so organized that the immediate learning goals were unclear, and in the other half the immediate learning goals were clear.

The four treatments involved were:

Treatment 1. Direct teacher influence: clear goals, 35 dependent-prone students.

Treatment 2. Direct teacher influence: unclear goals, 35 dependent-prone students.

Treatment 3. Indirect teacher influence: clear goals, 35 dependent-prone students.

Treatment 4. Indirect teacher influence: unclear goals, 35 dependent-prone students.

The experimental population of 140 dependent-prone students was part of a larger group of 560 students. The larger group was exposed to the preceding four treatments in groups of 20 as part of a larger study. The 560 eighth-grade students were selected at random from Minneapolis and St. Paul public schools. The 140 students were the top 25% in each treatment of the larger population according to their scores on the dependence-proneness test.

The students were brought, 20 per session, to a spare room in a public school. First, a pre-test of geometry achievement and a test of dependence-proneness were administered. Second, a tape recording was played introducing the basic concepts of C = D, Distance = Speed × Time, and geometric concepts and formulae concerning inscribed angles. In half of the groups the immediate goals were made clear because the recording explained how this information could be used to solve problems; in the other half the goals were less clear because the students were warned that they could not be sure how this information could be used. Third, in the direct treatments a teacher gave a 15-minute lecture, with a few questions, explaining the material and illustrating problems that could be solved. In the indirect treatments, a teacher conducted a 15-minute discussion explaining the material and illustrating problems that could be solved. The content coverage was the same in the contrasting treatments. Fourth, the students then had about 15 minutes to practice solving problems at their seats by working on a problem sheet. And fifth, the post-test of achievement was administered. The entire sequence lasted two hours.

At appropriate points in this procedure the students' perceptions of goal clarity and their perceptions of the teacher were measured by paper-and-pencil tests. The reliability of both of these scales was estimated by the use of the Hoyt-Stunkard (1952) analysis of variance technique. The estimated reliability of the student perception scale was 0.64, while the reliability found for the goal perception measure was 0.93 for the measure administered just before the discussion (Amidon, 1959). Whenever the teacher talked, an observer classified all teacher and student statements according to Flanders' (1960) system of Interaction Analysis. Later the validity and reliability of the observer's judgments were verified by studying the tape recording that was made of every experimental session.

RESULTS

Control teacher influence and goal perception

The manipulation of direct and indirect teacher influence occurred right after the tape recording when the teacher first came in contact with the students. The same role player acted as teacher in all treatments to avoid differences in personality and appearance. The differences between the direct and indirect approach are shown in Table 2–22 according to the percentage of statements classified into interaction categories.

The figures in Table 2–22 show that essential differences between the direct and indirect treatments are: the teacher lectures and gives more directions in the direct treatments; he asks more questions and gets more student participation in the indirect treatments; he praises, encourages, and clarifies student ideas more frequently in the indirect treatments; and he criticizes students more frequently in the direct treatments.

The fact that the teacher controlled his behavior successfully and created the two teacher styles is self-evident. A Darwin (1959) chi-square analysis of these same interaction data, after they were tabulated in a matrix of sequence pairs, was calculated to test the null hypothesis that there is no difference between interaction data of the direct and indirect combined treatments. The chi-square value found was 702.2 $(df = 90)$. This value, transformed to a z score of 24.1 indicates that the differences could have occurred by chance with a frequency of much less than 0.01.

The reliability of the observers who classified the statements in the live situation was higher than 0.90. It can be shown that the errors of observation, at this level of reliability, are extremely small compared with the difference shown in Table 2–22 between the direct and indirect patterns.

After the lectures and discussions and before the period devoted to problem sheets, the students responded to a number of opinion items combined into a scale which measured their perceptions of the teacher's behavior. An analysis of variance was made of these scale scores which indicated that the F ratio between the groups subjected to the direct and indirect influence treatments was 78.4 $(df = 1/136)$. This was significant at the 0.01 level of confidence. The mean scores indicated that students in the direct treatments more often saw the teacher as "telling us what to do," "firm and businesslike," "mak-

Table 2–22

Percentage of Tallies in Interaction Categories

Category definition	Treatment			
	1	2	3	4
Teacher talk:				
Praise and encouragement	1.35	1.61	17.04	14.90
Clarification and development of ideas suggested by students	2.48	0.92	15.78	16.10
Asks questions	2.58	1.73	28.07	30.04
Gives own opinions and facts (lectures)	63.10	61.40	13.52	15.97
Gives directions	8.67	10.36	0.28	0.27
Criticizes students	13.03	15.54	1.27	0.94
Student talk	5.07	5.29	16.47	17.17
No one talking	3.49	3.45	7.75	4.69
Total tallies on which the percentage figures are based	889	869	711	746

ing plans for us," "critical of our ideas," "talking more than the students," and "not using student ideas or suggestions." In the indirect treatments, students often marked: "finding out what we know," "relaxed and cheerful," "letting us make our own plans," "letting students talk," "using our ideas," and similar perceptions that were the opposite of the direct pattern. The means and F ratio are presented in Table 2–23.

Table 2–23

Student Perception of Teacher Influence

Group	Mean	F_{obs} between direct and indirect groups
Direct influence	11.74	78.40
Indirect influence	18.84	

As expected, an analysis of observation data and of student perceptions of the teacher comparing the clear and unclear goal treatments showed no significant ($p < 0.05$) difference in teacher behavior. Also, no significant ($p < 0.05$) interaction effects were found in the analysis of variance.

The interaction analysis data and measures of the students' perceptions of the teacher did show that the differences between the direct and indirect approach did exist as required by the experimental design, were clearly seen by a trained observer, and were noticed by the students.

Paper-and-pencil measures of the clarity of goals were made after the playback of the tape recording introducing the basic geometric concepts. Students responded to items such as: "Can you see all the steps necessary to finish your work?" "Right now can you see what you will be doing clearly?" "Can you picture your work so clearly that you could tell when you will be finished?" and similar items that were combined into a scale. An analysis of variance of these scale scores yielded an F ratio of 16.98 ($df = 1/136$, p < 0.01). An inspection of the means indicates that the results were consistent with the intended goal manipulation. The results show that the immediate response of students to the clear and unclear tape recording was significantly different. The means and F ratio are found in Table 2–24.

Table 2–24

Student Perception of the Goal

Group	Mean	F_{obs} between clear and unclear goals
Clear goals	21.40	16.98
Unclear goals	26.13	

RESULTS OF THE GEOMETRY ACHIEVEMENT

Since achievement in geometry was the fundamental outcome variable analyzed in this study, the post-achievement test was subjected to several analyses. The first analysis was the comparison of post-achievement scores between the indirect and direct teacher influence groups. The F ratio found in this analysis was 7.67, which was significant at the 0.01 level. The means of the indirect teacher influence groups were significantly higher than the means of the direct teacher influence groups on the post-achievement measure. In order to reduce unaccounted-for error in the analysis of post-achievement, two analyses of covariance controlling pre-achievement scores and intelligence scores were run. The F ratio between direct and indirect teacher influence groups was 10.03 when intelligence was controlled, and 9.62 when pre-test scores were controlled. Again, those F ratios were significant at the 0.01 level, indicating the superiority of the indirect teacher influence group. For each of the analyses of covariance $df = 1/137$.

The analyses of variance and covariance just discussed yielded insignificant (p > 0.05) results when the clear and ambiguous goal perception groups

Table 2–25

Analysis of Differences in the Means of Post-achievement Scores with Various Factors Controlled Statistically

Source of variation	df	F_{obs}	Null hypothesis
With no measure controlled:			
Interaction	1	—	Not rejected
Teacher influence	1	7.67	Rejected
Goal perception	1	—	Not rejected
Pre-achievement controlled:			
Interaction	1	2.71	Not rejected
Teacher influence	1	10.03	Rejected
Goal perception	1	—	Not rejected
Intelligence controlled:			
Interaction	1	1.08	Not rejected
Teacher influence	1	9.62	Rejected
Goal perception	1	1.13	Not rejected

were compared statistically. The interaction of goal perception and teacher influence also did not yield significant ($p < 0.05$) results. The F ratios found in these analyses are presented in Table 2–25.

The means of the indirect group were significantly higher than the means of the direct group. This is true when intelligence and pre-achievement were controlled, and it was also true when they were not controlled. The means of the direct and indirect teacher influence groups are presented in Table 2–26.

Table 2–26

Means of Direct and Indirect Groups for Post-achievement Measure

Mean	Not adjusted	Adjusted by pre-test scores	Adjusted by intelligence
Direct group	9.24	9.31	9.30
Indirect group	10.82	10.76	10.69

DISCUSSION

The measures of geometry achievement indicate that the dependent-prone students learned more in the classroom in which the teacher gave fewer directions, less criticism, less lecturing, more praise, and asked more questions which increased their verbal participation. This finding takes on added significance when compared with Flanders' (1960) findings that the total group of 560 students, those scoring high, average, and low on the dependence-proneness tests, failed to show the same significant differences under the same conditions. Moreover, when the independent-prone students (those in the lower 25% on the dependency scale) were compared separately, no differences were found.

Compared with students in general, dependent-prone students are apparently more sensitive to the influence pattern of a geometry teacher.

The authors are disposed to interpret these findings in terms of the probable effects of teacher influence on the dependent-prone student. We assume that dependent-prone students are more sensitive to the directive aspects of the teacher's behavior. As the teacher becomes more directive, this type of student finds increased satisfaction in more compliance, often with less understanding of the problem-solving steps carried out. Only when he is free to express his doubts, to ask questions and gain reassurance, does his understanding keep pace with his compliance to the authority figure. Lacking this opportunity, compliance alone may become a satisfactory goal and content understanding may be subordinated to the process of adjusting to teacher directives. It is interesting to note that this effect occurs even when the material being learned concerns an orderly, logical system, such as exists in geometry.

One implication of this study is that closer supervision through the use of direct influence, an all too common antidote to lower achievement, may be more harmful than helpful for dependent-prone students.

SUMMARY

The primary purpose of the study described here was to determine the effects of direct vs. indirect teacher behavior and of clear vs. unclear student perception of the learning goal on the achievement of eighth-grade geometry students. A specially trained teacher role-played both a very direct and a very indirect teacher in a laboratory situation involving 140 eighth-grade pupils chosen from a larger population on the basis of high scores on a test of dependency proneness. All students were randomly assigned to one of the following four experimental treatments: direct teacher influence with clear goals, direct teacher influence with unclear goals, indirect teacher influence with clear goals, and indirect teacher influence with unclear goals.

Students in the various classifications were then compared on the basis of pre- and post-achievement tests in geometry. No differences were found between the clear goal and unclear goal treatments, indicating that in this study, at least, achievement of dependent-prone students was not affected by perception of the learning goal. An analysis of the direct and indirect treatments indicated that the children taught by the indirect teacher learned more than did the children taught by the direct teacher.

The results of this study take on additional meaning when compared with the results of Flanders (1960) using the same experimental design. Flanders found no differences (among the four experimental conditions) on the total group of 560 students who ranged from very high to very low on the dependence scale. Apparently dependent-prone students are more sensitive to types of teacher influence than are independent-prone students or students who make average scores on the test for dependence proneness.

10

SOME RELATIONSHIPS AMONG TEACHER INFLUENCE, PUPIL ATTITUDES AND ACHIEVEMENT[28]

NED A. FLANDERS

This chapter is divided into two parts. The first is concerned with a research program, conducted at the University of Minnesota and supported by the U.S. Office of Education, in which an analysis was made of teacher statements, pupil attitudes, and achievement. At appropriate points, the findings of other research studies are cited to support or modify the evidence from Minnesota. The second part of the chapter is concerned with the implications of this research for the practical aspects of evaluating teaching.

RESEARCH ON TEACHER INFLUENCE, PUPIL ATTITUDES, AND ACHIEVEMENT

Teaching may be conceived of as a series of overt acts over a period of time. How many different kinds of acts to be seen depends upon what one is looking for. Suppose one restricted himself to verbal behavior and chose to classify communication into three categories; for example, teacher talk, student talk, and silence or confusion. For only three categories based on who was talking, observer reliability would be high, but the psychological usefulness of the data would be limited. Suppose one had a great number of categories based upon such microscopic detail that each verbal act was seen as slightly different from the next. With so much to keep track of, observer reliability would be very low or nonexistent; the efficiency of the observation process would be very low and tabulation problems high; and the data would be too complex to analyze.

---

[28] From *Contemporary Research on Teacher Effectiveness.* Ed. by Bruce J. Biddle and William J. Ellena, copyright © by Holt, Rinehart, and Winston, Inc. All rights reserved. Reprinted by permission of Holt, Rinehart and Winston, Inc., and the authors.

Somewhere between too many and too few categories is an optimum number of categories that will permit the observer to reach psychologically useful inferences by recording acts of influence as rapidly as they can be identified. The limitations of such a system will arise from the nature of categories and the skill of the observer, compared with the purposes of the observation.

In the research project to be described, ten categories were used to classify the statements of the pupils and the teacher at a rate of approximately once every three seconds. It was found that an observer can be trained to categorize at this rate with sufficient accuracy (Flanders, 1960b) and that, in a very short time, the teacher and students can adjust to the presence of the observer.

The ten categories included seven assigned to teacher talk, two to student talk, and one to silence or confusion. When the teacher was talking, the observer decided if the statement was: (1) accepting student feelings; (2) giving praise; (3) accepting, clarifying, or making use of a student's ideas; (4) asking a question; (5) lecturing, giving facts or opinions; (6) giving directions; or (7) giving criticism. When a student was talking, the observer classified what was said into one of two categories: (8) student response or (9) student initiation. Silence and confusion were assigned to category (10).

In practice, an observer also kept a record of the different periods of classroom activity. In an hour he collected observation data separately for all periods of routine administration, such as settling down to work, cleaning up, passing out materials, and collecting materials; for all periods of evaluation in which homework or tests were being corrected; for all periods in which new material was being introduced; for all periods in which the students and teacher planned activities together; for all other class discussions; and for all periods in which the students worked at their desks or in groups. Thus, at the end of an hour's observation, it was possible to add up the different kinds of statements for each of these six types of classroom activity separately and to combine these into a grand total for the entire hour.

This method of observation is called "interaction analysis" in the classroom, and it can be used to quantify the qualitative aspects of verbal communication. The entire process becomes a measure of teacher influence because it makes the assumption that most teacher influence is expressed through verbal statements and that most nonverbal influence is positively correlated with the verbal. Those who have worked with this technique are disposed to accept this assumption.

Interaction analysis is a specialized research procedure that provides information about only a few of the many aspects of teaching. It is an analysis of spontaneous communication between individuals, and it is of no value if no one is talking, if one person talks continuously, or if one person reads from a book or report. Unless additional records are kept, the following kinds of information will be ignored—right, wrong, good, or bad content information— whatever is being discussed, the variety of instructional materials being used; the various class formations during learning activities; the preparation of the teacher as revealed by lesson plans; and anything else not directly revealed by verbal communication. Of the total complex called "teaching," interaction analysis applies only to the content-free characteristics of verbal communication.

The point of departure

The early research designs were simple. It was merely assumed that, by identifying classrooms in which the students had constructive attitudes and those in which attitudes were less constructive, comparisons of the contrasting teacher influence patterns would reveal significant differences. This design worked well from 1954 to 1957, during the early phases of the research program.[29]

The student attitudes chosen for measurement are illustrated by the attitude inventory used in a 1957 study of New Zealand elementary-school classrooms.[30] The five scales used were: teacher attractiveness—liking the teacher; motivation—finding school work interesting; rewards and punishment—feeling that rewards and punishments were administered fairly; independence—feeling free to make some important decisions and to direct oneself while at work; and disabling anxiety—certain paranoid reactions to the teacher's authority.

After the New Zealand study the next logical step seemed to be an approach to the question of whether or not the constructive attitudes of the students would be positively correlated with measures of achievement. A contract with the Cooperative Research Program, U.S. Office of Education, 1958–1960, provided this opportunity.

First, 16 teachers were selected from a population of seventh-grade combined English–social studies classes. This, because test evidence was available indicating that the classes chosen would represent the wide range of teacher-influence patterns of the parent population. A similar sample of 16 eighth-grade mathematics classes was selected by the same methods. All of the instructional materials needed for a two-week unit of study were developed, and they included such a variety that each teacher could use his natural style of teaching. The teachers had adequate time to look over the materials and plan the unit before it was scheduled in one of their regular public school classes. No teacher saw the carefully prepared achievement tests before teaching. However, they did know the objectives of the tests and that the tests would be designed to measure not only the knowledge and skills of problem solving but also the application of knowledge and skills to unique and unusual problems. The tests were administered before and after each unit so that adjustments for initial ability could be made. In addition to the achievement test, the members of the research staff also administered an attitude inventory based on the earlier research instruments.

---

[29] During the early period the research program was sponsored by the Laboratory for Research in Social Relations, University of Minnesota, a department of the College of Science, Literature, and the Arts.
[30] The New Zealand study was made possible by a Fulbright Research Scholarship and the cooperation of the New Zealand Council for Educational Research, Mr. George Parkyn, Director. Results of the New Zealand study are reported in Flanders (1959).

During 1959–1962 a project concerned with the application of interaction analysis to the in-service training of teachers was completed with the support of a grant from the Educational Media Branch, U.S. Office of Education. Five sound filmstrips were developed to help teachers understand the purposes and limitations of interaction analysis, to use it as a tool for analyzing their own verbal behavior and the verbal behavior of their colleagues, and to see if carefully designed in-service training programs will result in actual changes in the spontaneous patterns of teacher influence. Heretofore, the appraisal of in-service training has been informal or, at best, analysis of possible changes in the attitudes of the participating teachers. Interaction analysis provides a tool to find out if changes in attitude result in differences in teaching behavior.

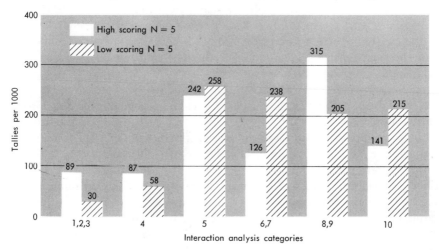

FIG. 2–18. Interaction analysis data from New Zealand standard, four classes scoring high and low on the student attitude inventory.

Theoretical principles of teacher influence and early research

The research program, up to 1958, was designed to find out if certain patterns of teacher influence could be associated with pupil attitude scores. When a distribution of verbal statements within the categories is plotted separately for classrooms in which scores on constructive pupil attitudes are low, in contrast with classrooms in which the same scores are high, a histogram (Fig. 2–18) results.

The two profiles in Fig. 2–18 show the proportion of different statements for two imaginary composite teachers. The percentage falling into each category is based on all the statements of five teachers whose classes scored highest and five whose classes scored lowest in a sample of 33 teachers of standard-four, in New Zealand. The data from earlier studies of elementary and secondary classrooms in Minnesota were similar but not identical.

Conclusions drawn from these earlier studies are consistent with each other in spite of differences in grade level and the fact that differences exist between New Zealand and Minnesota schools (Flanders, 1959).

All classrooms visited had in common a situation in which the teacher was clearly in charge, using his authority to control classroom activities. There was the impression that the teacher could do very little to avoid controlling classroom activities. When a teacher did succeed in withholding control or influence, there were predictable outcomes. The authority of the teacher was not only a psychological fact, it was the basis of school law. Later on, differences in the way teachers use their authority will be discussed at length. This will include discussion of the way in which some move in to control directly and others provide support to students who seem to control themselves.

Another element common to all classrooms was emphasis on subject matter. In both Minnesota and New Zealand, the knowledge, skills, and attitudes associated with content were given primary emphasis. The particular categories used for observation tended to ignore this primary emphasis and to concentrate, instead, on the management skills of the teacher. The way the teacher encouraged or restricted student participation was isolated for special attention by the very nature of the categories. The fact that these management skills can be shown to be related to subject-matter achievement indicates their importance to classroom learning even though they are not emphasized in classroom discourse.

The differences noted between the high and low scoring classrooms in Minnesota and New Zealand made possible the development of a set of hypotheses about teacher influence and student attitudes related to learning.

HYPOTHESIS 1. Restricting student freedom of participation early in the cycle of classroom learning activities increases dependence and decreases achievement.

HYPOTHESIS 2. Restricting student freedom of participation later in the cycle of classroom learning activities does not increase dependence but does increase achievement.

HYPOTHESIS 3. Expanding student freedom of participation early in the cycle of classroom learning activities decreases dependence and increases achievement.

Each concept used in the three hypotheses will be given an explicit theoretical meaning and the steps necessary to measure each will be outlined briefly.

Certain teacher statements inhibit student participation and others encourage it. Restrictions occur when a teacher lectures or expresses his own opinions (category 5), gives directions (category 6), gives criticism or justifies the use of his own authority (category 7). He uses these statements to exert direct control. He is directive in order to focus on a particular idea or problem, in order to achieve compliance, or in order to correct misbehavior. In doing this, he will talk more and will take a more dominant role in the classroom.

Expansion occurs when a teacher asks questions (category 4), clarifies student ideas and uses them in problem solving (category 3), praises and encourages student action (category 2), or makes constructive interpretations of student feelings or attitudes (catgeory 1). These statements express teacher authority indirectly through their support of selected patterns of student behavior. The teacher assumes a less dominant posture, and the proportion of student talk increases.

"Early and late in the cycle of classroom learning activities" refers to a sequence of events that occurs again and again in every classroom. First, an intellectual difference or problem is created. Second, the major dimensions of the problem are identified, and third, relationships within the problem are isolated. Fourth, work occurs, such as the gathering of information, the application of a formula, or the trial solution of a problem. Fifth, progress is evaluated and tested. Sixth, the new knowledge is applied to additional problems or interpreted in some meaningful way.

There are, of course, cycles within cycles. The solution of a single problem in mathematics is part of a unit of study. Both the problem and the unit follow a similar sequence, although a particular problem may involve only five minutes while a unit of study might last two weeks. In social studies, units of study for the entire class and the shorter, individual tasks illustrate these similar relationships. Observation data were obtained separately for the first two days, middle two days, and last two days of a two-week unit of study in order to make comparisons at different stages of the long cycles. Also isolated were short periods of time when new material was introduced, when homework was corrected, or when reports were given. This was done in order to make comparisons within the short cycles.

In order to understand increased or decreased dependence it is necessary, first, to understand what is meant by dependent behavior. A student who is dependent is concerned primarily with pleasing the teacher. As he works on a problem, he is more concerned about whether or not his method is what the teacher wants than he is with whether or not his method will solve the problem. Dependent behavior in a classroom is recognized when students unnecessarily check their work with the teacher to make sure they are on the right track, check their work before going on to the next step, or solicit teacher approval more often than is necessary. Sustained direct influence by a teacher results in increased compliance, and, when this is maintained over an extended period of time, patterns of dependent behavior increase.

The concept of achievement involves measurable differences in content understanding and skill in problem solving as revealed by pre- and post-achievement tests. In comparing the achievement of one class with another, adjustments were made for initial ability and knowledge of the subject matter being studied.

When classes in which achievement is high are compared with classes in which it is low, there are certain predictions that can be made as logical derivations from the hypotheses. Hypotheses 2 and 3 both predict high achievement yet require two quite different patterns of teacher influence. Taken together, more variable teacher influence in high achieving classes ought to be found. Early in a learning cycle, the teacher would use an indirect approach; later the teacher might shift to a more direct approach. This shift in influence pattern is called "flexibility of teacher influence." The sustained restriction of student participation by direct teacher influence is associated with low achievement, according to hypothesis 1; and if it is accurate, the prediction can be made that teachers in these classrooms will exhibit limited flexibility of teacher influence.

Considerable research is related to these hypotheses. H. H. Anderson and his colleagues (1939, 1945, 1946) carried out a series of projects with preschool and primary and elementary school children. This imaginative research effort has produced a series of internally consistent and significant findings. First, the dominative and integrative contacts of the teacher set a pattern of behavior that spreads throughout the classroom; the behavior of the teacher, more than that of any other individual, sets the climate of the class. The rule is that, when either type of contact predominates, domination incites further domination and integration stimulates further integration. The teacher's tendency spreads among pupils and persists even when the teacher is no longer in the room. Furthermore, the pattern a teacher develops in one year is likely to persist in his classroom the following year with completely different pupils. Second, when a teacher has a high proportion of integrative contacts, pupils show more spontaneity and initiative, voluntary social contributions, and acts of problem solving. Third, when a teacher has a high proportion of dominative contacts, the pupils are more easily distracted from school work and show more compliance to, as well as rejection of, teacher domination.

In a study by Filson (1957) direct measures of dependent acts by students were associated with different patterns of teacher influence. His study showed that during a task in which the goal is not clear, a condition similar to the early phases of learning cycles, more direct teacher influence elicited more requests for teacher approval and help during work periods even after considerable exposure to the task. The reverse was true when the teacher used an indirect pattern.

Previous research concerning the ways in which teachers modify their behavior to fit different situations and different students has been conducted by several researchers. Wispe (1951) and Smith (1955) have shown that, when college-age students are classified into different psychological types, each type has a different reaction to the same patterns of teacher influence. Gage *et al.* (1956) found that elementary school pupils' perceptions of the same teacher were different according to classification of the pupil as tending to seek "affective" or "cognitive" responses from the teacher. J. P. Anderson (1960) demonstrated that junior high school boys and girls have significantly ($p < 0.01$) different ideal expectations about teacher behavior and that students classified as "dependent-prone" tended to expect different teacher behavior than did the "independent-prone" (at the 0.05 level of significance). The girls and the dependent-prone preferred a pattern that was somewhat indirect.

In the laboratory experiment, Amidon and Flanders (1961) have shown that dependent-prone junior high school students are more sensitive than average students to differences in patterns of teacher influence and that the dependent-prone learned less geometry when exposed to a rigid, direct pattern of influence than they did with an indirect pattern. In this study, the different patterns were created by the same role-playing teacher.

Bales and Strodtbeck (1951) give support to the notion that different types of verbal communication occur naturally in adult group discussions at different states of a problem-solving cycle.

Other studies involving the classification of verbal statements by using different systems of interaction analysis have been conducted by Bales (1950), Mitzel and Rabinowitz (1953), Withall (1949), and others.

Each of the foregoing researchers has influenced the Minnesota research studies. By 1958, the following generalizations were established concerning patterns of teacher influence.

First, there is a direct relationship between teacher influence that encourages student participation and constructive pupil attitudes toward the teacher, the school work, and the class activities.

Second, different students will have different attitudes in the same classroom situation. In spite of these individual differences, the first generalization holds.

Third, when dealing with the class as a whole, all the evidence suggests a causal relationship, teacher behavior causes pupil attitudes.

Fourth, a number of different factors affect the patterns of influence teachers use. Among these are: (1) the subject matter being taught, (2) the age and maturity of the students, (3) the instructor's preferred style of teaching, and (4) the nature of the learning activities.

Fifth, all teachers employ a combination of statements, some that restrict freedom of participation and others that expand it. Given an extended period of observation, a fairly stable proportion or balance of indirect and direct statements can be identified for each teacher. This ratio, called the "I/D ratio," is positively correlated with the class average on an attitude inventory.

Teacher influence and achievement

In order to test the three hypotheses about teacher influence and achievement listed earlier, certain experimental controls were necessary. First, all teachers in each content area had access to the same instructional materials. They were provided in sufficient variety so that each teacher could use his natural style of teaching. Second, the procedure for testing achievement gain permitted the testers to adjust for initial ability and knowledge. Third, the teachers in each subject-matter area were selected from two large urban areas so that they would be representative of the wide range of teacher influence patterns found in the parent population. Fourth, a schedule was carefully worked out so that members of the research staff could administer the tests and make the necessary observations at the beginning, middle, and end of the two-week units of study. Fifth, mathematics and combined English–social studies were chosen in order to test the hypotheses under very different conditions; mathematics with its tight, logical, inductive–deductive reasoning, and social studies with less exact reasoning systems.

A choice was soon evident in designating the dependent and independent variables. High and low achieving classes could be isolated and then compared with the teachers' influence patterns, or teachers could be grouped according to their patterns of influence and then their achievement compared. If the hypotheses were valid, of course, there would be no difference in the results, but designating teacher influence as the independent variable and then predicting achievement was more consistent with the way the hypotheses were stated.

CONTROL OF THE INDEPENDENT VARIABLE. The job here was to identify the pattern of influence used by each teacher, to find out which teachers varied their proportion of direct and indirect influence within cycles of learning, and to group teachers according to the characteristics of their influence patterns. The research tool used was interaction analysis.

The first problem was to establish the reliability of the observers and maintain this reliability during the three-month data-collecting period. All observers began with twelve to eighteen hours of training before the first classroom visit. Preliminary training made use of tape recordings for which exact distributions were already known. Later, the observing team made use of one-way observation booths that permitted observers to talk out loud to one another as they classified statements in the adjoining "live" classroom. These procedures provided sufficient reliability, given intelligent graduate students who had previous counseling or teaching experience.

Once established, the maintenance of reliability required weekly discussions about unusual categorizing problems and spot-reliability checks with a fellow observer. Reliability may, of course, deteriorate unless maintained by additional training. A technical discussion of these procedures can be found in *Interaction Analysis in the Classroom: A Manual for Observers* (Flanders, 1960b, or pp. 158–166 of this volume).

An analysis of the statements of the 16 mathematics teachers and 15 social-studies teachers (one was dropped due to unusual circumstances) suggested that three groups of teachers would provide the most useful comparisons. In each subject, the teachers were classified as most indirect, average, and most direct. This division was based on a restricted proportion of indirect to direct statements, known as the i/d ratio, computed for each teacher for all hours of observation.[31] The composite distributions for the mathematics teachers are shown in Fig. 2–19, social studies in Fig. 2–20. In comparing these two histograms with Fig. 2–18, it can be seen that the differences between high and low scoring classes in New Zealand were similar to the group differences in social studies and mathematics even though there were some basic differences in the overall patterns.

Most seventh-grade social studies classrooms are quite different from eighth-grade mathematics classrooms, yet the similarities between Figs. 2–19 and 2–20

---

[31] The I/D ratio makes use of all seven teacher categories. Referring to the categories listed above, $I/D = (1 + 2 + 3 + 4)$ divided by $(5 + 6 + 7)$. The i/d ratio ignored categories 4 and 5, asking questions and lecturing, so that $i/d = (1 + 2 + 3)$ divided $(6 + 7)$. The i/d ratio is preferred in this application because it is independent of communication patterns (like drill) that are unique to subject matter.

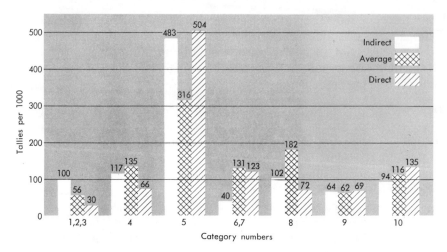

FIG. 2–19. Influence patterns of most indirect, average, and most direct mathematics teachers.

are quite remarkable. By comparing the bars above categories 1, 2, and 3, with 6 and 7, it is obvious that the i/d ratios of the three groups form a rank order that is consistent with the method of grouping the teachers. It was something of a surprise to find that the composite i/d ratio of the most indirect mathematics teachers was larger than the similar ratio for social studies teachers.

There were a number of characteristics that distinguished the most indirect teachers from the most direct in both social studies and mathematics. First, indirect teachers were more alert to, concerned with, and made greater use of statements made by students. These teachers went beyond mere clarification and acknowledgement of student ideas over periods longer than three seconds[32] occurred more frequently by a factor of 18 when the most indirect social studies teachers were compared with the most direct. For mathematics, the same factor is five.

Second, the most indirect teachers asked longer, more extended questions, and did this about four times more frequently than did the most direct teachers. Short questions usually elicited short student responses; long questions, long student responses. Ideas were dealt with in greater detail in the most indirect classrooms.

Third, the most direct teachers had more discipline problems and found it necessary to interrupt giving directions in order to criticize students three times more often than did the most indirect. The most direct teachers gave longer and more involved directions and often had to repeat directions. Stu-

---

[32] Interpretations from interaction analysis data made in this section are based on "matrix interpretation." The matrix has not been described here due to lack of space. An extended treatment of this method of tabulating and interpreting interaction data can be found in the first pages in this chapter.

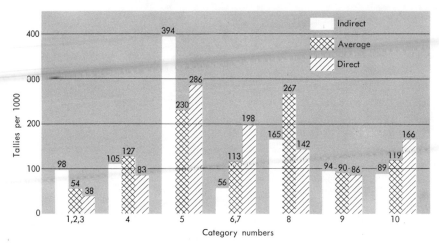

FIG. 2–20. Influence patterns of most indirect, average, and most direct social studies teachers.

dents more often tended to question or even to resist the directions given by the most direct teachers.

Some readers may conclude, at this point, that the most direct teachers in this study had the misfortune to be dealing with difficult classes at the time of the project. While it is true that some classes are more difficult than others, this did not affect research results to any great degree. In the first place, some of the most indirect teachers were assigned troublesome students as a regular policy. It was the testers' impression that sustained and rigidly employed patterns of above-average direct influence invited student resistance. This observation is supported by Anderson, Brewer, and Reed (1946). They found that teachers soon established, in the second year, the same or similar patterns observed during the first year in spite of different pupils. Anderson was observing primary classes, however; and there can be no doubt that, at older age levels, classroom interaction is the product of both teaching style and pupil reaction. The point, here, is that the teacher has the power, the experience, and the professional responsibility to establish the quality of the interaction.

The i/d ratios used to divide teachers into the most indirect, average, and most direct groups, as well as the profiles shown in Figs. 2–19 and 2–20, were based on data combined for all hours of observation. In the mathematics classes, there were six one-hour periods, and in combined English-social studies classes, six two-hour periods. However, during each classroom visit, a number of different learning activities occurred that could be clearly identified by the observer. In mathematics, these time-use categories included: (1) routine administration, such as taking roll, distributing or collecting materials, and so forth; (2) evaluation of the products of learning, such as discussion of home-work, test results, or student reports; (3) introducing new material, such as a class discussion of a new formula (or new facts about a country); (4) general

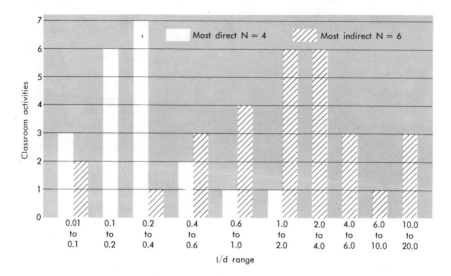

FIG. 2–21. Distribution of i/d ratios for different classroom activities in social studies.

discussion of old material or current problems; and (5) supervision of seat work, periods when students were busy doing homework or projects. The same five time-use categories were used in social studies plus a sixth not involved with mathematics, namely (6) teacher–pupil planning, or class discussions about the organization of work.

Inasmuch as the interaction analysis data were tabulated separately for each time-use category, providing it appeared, it was possible to calculate separate i/d ratios for each type of activity. Later will be shown the extent to which changes in i/d ratio across different learning activities supported the hypotheses of this study. However, a preliminary question to be asked, now, concerns the degree of variability in range of different i/d ratios when the most indirect is compared with the most direct. In Figs. 2–21 and 2–22, the frequency of different i/d ratios is shown for social studies and mathematics. Notice that the class intervals for each bar in the histogram are not equal.

All of the i/d ratios of the most direct teachers fall within the range of 0.01 to 2.0, with the majority below 0.4. For the most indirect teachers, the range for social studies is 0.01 to 18.0. For mathematics the range is 0.01 to 11.0. The majority of ratios for the most indirect fall above one. The distribution of i/d ratios for the two average groups falls midway between the two extreme groups and is not shown on the histograms.

These data neither support nor reject the three hypotheses of the study, but they do indicate that we can expect greater flexibility of teacher influence among the most indirect and less flexibility among the most direct. Clearly, the most indirect are making more dramatic shifts in their patterns of teacher influence as the classroom learning activities change from one time-use category to another.

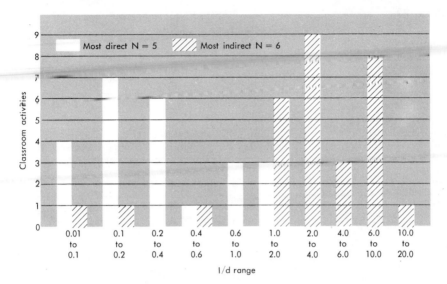

FIG. 2–22. Distribution of i/d ratios for different classroom activities in mathematics.

Results in terms of achievements

The first step in the analysis of achievement data was the making of adjustments for initial ability and differences in IQ. Adjustments were made by analysis of covariance based on pretest scores only. Since IQ was positively correlated with both pretest and posttest scores of achievement, the extra work of including IQ in the regression equation was not justified.

Next, in placing all teachers in each subject area in a rank order list according to over-all i/d ratio, it was noticed that a large break occurred between the seventh- and eighth-grade teachers in mathematics and that the social studies rank order progressed evenly. Consequently, a comparison of adjusted achievement scores was made for seven indirect versus nine direct mathematics teachers; a similar comparison was made for eight indirect and eight direct social studies teachers until one of the teachers was dropped, as indicated earlier, making a seven versus eight split. The results of these comparisons, not shown here, indicated superior achievement for the indirect classes, when compared with the direct, at a level of significance beyond 0.01.

The results of the analysis of adjusted achievement scores for the most indirect and most direct teachers are shown in Table 2–27. Achievement was significantly higher in the most indirect classes in both social studies and mathematics.

Results in terms of dependence and other attitudes

The testers were unable to develop a satisfactory system for observing spontaneous acts of dependence in the field. However, a long form of student attitude inventory was administered similar to the attitude tests used in the

Table 2–27

Adjusted Achievement Scores for the Most Indirect and Most Direct Social Studies and Mathematics Classes

| Teaching style | Mathematics | | | | Social Studies | | | |
| | Adjusted mean | Variance | N | | Adjusted mean | Variance | N | |
			Students	Teachers			Students	Teachers
Most indirect	28.9	42.3	156	6	36.4	20.4	156	6
Most direct	24.9	33.3	90	5	31.0	31.8	92	4
Critical ratio	5.00		$p < 0.01$		7.73		$p < 0.01$	

research prior to 1958. This long form contains items that indicate a student's perceptions of the teacher, the class, and the learning activities. Many items in the inventory were intended to be direct measures of independent perceptions. Additional items were keyed in a direction logically related to independence, although they dealt with the teacher, motivation, or other factors in the classroom. Thus, a high class average indicates favorable and constructive attitudes, in general, with minimum dependence on the teacher.

As with the achievement data, an analysis of attitude scores of all classes was prepared to reveal high scores ($p < 0.01$) for the indirect patterns of teaching. These differences were even more significant when the most indirect and most direct classes in social studies were analyzed separately. In mathematics, however, the degrees of difference between the most indirect and the most direct teachers were only slightly greater than for all teachers. The data on which these statements are based can be found in the U.S. Office of Education Terminal Contract Report (Flanders, 1965a).

In this field experiment, just as in the earlier studies not involving achievement, the most constructive and independent attitudes were found to be associated with the most indirect patterns of teacher influence. The relationship between these attitude measures and measures of adjusted achievement is expressed by a correlation of 0.44 for mathematics and 0.45 for social studies.

Results in terms of the major hypotheses

The theoretical considerations underlying the three hypotheses stated earlier have been developed in greater detail on the last page of Chapter One. The characteristics of the most indirect and most direct teaching patterns already have been described. It is now known that, in the indirect classrooms, students learned more and possessed more constructive and independent attitudes than in the direct. Furthermore, the indirect teachers were more flexible than the direct teachers in that they made more dramatic changes in their patterns of influence in the various time-use activity categories.

It is difficult to describe these results without leaving the impression that there *is* such a thing as an indirect teacher and a direct teacher. These labels were used to refer to the groups of teachers compared in these various research projects. It cannot be overemphasized, however, that there is no direct or indirect teacher. All teachers are either indirect or direct over only very short periods of time. Every teacher, over long periods of time, blends direct and indirect acts into some kind of balance. When all of the acts observed for a group of teachers are combined into a composite pattern, a comparison of teachers tending toward either direct or indirect teaching patterns reveals differences that total only 20 to 30% in certain crucial categories. These are shown in Fig. 2–18.

Even though the general differences between indirect and direct teaching are interesting and of practical importance to the profession, further analysis is required to support the three major hypotheses. These hypotheses predict certain consequences for pupil dependence and achievement from particular patterns of teacher influence. The rationale supporting these hypotheses involves the following logical steps.

First, the hypotheses describe shifts in teacher influence during the early and late phases of learning cycles. Therefore, these hypotheses could be tested only if some kind of shift took place over a period of time. Inflexible teaching patterns would not provide evidence one way or another.

Second, by isolating the most indirect teachers (who were shown to be more flexible) it would be possible to study the shifts these teachers made to see if they were consistent with the hypotheses. It was expected that the most direct teaching patterns, in which shifts of influence had been shown to be very small, would not support these hypothesized trends significantly (perhaps they would even make small shifts in the opposite direction).

Third, if the previous two steps proved fruitful it was then expected that learning would be significantly higher in those classrooms where theoretical predictions were supported; significantly less learning was expected in those classrooms where the hypotheses were not supported.

A comparison of the first two days, middle two days, and last two days of the two-week units of study provides evidence of changes in teacher influence patterns over the long-range cycles (Fig. 2–23).

Two histograms for social studies and two for mathematics are shown in Fig. 2–23. The percentages of total class time spent in either "expanding" or "restricting" activities are shown at the left. All situations observed that obviously permitted student freedom of action were classified as expanding. Those that obviously restricted student freedom of action were called restricting. Unless the observer's notes were clear and unequivocal, the interaction record was assigned to a neutral category for the time period coded. Situations that, typically, were classified as expanding included teacher–pupil planning with

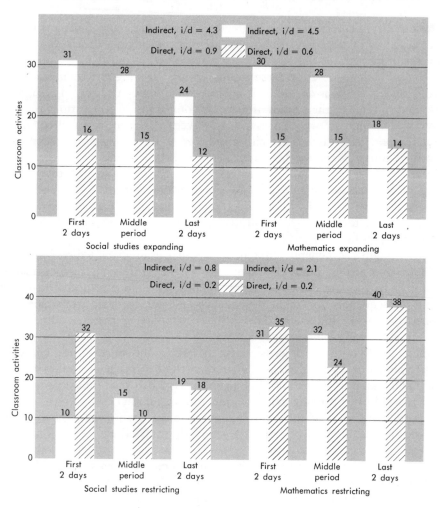

FIG. 2–23. Shifts in expanding and restricting learning activities.

high student participation, discussion designed to clarify the students' point of view, periods when the students directed their own discussion, and so on. Situations that, typically, were classified as restricting included assignment giving by the teacher, the telling of students how to do their work, and so on.

First, look at the absolute differences in height of the clear bars and the shaded bars in all four histograms of Fig. 2–23. The social studies and mathematics expanding histograms show that indirect teachers provided significantly more expanding activities at all stages of learning except for the last two days of mathematics units. In this one instance, the trend is consistent but not significant. These absolute differences are smaller for restricting activities as shown in the histograms. Here, all differences are statistically significant except for the first two days of mathematics and last two days of social studies.

The fact that expanding activities were significantly higher for the indirect teachers and restricting activities were not always consistently higher for the direct teachers confirmed results in the earlier studies. On several occasions, the differences between direct and indirect teachers did not appear in the direct aspects of the teaching–learning process but were present in the indirect aspects. This is interpreted to mean that indirect teachers can be direct, but direct teachers cannot be equally indirect.

Second, the trends predicted by the hypotheses are shown by the dash lines in each histogram. The decreasing use of expanding activities is clearly shown for the indirect teachers and is nonexistent, for all practical purposes, for the direct teachers, as shown in the histograms of expanding activities. The tendency to increase restricting activities is not only present for the indirect teachers (shown in the histograms), but the opposite trend appears to approximate better the shifts of the direct teachers.

Not only did the use of time support the hypothesized trends, but the i/d ratios, shown above each histogram, added further support. For example, expanding activities in social studies occurred more frequently and with a much more indirect pattern of teacher influence in the indirect classrooms, the direct classroom providing less time for this kind of activity, and, when it did occur, the teacher was much more direct.

Table 2–28

Median i/d Ratios for Direct and Indirect Teachers

Subject	Type	Planning	New material	Discussion	Work	Evaluation	Routine
Social Studies	Indirect	5.14	3.25	1.72	0.84	0.93	0.30
	Direct	1.3	0.23	0.51	0.03	0.20	0.17
Mathematics	Indirect	—	3.64	6.83	2.24	2.24	0.59
	Direct	—	0.72	0.21	0.15	0.25	0.14

Altogether, the four histograms support the three hypotheses. Hypotheses 1 and 2 predicted the increasing use of direct influence for increased learning and decreased dependence. This trend was followed by the indirect teachers; the opposite trend was followed by the direct teachers. Hypothesis 3 predicted indirect influence early in the cycle for increased learning and decreased dependence; these were clearly present in the indirect classrooms.

Finally, turn to cycles that occur during a single observer visit. A teacher conceivably can introduce some new material, discuss it with the class, and assign it as work, all within a period of 30 minutes or less. The dramatic changes in influence by the indirect teacher for different situations, and the smaller adjustments by the direct teachers, are shown in Table 2–28. The i/d ratios for the six different time–use categories in social studies and the five in mathematics show that indirect teachers made greater changes.

Summary and conclusions

The three major hypotheses were supported by an analysis of data from interaction analysis, attitude, and achievement scores in seventh-grade social studies and eighth-grade mathematics. Teachers who were able to provide flexible patterns of influence, by shifting from indirect to direct with the passage of time, created situations in which students learned more. The students of teachers who were unable to do this learned less.

There seemed to be four essential elements of teacher influence in the classrooms in which achievement and attitudes were superior. First, the teacher was capable of providing a range of roles, spontaneously, that varied from fairly active, dominative supervision, on the one hand, to reflective, discriminating support, on the other hand. The teacher was able not only to achieve compliance but to support and encourage student initiative. Second, the teacher was able to control his own spontaneous behavior so that he could assume one role or another at will. Third, he had sufficient understanding of principles of teacher influence to make possible a logical bridge between his diagnosis of the present situation and the various actions he could take. Fourth, he was a sensitive, objective observer who could make valid diagnoses of current conditions. All of these skills, which seemed to characterize the most successful teachers, were superimposed upon a firm grasp of the subject matter being taught.

Teachers in the studies who failed to approach these requirements appeared to be restricted to a limited number of roles producing a rigid sequence of actions. There was little variation from one classroom situation to the next. In particular, the inability to expand or restrict the freedom of action of the students through one's self-control of verbal influence seemed to characterize the unsuccessful teachers.

All of these conclusions are made from composite bits of teacher behavior for two groups of teachers. They are not conclusions based on the actions of a single teacher in an expanded case study. These generalizations also are restricted by what is best called "the limitations of current practice." Were it possible to give one year's training to a group of currently superior teachers, accentuating their awareness of influence patterns and helping them to develop even more self-control, the performance differences might be increased to become even more striking than those found in the present study.

SOME OBSERVATIONS CONCERNING THE EVALUATION OF TEACHER COMPETENCE

The research activities and conclusions presented in preceding sections of this paper involved past efforts. They summarize what happened in a series of projects concerned with the study of teacher influence; now to a contemporary interpretation of these past events.

The problems of evaluating teaching

There are those who say that teaching is an art; and certainly no one can deny that an exceptionally fine lesson has much in common with an artistic performance. Most artists would be the first to point out, however, that arduous, lengthy practice and attention to technical skill were prerequisite to a particularly fine performance. This last observation seems inconsistent with the old expression that teachers or artists are born, not made. The education and training of a teacher involves a science to the extent that there are logical relationships among what a teacher does, his own understanding of what he does, and his ability to organize these relationships into orderly principles.

Today, we are closer to a scientific understanding of teaching than ever before, and we are approaching a theory of teaching. Much more is known about teaching than a close study of current teacher preparation programs might suggest. The day is close at hand, if not already here, when prospective teachers can no longer be exposed to some facts about individual differences, some theories of learning, child growth and development, and so forth, and let the entire burden of translating this knowledge into teaching action fall on the practice-teaching experience.

In current situations, the evaluation of teaching is concerned not only with the improvement of current practices but with overcoming deficiencies in teacher preparation. In this section, some of the difficulties existing in current conditions will be dealt with briefly.

Attaining the cooperation of teachers

One problem met in both the evaluation of teaching and research on teacher influence involves the requirement of cooperation from the teachers. In this section, the procedures used for soliciting teacher cooperation will be reviewed, as they may be equally useful when teaching is evaluated.

Teachers will cooperate if they agree with the purposes of evaluation. They will resist if they mistrust these purposes. The decision to cooperate rests on *their* perceptions, not those of the administrators or researchers. The rule followed, when talking with the top administrators, the building principals, and the classroom teachers, was to approach each group as if the others did not exist. The principals knew that the project had cleared the superintendent's office, and the teachers knew that the principals had been consulted. However, it was emphasized that these clearances were for the purpose of *approaching* the next group, and that each group made its own decision to cooperate.

Stressed in meetings with administrators was the importance of creating an in-service training committee and a research steering committee (one for each project). For the in-service training project, the majority of committee members were classroom teachers; for the field experiments, there were two parents, two classroom teachers, two building principals, and two representatives of central administration. Each committee's functions were: (1) to review every paper-and-pencil test, observation technique, and experimental procedure; (2) to discuss these matters until they were understood, and then, either to endorse them or to incorporate appropriate modifications so that they could be endorsed with the committee decision being final; (3) to act as consultants to the research team, this involving research plans, implementation of plans, and possible approaches to the teachers; and (4) to act as a contact point for any teacher, pupil, parent, or administrator who became upset by the research activities.

The question each member of the committee asked himself, after reviewing research plans, was whether or not he could honestly say that he approved. It was important for the parents on the research committee to agree that their children be experimental subjects; it was necessary that the teachers be willing to participate, or to have their classes participate if asked; that the principals be willing to have the project in their schools; and it was important that the central office representatives approve from a system-wide point of view.

The steering committees were formed *before* talks with building principals and classroom teachers, in fact, the committees helped to plan these talks. In order to develop the field experiments, the author and associates met first with teachers in small groups of 15 to 25 at convenient, nearby schools. At most of these meetings, about one half of the teachers were willing to participate after listening to the explanation. A higher percentage required additional discussion. The lowest percentage of volunteers occurred at one meeting during which they questioned closely about whether or not this research was likely to be a first step toward merit pay evaluations.

The in-service training project was first described at two school-wide meetings. Next, all teachers were provided with a written brochure giving more detailed information. The day before teachers were to volunteer, a member of the research staff was available all day in the teachers' common room for private question-and-answer sessions. Many questions seemed to be directed only toward becoming better acquainted; but considerable concern was expressed about the purposes of the project, safeguards to prevent data from reaching the hands of administrators, and the amount of time the project would take. Even these informal contacts were not enough, however, to establish trust and cooperation among all interested teachers.

One incident sensitized the research team to the need for additional informal and private channels of communication. A teacher called a member of the in-service steering committee to indicate that the volunteer aspect of the participation did not exist. Those who did not volunteer automatically would be identified, and the administration would then classify them as not interested in professional development. This was discussed until the following solution was suggested. The teacher could volunteer for the in-service research project to show "professional interest," but when the hours for meetings were announced, he then could ask to be excused because of "a conflict of time caused by previous commitments." By means of expressions of disappointment, he could avoid being classified as not interested in professional growth. This alternative was sent back along the same informal channel of communication, and, when other teachers heard about it, the acceptance of the project probably was increased.

The following conclusions were reached: (1) the study of teacher behavior is acceptable to about one-half of the teachers, the rest require special approaches; (2) physical access can be provided by administrators, but genuine psychological access can come only from the teachers (for example, full access is not present when a teacher pretends something for an observer's benefit); (3) teacher control is provided by approval and veto powers on a "steering committee"; (4) not all teachers believe explanations of purpose; they require personal and private conversations during which they can speak freely; (5) a teacher is in the best position to solicit another teacher's cooperation; (6) the reduction of fear, suspicion, and skepticism occurs with frank and forthright communication among all concerned.

These observations probably apply, to some extent, to any program aimed at the evaluation of teaching.

Evaluation of teaching in order to improve instruction

In the final analysis, all evaluation of teaching has the ultimate purpose of improving instruction. A merit pay system seeks to do this by a special, formalized system of monetary and prestige rewards. In the in-service training program, rewards were individually created and recognized. Most of the teachers learned more about themselves, about their classroom behavior, and about their students' reactions. This was rewarding in itself. More than one half of the participating teachers were able to use this information to make changes in their classroom behavior; this, too, was rewarding. This project is believed to be the first attempt in education to judge the effectiveness of in-service training through a systematic analysis of spontaneous teacher behavior in the classroom. Heretofore, shifts in attitude, knowledge of teaching methods, or intentions (all measured by paper-and-pencil instruments) were used as evidence of progress before and after training. Just how much attitude change was translated into action was usually never known.

The approach began with the observation that most teachers have already established values in educational philosophy. These are not necessarily related to their behavior. Attempting to change these values is not the most direct approach to changing behavior. Qualified teachers have passed examinations that test their judgment of what "ought to be done in the name of good teaching"; they are very good at identifying democratic values. They have developed diagnostic skills at the paper-and-pencil test level and perform effectively at this level. However, the real issue is the relationship between the teacher's intent and his action. This issue was stressed in these studies by asking two questions: "What do you want to accomplish?" and "What did you do in order to achieve these ends?"

The most effective changes in method of instruction occur when a teacher can compare what he wanted to accomplish with a nonthreatening, objective summarization of his spontaneous behavior. Using proper procedures, the teacher can make his own discoveries and reach his own conclusions about what changes would reduce any discrepancy between intent and action.

These observations have suggested a few principles found helpful in the design of in-service training. First, do not consult with a teacher after a single visit because the teacher will initiate a series of defensive questions designed to obtain value judgments from the observer (for example, "What did *you* think of the lesson?"). Always schedule consultations after two or more visits so that comparisons can be made between different class sessions (for example, "Why was there more student participation in the first-period class?").

Second, the evidence and the criteria to be applied to evidence must be available equally to consultant and teacher. This means that all data-gathering procedures must be understood by the teacher. In the case of interaction analysis, teachers should have some experience as observers before being observed themselves. It means also that the data to be used in a particular consultation should be available to the teacher before the interview with a consultant. The teacher will need time to study the material in order to organize his own reactions.

The data to be collected for a consultation should be determined in advance by questions asked by the teacher. Questions to determine if something was good or bad and if certain changes ought to take place are poor questions at early stages. Questions should focus on what happened and how one situation differs from another.

Third, the major purpose of evaluating instruction is to create a sense of inquiry and experimentation in which one variable is a change in the teacher's behavior. A sample is to: (1) speculate about what might happen if the teacher acted first one way and then another in two somewhat similar situations, (2) try the variations with adequate data collection, and (3) analyze the results. With the right atmosphere, pairs or trios of teachers soon form teams and become more independent of consultant help.

The development of a sense of inquiry that includes experimentation with one's own behavior is the most important product of in-service training activities. Yet this emerges slowly as a characteristic of a school program. There are many restraints and inhibitions within a faculty to block the development of a sense of inquiry. Often, the teachers who could benefit most find it very difficult to experiment with their own behavior.

Fourth, creative tools for gathering a wide range of data are necessary to accommodate the range of questions teachers are prepared to ask. Teachers often ask two kinds of questions about pupil reactions and attitudes. The first has to do with long-range attitudes, such as those measured by attitude inventories. Second, they often like to collect opinions about a single lesson, a unit of study, or even a particular incident. Questions about teacher behavior were encouraged in our in-service training project, and they required complex systems of observation, such as interaction analysis.

There is no limit to the ways that data can be collected. One art teacher rated art products according to the degree to which the pupil copied an example executed by the teacher. This was done as a measure of pupil dependence on teacher influence. A mathematics teacher designed a "standardized" problem-solving experience for small groups of pupils as a measure of transfer from textbook problems to unique and unusual problems. Each teacher operates at his own level of sophistication in measurement, and this level changes with experience and training.

Evaluating teaching in order to classify teachers

Any system of merit pay, or other means of giving special recognition to individual teachers, must solve the problems associated with "single case decisions." These problems can be illustrated as follows.

A counselor collects test information about a single student to produce a profile of aptitudes and interests. Studies indicate that 80 out of 100 students with scores similar to those of the student succeed in the field of medicine. The crucial issue in making a recommendation involves determining if this particular student will be among the 20 who will fail or the 80 who will succeed.

The second illustration involves the assignment of grades by a classroom teacher. Suppose a teacher were blessed with achievement tests that were perfectly reliable and valid. Furthermore, the tests adequately sampled the major content objectives of learning. The test scores would then be valid indexes of each student's achievement, a condition that is approached only in practical situations. The fact is that even though a teacher can "scale" individual achievement accurately, he still faces an arbitrary, politico-social decision as soon as he assigns a grade. By what system of reasoning is one level of performance a failure, another set aside as an "A"?

These two problems are present in any system of classifying teacher performance. There will always be the question of whether or not the decision taken in a single case is the right one. Similarly, there will always be philosophical issues present in the use of evaluation data to classify teachers into categories of ability, and these will have personal consequences for the teacher and the school system.

Each person reading this material will have his own opinions about these problems, but there are some fairly objective observations that should be made.

First, in the studies of teacher influence, it was found that those teachers whose students had less constructive attitudes and who learned less than others were much more alike, as a group, than were the teachers classified as superior. It is easier to identify poor teaching than it is to identify superior teaching. The characteristics of the former are more consistent than the latter.

Second, the research on teacher influence compared groups of teachers, and the conclusions reached were based on comparisons of two hypothetical composite teachers whose acts of influence were, in fact, all the acts of several similar teachers. None of the comparisons were based on a single case. In addition, data were collected in situations that were carefully constructed in order to make them as similar as possible. It is interesting to note here that some of the correlations between interaction analysis data and scores of pupil attitudes collected in the heterogeneous classrooms of the in-service training project were lower than those collected in field experiments. That is, the interaction analysis data in a girls' physical education class are drastically different from those in a science class, which are, in turn, different from general shop.

One additional incident may be mentioned. While studying teacher influence patterns in New Zealand, it was possible to identify a rank order of ten teachers, based first on the attitude scores of the pupils, and second, on interaction analysis data that distinguished the top five from the bottom five in a fashion consistent with theories about teacher influence. Just before the author left New Zealand, the ratings that school inspectors had given to these teachers over the past few years became available. School inspectors in New Zealand give teachers a rating along a single scale of teaching effectiveness. This affects promotion and determines who receives desirable positions when they are open. The relationship between these ratings and the research data was quite low. Two out of five of the top teachers had received below-average ratings. Three out of five of the bottom teachers had received average or above-average ratings. An inspector normally visits a teacher for a half day and then writes a report based on a check list of classroom characteristics. The two systems produced contradictory results.

Third, the last issue in classification to be mentioned concerns the consequences of making an error. Before a surgeon will agree to a serious operation, he insists on evidence that is sufficiently conclusive to justify the risk. Standards nevertheless vary among surgeons. The same can be said about courts of law that must judge a man insane or guilty of some crime. Educators who choose to classify teachers according to their teaching ability must resolve issues inherent in the following questions: How large is the error of classification? What are the consequences of making a mistake? Will the entire process achieve the original goals of the evaluation program?

Finally, one finding from the in-service training project runs contrary to the thinking of some researchers who study the traits of teachers as an approach to evaluation of teaching. Storlie (pp. 262–270 of this volume) found that changes in classroom behavior resulting from in-service training, as measured by interaction analysis, were not correlated with eight different personality measures. These measures were selected as the most promising from Cattell's 16-factor personality tests, the eight scales in the Runner Questionnaire, and the Minnesota Teacher Attitude Inventory, a total of 25 scales. He concluded that the measures of personality he investigated did not help to predict which teachers would benefit most from in-service training. Another study (Davies, 1961) indicated that relationships between personality measures and pattern of influence, before in-service training, are sufficiently obscure so that an analysis of variance produced nonsignificant results. Perhaps a more sensitive analysis, such as the Johnson-Neiman technique used by Bowers and Soar (1961), may be more useful. Davies concluded, however, that so many factors influence the teacher's behavior that measures of teacher personality account for very little of the variance.

A point of view

We live in a society in which genuine, helpful evaluation is quite uncommon. Notice how uncomfortable we feel when someone pays us a compliment and how defensively we respond to almost any kind of criticism. As a group, teachers are isolated from systematic information about their own behavior. However, research indicates that teaching performance depends upon the range of behavior a teacher can produce, the self-control required to provide particular patterns of influence, a teacher's sensitivity in diagnosing the requirements of the moment, and his ability to predict the consequences of alternative actions.

The scientific study of teaching is so immature that, at this time, a particular pattern of teaching cannot be advocated as the most successful. Considerable improvement probably can be brought about by any program that provides reasonably intelligent teachers of average emotional adjustment with systematic information about their classroom behavior. If the information at hand increases, teachers will make modifications that can be tested, and, if satisfactory, adopted as improvements.

THE TEACHERS' BILL OF RIGHTS. First, each teacher needs the freedom to develop his own unique cycle of teaching. While teachers of the same subject matter and age level will often have much in common, there will always be unique differences as products of teacher-pupil interaction. No one can squeeze all teachers into the same mold.

Second, only the teacher himself can change his methods of teaching. Teachers can be told how to teach; they even can be ordered to teach in a particular manner; but stable changes in patterns of teacher influence, changes that result in improvements, are self-motivated. Surveillance is somewhat impractical. Only the changes that make sense to the teacher are maintained. A supervisor who helps a teacher to discover some better method for himself is of real help.

Third, helping a teacher to change his methods of teaching involves emotional as well as intellectual problems. Awareness of new material, access to new instructional resources, development of a new idea are all important in making changes. However, readiness for change must be considered as well as the fact that trying out new methods arouses emotional reactions in most teachers. Reactions that lead to constructive and positive viewpoints are essential for stable innovations. Reactions that are less than positive must be recognized, analyzed, and tested in situations free of threat if a realistic approach to innovation is to be taken.

Fourth, efforts toward change require social support, as well as intellectual stimulation, from one's peers. Two or three like-minded teachers, who have developed a sense of experimentation in their approach to teaching, may form a highly stable unit of change.

Taken all together, these four points suggest that any program for the improvement of teaching must be a voluntary, teacher-directed enterprise. Coercion and administrative fiats are not likely to succeed. Pressures for change can be generated in voluntary peer association, but compliance alone is not likely to lead to stable innovation.

THE NONTEACHERS' BILL OF RIGHTS. Nonteachers include supervisors, administrators, members of school boards, and the general public.

First, the long-established right of privacy within the four walls of the classroom cannot be used indiscriminately as a shield of academic freedom to block all possible approaches to change. Improvement of instruction takes place in the classroom, if it is to occur at all; and evidence of change must be available to all members of an improvement team, teacher and nonteacher alike.

Second, the fact that teaching is a complex social process, hard to define and evaluate, does not mean that all evidence is useless simply because it is incomplete. The tools and techniques for establishing criteria of teaching effectiveness are crude, but they can be improved only by further experimentation and development.

Third, nonteachers have a right to expect the teaching profession to take an active part in the development of successful methods for evaluating teaching effectiveness. The mark of a true professional is an active concern for developing criteria for professional effectiveness.

11

PUPIL NEEDS
AND TEACHER–PUPIL RELATIONSHIPS:
EXPERIENCE NEEDED
FOR COMPREHENDING READING[33]

ROBERT S. SOAR

INTRODUCTION

On a purely subjective basis, I think most of us would agree that the kind or the quality of the teacher–pupil relationships which exist in the classroom ought to make a difference in the rate at which children learn to read, or learn any subject, for that matter. This general topic has an important place in the writing of educational theorists, and a modest amount of research on the relationship of these aspects of the classroom to learning in general has been carried out. However, there has been a striking scarcity of research on teacher–pupil relationships and the development of reading skills. Rather, concern seems to have been devoted much more extensively to such questions as grouping, materials, procedures for building vocabulary, perceptual processes and specific teaching techniques. Perhaps the time is ripe for examination of some of these intangible influences.

There are a few studies which suggest that the kind of atmosphere which exists in the classroom is important in the teaching of reading. Among the most relevant studies, Delacato and Delacato (1952) found that a permissive group environment produced growth in reading skills, as well as more favorable attitudes, with a group of eleven boys referred for remediation. More recently, Perkins (1965), in a study of under-achievement with high-ability fifth graders, found that teacher lecturing and criticizing was related to loss in reading comprehension scores on the *California Achievement Test*. As he

---

[33] Paper read at the annual meeting of the International Reading Association, Detroit, Michigan, May 1965. Reprinted by permission of the author.

hypothesized, the factor of teacher lecturing and criticizing was also related to pupil withdrawal and inattention, as well as losses for certain subgroups in other academic areas, but gain in reading vocabulary. In contrast, Medley and Mitzel (1959) found only a slight relationship between growth in reading and Emotional Climate as measured by the *Observation Schedule and Record*.

Support for the idea that classroom atmosphere makes a difference in other kinds of learning comes from a study of Amidon and Flanders (1961) with geometry classes. They found that more "dependent-prone" pupils differed in how much they learned under different modes of teacher control behavior, whereas less "dependent-prone" pupils showed little change as a consequence of differences in teacher methods.

Again, McKeachie (1963), in reviewing research on college teaching concluded: ". . . the choice of instructor-dominated versus student-centered discussion techniques appears to depend upon one's goals. The more highly one values outcomes going beyond acquisition of knowledge, the more likely that student-centered methods will be preferred." (p. 1140)

These studies all point to the importance of classroom atmosphere broadly conceived as important in determining how much learning takes place. The way atmosphere is defined differs from study to study: in the Delacato and Delacato study the "permissive" environment appeared to involve both organization and control and emotional climate; in the Perkins study, "criticism" and "teacher lecturing" seem to involve both; Amidon and Flanders' "indirect" involved aspects of emotional climate, although control was more central; and McKeachie's summary seemed to involve primarily teacher control.

An integrating concept which may be useful in understanding the relations between the atmosphere of the classroom and the learning achieved may be found in work of Castaneda, Palermo, and McCandless (1956). They showed that children who were identified as high in anxiety level differed from children identified as low in anxiety level in their responses to two laboratory learning tasks. The high-anxious groups learned easy tasks more rapidly than the low-anxious, but the low-anxious learned difficult tasks more rapidly than the high-anxious. Runkel (1959) in a review of this area, concluded that the results of numbers of studies were clear in indicating the interaction of anxiety is higher for simple tasks than for complex, but that all tasks showed decrement with higher levels of anxiety. The conclusion from these studies appears to be that the more complex the learning task, the lower the level of anxiety that will interfere with it.

Support for the idea that anxiety can influence classroom learning has come rather indirectly from the work by Torrance (1962) on creativity. During the course of his analysis he found that children generally showed an actual decrease in creativity scores during the fourth grade, the "fourth-grade slump," which required on the average two years to make up. Torrance's explanation for this, based on interviews with students from different grade levels, and the developmental stages of the pupils, was that the transition to the fourth grade induced stresses on the pupils which had not existed before. This came about as a consequence of changes in classroom organization, and implicitly, their relationships with each other and the teacher. Whereas formerly they had commonly worked in small groups in informal furniture arrangements, beginning with the fourth grade they were expected to sit in rows, to be more adult in their behavior, and to be more organized and formal. They started doing homework, their papers were expected to be neat, without smudges, and they began having lessons in separate subject matters.

Although this finding may seem little related to learning in general and the development of reading skills in particular, the relevance of creative processes for reading have been pointed up by several writers. Russell and Fea (1963) suggest that the higher levels of reading may in themselves be creative, and that the reader "creates" from the ideas presented on the printed page. "Creative reading thus goes beyond literal comprehension of ideas explicitly stated by the author to 'reading between the lines' or to an individual, uncopied, novel response to the material." (p. 903)

Berg (1963) extended the idea of the relation of creativity to high level reading:

Creativity must be a part of the whole reading process, helping to set goals for the reading selection, continuing the direction of goal seeking during the reading, and acting as the integrative and constructive force after the reading is completed.

In some types of reading, modern poetry as a case in point, creativity is an absolute necessity. Yet, even here, we too often ask our students concrete questions only as if through these the true meaning could be elicited. I am of the opinion that the reason many persons do not like literary works is because the writer has given them only the building materials with which to work. The reader, never having been taught to build with words, does not know what to do with them if they do not present a highly concrete experience.

It seems reasonable to expect that the development of complex reading skills should be related to the development of creative processes, and therefore, should be influenced by the same environmental factors. Further, as a complex learning experience, it should be affected by stress or anxiety as the studies on anxiety and learning showed.

These researchers, all from the educational areas, suggest that the environment in the classroom is important in determining the ease with which different kinds of learning take place, but that the relationship is not simple.

There is the suggestion implied in these descriptions of classroom atmosphere that it has at least two aspects—the degree of control exercised by the teacher, and the degree of warmth or supportiveness of the emotional climate. Support for the existence of these two dimensions has emerged from factor analytic study of small group effectiveness, in which two factors were found which sound very much like these. Since our dimensions may not be identical to the small group factors, however, we shall identify them as "climate" and "control."

PROBLEM

This research, then, is a study of the development of vocabulary and reading skills in elementary pupils, in relation to the climate and control existing in the classroom. We hypothesize that reading and vocabulary, as complex learning, will be hampered by stress in the classroom, and that stress will be created both by direct teacher control, and by a negative emotional climate.

PROCEDURE

The general procedure was one in which the Vocabulary and Reading subtests of the *Iowa Tests of Basic Skills* were administered in the fall and spring in 56 elementary classrooms, grades three through six. During the year, teacher–pupil behavior in these classrooms was observed using two observation schedules, the *Interaction Analysis* (Amidon and Flanders, 1963) and another schedule made up of items from several revisions of the *Observation Schedule and Record* (Medley and Mitzel, 1958 and private communication) and the *Hostility-Affection Schedule* (Fowler, 1962).

The two dimensions of classroom behavior were taken from the results of the observation schedules on the basis of a factor analysis. The dimension of control behavior was measured by the revised i/d ratio for rows 8 and 9 of the *Interaction Analysis*. This is a ratio made up of teacher behaviors which occur immediately after a pupil stops talking. If the teacher praises or encourages, accepts feeling, or accepts or uses a student idea, these are identified as indirect, that is, they have the effect of expanding pupil freedom; but if the teacher criticizes, justifies his authority, or gives directions, this is classified as direct teacher behavior, and tends to limit pupil freedom. The measure used was a ratio of indirect to direct teacher behavior, so that a high score reflects more pupil freedom; a low score, more teacher control.

The clearest dimension of emotional climate which emerged from the analysis was made up of expressions of hostility, criticism, or negative feelings. These were counts of verbal and nonverbal pupil expressions of hostility, such as teasing, threatening, blaming, hitting, taking another's property, etc., and counts of hostile verbal teacher behavior, such as humiliating, threatening, and reproving comments, blaming a child, etc. The higher the score, the higher the incidence of critical or hostile comments or behaviors in the classroom.

Using these two dimensions of control and climate, four classrooms were then selected for study from each grade level, representing the extreme combinations of conditions: that is, direct control, high hostility; direct control, low hostility; indirect control, high hostility; and indirect control, low hostility.

The score of each child representing growth from fall to spring was adjusted statistically to minimize differences between children in ability to learn, so that the effects of the classroom could be seen more clearly. Differences in rates of growth from classroom to classroom attributable to emotional climate and control were then tested for significance.

Table 2–29

Analysis of Variance for Vocabulary Growth Scores*
for 16 Elementary Classrooms

Source	df	MS	F
A Hostility	1	167.17	10.22**
B Control	1	131.08	8.01**
C Grade	3	107.57	6.57**
A × B	1	105.20	6.43†
C × B	3	65.97	4.03**
A × C	3	16.22	0.99
A × B × C	3	72.53	4.43**
Error	417	16.36	
Total	432		

* In months, adjusted for regression effects and initial
standing.
† $p < 0.05$
** $p < 0.01$

Table 2–30

Vocabulary Growth* by Grade Level, Emotional Climate, and Teacher Control

		Grade level				
		3	4	5	6	Total
Hostility	High	6.58	5.78	7.91	7.24	6.87
	Low	7.73	6.51	8.80	9.40	8.22
	Total	7.17	6.10	8.38	8.39	7.55
Teacher	Direct	6.35	5.59	6.84	8.57	6.92
Control	Indirect	7.73	6.69	9.78	8.15	8.18
	Total	7.17	6.10	8.38	8.39	7.55

		Teacher control		
		Direct	Indirect	Total
Hostility	High	5.80	7.97	6.87
	Low	8.06	8.37	8.22
	Total	6.92	8.18	7.55

* In months, adjusted for regression effects and initial standing.

RESULTS AND DISCUSSION

The results for growth in vocabulary were as hypothesized (Tables 2–29 and
2–30). Indirect teaching produced greater growth than direct, classrooms in
which there was greater expression of hostility produced less learning than
those with warmer emotional climate, and the combination of indirect teaching
and low hostility produced the greatest gain of all. Grade level was also a

Table 2–31

Analysis of Variance for Reading Growth Scores*
for 16 Elementary Classrooms

Source	df	MS	F
A Hostility	1	36.72	0.86
B Control	1	183.28	4.32†
C Grade	3	29.57	0.70
A × B	1	1732.21	40.81**
B × C	3	29.04	0.68
A × C	3	70.44	1.66
A × B × C	3	121.11	2.85†
Error	417	42.45	
Total	432		

* In months, adjusted for regression effects and initial
standing.
† $p < 0.05$
** $p < 0.01$

significant factor in the development of vocabulary, with less growth in the
fourth grade than in any other. This is reminiscent of the "fourth grade
slump" in creativity mentioned earlier.

The results for reading were not clear cut, however, and present some
problems in interpretation (Tables 2–31 and 2–32). Differences in emotional
climate did not produce differences in reading growth, nor were there differences from grade to grade. Consistent with the findings for vocabulary, however, indirect teaching produced greater growth than direct.

Surprisingly, the greatest differences occurred under the joint influence
of climate and control; with indirect, high-hostile classroom producing greatest
growth, and direct, high-hostile the least growth. This does not square with
the hypothesis that both indirect teaching and a supportive emotional climate
should produce greater learning.

Yet a tentative *post hoc* reconciliation of the results can be formulated,
although it, like all *post hoc* explanations, is only a further hypothesis. There
are two problems to deal with, why the results for reading and vocabulary
differ, and why presumed less-than-optimal combinations of conditions produced most growth in reading. If, however, we refer to the principle of
simpler learning being facilitated by moderate levels of tension which hinder
more complex learning, as the studies on anxiety indicate, we would be led
to infer that the learning of reading, as measured here, is a less abstract function than learning vocabulary. This is a difficult assumption to accept, and
yet examination of the two tests makes this seem plausible; the vocabulary
items seem to deal often with abstractions (very few of the words are nouns,
for example) whereas the reading items appear to deal with relatively concrete ideas. If this assumption is accepted, then the interpretation would follow
that the reading skills tested were enough less abstract that they were facili-

Table 2–32

Reading Growth* by Grade Level, Emotional Climate, and Teacher Control

		Grade level				
		3	4	5	6	Total
Hostility	High	5.21	6.46	5.38	6.51	5.91
	Low	5.31	4.13	5.28	5.69	5.15
	Total	5.26	5.42	5.32	6.07	5.52
Teacher control	Direct	4.25	4.66	4.35	6.20	4.94
	Indirect	5.95	6.29	6.21	5.92	6.09
	Total	5.26	5.42	5.32	6.07	5.52

		Teacher control		
		Direct	Indirect	Total
Hostility	High	3.39	8.50	5.91
	Low	6.52	3.88	5.14
	Total	4.94	6.09	5.52

* In months, adjusted for regression effects and initial standing.

tated by a somewhat higher level of tension than was vocabulary. Related to this interpretation is the feeling of observers that these were schools, as a group, which were warmer and more supportive than many. By this hypothesis, if either the schools had been less supportive on the average (more tension producing), or if the test had measured more abstract reading functions, the results might have been as predicted.

I would like to propose another distinction which may be related to the differences, the idea of "inner-directed" vs. "teacher-directed" learning. Our field staff supervisor agrees that vocabulary was not so directly taught in these classrooms as reading, supporting the idea of more "inner-directed" learning.

Perhaps this kind of "inner-directed" learning is more easily influenced by both the climate and control aspects of the classroom, and an indirect, low-hostile classroom may create in the children a greater eagerness or desire to learn on their own. In contrast, the reading skills measured here may be ones which can be more directly teacher taught, and teacher influence replaced pupil "inner-direction."

Perhaps there is a further question, that of whether more complex, more abstract, higher-level kinds of learning are not of necessity more "inner-directed," rather than "outer" or "teacher-directed." It may be that the learning which involves the child's own motivation and interest is the learning which is most affected by the nature of the classroom.

Perhaps this interpretation offers a pointing finger toward resolving some of the disagreements in past research. If more teacher-directed learning is facilitated by tension levels which hamper more abstract or "inner-directed" learning, then the same task studied in classrooms which differ in tension level will produce different results; and if tasks which differ in abstractness are compared, the results may well be reversed from classroom to classroom, depending on tension level.

I would like to repeat my introductory sentence. On a purely subjective basis, I think that most of us would agree that the kind or the quality of the teacher–pupil relationships which exist in the classroom ought to make a difference in the rate at which children learn to read.

I still feel this way, but these results make clearer the enormous complexity of the classroom and difficulties involved in assessing factors related to growth in reading. They suggest that the most effective learning depends upon the tension the child feels, the emotional climate, and the teacher control present in the classroom, and that the optimum of each of these will differ with abstractness of the learning task. The issue would then become one of priority of objectives, and the decision would have to be made as to which are valued most.

This research, as some others, has examined how much a pupil has learned; few have examined how long he remembers what he has learned; and few are concerned with how he feels about what he has learned. Does he leave school in June with the glee of an escaped prisoner, or does he leave school reluctantly, to spend the summer with books from the library?

Clearly, the results of the researcher have not yet made easier the classroom teacher's job; but there is some support for the idea that if abstract, inner-directed learning is valued, it will be achieved best by indirect teaching and a supportive emotional climate.

chapter three

THE APPLICATION OF
INTERACTION ANALYSIS
TO PROBLEMS OF TEACHER EDUCATION

CHAPTER OVERVIEW

Those who have worked in a supervisory relationship with either student teachers or in-service teachers are aware of the difficulties involved in helping teachers become aware of and improve their teaching. For a teacher to improve his teaching three factors should probably be present: (a) the teacher should want to improve, (b) the teacher should have a model of the kind of teaching behavior that he wants to develop and (c) the teacher should get feedback regarding his progress toward the development of those teaching behaviors which he has conceptualized as his goal. Research on the training of teachers that has involved the use of interaction analysis has indicated that the second and third conditions necessary for change mentioned above are produced by interaction analysis. Not only do the category system and the matrix help teachers conceptualize the often abstract and nebulous phenomenon of patterns of verbal interaction, but in addition, when used as an observational system, interaction analysis provides the teacher with a means for receiving immediate feedback regarding his verbal teaching behavior.

Chapter One of this book dealt with the theory of social–emotional climate and its effects on student learning and behavior. Chapter Two dealt with a description of and explication of the system of interaction analysis and the empirical validation of the theory. This chapter contains thirteen papers each of which deals with the task of translating theory into practice. This chapter is devoted to the problem of the in-service and pre-service training of teachers, the purpose of which is the modification or shaping of flexible and effective patterns of verbal teaching behavior. Several of the papers in this chapter deal with the topic of helping teachers conceptualize models of verbal teaching behavior, while others discuss the concept of feedback and its use in teacher training. Most of the papers in this chapter, however, are reports of research studies which have been designed to measure the effects of training in interaction analysis on the verbal behavior of both in-service and pre-service teachers.

In the first paper in this chapter Ned Flanders discusses some problems of in-service training and describes several in-service training projects and the effect of such projects on the verbal behavior of in-service teachers. The second paper, by Theodore Storlie, reports in detail the findings from one of the projects discussed by Flanders. These two papers not only point up the importance of feedback, but in addition suggest that the nature of the verbal behavior (direct or indirect) used by the leader who had instructional responsibility for the in-service project was related to change in teacher verbal behavior.

The third paper, by Gertrude Moskowitz, reports a study that combined aspects of both in-service and pre-service training. In this case the in-service teachers were the student teaching supervisors of pre-service teachers. This paper sharply points up the importance of feedback and reports the effects of four different combinations of training patterns involving student teachers and their cooperating teachers. One of the more provocative findings from this study deals with the relationships between cooperating teachers and their student teachers when only the student teachers were trained in interaction analysis. The implications of this study for the concomitant in-service training of both student teachers and cooperating teachers are indeed profound.

In the fourth paper in this chapter Ned Flanders turns to a discussion of the problems of giving pre-service teachers feedback regarding their teaching intentions, and provides a rationale for an interpretation of the results of a number of the research articles that follow. Of particular importance in this paper is a delineation of the conditions that should be present, and by implication the conditions that should be avoided, in the post-observational feedback conference.

The next six papers are reports of research projects dealing exclusively with training of pre-service teachers in the skill and techniques of interaction analysis. Taken together these six studies represent an almost unprecedented occurrence in the field of teacher education; namely, consistent, replicated support for the effectiveness of a training technique used in the pre-service training of teachers. In each of these studies the criterion measure was the attitudes and/or the behavioral performance of pre-service teachers.

Though in one sense these six studies represent a consistent set of replications, each of the studies has a unique dimension. The study by Richard Zahn, for example, was designed to study the interactive effect of training in interaction analysis and the attitude change of open and closed student teachers. In this study, the effect of the openness or closedness of the belief–disbelief system of the student teacher was shown to be related to attiude change during student teaching, as was training in interaction analysis.

The study by Jeffery Kirk was the first involving pre-service, elementary teachers in which a body of interaction analysis data regarding the actual verbal behavior of student teachers was used as a dependent variable. Kirk reports data to suggest that training in interaction analysis did have an effect on the verbal behavior of teachers in his study.

The next study, by John Hough and Edmund Amidon, is included primarily because it was the first study in which interaction analysis was used as a training technique for pre-service teachers. In this case the teachers were secondary school teachers and the dependent variable of performance during student teaching was measured by student teaching supervisors using conventional rating scales rather than interaction analysis data gathered during the student teaching experience. One reason why no interaction analysis data were gathered by student teaching supervisors in this study was that at the time that this study was conducted in 1963, none of the student teaching supervisors had been trained in the use of interaction analysis. In the relatively few years since 1963 many supervisors at the university at which this research was conducted have been trained. This historical note is included to highlight the importance of training of college supervisors or cooperating teachers before interaction analysis can be used as a research technique.

An example of how the training of student teaching supervisors in inter-action analysis has had profound change on the measurement of the dependent variables of verbal behavior is illustrated in the paper by Norma Furst. One year following the conclusion of the study by Hough and Amidon, Mrs. Furst, one of the supervisors in the Hough and Amidon study, conducted a study of her own using interaction analysis data on student teachers as a dependent variable. In addition to testing the effect of training in interaction analysis on the verbal behavior of student teachers, she was the first researcher to study the effect of training in interaction analysis preceding student teaching. In all previous studies, the training of student teachers in interaction analysis had been done concurrently with student teaching.

The paper by John Hough and Richard Ober represents another example of research in which interaction analysis was taught to pre-service teachers in a general methods course prior to student teaching. In this study, the de-pendent variable of verbal teaching behavior was measured under simulated conditions of teaching at the conclusion of the general methods course.

The sixth paper in this group of studies of pre-service teacher education is an extension of the study by Hough and Ober. In this study Ernest Lohman, Richard Ober, and John Hough followed a representative sample of students from the Hough and Ober study into their student teaching to determine if the differences between the teaching behavior of those pre-service teachers trained in interaction analysis and those not so trained during a general meth-ods course preceding student teaching would persist four to twelve months later during their student teaching.

In the next two papers in this chapter Ned Flanders and John Hough present discussions conceptualizing verbal teaching behavior. In the eleventh paper Flanders presents a number of models of teacher behavior based on in-structional principles and represented on the interaction analysis matrix. In the twelfth paper, Hough discusses the relationships of reinforcement theory to patterns of teacher verbal behavior, and suggests some principles of teaching based on reinforcement theory, as described in the verbal behavior of teachers as represented in the interaction analysis matrix.

In the final paper in the book, Edmund Amidon and Elizabeth Hunter present an idea for the creation of flexible, expandable category systems that can be collapsed back into the basic ten category system of Flanders. Sug-gestions for using this approach in both research and teacher education are presented. In this paper the authors create categories from concepts developed by other researchers such as Taba, Hughes, and Gallagher and Aschner. The suggested approach would allow for a preservation of the type of classroom analysis developed by Flanders but would, in addition, provide a technique for using provocative ideas developed by others who have done research and theorizing in the field of analyzing classroom instructional behavior. A pos-sible outgrowth of this paper could be the development of a series of multi-dimensional category systems based on the fundamental concepts and pro-cedures of interaction analysis. Such an approach would seem to be a fruitful development from the present state of the analysis of spontaneous classroom behavior.

In summary, papers included in this chapter present evidence to support the assertion that training in interaction analysis does have an effect on the modification and shaping of the verbal behavior of teachers. Implications for current and future work in research and teacher education are presented.

TEACHER BEHAVIOR
AND IN-SERVICE PROGRAMS[34]

NED A. FLANDERS

CAN TEACHERS GROW THROUGH IN-SERVICE WORK?

Most in-service training programs are attempts to improve the quality of classroom instruction. Some programs attempt to accomplish this goal by introducing new curricular content; for example, the new mathematics curricula which are gaining increased acceptance. The assumption here seems to be that if more up-to-date or different material is taught, the quality of instruction is improved.

Other programs are built around some theme or particular aspect of teaching, such as "individualizing instruction," "improving the mental health of the classroom," or "teaching for creativity." The assumption of the "theme programs" may be that looking at old problems in a new light, that is, by developing new concepts for analyzing teaching, we can improve the quality of instruction.

There are two important questions that can be asked of any in-service training program, regardless of its origins, emphasis or point of view. First, will teachers be acting differently while teaching as a direct result of the in-service training? Second, if these changes do occur, has the quality of instruction really improved or is it just different? This article will consider these two questions without regard to the relative merits of one or another kind of in-service training.

EVALUATING IN-SERVICE TRAINING

Unfortunately very few in-service training programs are evaluated with enough care to tell whether or not the quality of classroom instruction has been affected. There are many reasons for this. Proper evaluation would more than double the costs of in-service activities. The technical problems are very difficult and the methodological advancements in research techniques neces-

---

[34] From *Educational Leadership* **21**, 1963, 25–29. Reprinted by permission of the A.S.C.D. and the author.

sary for such evaluation are only beginning to appear. Finally, thorough evaluation requires professional relationships between teachers, administrators, researchers and consultants that are free of suspicion, that are open and co-operative to a degree that is not easily achieved.

The steps of evaluation are very simple to state, but difficult to carry out. First, the objectives of the in-service training must be clearly stated as desired actions which occur in the classroom. Second, techniques for assessing these particular actions must be at hand. Third, sufficient experimental control must be exercised in the collection of the data so that cause and effect between train-ing and outcomes can be inferred. Fourth, the methods of training must be potent enough to produce changes that are considerably larger than the errors of measurement. And fifth, the validity of the process will depend on whether the changes in behavior produce more effective classroom learning.

When one takes a long, subjective look at current programs of in-service training across the country, it would appear that most programs fall short at each of the five steps outlined here. At its worst, in-service training is a gi-gantic spectator sport for teachers costing at least twenty million dollars[35] annually. As spectators, teachers gather to hear speeches, usually choosing seats in the rear of the room. They play a passive role in which their own ideas and questions are not adequately considered. They react as one does to any performing art and are more impressed or disappointed by the quality of the performance than with how much they may have learned. One wonders how the speech makers, the program chairmen who make the arrangements, the administrators and school board members who sign the checks, the teachers who are usually compelled to listen, and particularly the professional organiza-tions such as the NEA and the ASCD which seem to perpetuate this pattern at their national conferences, go about determining if classroom instruction is improved thereby.

At its best, in-service training is the opposite of a spectator sport since the teachers leave the grandstand and join the arena of activities. The training becomes a problem-solving process which explores new ways of teaching, new materials that can be used, new content that can be covered, and, perhaps most important, new ways of helping the teacher control his own behavior for pro-fessional purposes. It is not a single shot taken at the beginning of the year, but becomes a part of the teachers' professional responsibilities, directed by teachers, regularly scheduled during a week.

A PROJECT IN HUMAN RELATIONS TRAINING

Two recently completed in-service training projects attempted to measure changes in teacher behavior as part of the program evaluation. They will now be described to illustrate some of the difficulties involved in the five steps listed earlier.

---

[35] Estimated by the author: assume an average cost of $500 per year for 40,000 school districts.

Bowers and Soar (1961) completed a project in human relations training involving 54 elementary school teachers, 25 in an experimental group and 29 in a control group.

CONCEPTUALIZATION OF OBJECTIVES. The purpose of the in-service training was to help teachers achieve their own preferred degree of democratic classroom management by (a) increased sensitivity to their own behavior, (b) increased sensitivity to the factors causing pupil behavior, and (c) greater self-direction by pupils working in study groups.

TECHNIQUES FOR ASSESSING BEHAVIORS. The Medley and Mitzel OScAR instrument was used to observe and classify classroom interaction and activities. The Russell Sage Social Relations Test was used as a measure of pupils' skill in cooperative group planning and action. Two questionnaire instruments provided information about classroom activities; one was reported by the teacher, and the other was a report from the project staff.

EXPERIMENTAL CONTROL. The teachers were divided into two control and experimental groups, the latter being exposed to in-service training. Further control was established by classifying teachers on the basis of personality and attitude data collected by administering the Minnesota Teacher Attitude Inventory, the Minnesota Multiphasic Personality Inventory and the Bowers Teacher Opinion Inventory. Such classification permitted an investigation of whether different "types" of teachers benefited more or less from the in-service training. A very creative application of the Johnson-Neyman Technique was used in the analysis of data to give additional experimental control. This procedure permitted outcome variables to be compared between teachers in the control and in experimental groups who had similar personality traits, a kind of statistical matching process.

METHODS OF TRAINING. The training took place either right after the spring semester or just before the fall semester; an experimental teacher participated in one program, not both. Each program was three weeks long, one-half day sessions, five days a week. There was a theory session, skill practice session, and training group meeting each day. The emphasis was on active participation, developing new concepts, identifying possible teacher roles, and practicing the skills required by new teacher roles.

The control group was given the option of free tuition summer school courses and participated in a number of activities designed to reduce a possible Hawthorne effect.

CLASSROOM VALIDITY MEASURES. The OScAR observation of classroom interaction and testing pupil performance by the Russell Sage Social Relations Test were direct measures of the in-service objectives, occurring in the classrooms, before and after training. The data collecting required a team of observers and test administrators whose inter-reliability was known. The careful statistical analysis rejected comparisons unless the differences exceeded those that could have occurred by error and chance.

DISCUSSION. Whether or not one approves or disapproves of spending time on human relations training, this project illustrates attention to each of the steps outlined in the fourth paragraph of this article. Because of the careful research design, the results showed that not all teachers can benefit from this kind of training while others can. In general, teachers whose personality measures initially were correlated with more effective classroom practices, in turn, gained most from the training program.

TRAINING INVOLVING FEEDBACK TO TEACHERS

Flanders (1963) conducted a project in which teachers were trained to observe classroom interaction with a set of categories emphasizing different patterns of teacher influence. Fifty-one junior high school teachers participated in two different types of in-service training programs, each lasting nine weeks in the middle of the academic year.

CONCEPTUALIZATION OF OBJECTIVES. The purpose of the in-service training was to increase the flexibility of teacher influence and to increase the use of those teacher behaviors which support pupil participation in the classroom learning activities. Emphasis was given to principles of teacher influence which were concerned with when a teacher should purposely increase or decrease the freedom of pupil participation.

TECHNIQUES FOR ASSESSING BEHAVIORS. Every teacher practiced observation, recording types of verbal statements at three-second intervals, tabulating observed events into a matrix, and interpreting matrices in terms of teacher influence patterns. Each teacher was observed by specially trained staff observers before and after in-service training. The specific objectives of training were assessed as pre-training and post-training measures of spontaneous teaching acts in the teacher's regular classes.

EXPERIMENTAL CONTROL. Control was created by testing certain compatibility hypotheses. The two training programs were different because of the role taken by the in-service training instructor. It was hypothesized that a teacher would gain most from in-service training when his own style of teaching before training was compatible with that used by the training instructor. Thus, the question was whether a particular type of teacher would gain more or less from a particular type of in-service training.

METHOD OF TRAINING. All teachers spent a minimum of 30 hours in the formal training sessions. Most spent additional time exploring different patterns of influence in their own classrooms. The basic design was to provide opportunities in which teachers could secure feedback information about their own spontaneous behavior while teaching. These opportunities occurred during a three week application period in the middle of the training program. A teacher could obtain objective feedback from a staff observer, from a team formed with several colleagues, or he could make a tape recording of his own teaching and analyze this himself. In each case, the question was whether a teacher was acting in a fashion that was consistent with his intentions.

CLASSROOM VALIDITY MEASURES. An effort was made to measure attitudes of the pupils toward their teacher and the schoolwork before, during, and after in-service training. Earlier research had shown that such attitude measures were correlated with patterns of teacher influence and, in turn, with content achievement. The question as to whether changes in teacher behavior actually created more effective classroom learning rested on changes measured in pupil attitudes which, in this instance, were not significant.

DISCUSSION. This study showed that consistency between a teacher's own preferred style of teaching and the methods used will influence the progress made by a teacher in training. It also showed that some teachers, those who were most active in training, did make changes in their classroom behavior in a direction that was consistent with the objectives of the program. One training program was shown to be more effective than the other with most teachers.

SOME ASSUMPTIONS ABOUT CHANGING TEACHER BEHAVIOR

Many assumptions about in-service training can be inferred from the two projects just described. Three assumptions are discussed here because they are most often ignored in current in-service training activities.

First, ideas about teaching and learning must be organized into concepts which have meaning in terms of overt behavior. Ideas about teaching which cannot be related to overt actions are less likely to maintain a consistent meaning when the talking stops and the teaching starts.

Second, concepts about teaching and learning become useful to the extent that they can be applied personally. Concepts about teaching must ultimately be coordinated with one's own behavior. Concepts about pupil behavior must ultimately be applied to one's own class. Concepts about how to use instructional materials must ultimately be explored in one's own classroom.

Third, insight into principles of effective teaching comes about through personal inquiry. Teaching must be seen as a series of acts which occur with the passage of time. Instantaneous decisions must be made which have immediate consequences. Teachers can learn to recognize decision points, to become aware of more alternatives, to predict consequences accurately a higher proportion of the time, and to develop plans for controlling their own authority.

SOME QUESTIONS THAT NEED TO BE ANSWERED

A central issue, then, is how much of this overall process should be included in an in-service training program? Is actual practice or "acting-out" to be a part of in-service training? Or is this something that teachers will do by themselves, in the privacy of their own classrooms?

Current patterns of in-service training suggest a number of questions that should be answered.

For example, how will introducing a new curriculum in mathematics improve learning? Surely the pupils will learn things that they would otherwise not have learned, but will the new content necessarily stimulate more effective teaching methods? More skill in problem-solving?

Second, is it better to spend $200 to provide an inspirational speech for 100 teachers at the beginning of the semester, or spend the money during the year so that one teacher will have the resources to make changes in his teaching methods?

Third, since surveillance of teachers is neither desirable nor practical, is there any justification for compulsory participation in any form of in-service education? In the long run, will a higher proportion of faculty members explore more effective teaching practices through curiosity and contagion?

What little research has been accomplished so far suggests the tests that can be used for selecting teachers who can benefit more from in-service training. This research has also shown that compatibility between preferred patterns of learning and in-service training procedures will affect the progress of the teacher, and that changes, when observed, were the result of a continuing program of training. Opportunities for applying new insights immediately in the classroom and for obtaining feedback about one's behavior were found to be helpful.

2

APPLICATIONS OF INTERACTION ANALYSIS TO THE IN-SERVICE TRAINING OF TEACHERS[36]

THEODORE R. STORLIE

OVERVIEW

Few objective evaluations of the results of in-service programs have been reported. Some have attempted to evaluate in-service programs on the basis of objective evidence using pupil achievement or adjustment as criteria. Other studies have been concerned with evaluating in-service programs in terms of process criteria (change in teacher's behavior). One such study was conducted by Perkins (1951). He found a significantly higher ratio of expressed child development concepts following group-centered in-service study. Bowers and Soar (1961) have studied both product and process criteria.

The present study was concerned with change in the teacher's verbal behavior following an in-service course. There were three main purposes of this project: (1) to develop a series of five sound-filmstrips to serve as a basis for a 30-hour in-service course concerned with the study of teacher's use of verbal influence, (2) to determine whether participation in a course using these materials would produce a change in the verbal influence behavior of teachers, (3) to determine whether a teacher is more likely to change his behavior if he participates in a course in which the instructor's style is similar to his own teaching style.

Several suburban school districts near Minneapolis volunteered to participate in the project. One was selected which had two junior high schools and one senior high school. It was a typical suburban community. Volunteers for the project were sought and others were recruited for the course. A stipend of $75.00 or three credits was offered as an inducement to draw in a more typical

---

[36] Paper read at the annual meeting of the American Educational Research Association, Chicago, Illinois, February 1963. Reprinted by permission of the author.

sample. A research advisory council was established. This group approved all materials and plans for the course. Fifty-one teachers participated in the training out of a total of 150 secondary school teachers in the district. The partici pants came from the fields of English, social studies, science, mathematics, two art teachers, and one foreign language teacher. There were 33 men and 18 women in the sample. All had at least a B.S. and at least one year of experience. Twenty of the subjects had Master's degrees. Over two-fifths of the teachers in each junior high school and over one-fifth of the senior high school teachers participated.

The course was concerned with the analysis of teachers' use of authority in the classroom. It included practice in controlling the use of authority to achieve teacher goals; for example, using direct influence to focus pupils' attention on a particular phase of the learning activity and using indirect influence to help pupils to diagnose difficulty in the learning process. Teachers' verbal behavior is not always consistent with the intention of the teacher. Interaction analysis describes what a teacher has done so that he can determine if his actions have coincided with his intentions, and, if not, how his actions might be changed. Four weeks were devoted to teaching the basic concepts of interaction analysis, three weeks to application of these concepts with a consultant available to work with teachers upon request, and two weeks to the evaluation of the course.

The data collected for the project are listed in Fig. 3-1. Teachers were observed in the Fall for up to six hours. The in-service course was taught during the winter quarter and the teachers participating were observed again in the Spring. The Minnesota Student Attitude Inventory was administered in two classes of each teacher in the Fall, Winter, and Spring. This was done as a check on the interaction analysis data since other research indicated a relationship between teachers' verbal behavior and student attitudes. The MTAI was administered to nearly all the secondary teachers in the school district. Cat-

Observation with Interaction Analysis (experimental and control teachers)	Fall and spring
Minnesota Student Attitude Inventory (administered to a morning and afternoon class of each of the experimental and control teachers)	Fall, winter, and spring
MTAI (administered to experimental, control and nonparticipating teachers)	Fall
IPAT 16PF (Cattell, Saunders, and Stice) (experimental teachers)	Fall
Runner studies in attitude patterns (experimental teachers)	Fall
Post-meeting reaction sheets	At each session of training course

FIG. 3–1. Data collected.

tell's 16 PF test was administered to the participating teachers as was Runner's Studies in Attitude Patterns. Post Meeting Reaction Sheets were collected from each teacher at the close of every in-service session.

DIFFERENCES BETWEEN SATURDAY AND MONDAY

Two different training programs were established in order to determine whether change in the participating teachers would be related to the type of instruction and the teacher's own teaching style. These were designated as the Monday and Saturday groups respectively. In the Monday Group (the direct training program) the instructor planned and directed all activities. He did not offer much encouragement to teachers to express their own ideas and usually did not develop the ideas that were contributed. Thus the influence of the Monday instructor could be described as consistently direct throughout the course.

In the Saturday Group (the indirect treatment) the instructor encouraged the teacher participants to express their own ideas, to experiment with different patterns of influence, and to discuss the results with the class. On Saturday, the instructor was more flexible. That is, he used more indirect influence at certain points in the course. For example, at the first session, when the goals of the course were being clarified, he asked questions of the teacher participants and developed their ideas. In contrast, the Monday class first session was devoted more to telling what the course was about. Enthusiasm and initiative became greater in the Saturday group. In the Monday group some resentment developed over the greater enthusiasm of the Saturday group. For example, a teacher once asked a staff member, "What is wrong with us?"

We have two kinds of evidence that two different training programs existed: one from the interaction analysis data collected at the first, second, fourth, and seventh meetings of the course. These data are reported in Table 3–1. The interaction analysis data showed that the instructor talked 82% of the time on Monday but only 68% of the time on Saturday. The teachers talked 15% of the time on Monday and 28% of the time on Saturday. Thus, we see a 19% reduction in the amount of instructor talk resulted in almost doubling the participation by the teacher participants.

Qualitative differences in the teacher talk are indicated by the I/D ratio. On Monday it was 0.08 and on Saturday 0.22, indicating that the instructor used three times as much indirect influence on Saturday. The revised i/d ratio follows about the same trend. Even the Monday sessions allowed more teacher talk than is found in a typical college class. The instructor used twice as many twos (encouragement), and threes (acceptance of ideas) on Saturday as he did on Monday.

THE DIFFERENCES BETWEEN MONDAY AND SATURDAY SESSIONS AS INDICATED BY TEACHER REACTIONS. A second kind of data indicating that there were differences between the two in-service courses is supplied by the reactions of the teachers participating in the courses. Post Meeting Reaction Sheets (PMRS)

Table 3–1

Differences Between Direct and Indirect Courses*

	Monday (direct)	Saturday (indirect)
	Percent of total verbal communication	
Instructor talk	82%	68%
Teacher talk	15%	28%
Silence	3%	4%
	Ratio of indirect to direct influence	
I/D $\dfrac{\text{(Col. 1, 2, 3, \& 4)}}{\text{(Col. 5, 6, \& 7)}}$	0.08	0.22
i/d $\dfrac{\text{(Col. 1, 2, \& 3)}}{\text{(Col. 6 \& 7)}}$	1.79	4.43

* From Interaction Analysis data collected at the first, second, fourth, and seventh meetings of the course.

Table 3–2

Teachers' Perceptions of the Instructor's Role

Item	Group	Combined mean perception scores		
		First four weeks	Remaining five weeks	Total program
Four-item cluster (2A, 5A, 7A, 9A) on instructor (a)	Saturday (indirect)	4.63	4.71	4.68
	Monday (direct)	6.25	5.49	5.83
Kolmogorov-Smirnov Test		$X^2 = 69.19$ 0.001	$X^2 = 19.18$ 0.001	$X^2 = 69.59$ 0.001
Formal (b) vs. informal	Saturday (indirect)	3.06	2.93	2.99
	Monday (direct)	3.91	3.82	3.86
Kolmogorov-Smirnov Test		$X^2 = 8.88$ 0.02 0.01	$X^2 = 6.12$ 0.05 0.02	$X^2 = 12.25$ 0.01 0.001

(a)—Score on four items combined; scale from 1 to 10, higher scores refer to instructor-dominated.
(b)—Scores for single item; scale from 1 to 10, higher scores refer to more formal.

Table 3–3

Type of In-service Training Instruction and General Reactions to the In-service Training Program

| Item | Group | Combined mean evaluations* | | |
		First four weeks	Remaining five weeks	Total program
(1) Compared with an equal amount of time in an average education course, I would rate today as follows.	Saturday (indirect)	7.24	6.46	6.80
(2) I would rate the material and experiences of today's session —in terms of helping me with my own teaching —as follows.	Monday (direct)	6.33	5.04	5.60
Kolmogorov-Smirnov Test		$\chi^2 = 24.53$ 0.001	$\chi^2 = 53.11$ 0.001	$\chi^2 = 76.08$ 0.001

* Evaluation Scale: from 1 (very poor) to 10 (magnificent).
Scores for both reaction questions combined into one score.

were completed at the end of each session by the participants. The data from the first four sessions were used to try to create two different training programs. The data from the last five weeks were also combined to make one score for the time when the teachers faced the same two teaching styles as in the initial sessions.

Four intercorrelated items were combined to make a single score indicating teachers' perceptions of the instructor. Briefly, the content of these items was as follows: (a) Were the ideas before the group determined by the instructor or the participants? (b) Were the activities of the session controlled primarily by the instructor or was it primarily controlled by the teachers? (c) Was your participation stimulated primarily by the instructor or was it primarily self-generated? (d) Was the progress made at this session primarily due to the instructor or your own determination? There was a significant difference between the teachers' perception of the instructor's role the first four weeks. Monday teachers saw the sessions as significantly more instructor dominated. The same was true for the last five weeks. This is shown in Table 3–2 reporting the teachers' perception of the instructor's role. The Kolmogorov-Smirnov Test was used due to the lack of homogeneity of variance. The scale used ran from one to ten, higher scores indicating instructor domination.

Table 3–4

Type of In-service Training Instruction and Evaluations of In-service Activities that were Part of the Regular Sessions

Item	Group	First four weeks		Remaining five weeks	
		Mean evaluation*	K-S Test†	Mean evaluation*	K-S Test†
Demonstrations, role playing or panel discussions	Saturday (indirect)	7.07	$X^2 = 10.11$ 0.01 0.001	6.71	$X^2 = 14.30$ 0.001
	Monday (direct)	5.59		5.38	
Filmstrips or tape recordings	Saturday (indirect)	5.55	$X^2 = 1.87$ N.S.	5.67	$X^2 = 58.16$ 0.001
	Monday (direct)	5.04		2.07	
Lectures and talks given by the staff	Saturday (indirect)	7.05	$X^2 = 1.97$ N.S.	6.07	$X^2 = 9.73$ 0.01 0.001
	Monday (direct)	6.76		5.91	
Group discussions that were a part of the regular sessions	Saturday (indirect)	7.18	$X^2 = 12.22$ 0.01 0.001	7.19	$X^2 = 25.37$ 0.001
	Monday (direct)	6.22		5.89	

* Evaluation Scale: Ranges from 1 (lowest value) to 10 (highest value).
† Kolmogorov-Smirnov Test of Significance (at 2 degrees of freedom).

The scores on two other questions were combined to give a general reaction to the course. This is shown in Table 3–3. It is evident that the Saturday teachers rated the course significantly higher than Monday. On the PMRS the teachers were also asked to evaluate the various activities of the course. The results of this are reported in Table 3–4. The Saturday teachers rated the demonstrations, role-playing, and panels significantly higher during the first four weeks, as they did the group discussions, but there were no significant differences in the teachers' attitudes toward the lectures by the staff and the filmstrips and tape-recordings during the first four weeks. This supports the idea that the differences were in the instructor's influence patterns which would show up more in the demonstrations, role-playing, and group discussions. However, it appeared that the teachers' reaction to this influence colored their perception of the other materials during the last five weeks of the course.

At the last session of the course, the teachers were divided into three groups, according to their verbal participation on a self-selection basis and given a chance to discuss their reactions to the course. Some of these subjective reactions give an idea of what took place.

The following is a quote from one of the three groups in the Monday sessions, "And for the first three weeks, he (Flanders) didn't use a one, two, or three in our class and he was using *just all sorts of them* in the Saturday morning class (peevishly) and they got all this exuberance and hooray and 'let's go' and we got (ugh!)" (pause) "That group! They're running around with tape recorders and going into each other's room and helping each other out. I don't care if any ever come into my room" (laughter).

Differences in the verbal influence of the instructor were shown by the I/D ratio and the specific areas of the matrix. The PMR's showed that the teachers perceived the differences between the groups during the first four weeks. They saw the instructor as more direct on Monday.

EVIDENCE THAT THERE WERE DIFFERENT TYPES OF TEACHERS IN BOTH GROUPS

The Fall observation data showed that there were both direct and indirect teachers in the Monday and Saturday groups. This is indicated in Table 3–5. There were more indirect teachers in the Monday group, 16 versus 10 in the Saturday group, and more flexible teachers, 18 versus 7. However, there was no significant difference between the Monday and Saturday group before training in I/D or in i/d as shown by Chi-Square. The fact that the Monday group had more indirect and more flexible teachers makes the test of the hypothesis

Table 3–5

Summary of Comparisons between Groups before In-service Training

Group	Split	Fall I/D	Fall i/d	Fall flex. index	Fall MSAI A.M.	Fall MSAI P.M.	16 P.F.	MTAI
Saturday	Above Mdn	10	11	7	12	11	11	12
	Below Mdn	15	14	17	13	12	13	12
Monday	Above Mdn	16	16	18	12	11	14	13
	Below Mdn	10	10	8	14	13	12	13
Control	Above Mdn	5	4	6	7	7	b	b
	Below Mdn	6	7	5	4	3	b	b

regarding compatibility between teaching style and instructor style in the course much more rigorous.

The question arises as to whether there were differences between the groups in the personality characteristics of the teachers participating. This did not appear to be relevant as it had been found that there were no significant relationships between the 13 personality characteristics which seemed most relevant to predicting change in verbal behavior following a course in interaction analysis.

THE COMPATIBILITY HYPOTHESES

The rationale behind the compatibility hypotheses was as follows: previous research indicated that teacher flexibility in the use of verbal influence resulted in higher average I/D ratios and that student attitudes were more positive in such classrooms. It was also found that in seventh-grade social studies and in eighth-grade mathematics, content achievement was also superior when the I/D ratios of the teachers over an entire unit were higher. Thus we would expect teacher participants in a course where the instructor was more indirect, that had a higher I/D ratio, to make greater progress in changing their classroom verbal behavior than teachers in a course where an instructor was more direct.

Hypotheses	Teaching style	Treatment	Predicted results
A	Indirect	Indirect	Most gain
B	Direct	Direct	Second highest gain
C	Direct	Indirect	Less gain
D	Indirect	Direct	Least gain

FIG. 3–2. Compatibility hypotheses.

However, since the subject of the course was teaching and the participants were mature teachers, we might expect their own pre-training teaching style to influence their perceptions and evaluations of the course instructor's teaching and thus affect change in their behavior. Therefore, four hypotheses were developed regarding the relationship between the type of in-service course and the teacher's pre-training style of teaching. These hypotheses are summarized in Fig. 3–2. Hypothesis A: Indirect teachers, i.e., above the median in I/D in their own teaching, will gain the most when exposed to an indirect in-service program. Hypothesis B: The teachers below the median on being direct, who might be called direct, will gain the most when exposed to a direct program of in-service training. Hypothesis C: Direct teachers, when exposed to an indirect in-service training program, will show less gain than the above two groups, i.e., when there is incompatibility between their style and that of the instructor. Hypothesis D: Indirect teachers who are exposed to a direct in-service program will show the least gain. It was believed that teachers who were indirect would be more disturbed by being subjected to a direct treatment than direct teachers would be by being subjected to the indirect treatment. Part of the rationale behind the hypotheses was the belief that satisfaction with courses would be, in part, related to compatibility between the teachers' teaching style and the instructor's style and that greater satisfaction would lead to more change. This leads to Hypothesis E, that teachers who show the most gain in indirect teaching behavior will be most satisfied with the course. To gain more means increasing the use of indirect influence from fall to spring more than other teachers in the course.

3

THE ATTITUDES
AND TEACHING PATTERNS
OF COOPERATING TEACHERS
AND STUDENT TEACHERS
TRAINED IN INTERACTION ANALYSIS[37]

GERTRUDE MOSKOWITZ

When questioned as to what course has been the most helpful to them in their teaching, education students generally reply that it is their student teaching experience. At the same time, critics of education and educators themselves register dissatisfaction with the many prevailing arrangements for student teaching and its supervision. Although it is the college supervisor who assigns the grade to the student teacher, it is the cooperating teacher who has decidedly more contact hours with the student teacher, and who has the greater opportunity to become influential in shaping the actual attitudes and teaching patterns that develop in the novice. Yet there appears to be little that is either uniformly or specifically recommended concerning what the role of the cooperating teacher is or ought to be. This lack of information leaves many cooperating teachers wondering what types of experiences they should provide to be helpful to student teachers.

If the student teacher is indeed influenced by the cooperating teacher, then the cooperating teacher ought to be very much aware of his own particular teaching patterns and his attitudes toward teaching. The point in question, then, is whether or not cooperating teachers are sufficiently aware of their classroom behavior and its results. It would appear, therefore, that cooperating teachers need an objective way of getting data about their teaching behaviors; otherwise, it would be difficult for them to predict what is likely to be passed on to, and perhaps emulated by, their student teachers. Such data should also help the cooperating teachers to see more clearly the interaction patterns of the student teachers they are guiding. To date, most supervision by cooperating teachers has been left largely to intuition.

[37] This paper was prepared specially for this book.

The student teaching experience, however, is more than a practicum in teaching; it is a human-relations experience as well. A common complaint arising both from student teachers and cooperating teachers is that of dissatisfaction with one another because of differences in personality or varying viewpoints about teaching. Such differences have often led to anxieties and unprofitable experiences, and may even have caused some student teachers to decide not to go into teaching at all.

One way to obtain objective data concerning teaching behavior is through use of the Flanders system of interaction analysis, which categorizes the verbal behaviors of teachers as they interact with pupils in their classrooms. When the data have been collected and used as a feedback device, teachers have often developed new insights into their teaching and have subsequently made changes in their teaching patterns. Two assumptions might be made about teachers trained to use interaction analysis:

1. They could become better aware of their own patterns of interaction and would perhaps make changes where changes are desirable.

2. They could apply their knowledge of interaction analysis to the interaction between their student teachers and themselves, thereby improving the interpersonal relationship and ensuring a more profitable experience for both of them.

Very little experimental research has been conducted concerning cooperating teachers or cooperating teachers and their student teachers. In the recent studies of Hough and Amidon (1963), Kirk (1964), Zahn (1965), Furst (1965), and Amidon (1966), the conclusion was drawn that the attitudes and teaching patterns of student teachers were influenced in a positive direction by instruction in interaction analysis. The findings of Dunham (1958), Osmon (1959), McAulay (1960), and Price (1961) indicated that cooperating teachers influenced either the attitudes of their student teachers or the way in which they taught. The findings of such studies led to the following questions: (1) Would the teaching patterns of cooperating teachers be influenced if they were trained in interaction analysis? (2) If the teaching patterns of cooperating teachers trained in interaction analysis changed, would the new patterns be emulated by their student teachers? (3) Would the attitudes of the cooperating teachers and the student teachers toward one another be influenced if one or both of them received training in interaction analysis? (4) Would there be a relationship between the teaching patterns of student teachers and their cooperating teachers if one or both of them received training in interaction analysis?

To study these problems the following questions were investigated:

1. Does training of the cooperating teacher in interaction analysis result in attitudes and teaching patterns different from those of the cooperating teacher untrained in interaction analysis?

2. Does training in interaction analysis make a difference in the attitudes and teaching patterns of the cooperating teacher and/or the student teacher when:

   a) Both the cooperating teacher and the student teacher are trained in interaction analysis?

   b) Only the student teacher is trained in interaction analysis?

   c) Only the cooperating teacher is trained in interaction analysis?

   d) Neither the cooperating teacher nor the student teacher is trained in interaction analysis?

PROCEDURES

Forty-four secondary-education student teachers from Temple University and their cooperating teachers were selected as subjects of the present study, which was conducted during the 15-week spring semester of 1965. One-half the cooperating teachers and one-half the student teachers received training in interaction analysis. Subjects were assigned to one of the four possible combinations of training or no training in interaction analysis. In the present study, "trained" means that the subject received training in interaction analysis; "no training," or "untrained," means that the subject did not receive such training. Figure 3–3 illustrates the groups that evolved for the present study.

Group I	Group II
Trained cooperating teachers	Untrained cooperating teachers
Trained student teachers	Trained student teachers
Group III	**Group IV**
Trained cooperating teachers	Untrained cooperating teachers
Untrained student teachers	Untrained student teachers

FIG. 3–3. Experimental design of the study.

The trained cooperating teachers received, gratis, a two-credit graduate course in which they were given 25 hours of training in the use of interaction analysis as a supervisory tool in working with student teachers. Application of the insights gathered from the study of interaction analysis to the teaching of the cooperating teachers was not discussed in their course, since the focus was on helping student teachers to gain the insights. The student teachers trained in interaction analysis focused on its applicability to their own teaching. These student teachers received a total of 60 hours of training in interaction analysis, consisting of a two-hour lecture and a two-hour laboratory period each week for one semester.

Cooperating teachers who did not take the course in interaction analysis but who were supervising Temple student teachers were asked to be participants in the study. These cooperating teachers and the student teachers not trained in interaction analysis formed the untrained groups. Both groups of cooperating teachers, trained and untrained, were volunteers.

The study included teachers of English, social studies, science, and mathematics, with an equal number of teachers from each subject area being assigned to each of the four groups. The schools served either lower or middle socioeconomic areas. All college supervisors of student teaching were trained in the use of interaction analysis. Student teachers were grouped in their student teaching seminars according to whether or not they had been trained in interaction analysis.

Two instruments, the *Cooperating Teachers' Attitude Questionnaire* (CTAQ) and the *Student Teachers' Attitude Questionnaire* (STAQ), were devised to assess the attitudes of cooperating teachers and their student teachers toward each other and the degree of their satisfaction with one another. These questionnaires consisted of items that had been excerpted from favorable and unfavorable comments made by student teachers and cooperating teachers about one another. The Hoyt technique for estimating reliability by analysis of variance (Hoyt, 1941) gave the CTAQ a reliability of 0.92 and the STAQ a reliability of 0.87. These two questionnaires, plus the *Teaching Situation Reaction Test* (TSRT), which assesses teacher performance along an indirect–direct continuum, were used to collect attitudinal data from the subjects of the study.

The Flanders system of interaction analysis was used to collect the classroom observational data of each cooperating teacher and each student teacher as they taught two periods of discussion-type lessons. There are ten categories in the Flanders system; seven designate teacher behavior, two are for student behavior, and one is for silence or confusion. The teacher behaviors are divided into two types of influence, indirect and direct. The indirect categories of the Flanders system are those which expand the freedom of the students to participate. The categories of indirect teacher influence are: (1) accepts feelings of pupils, (2) praises or encourages, (3) accepts ideas of pupils, (4) asks questions. The categories of direct teacher influence limit the freedom of the students to participate. They are: (5) gives information, (6) gives directions, (7) criticizes or justifies authority one has as a teacher. The two categories of student talk are: (8) teacher-initiated response, (9) student-initiated response. (See "Interaction Analysis as a Feedback System" by Amidon and Flanders in Chapter 2 of this book.)

Eleven measures gathered by means of the Flanders system were used in comparing the teaching behaviors of the subjects in the study. The attitude questionnaires were administered the last week of the semester and the classroom observations were made during the last few weeks of the spring term. The observers who tallied the classroom interaction data did not know which of the subjects were trained in interaction analysis.

Several statistical tests of significance were used in the treatment of the data. The *F* test was used to test the significance of differences between variances; the *t*-test was used to test the hypotheses when the variance ratio was not significant. When the variance ratio was significant at the 0.05 level, indicating that the variances were not equal, the Mann-Whitney *U* test was used.

FINDINGS AND CONCLUSIONS

TEACHING PATTERNS OF COOPERATING TEACHERS. Between the classes of trained and untrained cooperating teachers there were no significant differences in the amounts of teacher talk and student talk. However, there were significant differences in the type of teacher talk. The trained cooperating teachers used significantly more indirect teaching patterns than did the untrained cooperating teachers. They also used significantly more extended indirect communication; that is, they tended to follow one indirect behavior with another.

TEACHING PATTERNS OF STUDENT TEACHERS. There were significant relationships between the teaching patterns of student teachers and their cooperating teachers.

1. Trained cooperating teachers and trained student teachers who worked together used significantly more indirect teaching patterns than untrained cooperating teachers and untrained student teachers who worked together (Group I versus Group IV).

Examination of the teaching patterns of the student teachers in Groups I and IV indicated a consistent tendency for the student teachers to develop teaching patterns similar to those of their cooperating teachers. Both the training of cooperating teachers and student teachers in interaction analysis and the influence of the cooperating teachers on the student teachers (and perhaps that of the student teachers on the cooperating teachers) appear to have been operating in these comparisons to make the teaching patterns of Group I more indirect than those in Group IV.

2. Trained student teachers used significantly more indirect teaching patterns than their untrained cooperating teachers. (Group II).

The fact that the student teachers were trained in interaction analysis and the cooperating teachers were not seemed to contribute to the use by student teachers of teaching patterns different from those of their cooperating teachers, the difference being in the use of more indirect patterns. It appears that the trained student teachers resisted the tendency to emulate their untrained cooperating teachers and therefore resisted becoming direct. Training in interaction analysis seemed to be a more potent influence on the teaching patterns of the student teachers in Group II than were the teaching patterns of their untrained cooperating teachers.

3. There were no significant differences between the teaching patterns of untrained student teachers and their trained cooperating teachers (Group III).

The influence of the trained cooperating teachers on the untrained student teachers seemed to be great (Group III). All trained cooperating teachers (i.e., those in Groups I and III) were compared with all untrained cooperating teachers (i.e., those in Groups II and IV), and the comparisons indicated that the trained groups were significantly more indirect than the untrained groups. It seems reasonable to infer, therefore, that the student teachers in Group III, being not significantly different from their cooperating teachers, incorporated the teaching patterns of those teachers, thereby tending to become indirect. Inspection of the means indicated that the untrained student teachers whose cooperating teachers were trained (Group III), were more indirect than the untrained student teachers whose cooperating teachers were also untrained (Group IV).

ATTITUDES OF COOPERATING TEACHERS TOWARD TEACHING. There were no significant differences between the scores of trained and untrained cooperating teachers on the *Teaching Situation Reaction Test*. The TSRT is a paper-and-pencil measure of how teachers believe they would react in various classroom situations, along the indirect–direct dimension. The teaching patterns of the trained and untrained cooperating teachers were compared, and an attempt was made to carry this dimension from the written response to the actual behavioral responses the teachers made in the classroom.

It cannot be generalized that the TSRT and the measures of indirect teacher influence used in comparing the teaching patterns of the trained and untrained groups assess precisely the same thing. However, the scores of the trained cooperating teachers showed them to have a tendency to be more positive or indirect on the paper-and-pencil test, although not significantly so, while actual classroom performance showed that the trained group was indeed more indirect than the untrained group, and significantly so. To put it another way, the teachers who were not trained in interaction analysis were more direct in their actual classroom teaching than their paper-and-pencil tests indicated. Comparison of the results of the TSRT with classroom observations showed that the differences between the two groups were greater in the classroom than on the written test.

ATTITUDES OF COOPERATING TEACHERS TOWARD STUDENT TEACHERS. A *t*-test indicated no significant differences between the attitudes of the trained and untrained cooperating teachers toward their student teachers, although the trained groups did have more positive attitudes. The difference was at the 0.15 level of probability. All cooperating teachers in the study were volunteers, and, as such, they knew that they were part of a study which dealt with their role as cooperating teachers. One speculation that can be made is that the attitudes of these volunteer cooperating teachers toward their student teachers might have been "above average" to begin with. In other words, these cooperating teachers might have had very satisfactory attitudes toward their student teachers in the past which led them to volunteer to participate in the study. As a matter of fact, this speculation may have greater applicability to

Table 3–6

Mean Scores for All Four Cooperating Teacher and Student Teacher Groups on Attitude Questionnaires

	N	TSRT	CTAQ	STAQ
Cooperating teachers and student teachers trained (Gr. I)	10	81.60*	82.90*	80.80
Cooperating teachers trained, student teachers untrained (Gr. III)	11	82.91	81.45	83.18*
Cooperating teachers untrained, student teachers trained (Gr. II)	11	86.73	78.00	65.27†
Cooperating teachers and student teachers untrained (Gr. IV)	12	88.42†	75.92†	75.08

* Most positive attitude.
† Least positive attitude.

the untrained group than to the trained group, since its members were not taking the free two-credit graduate course dealing with interaction analysis, and in effect received nothing tangible for their participation in the study. In spite of the above-stated possibilities, the differences that were present were in the direction of more positive attitudes in the trained group.

Table 3–6 presents the mean scores of each of the four groups of cooperating teachers on the TSRT and the CTAQ. Although the differences are not significant, several interesting relationships are apparent:

1. The most positive mean scores were those of the cooperating teachers in Group I, in which both cooperating teachers and student teachers were trained.

2. The next most positive mean scores were those of the cooperating teachers in Group III, in which only cooperating teachers were trained.

3. Third came Group II, in which the cooperating teachers were not trained but their student teachers were trained.

4. The least positive mean scores were those of the cooperating teachers in Group IV, in which neither cooperating teachers nor student teachers were trained.

In other words, the attitudes of the cooperating teachers toward teaching and toward their student teachers were most positive when both cooperating teachers and their student teachers were trained, and these attitudes decreased successively in positiveness as the degree of contact of the cooperating teachers with interaction analysis diminished.

ATTITUDES OF STUDENT TEACHERS TOWARD COOPERATING TEACHERS. A significant difference at the 0.01 level of significance was found in the attitudes of student teachers toward trained and untrained cooperating teachers. Student teachers whose cooperating teachers were trained had significantly more positive attitudes toward their cooperating teachers than student teachers whose cooperating teachers were not trained. Both trained and untrained student teachers held positive attitudes toward trained cooperating teachers.

In three of the four groups, the means of the cooperating teachers on the CTAQ and the means of the student teachers on the STAQ reveal that the attitudes within each group of cooperating teachers and student teachers were close to each other (Table 3–6). The exception was Group II, in which the attitudes of the cooperating teachers were much more positive toward the student teachers than were those of the student teachers toward the cooperating teachers. Of the four groups of student teachers, then, *the student teachers in Group II, who had been trained in interaction analysis, had the least positive attitudes toward their cooperating teachers.* It may be that this group of student teachers acquired a certain awareness that caused them to have particular expectations of their cooperating teachers; perhaps the fact that the cooperating teachers in that group were not trained in interaction analysis made it impossible, or at least difficult, for them to fulfill those expectations. This, of course, would lessen the rapport between the student teachers and the cooperating teachers because of their inability to communicate via a common frame of reference. In effect, the student teachers knew something that the cooperating teachers didn't; they may have wanted to try out new behaviors and found it a bit frustrating to be working with someone less experimentally inclined.

On the other hand, the untrained cooperating teachers in Group II held more positive attitudes toward their trained student teachers than the untrained cooperating teachers in Group IV held toward their untrained student teachers. In other words, the attitudes of untrained cooperating teachers were more positive toward trained student teachers than they were toward untrained student teachers. It appears as though training of the cooperating teachers in interaction analysis increased the rapport between them and their student teachers. Training of only the cooperating teachers accounted for very positive attitudes in their student teachers, while training of only the student teachers seemed related to very negative attitudes toward the cooperating teachers.

Although the training in interaction analysis did not significantly affect the attitudes of the cooperating teachers toward their student teachers, it appears to have significantly affected the attitudes of the student teachers toward the cooperating teachers. If the attitudes of the cooperating teachers were quite positive to begin with, the effect of the training may have been not so much to improve their attitudes as to increase their sensitivity in communicating with the student teachers.

VARIABILITY OF THE TEACHING PATTERNS. An unexpected outcome of this study concerned the variability of the teaching patterns of the teachers. There was significantly more variability in the teaching patterns of cooperating teachers and student teachers who were trained than in those of cooperating teachers and student teachers who were untrained. Not only did the trained groups of teachers use more indirect teaching patterns, but they used these patterns in a wider range of ways. This finding may indicate that the training in interaction analysis tended to produce individuality in the trained groups, in that there were greater individual differences in their teaching behaviors. Although training in interaction analysis appeared related to the increasing indirectness of cooperating teachers and student teachers, it did not make the individuals in the trained groups more alike. On the contrary, it appeared that the trained teachers became more individualistic in their teaching patterns.

These significant variances are reminiscent of the findings of Flanders (1965a) concerning high achieving and low achieving teachers. Flanders found that the matrices of low achieving teachers contained identical teaching patterns, while the matrices of high achieving teachers contained repertoires of varied patterns that differed from teacher to teacher. Swineford (1964), too, found that analysis of the teaching behaviors of the highest-rated student teachers disclosed no single characteristic pattern. The significant variability between the trained and untrained groups of teachers in the present study may indeed be an encouraging finding, if it indicates that trained teachers become more varied and experimental in their behavior, and if the variability is at all related to the findings of Flanders and Swineford.

DISCUSSION

There are several additional points concerning the present study that seem worth noting. To begin with, the investigator had reason to believe that there might be no significant differences between the trained and untrained cooperating teachers in this study. Since all of the cooperating teachers had volunteered to participate in a study which they knew involved student teachers, they probably already had favorable attitudes toward student teachers. It seemed likely, therefore, that these might be "above-average" cooperating teachers. They also knew that their classes would be visited by observers, and, as they felt no hesitancy about permitting observations, it might be that they were exceptional teachers. It should be mentioned that some cooperating teachers did refuse to participate in the study.

A second relevant point is that the trained cooperating teachers were presented with the Flanders system as a supervisory tool *for use with student teachers;* at no time was the information acquired by the system directly applied to their own classroom teaching. No tapes of their classrooms or analyses of their own teaching were required of the cooperating teachers, so they did not get any direct feedback on their own teaching patterns. This may account in part for the fact that between the classes of the trained cooperating teachers and those of the untrained cooperating teachers there were no significant differences in the amount of teacher talk or in the amount or kind of student talk. Yet, the trained cooperating teachers appeared to have acquired certain insights, and to have applied them both to their own teaching behavior and to the interpersonal relations between them and their student teachers. It seems that the odds were against the occurrence of significant differences between the trained and untrained cooperating teachers, which may have increased the significance of the differences that did occur.

Why did differences occur? One permissible speculation is that the training received by some of the cooperating teachers made them more aware of the classroom behavior of teachers in general and provided them with a framework for its study and analysis. They thus became more conscious of the effect of their own verbal behavior on their pupils and were better able to control it. The background in education and/or psychology that teachers receive often emphasizes the value of a climate of acceptance and student involvement to the learning process. Although many teachers believe in such concepts as being indirect and encouraging student participation, they may not necessarily know how to put these behaviors into operation. Once the teachers have the Flanders system as a frame of reference and understand the cause–effect relationship of their behavior on pupils, they acquire an understanding of how to produce desired behaviors. Research has indicated that trained teachers tend to become more indirect in their teaching. It is consistent with the findings of such research that having gained more awareness of the socio-emotional dynamics of teaching and having acquired a structure for its analysis, the trained cooperating teachers tended to use significantly more indirect teaching patterns than did the untrained cooperating teachers. In addition, the trained cooperating teachers seemed to transfer what they had learned to the one–to–one relationship with their student teachers, thereby increasing their sensitivity to the student teachers and improving communication with them.

In the comparisons made between the groups, seven different measures were used to determine whether there were significant differences in indirectness between the trained and untrained groups. Two of the measures used were selected in light of the recent findings of a yet unpublished study by Soar,[38] who revealed that in a ten-factor rotation of factor analysis, the 3-3 cell (extended use of student ideas) and the extended indirect area (buildup of an indirect behavior followed by indirect behavior) were the measures that loaded most heavily on a factor which appeared to identify indirect teacher behavior. In each of the five different sets of teaching-pattern comparisons in the present study, the trained cooperating teachers and trained student teachers used significantly more of either or both of these two critical measures of indirectness than did those who were untrained. This may be considered additional evidence of the presence of indirectness in the trained groups.

Another point of interest is that Flanders (1965a), in comparing teachers whose pupils had favorable attitudes and high achievement with teachers whose

---

[38] Robert S. Soar, personal communication, November, 1965.

pupils had unfavorable attitudes and low achievement, found that the cell that contained the greatest difference between these two groups was the 3-3 cell. In the present study, Group I, in which both the cooperating teachers and the student teachers were trained in interaction analysis, used the 3-3 cell significantly more than Group IV, in which neither the cooperating teachers nor the student teachers had received this training. If extended use of this cell is related to student achievement, then this difference between Groups I and IV may take on added significance.

IMPLICATIONS

A major assumption underlying this study was that both the cooperating teachers and interaction analysis are forces of influence on the behavior of student teachers. These forces were distributed in different combinations among the groups so that it might be determined to what degree the cooperating teachers and/or interaction analysis influenced the attitudes and the teaching patterns of the student teachers. In this case it was assumed that the greatest influence in a positive direction will be brought to bear on the student teachers when both the cooperating teachers and the student teachers are trained in interaction analysis.

The findings of this study seem to support these assumptions:

1. The fact that both cooperating teachers and student teachers were trained appeared related to:

    a) Their use of more indirect teaching patterns, or of teaching patterns more in accord with the generally accepted goals of education.

    b) The development of more positive interpersonal relationships between the cooperating teachers and their student teachers.

2. The training of cooperating teachers in interaction analysis appeared to have a positive effect on:

    a) The way in which they taught.

    b) The way in which their student teachers taught.

    c) The interpersonal relationships between them and their student teachers.

3. Training only the student teachers appeared to affect:

    a) Their teaching patterns in a positive direction.

    b) The attitudes toward their cooperating teachers in a negative direction.

The findings of this study suggest that more indirect, individualistic teaching will be promoted, and more positive interpersonal relationships will be developed during the student teaching experience, if both the cooperating teachers and their student teachers are trained in interaction analysis. It also appears that if a choice had to be made to train either cooperating teachers or student teachers, it is the cooperating teachers that should be trained, since their student teachers might thereby develop more positive attitudes toward their cooperating teachers and somewhat more indirect teaching patterns. It does not seem desirable to train only the student teachers, inasmuch as the attitudes developed by the trained student teachers toward their untrained cooperating teachers tended, in this study, to be extremely negative.

The overall results of this study are encouraging, as they seem to indicate that within a brief but concentrated period of time, the student teaching experience can be tangibly affected and improved, both in the area of human relations, in which improvement is sorely needed, and in the place in which it is hoped that effective changes will occur, that is, the actual classroom setting.

4

INTENT, ACTION, AND FEEDBACK: A PREPARATION FOR TEACHING[39]

NED A. FLANDERS

THE PROBLEM

The point is that much of what is learned in education courses is neither conceptualized, quantified nor taught in a fashion that builds a bridge between theory and practice. Education students are only occasionally part of an exciting, systematic exploration of the teaching process, most infrequently by the instructor's example. How can we create, in education courses, an active, problem-solving process, a true sense of inquiry, and a systematic search for principles through experimentation? At least one factor favors change and that is the lack of solid evidence that anything we are now teaching is clearly associated with any index of effective teaching, with the possible exception of practice teaching.

A great many factors resist curriculum change in teacher education. Perhaps the most important is that genuine curriculum innovation, to be distinguished from tinkering with content and sequence, would require that existing faculty members, old and new alike, think differently about their subject matter, act differently while teaching, and relate differently to their students. For some this is probably impossible, for all it would be difficult. Yet changes do occur when enough energy is mobilized and convictions are strongly held.

It is a serious indictment of the profession, however, to hear so many education instructors say that their students will appreciate what they are learning *after* they have had some practical teaching experience. What hurts is the obvious hypocrisy of making this statement and then giving a lecture on the importance of presenting material in such a way that the immediate needs and interests of the pupils are taken into consideration. Such instances reveal a misunderstanding of theory and practice. To be understood, concepts in educa-

---

[39] From *Journal of Teacher Education* 14, 1963, 251–260. Reprinted by permission of the National Education Association and the author.

tion must be verified by personal field experiences; in turn, field experiences must be efficiently conceptualized to gain insight. With most present practices, the gorge between theory and practice grows deeper and wider, excavated by the very individuals who are pledged to fill it.

One stumbling block is our inability to describe teaching as a series of acts through time and to establish models of behavior which are appropriate to different kinds of teaching situations. This problem has several dimensions. First, in terms of semantics, we must learn how to define our concepts as part of a theory. We also need to organize these concepts into the fewest number of variables necessary to establish principles and make predictions. Too often we try to teach the largest number of variables; in fact, as many as we can think of for which there is some research evidence. Second, in terms of technology, we must develop procedures for quantifying the qualitative aspects of teaching acts so that our students will have tools for collecting empirical evidence. Third, in terms of philosophy, we must decide whether our education students are going to be told about teaching in lectures and read about it in books or if they are going to discover these things for themselves. This paper will be devoted to these three issues, in reverse order.

A PHILOSOPHY OF INQUIRY

When Cantor (1953) published his nine assumptions of orthodox teaching, there was little evidence to support his criticism. Must pupils be coerced into working on tasks? In what way is the teacher responsible for pupils' acquiring knowledge? Is education a preparation for later life rather than a present, living experience? Is subject matter the same to the learner as it is to the teacher? The last decade has provided more evidence in support of Cantor's criticism than it has in defense of existing practice.

H. H. Anderson and his colleagues (1939, 1945, 1946) first demonstrated that dominative teacher contacts create more compliance and resistance to compliance, that dominative teacher contacts with pupils spread to the pupil-to-pupil contacts even in the absence of the teacher, and that this pattern of teaching creates situations in which pupils are more easily distracted and more dependent on teacher initiative.

Flanders and Havumaki (1960) demonstrated that dominative teacher influence was more persuasive in changing pupil opinions but that such shifts of opinion were not stable since inner resistance was so high.

A research team in Provo, Utah (Romney et al., 1958, 1961) believes that patterns of spontaneous teacher action can be identified and that more effective patterns can be distinguished from less effective patterns. The difference is that more dominative patterns are less effective.

Our own eight-year research program which involved the development of interaction analysis as a tool for quantifying patterns of teacher influence lends further support to Cantor. The generalizations to follow are based on all teachers observed in our different research projects. This total is only 147 teachers, representing all grade levels, six different school districts in two counties; but these teachers came from the extremes of a distribution involving several thousand teachers. The total bits of information collected by interaction analysis are well in excess of 1,250,000.

The present, average domination of teachers is best expressed as the rule of two-thirds. About two-thirds of the time spent in a classroom, someone is talking. The chances are two out of three that this person is the teacher. When the teacher talks, two-thirds of the time is spent by many expressions of opinion and fact, giving some direction and occasionally criticizing the pupils. The fact that teachers are taking too active a part for effective learning is shown by comparing superior with less effective classrooms. A superior classroom scores above average on constructive attitudes toward the teacher and the classwork. It also scores higher on achievement tests of the content to be learned, adjusted for initial ability. In studies (Flanders, 1960) of seventh-grade social studies and eighth-grade mathematics classes, it was found that the teachers in superior classrooms spoke only slightly less, say 50 to 60% of the time, but the more directive aspects of their verbal influence went down to 40 to 50%. These teachers were much more flexible in the quality of their influence, sometimes very direct, but on more occasions very indirect.

To describe the classrooms which were below average in constructive pupil attitudes and in content achievement (they are positively correlated), just change the rule of two-thirds to the rule of three-fourths plus.

The foregoing evidence shows that no matter what a prospective teacher hears in an education course, he has, on the average, been exposed to living models of what teaching is and can be that are basically quite directive. After 14 or so years he is likely to be quite dependent, expecting the instructor to tell him what to do, how to do it, when he is finished, and then tell him how well he did it. Now it is in this general context that we turn to the question of how we can develop a spirit of inquiry with regard to teaching.

Thelen has described a model of personal inquiry, as well as other models, and the question is whether teacher education can or should move toward this model. He describes this model as follows (Thelen, 1960, p. 89):

. . . (personal inquiry) is a process of interaction between the student and his natural and societal environment. In this situation the student will be aware of the process of which he is a part; during this process he will be aware of many choices among ways he might behave; he will make decisions among these ways; he will then act and see what happens; he will review the process and study it with the help of books and other people; he will speculate about it, and draw tentative conclusions from it.

Returning to the education course, the student will be aware of the learning process of *that* classroom, he will confront choices, he will make decisions among the choices, he will act and then evaluate his actions, and then he will try to make some sense out of it with the help of books, the instructor, and his peers. This is a tall order, but who knows, it may be the only route to discovery and independence for the prospective teacher.

Occasionally we hear of exciting learning experiences in which education students attain a sort of intellectual spirit of inquiry. A unit on motivation can begin with an assessment of the motivation patterns of the education students. The same assessment procedures can then be used at other grade levels, permitting comparisons and generalizations. Principles of child growth and development can be discovered by observation and learned more thoroughly, perhaps, than is possible with only lecture and reading. But this is not what is meant by inquiry.

Inquiry in teacher education means translating understanding into action as part of the teaching process. It means experimenting with one's own behavior, obtaining objective information about one's own behavior, evaluating this information in terms of the teacher's role; in short, attaining self-insight while acting like a teacher.

Procedures for obtaining self-insight have been remarkably improved during the last decade in the field of human relations training. Two characteristics of these training methods seem relevant to this discussion. First, information and insights about behavior must become available in a way that can be accepted and in a form that is understood. Second, opportunities to utilize or act out these insights must be provided. Our ability to accept information about ourselves is a complex problem, but it helps if we believe the information is objective, valid, and given in an effort to help rather than hurt. Our understanding of this information will depend a great deal on our ability to organize the information conceptually. Freedom to act at least requires freedom from threat or embarrassment.

From all of these things, a spirit of inquiry develops.

THE TECHNIQUE OF INTERACTION ANALYSIS

Interaction analysis is nothing more and nothing less than an observation technique which can be used to obtain a fairly reliable record of spontaneous verbal statements. Most teacher influence is exerted by verbal statements, and to determine their quality is to approximate total teacher influence. This technique was first developed as a research tool, but every observer we ever hired testified that the process of learning the system and using it in classrooms was more valuable than anything else he learned in his education courses. Since interaction analysis is only a technique, it probably could be applied to teacher education in a fashion that is consistent with a philosophy of personal inquiry. How it is used in teacher preparation is obviously as important as understanding the procedure itself.

The writing of this manuscript followed the completion of a terminal contract report of a U.S. Office of Education sponsored, in-service training program based on interaction analysis as a tool for gathering information. How we used interaction analysis is illustrated by the conditions we tried to create for the 55 participating teachers, most of whom represented about one-half of the faculties of two junior high schools:[40]

1. Teachers developed new (to them) concepts as tools for thinking about their behavior and the consequences of their behavior. These concepts were used to discover principles of teacher influence. Both types of concepts were necessary: those used for describing actions and those used for describing consequences.

2. Procedures for assessing both types of concepts in practical classroom situations were tried out. These procedures were used to test principles, to modify them, and to determine when they might be appropriately applied.

3. The training activities involved in becoming proficient in the assessment of spontaneous behavior, in and of themselves, increased the sensitivity of teachers to their own behavior and the behavior of others. Most important, teachers could compare their intentions with their actions.

4. By avoiding a discussion of right and wrong ways of teaching and emphasizing the discovery of principles of teacher influence, teachers gradually became more independent and self-directing. Our most successful participants investigated problems of their own choosing, designed their own plans, and arranged collaboration with others when this seemed advantageous.

Five filmstrips and one teacher's manual have been produced and written. These materials would have to be modified before they could be used with undergraduate students. Before asking how interaction analysis might be used in teacher preparation, we turn next to a description of the procedures. [*Editors' note:* For a more detailed description, see Amidon and Flanders, *Interaction Analysis as a Feedback System*, the first paper in Chapter II.]

THE PROCEDURE OF OBSERVATION

The observer sits in a classroom in the best position to hear and see the participants. At the end of each three-second period, he decides which category best represents the communication events just completed. He writes this category number down while simultaneously assessing communication in the next period and continues at a rate of 20 to 25 observations per minute, keeping his tempo as steady as possible. His notes are merely a series of numbers written in a column, top to bottom, so that the original sequence of events is preserved. Occasionally marginal notes are used to explain the class formation or any unusual circumstances. When there is a major change in class formation, the

---

[40] Interaction analysis as a research tool has been used ever since R. F. Bales first developed a set of categories for studying groups. Most of our research results can be found in the references at the end of this book.

communication pattern, or the subject under discussion, a double line is drawn and the time indicated. As soon as the total observation is completed, the observer retires to a nearby room and completes a general description of each separate activity period separated by the double lines, including the nature of the activities, the class formation, and the position of the teacher. The observer also notes any additional facts that seem pertinent to an adequate interpretation and recall of the total visit.

The numbers that an observer writes down are tabulated in a 10 × 10 matrix as sequence pairs, that is, a separate tabulation is made for each overlapping pair of numbers. An illustration will serve to explain this procedure.

Teacher: "Class! The bell has rung. May I have your attention please!" (6) During the next three seconds talking and noise diminish. (10)

Teacher: "Jimmy, we are all waiting for you." (7) Pause.

Teacher: "Now today we are going to have a very pleasant surprise, (5) and I think you will find it very exciting and interesting. (1) Have any of you heard anything about what we are going to do?" (4)

Pupil: "I think we are going on a trip in the bus that's out in front." (8)

Teacher: "Oh! You've found out! How did you learn about our trip?" (4)

By now the observer has written down 6, 10, 7, 5, 1, 4, 8, and 4. As the interaction proceeds the observer will continue to write down numbers. To tabulate these observations in a 10 × 10 matrix, the first step is to make sure that the entire series begins and ends with the same number. The convention we use is to add a 10 to the beginning and end of the series unless the 10 is already present. Our series now becomes 10, 6, 10, 7, 5, 1, 4, 8, 4, and 10.

These numbers are tabulated in a matrix one pair at a time. The column is indicated by the second number, the row is indicated by the first number. The first pair is 10-6; the tally is placed in row ten, column six cell. The second pair is 6-10; tally this in the row six, column ten cell. The third pair is 10-7, the fourth pair is 7-5, and so on. Each pair overlaps with the next, and the total number of observations, 'N,' always will be tabulated by 'N-1' tallies in the matrix. In this case we started a series of ten numbers, and the series produced nine tallies in the matrix.

THE PROBLEM OF RELIABILITY

The problem of reliability is extremely complex, and a more complete discussion can be found in two terminal contract reports (1963, 1965a) one of which was published as a research monograph in the 1963 series of the Cooperative Research Program [or in the fourth paper of Chapter II of this book (Eds.)]. Education students can learn how to make quick field checks of their reliability and work toward higher reliability under the direction of an instructor.

Table 3-7

Matrix analysis

Category	Classification		Category	1	2	3	4	5	6	7	8	9	10	Total
Accepts feelings	Teacher talk	Indirect influence	1	Area E										
Praise			2											
Student idea			3											
Asks questions			4	"Content cross"							Area I			
Lectures			5											
Gives directions		Direct influence	6						Area F					
Criticism			7											
Student response	Student talk		8	Area G					Area H		Area J			
Student initiation			9											
Silence			10											
			Total	Area A			Area B			Area C		D		
				Indirect teacher talk			Direct teacher talk			Student talk				

THE INTERPRETATION OF MATRICES

A matrix should have at least 400 tallies, covering about 20 minutes or more of a homogeneous activity period, before an interpretation is attempted.

Certain areas within the matrix are particularly useful for describing teacher influence. Some of these areas will now be discussed by making reference to Table 3-7.

The column totals of a matrix are indicated as Areas "A," "B," "C," and "D." The figures in these areas provide a general picture by answering the following questions: What proportion of the time was someone talking compared with the portion in which confusion or no talking existed? When someone was talking, what proportion of the time was used by students? By the teacher? Of the time that the teacher talked, what proportion of his talk involved indirect influence? Direct influence?

The answers to these questions form a necessary backdrop to the interpretation of the other parts of the matrix. If student participation is about 30 or 40%, we would expect to find out why it was so high by studying the matrix. If the teacher is particularly direct or indirect, we would expect certain relationships to exist with student talk and silence.

The next two areas to consider are areas "E" and "F." Evidence that categories 1, 2, and 3 were used for periods longer than three seconds can be found in the diagonal cells, 1-1, 2-2, and 3-3. The other six cells of Area E indicate various types of transitions among these three categories. Sustained praise or clarification of student ideas is especially significant because such elaboration often involves criteria for praise or reasons for accepting ideas and feelings. The elaboration of praise or student ideas must be present if the student's ideas are to be integrated with the content being discussed by the class.

Area F is a four-cell combination of giving directions (category 6) and giving criticisms or self-justification (category 7). The transition cells 6-7 and 7-6 are particularly sensitive to difficulties that the teacher may have with classroom discipline or resistance on the part of students. When criticism follows directions or direction follows criticism, this means that the students are not complying satisfactorily. Often there is a high loading on the 6-9 cell under these circumstances. Excessively high frequencies in the 6-6 cell *and* 7-7 cell indicate teacher domination and supervision of the students' activities. A high loading of tallies in the 6-6 cell alone often indicates that the teacher is merely giving lengthy directions to the class.

The next two areas to be considered are Areas G and H. Tallies in these two areas occur at the instant the student stops talking and the teacher starts. Area G indicates those instances in which the teacher responds to the termination of student talk with indirect influence. Area H indicates those instances in which the teacher responds to the termination of student talk with direct influence. An interesting comparison can be made by contrasting the proportion G to H versus the proportion A to B. If these two proportions are quite different, it indicates that the teacher tends to act differently at the instant a student stops talking compared with his overall average. Often this is a mark of flexible teacher influence.

There are interesting relationships between Area E and Area G and between Area F and Area H. For example, Area G may indicate that a teacher responds indirectly to students at the instant they terminate their talk, but an observer may wish to inspect Area E to see if this indirect response is sustained in any way. The same question with regard to direct influence can be asked of Areas F and H. Areas G and H together usually fascinate teachers. They are often interested in knowing more about their immediate response to student participation.

Area I indicates an answer to the question, What types of teacher statements trigger student participation? Usually there is a high tally loading in cells 4-8 and 4-9. This is expected because students often answer questions posed by the teacher. A high loading on 4-8 and 8-4 cells alone usually indicates classroom drill directed by the teacher. The contrast of tallies in columns 8 and 9 in this area gives a rough indication of the frequency with which students initiate their own ideas versus respond to those of the teacher.

Area I is often considered in combination with Area J. Area J indicates either lengthy student statements or sustained student-to-student communication. An above-average frequency in Area C, but not in Area J, indicates that short answers, usually in response to teacher stimulation, have occurred. One would normally expect to find frequencies in Area E positively correlated with frequencies in Area J.

CONCEPTS AND PRINCIPLES OF TEACHER INFLUENCE

It may be too early to determine what are the *fewest* number of concepts which, if organized into logically related principles, can be used by a teacher to plan how he will use his authority. Surely he will need concepts that refer to his authority and its use. He will need concepts to describe learning goals and pupil tasks. He will need concepts to classify the responses of students. He may also need concepts to characterize class formations and patterns of classroom communication. These concepts are at least minimum.

Concepts that refer to teacher behavior

CLEAR GOALS. Goal perceptions are defined from the point of view of the pupil, not the teacher. "Clear goals" is a state of affairs in which the pupil knows what he is doing, the purpose, and can guess at the first few steps to be taken. It can be measured by paper-and-pencil tests, often administered at different points in a problem-solving sequence.

AMBIGUOUS GOALS. "Ambiguous goals" describes a state of affairs in which a pupil is not sure of what he is expected to do, is not sure of the first few steps, or is unable to proceed for one reason or another. It can be measured as above.

Other concepts in this area include: attractive and unattractive clear goals, pupil tasks, task requirements, and similar concepts.

Concepts that refer to pupil responses

DEPENDENT ACTS. Acts of dependence occur when a pupil not only complies with teacher influence but solicits such direction. A pupil who asks a teacher to approve of his work in order to make sure that it is satisfactory, before going on to the next logical step, is acting dependently. This type of response can be measured by observation techniques and by paper-and-pencil tests on which he indicates what kind of help he would like from the teacher.

INDEPENDENT ACTS. Acts of independence occur when the pupils react primarily to task requirements and are less directly concerned with teacher approval. The measurement of this concept is the same as for dependent acts.

Other concepts include: dependence proneness (a trait), compliance, conformity, counter-dependence, and similar concepts.

Some principles that can be discovered

We discovered in our research (Flanders, 1965a) that, during the first few days of a two-week unit of study in seventh-grade social studies and when introducing new material in eighth-grade mathematics, superior teachers are initially more indirect, becoming more direct as goals and associated tasks become clarified. We also suspect that these same teachers are more indirect when helping pupils diagnose difficulties, when trying to motivate pupils by arousing their interest, and in other situations in which the expression of pupil perceptions is helpful. On the other hand, the average or below average teacher did exactly the opposite.

Now the problem in teacher education is not only to create a situation in which education students could verify these relationships but could practice controlling their own behavior so as to become indirect or more direct at will. One place to begin is to have two, six-man groups work on a task under the direction of a leader. One task is something like an assembly line; it has a clear end product and sharp role differentiation. The other task is much more difficult to describe and does not have clear role differentiation. Now let the class superimpose different patterns of leader influence. Let them interview the role players, collect interaction analysis data by some simplified system of categories, and discuss the results. When undergraduate students first try to classify verbal statements, it sometimes helps to use only two or three categories. In one instance, the issue was the effect of using broad questions versus narrow questions. A broad question was one to which it was hard to predict the type of answer. Which type of question was more likely to increase pupil participation? The students role-played this and kept a record of broad questions, narrow questions, and the length of the response. The fact that they verified their prediction correctly for this rather superficial problem was much less important compared with the experience that they gained. They learned how to verify a prediction with empirical evidence, and some had a chance to practice control of their own behavior for professional purposes.

There is no space here to list a complete set of principles that can be investigated by systematic or intuitive data-collecting procedures. The following questions might stimulate useful learning activities. Does dependence always decrease as goals become clear? Is the final level of dependence determined by the pattern of teacher influence when goals are first formulated? Are measures of content achievement related to the pupils' attitudes toward the teacher and the schoolwork? What effects can you expect from excessive and pedantic clarification of pupil ideas and feelings? And many others.

APPLICATIONS OF INTERACTION ANALYSIS TO TEACHER EDUCATION

Suppose that before education students were given their practice teaching assignment, they had been exposed to a variety of data-collecting techniques for assessing pupil perceptions, measuring achievement, and quantifying spontaneous teacher influence. Suppose, further, that these skills had been taught in a context of personal inquiry as described earlier. What effect would this have on their approach to practice teaching?

One of their suggestions might be that two students should be assigned as a team to the first assignment. While one took over the class the other could be collecting information; the next day or so, the roles could be reversed.

Together they would work out a lesson plan, agree on the data to be collected, go over the results with the help of the supervising teacher who might also have the same data-collecting skills. This situation could approach the inquiry model described earlier. The practice teacher might discover that his failure to clarify the pupils' ideas restricted the development of curiosity or that his directions were too short when he was asked for further help; both of these inferences can be made from an interaction matrix with reasonable reliability and objectivity.

Later on a student may wish to take a practice teaching assignment by himself and turn to the supervising teacher for aid in feedback. In either case, the requirement is that the learner be able to compare his intentions with feedback information about his actions and analyze this information by using concepts which he found useful in his earlier courses in education.

There are some precautions that can already be stated with regard to the use of interaction analysis in such a situation.

First, no interaction analysis data should be collected unless the person observed is familiar with the entire process and knows its limitations.

Second, the questions to be answered by inspecting the matrix should be developed before the observation takes place.

Third, value judgments about good and bad teaching behavior are to be avoided. Emphasis is given to the problem being investigated so that cause-and-effect relationships can be discovered.

Fourth, a certain amount of defensive behavior is likely to be present at the initial consultation; it is something like listening to a tape recording for the first time.

Fifth, a consultation based on two observations or at least two matrices helps to eliminate value judgments or at least control them. Comparisons between the matrices are more likely to lead to principles.

Just how experiences of the type we have been discussing will fit into the present curricula is difficult to know. If activities of the sort described in this paper are valuable, are they to be superimposed on the present list of courses or is more radical surgery necessary?

Perhaps this is the point to risk a prediction, which is that teacher education will become increasingly concerned with the process of teaching itself during the next few decades. Instead of emphasizing knowledge which *we think* teachers will need in order to teach effectively, as we have in the past, we will turn more and more to an analysis of teaching acts as they occur in spontaneous classroom interaction. We are now at the point in our technology of data collecting at which procedures for analyzing and conceptualizing teaching behavior can be developed. Systems for doing this will become available regardless of whether they are similar or dissimilar to the procedures described in this paper. When this fine day arrives, the role of the education instructor will change, and the dichotomy between field and theory will disappear. The instructor's role will shift from talking about effective teaching to the rigorous challenge of demonstrating effective teaching. The process of inquiry will create problem-solving activities that will produce more independent, self-directing teachers whose first day on the job will be their worst, not their best.

These changes will be successful to the extent that the graduates of teacher education can learn to control their own behavior for the professional purpose of managing effective classroom learning. It will be the responsibility of the education instructor to help prospective teachers discover what their teaching intentions should be and then create training situations in which behavior gradually matches intentions with practice. Teaching will remain an art, but it will be studied scientifically.

5

THE USE OF INTERACTION ANALYSIS IN SUPERVISING STUDENT TEACHERS[41]

RICHARD D. ZAHN

STATEMENT OF THE PROBLEM

The problem in this study was to determine what effect instruction in and supervision with Flanders' system of interaction analysis would have on the attitudes and performance of student teachers. Specifically, the purposes of the study were: (1) to compare the use of conventional supervisory techniques with pre-service student teachers with the use of interaction analysis as a supervisory technique, (2) to determine the effect of using interaction analysis as a supervisory technique on student teachers' attitudes and performance in a student teaching experience, and (3) to determine the effects of the cooperating teachers' attitudes toward teaching on the professional attitudes of the student teachers.

METHOD OF THE STUDY

Selected for this study were 92 elementary-education students, and their cooperating teachers, who were undergoing their junior-year student-teaching experience. The 92 students were assigned to four equal groups, three of which received conventional instruction and supervision. The fourth group received instruction and supervision using interaction analysis. One group experiencing conventional instruction and supervision was instructed and supervised by the investigator. So was the group with which interaction analysis was used.

Instruments to be used for the collection of data were selected. One personality inventory was chosen: the *Dogmatism Scale* (D-Scale). The teacher attitude inventory used was the *Teaching Situation Reaction Test* (TSRT).

---

[41] This paper was prepared specially for this book.

Student-teacher performance was rated through the use of the *Cooperating Teacher's Evaluation Form to be Used in Evaluating Classroom Participation of Practicum Students.*

All four groups were given the *Dogmatism Scale* and the TSRT prior to instruction and supervision in their teaching assignments. On completion of their student teaching assignments all subjects again received the TSRT. The cooperating teachers were given the TSRT during the initial stages of the student-teachers' assignment to the classroom. They completed the *Cooperating Teachers Evaluation Form to be Used in Evaluating Classroom Participation of Practicum Students* at the end of the student's teaching assignment.

The study provided for the input variable of instruction and supervision using interaction analysis. Prior to commencing the student teaching experience, the experimental group received approximately 15 hours of instruction in interaction analysis. The student teachers in this group were taught how to build matrices from raw data and to interpret the matrices. They also discussed research related to interaction analysis. The control groups were given the usual instruction prior to commencing classroom teaching experience.

The supervisor, when working with the interaction analysis group, could be best described as a feedback observer. In this role the observer furnished the student teacher with objective data about the lesson taught. The student teacher constructed his matrix from the interaction analysis data and met with the investigator to discuss the lesson. These conferences focused on analysis of data available from the tallies and the matrix. The student was encouraged to arrive at his own conclusions concerning the effectiveness of the lesson taught.

The control groups were observed by the college supervisor, who would commonly meet with the student following the lesson to discuss it, emphasizing achievement of objectives and problems in methodology and discipline. The supervisor indicated to the student the strengths and weaknesses of the lesson taught and made suggestions for improvement. He commonly evaluated the student teacher's lesson as poor, fair, good, or excellent.

The *t*-test was used to analyze differences in the data on attitude and teaching performance which were collected in the various groups. Chi-square tests of significance were chosen to analyze the number and direction of the subject's changes in teaching attitude.

On the basis of the findings, a number of conclusions and recommendations were made concerning the use of interaction analysis as an instructional and supervisory tool with student teachers.

SUMMARY OF THE RESULTS OF THE EXPERIMENT

On the basis of the results of the study there appeared to be a relationship between the type of instruction and supervision the student teachers received and attitude change. There also appeared to be a relationship between the strength of the student teacher's belief system and his teaching performance as rated by the cooperating teacher. The following results emerged from the study:

1. Student teachers undergoing instruction and supervision using interaction analysis had more positive teaching attitudes after student teaching than those students undergoing conventional supervision and instruction.

2. The student teachers undergoing instruction and supervision using interaction analysis tended to modify their teaching attitudes more positively than student teachers undergoing conventional instruction and supervision, regardless of the attitude of the cooperating teacher.

3. Student teachers with *Dogmatism Scale* scores that were above average but not more than one standard deviation above the mean tended to change their teaching attitudes positively if they experienced instruction and supervision using interaction analysis.

4. Student teachers with *Dogmatism Scale* scores one standard deviation below the mean (relatively open belief system) were judged to be significantly more proficient in their student teaching performance than those student teachers one standard deviation above the mean (relatively closed belief system), regardless of the kind of supervision received.

CONCLUSIONS

In relation to the purposes of this study and within the limitations established, these conclusions appear to be appropriate:

1. The use of interaction analysis in the instruction and supervision of student teachers appears to be related to a positive change in the teaching attitude of the student. The use of interaction analysis as an instructional and supervisory tool with student teachers seems to have a predictable and measurable effect on improved attitude change with students not limited by very strong belief systems.

2. The amount and direction of change in teaching attitude that is experienced by the student teacher receiving instruction and supervision using interaction analysis is limited by the strength of his belief system. The results indicate that interaction analysis as a supervisory technique for students with strong belief systems is particularly related to positive attitude change. This relationship may be caused by the need of these students for structure, which is met by the objective nature of the feedback provided by interaction analysis technique. The student teacher's attention is focused on classroom interaction that he has caused to occur. The desires and value orientation of the supervisor are forced into a position at least secondary to the relatively objective data furnished by the matrix. Through the analysis of these data, with the supervisor serving as clarifier, the student can better understand his style of teaching in relation to desired objectives.

3. While the personality of the supervisor appears to have an effect on the attitude of the student teacher, the method of instruction and supervision used by the supervisor has an effect as well.

To ascertain the relative effect of the supervisor versus the cooperating teacher appears to be a difficult task. The data furnished by this study indicate that the supervisor, through a specific technique of supervision, can influence the student's teaching attitude. This point of view was illustrated by the investigator who used both conventional techniques and the method of interaction analysis as a supervisory tool. The personality of the investigator seemed to make some difference in positive attitude change, but when he used interaction analysis as an instructional and supervisory tool the investigator appeared to be related to a greater positive change.

4. The effect of the cooperating teacher on the attitude of the student teacher seems to be greater when students are supervised by conventional techniques than it is when the college supervisor uses the techniques of interaction analysis.

5. The quality of the student teacher's performance appears to be related to the strength of his belief–disbelief system.

6

ELEMENTARY SCHOOL STUDENT TEACHERS AND INTERACTION ANALYSIS[42]

JEFFERY KIRK

The study described here had two purposes: to determine whether interaction analysis (Flanders, 1963) could discover elements of teaching style common to student teachers of intermediate grades, and to determine whether knowledge of interaction analysis would lead student teachers to alter their teaching styles in any manner; there was concern neither with pupil achievement nor with the cognitive aspects of the social-studies classes analyzed. The study was designed to produce temporary norms which might be validated by further studies, and the norms were to describe two shifts: (1) As student teachers led free-discussion classes in social studies, what changes in verbal patterns occurred between the beginning and the end of a placement? (2) If student teachers were taught the fundamentals of interaction analysis and were able to analyze several of their own classes, how would the normal shift in the pattern be influenced?

Fifteen student teachers were selected as an experimental group to be taught interaction analysis. Fifteen other student teachers, comparable in age, professional experience, basic personality, and attitude toward teaching, were allowed, as a control group, to proceed through their placement without contacting the ideas of interaction analysis in any way. Each group was observed initially for ten hours as they taught their fourth-, fifth-, and sixth-grade children; six and seven weeks later similar observations occurred. Thus each individual student teacher was observed, on the average, for one hour and 24 minutes total, or for two 21-minute periods on separate days during pretraining and for two separate 21-minute periods during posttraining. For purposes of group comparison, all individual matrices were combined into four master matrices; two for the pretraining groups and two for the posttraining groups.

---

[42] This paper was prepared specially for this book.

Chi-Square was used to deal with the frequency data contained in these matrices, all data being treated to hold the time factor constant.

The experimental treatment consisted of teaching the student teachers to notate, construct, and interpret the records presented by interaction analysis, including records of their own teaching efforts. Five hours of semester time were given to discussion of and training in interaction analysis, and six individual conferences, occurring immediately after weekly visits by the college supervisor, who was running the experiment, focused, at least in part, on the tally sheet of the lesson just observed. No prescriptive statements were made by the supervisor at any time, though there was some discussion of previous research results.

Several results of this study will now be reviewed in terms of the original two questions: First, the apparent norms that student teachers produce in their handling of open-discussion social-studies classes will be examined, as well as the way in which knowledge of interaction analysis affects these norms. Second, wherever possible, an attempt will be made to compare these norms with previous results as reported by Ned Flanders.[43] It should be recalled that Flanders' investigation was with in-service teachers of social studies in a junior high school in Minnesota, while the present study was with pre-service intermediate teachers in Philadelphia.

Lastly, an ideal curve will be imposed on occasional actualized figures, a curve which should be considered at this time to be more aesthetically suggestive than scientifically approbative. For just as the generalizations induced here refer only to the student teachers of this study, the ideals deduced refer only to a possible world, and perhaps not to the best of these.

Who does the talking?

Student teachers talk more than their pupils and tend to speak less as time goes on. They begin their placement by commanding nearly 60% of the total class time and end by speaking about 56% of the time. Meanwhile their pupils tend to increase the amount of their contributions, beginning around 29% and consuming 32% or more by the conclusion of their student-teachers' placement. The relationship between the pupils' and the student teachers' total amount of talking may be shown by a P/T ratio, the ideal ratio being arbitrarily set at 1.0, a 50–50 relationship.

Table 3–8 and Fig. 3–4 show how the experimental group in this study compares with the control group and with Flanders' teachers. Their P/T ratio of 0.76 was significantly higher (0.01) than that of the control group. Knowledge of interaction analysis seems to lead toward fuller pupil participation, a decline in teacher talk, or both.

---

[43] The Flanders figures are taken from *Teacher Influence, Pupil Attitudes, and Achievement* (1963) and from his chapter, "Some Relationships Between Teacher Influence, Pupil Attitudes, and Achievement." See the last papers in Chapter Two.

Table 3–8

Pupil Talk–Student Teacher Talk Relationships*

| | Student-teacher norms | | | In-service norms | | | |
	Pre.†	Post.	Exp.	Dir.	Av.	Ind.	Ideal
Pupil talk							
Percent of total time	29	32	40**	23	36	32	—
Percent of talk time	32	37	43**	27	41	36	50
Student-teacher talk							
Percent of total time	60	56	53**	61	52	57	—
Percent of talk time	68	63	57**	73	59	64	50
P/T ratio	0.48	0.58	0.76**	0.38	0.68	0.56	1.00

* All percentages in the tables and figures in this article have been rounded to the nearest whole percentage. More accurate percentages as well as the statistical evidence for significance of reliability claims may be found in (Kirk, 1964).

† Pre. = pretraining; Post. = posttraining; Exp. = experimental group; Cont. = control group; Dir. = direct teachers; Av. = average teachers; Ind. = indirect teachers.

** 0.01 level of probability

Key; ▨ Minnesota Teachers
  — Ideal curve of improvement (0.33 — 0.50 — 1.00)
  ← Experimental group
  → Control group

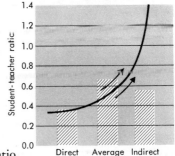

FIG. 3–4 P/T ratio.

What do they talk about?

As the student teachers become more familiar with their classes, they spend more time discussing the topic at hand and less time motivating and controlling. Examination of the content-cross area of the matrix shows that, as given in Table 3–9, both groups of student teachers became remarkably similar to Flanders' (1960, p. 19) average teachers, as they fitted their content communications precisely within his predicted range of 75–80% of total talk. There was no significant difference between the groups in this regard.

Table 3–9

Content-Cross Percentages*

| | Pretraining | | Posttraining | |
	Control	Experimental	Control	Experimental
Percent of total time	39	40	42	41
Percent of total talk	67	66	75	77

* Percentages found in Flanders' categories 4 and 5 summed.

Table 3–10

Indirect–Direct Ratios (I/D)

	Student teachers			In-service teachers			
Pretraining		Posttraining					
Cont.	Exp.	Cont.	Exp.	Dir.	Ave.	Ind.	Ideal
0.89	0.79	0.74	0.73	0.25	0.53	0.73	1.00

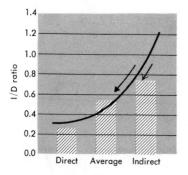

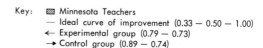

Key: ▨ Minnesota Teachers
      — Ideal curve of improvement (0.33 — 0.50 — 1.00)
      ← Experimental group (0.79 — 0.73)
      → Control group (0.89 — 0.74)

FIG. 3–5. I/D ratio.

How does the student teacher talk?

Though they talk less as their experience broadens, student teachers seem to lecture more. Roughly a quarter of all class time is consumed by lecturing, the overall percentages moving from 22 to 26. In terms of their own talk, student-teacher lecture time increases from slightly more than one-third to nearly one-half, i.e., from 37 to 48%. The great majority of all lecturing is continuous, taking longer than three seconds to deliver, as indicated by tallies in the 5-5 cell. In other words, 66% of all lecturing at the beginning of the placement is continuous; by the end it is 70%. Therefore, the general conclusion regarding lecturing by student teachers is that as time goes on they become more informative, doing so with fewer moves of longer duration. All other categories of student-teacher talk decrease. The ramifications of this fact are dealt with in the next section.

Do student teachers become more or less direct?

The answer to this question depends on the segments of interaction being considered, as well as on the definition of directness. The direct–indirect continuum relates to theoretical assumptions regarding pupil freedom of verbal participation as quantified in categories which, again theoretically, enhance or curtail this freedom. The P/T ratio previously discussed shows student teachers as becoming less direct, with the experimental group allowing even significantly greater pupil participation. The lecture increase, however, identifies as an opposing tendency: in their general use of language, student teachers tend to

---

Table 3–11

Indirect–Direct Ratios (i/d)

Student teachers				In-service teachers			
Pretraining		Posttraining					
Cont.	Exp.	Cont.	Exp.	Dir.	Av.	Ind.	Ideal
0.97	1.01	1.24	1.83	0.19	0.48	1.52	1.50

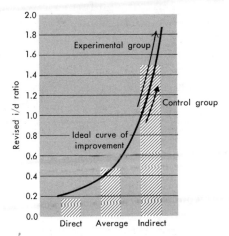

FIG. 3–6. i/d ratio.

become more direct. This is demonstrated in the I/D ratio as portrayed in Table 3–10 and Fig. 3–5. When an ideal balance is hypothesized between the use of the direct (as opposed to the indirect) categories, the student teachers gradually swing toward weighting the former. They remain in the indirect–superior area of Flanders' in-service teachers, though the swing is toward the average.

In this tendency toward directness there is no essential difference between that of the control group and that of the experimental group. A signal difference does appear in the i/d ratio, however.

The i/d ratio comparing the teachers' praise statements and acceptance of pupils' ideas and feelings with their corrective and directive statements again shows the growth toward indirectness. Though all categories other than lecture are used less at the end of the placement than at the beginning, the decrease in the direct categories is sharper than the decrease in the indirect categories. Student teachers give fewer directions and criticisms, while giving more praise, commendations, and recognition to their pupils, so that, comparatively, their protracted use of encouraging language waxes as their prolonged use of restrictive language wanes. The resulting shift in i/d ratios, seen in Table 3–11 and Fig. 3–6, allows the conclusion that student teachers tend to become more indirect in their attempts to motivate and control their pupils.

Several conclusions may be drawn from the figures on i/d ratio. First, the i/d ratio seems to be the most accurate of the three ratios here discussed, for it more surely unites theory with practice. Its 0.25–0.50–1.50 projected curve virtually coincides with the 0.19–0.48–1.64 actualized curve of Flanders' teachers. The I/D ratio is also essentially true to life, although the superior-achievement teachers did not show the overall language indirectness expected. The P/T ratio projection was definitely inaccurate for the superior teachers; an actual decline occurred, rather than an increment. Thus the I/D and P/T ideal curves (both 0.33–0.50–1.00) must either be modified to fit reality or shown to be indicative of reality through further research.

Second, as mentioned above, student teachers seem to tend naturally toward increasing indirectness in their verbal social skills.

Third, when student teachers are taught the rudiments of interaction analysis, a significant increase in their use of the indirect social skills seems to be an unsolicited result. The normal increment is accelerated. If this is indeed the case and if indirectness is a goal of educators, then longer and more intensive study of interaction analysis by student teachers might improve the condition of teacher training.

In the interest of space, no other indirect-direct ratios discernible within the interaction matrix will be discussed here. The "immediate response to pupil participation I/D" and the "extended use of motivating language i/d," for example, are also sensitive indicators of teacher influence; the harmony between data and ideal shown in them will have to be explained in another place. Of the myriads of facts discovered in the present study, only three more will be mentioned; one is an element of style, and the second and third are specific effects of learning interaction analysis.

What happens when the lecture stops?

Eighty-five percent of the time that a student teacher stops lecturing, three activities prevail: a question is asked of the pupils, a pupil responds without being asked, or a direction is given by the student teacher. As the placement matures, pupil response gradually outweighs teacher direction, though together response and direction continually constitute 40% of after-lecture activity. The element of style is this, that nearly every other time a student teacher discontinues lecturing, she asks a question. This 45% lecture–question sequence is held throughout the experience and shows no variance. Whether the tendency to top statements with queries is an effective teaching pattern depends undoubtedly on the quality of the questions, but a quantitative variation, allowing for other types of verbal activity on the part of the teacher and including intentional silence, might be worthy of some research.

What would be the effect, for instance, of teachers consciously dropping the questions from 45 to 33% and saying *nothing* occasionally when they stop talking? The present study indicates that, under the traditional standards of teacher practice, the chance that there will be some extended silence following a lecture bit is only one in 31 (a 3.2% chance). Why not give silent thought a chance, say one in ten?

What interaction patterns develop?

Close analysis of the "conversation" cells of the matrix (cells 5-9, 9-5, 3-9, and 9-3), the "continuous-lecture" cell (5-5), and the "continuous-initiation" cell (9-9) shows some interesting differences between the two groups in this study. In addition to the previously mentioned general tendency for the student teachers to lecture more, there is a general tendency for the pupils in both groups to loosen up as time goes on, to speak more freely and at greater length. The probability that a pupil's freely initiated statement will follow lecturing increases by nearly two, i.e., at the end of the placement there is nearly twice the chance that student-teacher lecturing will be followed with a volunteered pupil contribution than there is at the beginning. Nevertheless, significant differences were found in the conversation patterns of the two groups:

1. Spontaneous pupil talk (category 9) as well as continuous spontaneous pupil talk (cell 9-9) increased more than expected in the experimental group.

2. Continuous lecture (cell 5-5) of the experimental group did not show the expected increase but in fact declined slightly.

3. The experimental pupils interjected comments and questions into their student teachers' lecturing more frequently than expected (cell 5-9).

4. The experimental student teachers reacted to their pupils' spontaneous participation with more content-oriented material than expected (cell 9-5). In other words, although they lectured more as time passed, the experimental student teachers were not more lengthy in their lectures. They spoke rather in response to unelicited pupil statements, in "bursts," their discourse interrupted by other forms of verbal behavior. The pattern of interaction was consequently more conversational than lectorial, the pupils evidently feeling quite free to enter into the exchange of ideas at will.

That this more conversational pattern appears in the experimental group may be attributed to their more indirect i/d ratio. There may have been a more mutually functional relationship between the two sets of facts. It was one of the conclusions of this study, however, that a definite connection exists between the learning of interaction analysis and the two favorable results.

Do the pupils perceive any change in teaching style?

A "Student Perception of Teacher Attitude" inventory (Anderson, 1960), run both at the beginning and at the end of the placement, showed that the 449 children taught by the experimental group felt some slight but significant (0.01 level) differences in classroom procedure and climate when compared with the feelings of the 427 pupils taught by the control group. Though the results of the inventory were similar during the pretraining period, the later inventory showed the experimental pupils shifting toward a perception of indirectness when forced to choose descriptions in such items as "The teacher seems to be mostly concerned with explaining the material—or finding out what we know," and "The attitude of the teacher seems to be firm and businesslike—or relaxed and cheerful." A second section of this inventory failed to discriminate between the groups, except in one item; "Does this teacher talk more than the students?" The experimental pupils here shifted from the mean "about the same" toward the higher P/T ratio of "less than the students." These findings are in harmony with those of the interaction analysis.

We reach the conclusion, then, that indirect student teaching and training in interaction analysis appear to be related, though how strong the relationship is and whether it is entirely good cannot be unequivocally expressed. All that we can say with certainty is that the student teachers in one group were made more aware of what they did in class and of what is possible than did the other group, and that they achieved a relaxed, conversational, and content-centered atmosphere without being ordered to. Other student teachers individually achieved the same result through the graciousness of their own proclivities, but those who learned interaction analysis became indirect through positive reactions to the objective instrument, changing as a group and thus statistically.

7

BEHAVIORAL CHANGE
IN STUDENT TEACHERS[44]

JOHN B. HOUGH and EDMUND AMIDON

This article reports a portion of a larger study of behavioral change in pre-service teacher education done at Temple University during the Spring semester 1963 (Hough and Amidon, 1964). The purpose of the aspect of the study reported here was to test the effectiveness of an experimental pre-service experience on student-teaching performance. The authors recognized from the outset of this study that one of the major problems involved in effecting behavioral change is getting people to "do" in terms of what they "know." Combs (1958) summarizes one dimension of this problem when he says, "Modern psychology tells us that it is only when knowledge becomes meaning that behavior is affected. If it is meaning that affects human behavior, then it is meaning with which educators must deal."

If the above statement is true, then the key to changing the behavior of teachers seems to lie in finding ways of helping teachers discover personal meaning in cognitive knowledge regarding the teaching–learning process. The problem for the investigators in this study thus became that of finding a means by which student teachers could (a) gain knowledge about principles of teaching and learning, (b) make use of such knowledge in a situation characterized by personal meaning, (c) get immediate feedback regarding the effects of their behavior in the classroom, and thus (d) discover for themselves more effective patterns of teaching behavior.

In the process of creating an experience which would meet the four criteria described above, several assumptions were formulated. First, it was assumed that if the Flanders system of interaction analysis (Amidon and Flanders, 1963) were learned by student teachers, it would provide them with a feedback mechanism which would increase the accuracy with which they could view their own behavior in student teaching. Second, it was assumed that a concomitant learning situation that focused on the teaching of understandings regarding the teaching–learning process would provide the student teachers

---

[44] This paper was prepared specially for this book.

with a concomitant set of learnings concerning the teaching–learning process that would transfer to the student teaching situation. Third, it was assumed that a concomitant laboratory experience in which student teachers could explore ideas regarding the teaching–learning process, and thus develop for themselves a structure of understanding and attitude to support their teaching behavior, would serve as an integrating and supporting experience both for the student-teaching experience and for the class in teaching–learning principles.

The investigators recognized, however, that for such a set of experiences to make an impact on student teachers, these teachers must be open to the many stimuli available in student teaching, the teaching–learning principles class, and the laboratory. The richest environment of stimuli is of questionable use to a person if he is unable to perceive accurately the stimuli that characterize that environment. Prior experience and the condition of receptors are two factors that influence perception. A third factor may be found in the relative openness or closedness of the person's belief–disbelief system as defined by Rokeach (1960). Ideas that pose a threat to the person's belief–disbelief system are likely to be distorted to harmonize with that system or to be subconsciously screened out. According to Rokeach, the belief–disbelief system seems to act as a filter which distorts the reality of some stimuli and screens out others. It would seem, therefore, that there would be a relationship between the relative openness of a person's belief–disbelief system and his ability to accurately perceive stimuli and profit from experience.

Previous research seemed to support both the teaching of interaction analysis to student teachers as a feedback mechanism for viewing the effects of their teaching behavior and the use of a concomitant human-relations laboratory in which ideas about the teaching–learning process could be tested in a relatively threat-free situation. In a study of the effects on teaching behavior of an in-service workshop that taught interaction analysis, Flanders (1963) found improved teaching performance, particularly for teachers who were indirect in the classroom. Bowers and Soar (1961) used an experimental human-relations training design in a workshop experience for in-service teachers. They found that only some teachers showed positive change as a result of the experience, but that change was related to personality factors as measured by the Minnesota Multiphasic Personality Inventory. Similar findings were reported by Engle (1961) in a study that showed the behavioral change of teachers and administrators who participated in a workshop experience to be related to self concept and openness to experience, as measured by the Index of Adjustment and Values. The dimension of personality used in the study reported in this article was the relative openness or closedness of the belief–disblief system, as measured by Form E of the Dogmatism Scale (Rokeach, 1960).

The four hypotheses for this study were as follows:

1. Students in the experimental group of student teachers will be observed by their student-teaching supervisors as being more effective in their student teaching than student teachers in the control group.

2. Over a semester period of time, students in the experimental student teaching group will become more empathic in their relationship with their students, more objective in their use of data about students, more experimental in their use of methodology, and more positive in their use of control measures (as measured by the Teaching Situation Reaction Test).

3. Over a semester period of time, students in the student-teaching control group will become more empathic in their relationship with students, more objective in their use of data about students, and more experimental in their use of control measures (as measured by the Teaching Situation Reaction Test).

4. Student–teacher change in the direction of more empathic relationships with students, more objective use of data about students, more experimental use of methodology, and greater use of positive control measures (as measured by the Teaching Situation Reaction Test) will be positively related to the relative openness or closedness of the student teacher's belief–disbelief system (as measured by Form E of the Dogmatism Scale).

METHOD

Procedures

In the Spring semester of 1963 the authors introduced an experimental section of a course in the teaching–learning process in the secondary-education teacher-preparation program at Temple University. This experimental section of the course was taught in conjunction with the regular student-teaching experience, and it combined the teaching of the Flanders system of interaction analysis with the teaching of instructional theory and an experimental human-relations laboratory. The term "instructional theory" is used here to mean principles of teaching derived from learning theory and transferred into descriptive statements of teacher and student behavior. Wherever such statements of teacher and student behavior were translatable into categories of the Flanders system of interaction analysis, such parallels were drawn. An example of an instructional principle translated into the categories of the Flanders system would be, "all other things being equal, teacher acceptance (Flanders category 3) or praise (Flanders category 2) of student responses (Flanders category 8) to teacher questions (Flanders category 4) will result in an increase in the probability that such student responses will be emitted in the future."

The initial teaching of interaction analysis and instructional principles was done in a two-hour lecture. An experimental laboratory in human relations and teaching was scheduled each week in which students perfected their skills in interaction analysis, explored hypothetical and actual applications of instructional principles in their student teaching, and sought through informal discussion to find personal meaning in instructional principles as they might apply to their behavior in the laboratory and the problems they were having in their student teaching. A climate of relative permissiveness was established in the laboratory to encourage the student teachers to feel free to explore the personal meaning of ideas both with their peers and with the laboratory instructor. The total experimental course, composed of two hours of lecture and two hours of laboratory each week, was scheduled by 20 S's who were concurrently scheduled for student teaching. These S's constituted the experimental group. Eight of these 20 S's were scheduled for preliminary student teaching and 12 for final student teaching. Students scheduling preliminary student teaching are usually juniors. They teach one class per day, five days a week, for a full semester. Students taking final student teaching are seniors. They teach two classes a day, five days a week, for a full semester.

In addition to the experimental treatment described above, the design of this study included a student teaching control group. The control group consisted of 20 student teachers drawn as a stratified random sample from 54 student teachers who were not scheduled for the experimental course. This sample was drawn in such a way as to equate the experimental and control groups on such variables as (a) number of preliminary and final student teachers, (b) supervisors responsible for evaluating student teachers, and (c) type of class and grade level taught in student teaching. Thirteen of the S's in the control group were scheduled for final student teaching. All of these S's had taken the conventional course in instructional principles (four class hours per week) the previous semester. Seven S's who were preliminary student teachers and had not taken the instructional-principles course were assigned to a general-methods seminar concurrently with their student teaching. The course experiences of the control group represented the typical pattern of courses and student teaching taken by secondary-education majors at Temple University. No S's in the control group had learned interaction analysis.

Tests and measures

At the beginning of the semester all S's were pre-tested on the Teaching Situation Reaction Test and Form E of the Dogmatism Scale. They were post-tested at the end of the semester on the Teaching Situation Reaction Test. The Teaching Situation Reaction Test is a 36-item forced-choice instrument which requires the S to rank four possible choices of action from most desirable to least desirable. These 36 items are problem situations, and all are related to one ongoing classroom situation that extends over several months. The Teaching Situation Reaction Test is designed to measure such attitude and understanding variables as empathic relationships with students, objective use of data about students, experimental use of methodology, and the use of positive control measures. Scores on this test have been found to relate positively to performance in student teaching (Hough and Amidon, 1964).

Performance in student teaching was measured by two instruments developed for this study. The first of these instruments was the TSRT Observational Rating Scale (a 20-item rating scale used to rate student teachers on behaviors associated with the construct of the Teaching Situation Reaction Test). The second instrument was the General Supervisory Rating Scale (a six-item rating

Table 3–12

Means and Standard Deviations for the Groups on the Control Variables

Variable	Experimental group (N = 20)		Control group (N = 20)	
	M	SD	M	SD
Teaching Situation Reaction Test	60.70	8.76	61.00	8.65
Dogmatism Scale	117.54	25.28	117.55	25.28
Cumulative point hour ratio	2.67	0.46	2.39	0.73
Education point hour ratio	2.75	0.41	2.65	0.91
Teaching field point hour ratio	2.68	0.64	2.54	0.33
Semester hours in teaching field	29.55	8.55	33.05	8.44

scale used to rate student teachers on such factors as organization and presentation of lessons, handling of classroom routine, and the development of a classroom climate conducive to learning). All the S's were rated on these instruments by their student-teaching supervisors at the conclusion of their student teaching.

At the beginning of the semester the experimental and control groups were found not to differ on the Teaching Situation Reaction Test scores, on Dogmatism Scale scores, on cumulative point–hour ratio, education course point–hour ratio, teaching field point–hour ratio, or in the number of semester hours of credit earned in their teaching fields, as shown in Table 3–12. (Ratios are not reported in Table 3–12, but none were significant.)

RESULTS

The reliability of the Teaching Situation Reaction Test was computed by using the split-half method suggested by Ross and Stanley (1954). The reliability was computed for the pre-test using an N of 60, and was found to be 0.94. Using the formula for the standard error of a test as suggested by Guilford (1956), the SE was found to be 1.97.

The hypothesis was that student teachers in the experimental group would be observed by their supervisors as being more effective in student teaching than student teachers in the control group, and it was supported both for supervisory ratings on the TSRT Observational Rating Scale ($t = 1.75$, $P < 0.05$) and on the General Observational Rating Scale ($t = 1.73$, $P < 0.05$), as shown in Table 3–13.

Table 3–13

Groups Compared on Supervisors' Ratings

	Experimental group (N = 20)		Control group (N = 20)		Significance level[a]	
	M	SD	M	SD	t	P
TSRT observation rating scale[c]	38.25	13.27	46.05	14.25	1.75	0.05
General observation rating scale[d]	42.65	6.93	38.14	12.16	1.73[b]	0.05

[a] Using a one-tail test.
[b] Using 19 d.f. (F = 3.62, <0.01).
[c] Low scores on this rating scale indicate more positive ratings.
[d] High scores on this rating scale indicate more positive ratings.

Table 3–14

Groups Compared on Teaching Situation Reaction Test Change Scores

	M	SD	t	Significance level*
	Pre- to post-test change	Change score		
Experimental group (N = 20)	−3.85†	6.93	2.42	0.01
Control group (N = 20)	−0.45	6.85	0.29	NS

* Using a one-tail test.
† Negative score indicates positive change.

Of the two hypotheses that predicted change on the Teaching Situation Reaction Test over a semester period of time, only hypothesis number two could be supported. While the experimental group did show a significant change ($t = 2.42$, $P < 0.01$), the control group did not show significant change. These data are presented in Table 3–14.

Hypothesis number four, that Teaching Situation Reaction Test pre- to post-change scores would be positively related to Dogmatism Scale scores, could be supported only for the experimental group ($r = 0.38$, $P < 0.05$), as shown in Table 3–15. Table 3–16 presents data to show that when the ten S's in the experimental group who were below the mean on the Dogmatism Scale were compared with the ten S's in the control group who were below the mean on the Dogmatism Scale, it could be seen that those in the experimental group had made a significantly greater change ($t = 1.81$, $P < 0.05$).

Table 3–15

Correlation of Dogmatism Scale Scores and Teaching Situation
Reaction Test Change Scores

	Experimental group	Control group
Dogmatism Scale scores with Teaching Situation Reaction Test pre- to post-change scores	0.38*	−0.04

*Significant <0.05 using a one-tail test with 18 d.f.

Table 3–16

Comparison of the Ten Students Below the Mean on the Dogmatism Scale in Each Group
on Teaching Situation Reaction Test Change Scores

	Experimental group (N = 10)		Control group (N = 10)		Significance level*	
	M	SD	M	SD	t	P
Teaching Situation Reaction Test pre- to post-change scores	−4.40†	8.36	1.70	6.00	1.81	< 0.05

* Using a one-tail test.
† Negative score indicates positive change.

Discussion

The findings of this study seem to indicate that the combination of experiences provided for the experimental group was effective in that it had the predicted effect on the behavior of student teachers and on the changes in attitudes and understandings associated with effective teaching. However, the limitations of the experimental design of this study make it impossible to make a definitive statement of the causes of the superiority of the experimental group.

Was the superiority of the experimental group in their student teaching a function of the students' use of interaction analysis as a feedback mechanism? Did the experimental laboratory provide an experience in which students could, in fact, analyze their own teaching behavior and thus develop a structure of attitude and understanding which served as a basis for their behavior in student teaching? Without such a tool as interaction analysis for viewing their behavior, could such an attitude and understanding structure have been internalized in their teaching behavior? Was the apparent superiority of the experimental group in student teaching and their development of attitudes and understandings which have been found to be related to effective teaching a function of only one of the experimental variables, or of several of these variables interacting with one another?

At the outset of this study the experimenters knew that the limitations of the design would not allow such questions to be answered. But if the effectiveness of the combination of variables characteristic of the experimental condition could be demonstrated, a future study could be designed to answer such questions.

Were the conditions of the experimental treatment equally effective for all students? There seems to be some evidence that they were not. Data have been presented to show that students in the experimental group gained significantly in the direction of attitudes and understandings associated with effective teaching as measured by the Teaching Situation Reaction Test. However, data have also been presented to show that this change occurred primarily in those student teachers who scored below the mean on the Dogmatism Scale. This would seem to indicate that the combination of experiences characteristic of the experimental condition was most effective for the ten students who had the most open belief–disbelief systems. Certainly this study should be replicated with more controls, but these findings are really not surprising. One would expect the more open students to be the ones who would most profit from the rich environment characteristic of the experimental condition.

It is of significance to note that the student teachers in the control group showed no significant change during their student teaching experience in the direction of becoming more empathic in their relationships with students, more objective in their use of data about students, more experimental in their use of methodology, or more indirect in their use of control measures as measured by the Teaching Situation Reaction Test. The failure of the experiment to support hypothesis three raises more questions than it answers. Certainly one interpretation of these data could be that the conventional student teaching program without a supporting human-relations laboratory results in a rather traumatic and perhaps threatening experience which for many student teachers results in an attitudinal regression in terms of those variables measured by the Teaching Situation Reaction Test.

If future research continues to support the findings of this study, and if future studies can be designed to isolate the effects of the experimental variables used in this study, such research would have broad implications for both teacher-education programs and the selection of candidates for such programs.

8

THE EFFECTS OF TRAINING IN INTERACTION ANALYSIS ON THE BEHAVIOR OF STUDENT TEACHERS IN SECONDARY SCHOOLS[45]

NORMA FURST

BACKGROUND OF THE STUDY

During the 1962–63 academic year, Hough and Amidon (1964) attempted to test certain hypotheses regarding the effect of an experimental pre-service experience on change in classroom behavior of secondary education student teachers.

They instituted a pre-service course called, "The Teaching–Learning Process," which consisted of a two-hour lecture and two-hour laboratory experience. The laboratory section was primarily designed to help students discover personal meaning in student teaching. Effects of their own teaching behavior were discussed and integrated with accepted learning principles. The experimental section of this course combined traditional learning theory content with instruction in the use of interaction analysis as developed by Ned Flanders (Amidon and Flanders, 1963). All the students in the experimental section were concurrently enrolled in student teaching. While control group students received instruction in conventional learning theory during a two-hour lecture and two-hour laboratory experience, they received no training in interaction analysis.

Hough and Amidon found evidence to support their hypothesis that student teachers in the experimental group would be rated by their college supervisors as more effective than student teachers in the control group. They also found evidence that the students in the experimental group showed significant positive pre-test to post-test change scores on a survey of attitudes toward the teaching situation.

---

[45] Paper read at the Annual Meeting of the American Education Research Association, Chicago, Illinois, February, 1965. Reprinted by permission of the author.

Hough and Amidon concluded that the combination of experiences which comprised the experimental treatment in this study was effective. In general, it had the predicted effects on student behavior.

This study raised some questions in the mind of the present researcher. Hough and Amidon accepted as evidence of behavior change, scores on a pencil-and-paper attitude survey and ratings made by college supervisors of student teaching. Workers in pre-service education are often aware of the limitations of these criteria. Opinions, philosophies and objectivity of college supervisors often differ significantly and student teachers often are fully able to verbalize positive attitudes toward their roles as teachers while at the same time having great difficulty making their strategies operational in the classroom.

The present study was therefore designed to actually observe classroom behavior of student teachers by a trained observer using an objective tool. The actual, overt teaching behavior of students who had been trained in the use of Flanders' interaction analysis would be compared with the actual, overt teaching behavior of student teachers who had been more conventionally trained.

This study was further designed to gather data to help make an intelligent administrative decision as to the best time to schedule the experimental course during pre-service education. Hough and Amidon had scheduled their experimental sections concurrently with student teaching. However, due to University scheduling problems, many students had later elected to take the course, "The Teaching–Learning Process," sometime during the several semesters which intervened between their first and final student teaching experiences. The two instructors handling the laboratory sections of the course during which the bulk of the interaction analysis was taught could offer nothing more than "hunches" as to which group seemed to be benefitting the most from the treatment. It seemed easier to interest the students who were faced daily with actual teaching problems than those who were relying on their memories of problems a year old. The groups who were not student teaching had to rely more on observations of other teachers and simulated teaching experiences for analysis. The student teachers, on the other hand, could tape their actual classes and analyze themselves. However, there were no actual data to support any one time sequence over another.

This study was also undertaken to gather information as to the feasibility of working with a new system for classifying verbal interaction in the classroom —the Verbal Interaction Category System (Amidon and Hunter, 1966).

In summary, this study was undertaken for three reasons:

1. To gather actual behavioral data along with pencil-and-paper attitude scores to show whether or not there are significant differences between student teachers trained in interaction analysis and those not so trained.

2. To gather evidence to help decide if the timing of instruction in interaction analysis makes any significant difference in the behavior and/or attitudes of student teachers.

3. To gather evidence as to the usability of the Verbal Interaction Category System.

HYPOTHESES

The study was designed to test the following null hypotheses:

1. a) There is no significant difference on post-student-teaching attitude scores between student teachers trained in Flanders' interaction analysis and those not so trained.

   b) There is no significant difference on post-student-teaching attitude scores between student teachers trained in Flanders' interaction analysis *before* student teaching and those trained *while* student teaching. (Attitude is defined as the student teacher's score on the Teaching Situation Reaction Test.)

2. a) There is no significant difference in pre and post attitude change scores between student teachers trained in Flanders' interaction analysis and those not so trained.

   b) There is no significant difference in pre and post attitude change scores between student teachers trained in Flanders' interaction analysis *before* student teaching and those trained *while* student teaching. (Attitude change scores are defined as the difference in scores on the pre-student-teaching Teaching Situation Reaction Test and the post-test scores on the same test.)

3. a) There is no significant difference in "self-awareness" between student teachers trained in Flanders' interaction analysis and those not so trained.

   b) There is no significant difference in "self-awareness" between student teachers trained in Flanders' interaction analysis *before* student teaching and those trained *while* student teaching. (Self-awareness defined as score achieved on the "My Classroom" questionnaire.)

4. a) There is no significant difference in verbal behavior of student teachers trained in Flanders' interaction analysis and those not so trained.

   b) There is no significant difference in verbal behavior of student teachers trained in Flanders' interaction analysis *before* student teaching and those trained *while* student teaching. (Verbal behavior of student teachers is defined by use of the following categories and/or combination of categories of the Verbal Interaction Category System:

   > lecture, direction giving, asking narrow questions, asking broad questions, accepting student ideas, accepting student behavior, accepting student feelings, rejecting student ideas, rejecting student behavior, rejecting student feelings.

   > total teacher talk, total teacher questioning, total teacher accepting behavior, total teacher rejecting behavior, teacher accepting behavior which lasts more than three seconds, teacher rejecting behavior which lasts more than three seconds.)

5. a) There is no significant difference in pupil verbal behavior between classes taught by student teachers trained in Flanders' interaction analysis and those in classes taught by student teachers not so trained.

b) There is no significant difference in pupil behavior between classes taught by student teachers trained in Flanders' interaction analysis *before* student teaching and those trained *while* student teaching. (Pupil verbal behavior is defined as the use of the following categories and/or combination of categories of the Verbal Interaction Category System:

> pupil response to teacher, predictable; pupil response to teacher, unpredictable; pupil initiation to teacher; pupil initiation to student; pupil response to student; total student talk; total student response talk; total student initiatory talk.

6. a) There is no significant difference in the amount of silence between classes taught by student teachers trained in Flanders' interaction analysis and those not so trained.

b) There is no significant difference in the amount of silence between classes taught by student teachers trained in Flanders' interaction analysis *before* student teaching and those trained *while* student teaching.

7. a) There is no significant difference in the amount of confusion between classes taught by student teachers trained in Flanders' interaction analysis and classes taught by student teachers not so trained.

b) There is no significant difference in the amount of confusion between classes taught by student teachers trained in Flanders' interaction analysis *before* student teaching and those trained *while* student teaching.

PROCEDURE

All English and social studies student teachers enrolled in the Secondary Education Department of Temple University for the Spring semester, 1964, were grouped by the following criteria:

EXPERIMENTAL GROUPS:

Group A: had taken the experimental course which included Flanders' interaction analysis *before* their final student teaching.

Group B: were taking the experimental course *at the same time* that they were student teaching.

CONTROL GROUP:

Group C: had not taken the experimental course nor were they presently enrolled in it. (These students had either taken the conventional learning theory course or were Liberal Arts students completing certification requirements through the Secondary Education Department and had taken all the same courses as had the other two groups of students with the exception of either the conventional or experimental course in the Teaching–Learning Process.)

All student teachers had achieved a minimum cumulative point hour ratio of 2.0 in all of their work, and 2.5 in their subject matter field. Each group contained approximately 30 to 35 students.

To make up our sample, 10 students were chosen at random from each group. All students chosen were teaching average ability groups and none were in schools considered "extreme" from a socio-economic point of view.

It should be noted that none of the student teachers who had been or were being trained in Flanders' interaction analysis were required or even necessarily encouraged by the college supervisors to use the technique. At this time, the experimental course was being treated as a separate entity.

Since Hough and Amidon had shown evidence that a student teacher's "openness or closedness" (as measured by a Rokeach Dogmatism Scale) seemed to be a significant factor in attitude formation and change, it seemed important to make sure that the three groups did not differ significantly on this variable. Therefore, all subjects were given a Rokeach Dogmatism Scale.

Group A had been taught interaction analysis *before* their student teaching experience. It might, therefore, be argued that the student teachers in this group had a more positive attitude toward teaching before their student teaching experience than did the student teachers in the other two groups. The Teaching Situation Reaction Test was therefore given to all groups the week before student teaching.

Our three groups did not differ significantly in the Dogmatism Scale scores or on the Teaching Situation Reaction Test (TSRT) given prior to student teaching (see Table 3–17).

During the month of May 1964, all the student teachers were observed in their classrooms for a full period by an observer trained in the Verbal Interaction Category System (VICS). The student teachers were notified that a researcher would be visiting. However, they did not know the purpose of the project, what was being observed, or when they would be visited.

At the end of the observation, the student teachers were asked to complete a "My Classroom" questionnaire regarding their own classroom behavior.

Table 3–17

Comparison of Experimental and Control Student-Teaching Groups on the D-Scale and TRST Test Given *before* Student Teaching

	Group A (n = 10)	Group B (n = 10)	Group C (n = 10)	F	Level of significance*
	$\bar{X}$	$\bar{X}$	$\bar{X}$		
D scale scores	105.2	105.0	117.6	1.31	n.s.
TSRT pre-test†	56.5	62.7	57.5	2.21	n.s.

* Analysis of variance with d.f. of 2, 27.

† Lower scores indicate more positive attitudes.

MEASUREMENT INSTRUMENTS USED

The principal instrument used was the Verbal Interaction Category System. Like Flanders', the VICS is used to analyze verbal behavior in the classroom. In both, a trained observer sits in the classroom and tallies the ongoing behavior every three seconds or at every change in behavior. At the end of the session the observer transfers the information he has gathered to a matrix in overlapping fashion. A finished matrix gives a numerical description of general patterns of interaction. (Figure 3–7 gives the category descriptions of both systems.)

VICS	Flanders System
Teacher-initiated talk:	Teacher talk:
1. Presents information or opinion	Indirect influence
2. Gives direction	1. Accepts feeling
3. Asks predictable response question	2. Praises or encourages
4. Asks unpredictable response 'questions'	3. Accepts or uses ideas of student
	4. Asks questions
Teacher response:	Direct influence
5. Accepts a) ideas, b) behavior, c) feeling	5. Lecturing
6. Rejects a) ideas, b) behavior, c) feeling	6. Giving directions
	7. Criticizing or justifying authority
Pupil response:	Student talk:
7. Responds to teacher	8. Student-talk response
a) predictably	9. Student-talk initiation
b) unpredictably	10. Silence or confusion
8. Responds to another pupil	
Pupil-initiated talk:	
9. Initiates talk to teacher	
10. Initiates talk to another pupil	
Other:	
11. Silence	
Z. Confusion (Z may be used alone when con-	(Numbers may be placed to the right of and
fusion drowns out verbal behavior, or	slightly above the category numbers to indicate
alongside another category to indicate inter-	change in pupils who are participating)
fering disruption while someone is talking)	

FIG. 3–7. The Flanders and Verbal Interaction Category Systems.

Some differences between Flanders' system and VICS are discussed by Amidon and Hunter (1966).

Perhaps the primary differences between the Flanders System and the system here discussed is that the dimension of teaching behavior pointed up in the Flanders System is directness as opposed to indirectness. Does the teacher use more direct or indirect influence in his teaching? Although the point is made that no values are implied, there is argument about whether direct or indirect behavior is more desirable. Direct teacher influence as opposed to indirect is not a dimension of the VICS

System. The teacher categories are looked at rather in terms of initiation and response.

The Flanders System does not provide a method for differentiating the type of teacher question. There is only one category, the category 4: "asks questions." The VICS, on the other hand, allows for the division of teacher questions into those which bring forth predictable responses and those which elicit unpredictable responses. In other words, the VICS allows teacher questions to be categorized into those which are broad and those which are narrow in scope.

A third difference between these two systems is in the area of pupil talk. The VICS includes five categories for pupil talk, and distinguishes between that conversation which a pupil has with the teacher and that which he has with another pupil. Both systems indicate whether or not the pupil's talk with the teacher is initiatory or responsive, but the VICS adds the dimension of predictable or unpredictable response.

The Flanders System has one category to indicate silence or confusion while the VICS separates these two. . . .

A fifth difference between the two systems is the manner in which teacher response to pupil behavior is noted. The Flanders System has three categories for reacting positively to pupils, but only one for reacting negatively. The VICS has three for each: accepting or rejecting pupils' *ideas, behavior,* or *feeling* . . . .

The Dogmatism Scale is a test developed by Milton Rokeach and his associates as a device for measuring the relative openness or closedness of an individual's belief–disbelief system. A discussion of the test construct and validating procedures is available in *The Open and Closed Mind* (Rokeach, 1960). A discussion of the form of the test used in this study may be found in Hough and Amidon (1964).

The Teaching Situation Reaction Test (TSRT) is a test made up of 36 items each of which requires the subject to respond to classroom oriented situations by ranking a set of four items representing possible responses to the situation. Specifically, the construct of the test includes the following dimensions: (1) the type of control a teacher would use in the classroom, direct or indirect, (2) the relationship the teacher would have with students in the classroom, empathetic or self-oriented, (3) the approach a teacher would take to classroom problems of instruction and control, objective or subjective, and (4) the approach the teacher would have to classroom methodology, experimental or conservative. For a further discussion of the test and its validity, see Hough and Amidon (1964).

A questionnaire was designed for this study to parallel the Amidon System categories and to assess how "aware" the student teacher was of his verbal behavior.

TREATMENT OF DATA

The data were subjected to analyses of variance. The level of significance accepted was either the 0.05 or 0.01 level. Where the overall F turned out to be significant, the Tukey Gap Test was used.

Table 3–18

Comparison of Experimental and Control Student Teachers on TSRT Test Given *after* Student Teaching

	Group A (n = 10)	Group B (n = 10)	Group C (n = 10)	F	Level of significance*
Post-student teaching TSRT scores†	$\bar{X}$ 57.0	$\bar{X}$ 55.8	$\bar{X}$ 60.6	1.2	n.s.

* Analysis of variance with d.f. of 2,27.
† Lower scores indicate more positive attitudes.

Table 3–19

Comparison of Experimental and Control Student Teachers on Differences in Scores on Pre- and Post-Student-Teaching TSRT Tests

	Group A (n = 10)	Group B (n = 10)	Group C (n = 10)	F	Level of significance*	Gap	Level of significance†
Differences in pre- and post-student teaching TSRT scores**	$\bar{X}$ 0.5	$\bar{X}$ −5.7	$\bar{X}$ 10.5	16	0.01	10	Group A 0.01 Group C Group B
						6.2	0.05 Group A

* Analysis of variance at the d.f. of 2,27.
† Tukey Gap Test used.
** Minus scores indicate a change toward more positive attitudes.

RESULTS

Null hypothesis 1(a) was *accepted*, indicating that there was no significant difference in attitude toward teaching after a student teaching experience between students trained in Flanders' Interaction Analysis System and those not so trained. Null hypothesis 1(b) regarding differences between the experimental groups was also *accepted* (Table 3–18).

Null hypothesis 2(a) was *rejected*. There was a significant difference at the <0.01 level of significance in difference scores between the pre-student-teaching TSRT test and the post TSRT in favor of the experimental groups. Null hypothesis 2(b) was also *rejected*. There was a significant gap at the <0.05 level of significance in favor of the group trained *while* student teaching (Table 3–19).

Null hypothesis 3(a) concerning "self-awareness" of student teachers was *rejected* at the <0.05 level of significance. Null hypothesis 3(b) was also

Table 3–20

Comparison of Experimental and Control Student Teachers on "My Classroom" Questionnaire

	Group A (n = 10)	Group B (n = 10)	Group C (n = 10)	F	Level of significance*	Gap	Level of significance†
"My Classroom" scores**	X̄ 74.2	X̄ 63.2	X̄ 66.4	4.53	0.05	7.8	Group A 0.05 Group C

* Analysis of variance with d.f. of 2,27.
† Tukey Gap Test.
** Higher scores indicate more "self-awareness."

rejected. There was a significant gap between Group A and Group B in favor of the group which had had training in interaction analysis *before* student teaching (Table 3–20).

Null hypothesis 4(a) concerning significant differences between the verbal behavior of teachers trained in interaction analysis and those not so trained was *accepted* for the following behaviors for which no significant differences were found:

teacher: lecture, direction giving, asking narrow questions, asking broad questions, accepting student behavior, accepting student feelings, rejecting student ideas, rejecting student feelings, total teacher talk, teacher rejecting behavior which lasts more than three seconds.

Null hypothesis 4(a) was *rejected* at the <0.01 level of significance for the following verbal behaviors:

Interaction analysis groups used *more* teacher acceptance of students' ideas and *more* total teacher accepting behavior than non-interaction analysis groups. Null hypothesis 4(a) was also *rejected* at the <0.05 level of significance for the following verbal behaviors:

Interaction analysis groups used *less* rejecting of student behavior and *less* total teacher rejection.

The student teachers in the interaction analysis groups also tended to use more total teacher questioning and more teacher acceptance which lasts longer than three seconds.

Null hypothesis 4(b) was *accepted.* There were no statistically significant gaps between the two experimental groups in verbal behavior. [Table 3–21 concerns null hypotheses 4(a) and 4(b).]

Null hypothesis 5(a) concerning pupil verbal behavior between classes taught by student teachers trained in interaction analysis and those not so trained

Table 3–21

Comparison of Experimental and Control Groups of Student Teachers in Verbal Behavior Categories as Measured by VICS

VICS categories Teacher:	Group A (n = 10)	Group B (n = 10)	Group C (n = 10)	F	Level of significance†	Significant gap	Level of significance of gap**
	$\bar{X}$*	$\bar{X}$*	$\bar{X}$*				
1 lectures	26.0	25.7	24.0	0.04	n.s.		
2 gives directions	5.8	7.25	8.20	0.53	n.s.		
3 asks narrow question	15.3	10.3	9.80	1.7	n.s.		
4 asks broad question	3.8	4.5	1.8	1.46	n.s.		
5a accepts students' ideas	12.8	11.0	6.1	7.98	<0.01	4.90	AB <0.01 C
5b accepts students' behavior	0.55	0.7	0.2	0.2	n.s		
5c accepts students' feelings	0.5	0.3	0.42	0.18	n.s.		
6a rejects students' ideas	1.1	0.6	1.8	1.00	n.s.		
6b rejects students' behavior	1.1	0.9	3.45	3.71	<0.05	2.35	AB <0.01 C
6c rejects students' feelings	0	0	2.2	0.2	n.s.		
Total teacher talk (1–6c)	66.7	61.2	57.9	1.1	n.s.		
Total teacher acceptance (5a, b, c)	13.85	12.0	6.72	7	<0.01	5.24	AB <0.05 C
Total teacher rejection (6a, b, c)	2.2	1.5	7.45	4	<0.05	5.25	AB <0.05 C
Teacher acceptance > 3 sec.	3.8	2.45	1.16	4.5	<0.05		n.s. gaps
Total teacher questioning	19.1	14.8	11.6	4.1	<0.05		n.s. gaps
Teacher rejections > 3 sec.	0.8	0.6	0.4	0.5	n.s.		

* Adj. to 100.   † ANOV-d.f. = 2,27.   ** Tukey Gap Test.

Table 3–22

Comparison of Pupil Verbal Behavior in Classes Taught by Student Teachers in Experimental and Control Groups

VICS categories	Group A (n = 10)	Group B (n = 10)	Group C (n = 10)	F	Level of significance†	Significant gap	Level of significance of gap**
	$\bar{X}$*	$\bar{X}$*	$\bar{X}$*				
P responds to T predictably	13.9	19.0	11.9	2.19	n.s.		
P responds to T unpredictably	5.6	8.0	3.7	0.57	n.s.		
P responds to other P	2.5	0.6	0.35	0.6	n.s.		
P initiates to teacher	4.6	8.1	2.9	2.59	n.s.		
P initiates to other P	0.45	0.4	0.3	0	n.s.		
Total student talk	25.55	39.7	21.05	6.0	<0.01(a)	14.15	B <0.05 AC
Total student response	17.8	27.6	17.8	3.8	<0.05(b)	9.8	B <0.05 AC
Total student-initiated talk	5.05	8.5	3.2	2.2	n.s.		

* Adj. to 100.   † ANOV d.f. = 2,27.   ** Tukey Gap Test.

was accepted for the following pupil behaviors:

pupil: responds predictably, responds unpredictably, responds to student, initiates talk to teacher, initiates talk to another student, total student-initiated talk.

However, this null hypothesis may be rejected at the <0.01 level of significance for *total* student talk and may be rejected at the <0.05 level of significance for *total* student response. Although not statistically significant, there is a trend toward more pupil initiation to teacher and predictable response to teacher in the experimental groups.

Null hypothesis 5(b) may be *rejected* at the <0.05 level of significance in favor of more total student talk and more student response talk in classes taught by student teachers who had training in Flanders' interaction analysis *during* student teaching. [Table 3–22 shows results of analysis of data concerning null hypotheses 5(a) and 5(b).]

Null hypothesis 6(a) regarding silence in the classroom may be *rejected* at the <0.01 level of significance. Null hypothesis 6(b) may be *accepted*. Although there is a statistically significant difference in the amount of silence in classes of student teachers who do not know interaction analysis (they have less of it), there is no statistically significant difference between the two groups who know the system (Table 3–23).

Table 3–23

Comparison of Experimental and Control Groups of Student Teachers in the Amount of Silence and Confusion Used

VICS categories	Group A (n = 10)	Group B (n = 10)	Group C (n = 10)	F	Level of significance†	Significant gap	Level of significance of gap**
	$\bar{X}$*	$\bar{X}$*	$\bar{X}$*				
Silence	7.8	2.8	18.6	15.63	<0.01	10.20	C <0.01 AB
Confusion	2.4	0.8	24.5	0.09	n.s.		

* Adj. to 100.   † ANOV d.f. = 2,27.   ** Tukey Gap Test.

Null hypotheses 7(a) and 7(b) regarding confusion in the classroom may be accepted (Table 3–23).

SUMMARY AND CONCLUSIONS

In summary, we may say that student teachers taught interaction analysis do differ significantly from a control group not taught interaction analysis in their:

Use of *more* total teacher acceptance of student ideas
    total teacher acceptance behavior
Use of *less* teacher rejection of student behavior
    teacher total rejecting behavior

Students trained in Flanders' interaction analysis tend to use *more* accepting behavior which lasts longer than three seconds, and *more* total questioning.

The timing of the training in interaction analysis seems to have *no* effect on these behavior differences.

Student teachers trained in interaction analysis *during* student teaching have *more* total student talk and *more* pupil response talk than those student teachers who are trained before student teaching and those not so trained at all.

Student teachers trained in Flanders' interaction analysis show statistically significant evidence of *more* positive change scores on an attitude inventory of Teaching Situation Reactions (the TSRT), than those not so trained. In this case, the student teachers trained *while* student teaching show more significant positive changes than those trained either before student teaching or not so trained at all.

Student teachers trained in Flanders' interaction analysis before student teaching seem more "aware" of their own verbal behavior than those trained during student teaching or those not so trained at all.

The Verbal Interaction Category System was found to be an easy, usable system. The two observers had no difficulty in achieving a Scott coefficient of reliability of 0.97 after a very short training period. One difficulty may be pointed out: Amidon and Hunter's idea of making note of the number of the child who speaks along with the category of response was found to be most impractical for an observer unfamiliar with the children. Beyond the first five children it became a "guessing game" as to what number belonged to which child. Perhaps a teacher using the system on a taped lesson of her own class would have less difficulty differentiating the children.

Student teachers who were shown their VICS matrix for feedback purposes were especially pleased with the differentiation between student talk to teacher and student talk to other pupils. Differences between narrow and broad questions also seemed to interest the student teachers.

IMPLICATIONS OF THE STUDY

The results of this study seem to indicate that training in Flanders' Interaction Analysis System does lead to both attitude and behavior differences. The student teachers in our experimental groups were able to evidence more use of accepting teaching behaviors and less use of rejecting teaching behaviors than those teachers more conventionally trained. They also had more student talk in their classes. Further, students trained in interaction analysis before student teaching were more "aware" of what they were doing than those student teachers not so trained.

Those who believe that this "awareness" and use of more accepting teaching strategies may be positive approaches to the role of the teacher should be greatly encouraged by this pilot study.

Several interesting questions may be raised:

1. What would follow-up work with interaction analysis by college supervisors of student teaching show?

2. Did student teachers in the control group have more behavior problems and, therefore, use more teacher rejection of student behavior category, or did they use less "variety" in handling student control problems than did students trained in interaction analysis?

Skeptics are certain to notice that the areas of behavior differences seem to appear in the categories of the VICS that are most like the Flanders' system. This might be interpreted to show that the experimental teachers were more aware of these categories and, therefore, using them for the observers' benefit. This, however, overlooks the fact that these student teachers *were practicing,* if even for that one day, what they had been taught. Do other courses in education show this transfer? After all, the control group of student teachers undoubtedly had discussed the value of student talk and a positive teacher approach somewhere in their pre-student teaching course work. They, however, did *not* make the transfer to their actual teaching behavior.

It might be interesting to see how student teachers trained in other systems for self-analysis behave. It is conceivable to hypothesize that those familiar with the VICS might use more "broad questions." They might differentiate more between accepting a student's ideas vs. rejecting his behavior. Other systems might focus the prospective teacher onto other areas of interest.

Colleges of education might seriously consider the type of experience which gives the pre-service teacher training in the use of an observational system for self-analysis. The possibilities seem almost limitless for effective pre-service training which closes the gap between conceptualizations of teaching and operational performances in the classroom.

9

THE EFFECT OF TRAINING
IN INTERACTION ANALYSIS
ON THE VERBAL TEACHING BEHAVIOR
OF PRE-SERVICE TEACHERS[46]

JOHN B. HOUGH and RICHARD OBER

This paper reports findings from a two-year course revision and institutional research project designed to create a more effective general methods course in Ohio State University's program for the preparation of secondary school teachers (Hough, 1965a). As currently envisioned, this introductory course (Education 535, Theory and Practice in Secondary Education) is designed as an introduction to the instructional role of the teacher in the secondary school classroom. The primary behavioral outcomes of this course lie in the areas of human relation skills and skill in the appropriate use of a representative variety of verbal teaching behaviors.

There are, of course, several assumptions that underlie the purposes of this general methods course (Education 535). It is assumed that, all other things being equal, teachers who are (a) more accepting, unconditional and less rejecting in their relationships with students and (b) who are aware of and able to use a variety of appropriate teaching behaviors will be able to facilitate more learning in their classrooms. If these assumptions are true, then teacher training programs should provide experiences by means of which prospective teachers can improve their human relations skills and become more aware of and flexible in the use of a variety of appropriate teaching behaviors that have been found to be related to positive student attitudes toward school and their teachers, and increased student achievement.

The use of effective human relations skills and flexibility in the use of appropriate verbal behaviors do not constitute the entirety of effective teaching. It is asserted, however, that these two areas of competence are needed by most, if not all, secondary school teachers, and thus are appropriate objectives for a general methods course.

---

[46] Paper read at the annual meeting of the American Educational Research Association, Chicago, Illinois, February, 1966. Reprinted by permission of the authors.

Literature in the field gives some support to the assumptions underlying the purposes of this introductory course in Ohio State's program for the preparation of secondary school teachers. Rogers (1959a) has stated that student learning is enhanced by teachers who are congruent, and are capable of expressing unconditional positive regard and empathy to their students. Rogers (1959) has also postulated a personality continuum from closedness to experience (stasis) to openness to experience (process). He suggests the possibility that the ability of a person to enter into a helping relationship with other persons may be directly related to this stasis-process factor and the person's ability to show to others the conditions of empathy, congruence and unconditional positive regard. Teacher empathy and acceptance and rejection of students can be observed in the verbal behavior of teachers by means of observational systems such as Flanders' system of interaction analysis.

In a pilot study of the effectiveness of dyadic programmed human relations training, Hough (1965) reported that ten hours of such instruction significantly increased pre-service teachers' ability to show to others the conditions of empathy, congruence and unconditional positive regard as measured by the Relationship Inventory. Such change was found to be related to the openness or closedness of the belief–disbelief system of significant others with whom the person interacted during human relations training. It should be pointed out that in this study, human relations skills were restricted to those used in a dyadic relationship and were measured by a rating scale. No attempt was made to measure the use of empathic, accepting or rejecting behavior in a teaching situation.

In a study of teacher effectiveness, Flanders (1965a) found that teachers' use of indirect verbal behavior such as acceptance and clarification of student ideas and feelings, and encouragement and praise were associated with more positive attitudes toward school and higher student achievement in junior high school social studies and mathematics classes. He also found that teacher criticism, rejection, and extended verbal directness were associated with less positive attitudes and lower student achievement. Similar findings were reported by Amidon and Flanders (1961) in a study in which eighth grade students were found to have learned more geometry when taught by an indirect teaching style than by a more direct teaching style.

In a study of the feasibility of changing verbal teaching behavior of in-service teachers, Flanders (1963a) found that teachers could become more indirect in their teaching style by experiencing a workshop in which interaction analysis was taught as a technique for analyzing their verbal teaching behavior.

In a study of the effect of teaching interaction analysis to student teachers, Hough and Amidon (1963) found that student teachers who were taught interaction analysis were seen by student teaching supervisors as being more effective in their student teaching than student teachers who had not been taught interaction analysis. In the same study Hough and Amidon found that supervisor ratings of student teachers were related to student teachers' scores on the Teaching Situation Reaction Test (a situational test designed to measure a teacher's human relations ability, openness to new experience, and feelings of comfort in using a direct or indirect teaching style). In an extension of the work of Hough and Amidon, Furst (1965) found that student teachers who were taught interaction analysis used significantly more accepting verbal behavior and questions and significantly less criticism than student teachers not taught interaction analysis. Furst also found that those student teachers who were taught interaction analysis scored more positively on the Teaching Situation Reaction Test, a test that has been shown to be predictive of success in student teaching (Hough and Duncan, 1965).

In summary, improved human relations skill and control of appropriate verbal teaching behavior constitute the basic behavioral objectives of Ohio State University's introductory general methods course for the preparation of secondary school teachers. Literature in the field gives support for the purposes of this course and in addition suggests the feasibility of attaining the intended behavioral outcomes.

It was the purpose of this study to test the effect on verbal teaching behavior of (a) three methods of teaching human relations skills, and (b) two methods of teaching pre-service teachers to analyze and control their verbal teaching behavior.

HYPOTHESIS

The hypothesis for this study proposed to test whether certain experimental treatments used in this study were more effective than others in facilitating the use of verbal teaching behaviors that have been found to be associated with increased student achievement and more positive attitudes toward school. Though the literature would suggest certain predictions, the hypothesis for this study was stated in the null-operational form as follows:

Subjects experiencing the five experimental treatments used in this study will not differ in regard to the percentages of verbal behaviors they and their students use during a half-hour simulated lesson (as measured by observers using a 13-category modification of the Flanders system of interaction analysis).

MEASURING INSTRUMENTS

Four instruments were used in this study. One was used to measure the dependent variable of verbal teaching behaviors used during simulated teaching. Three additional instruments were used to measure control variables that have been found in other research studies to be associated with growth in human relations skill and a person's use of selected verbal teaching behaviors.

Measurement of the dependent variable

Verbal teaching behaviors used by subjects during simulated teaching were measured by trained observers using a 13-category modification of the Flanders system of interaction analysis. The development and validation of interaction analysis as an observational technique is reported by Flanders in *Teacher Influ-*

Table 3-24

Summary of the Thirteen Categories of Verbal Behavior Used in This Study*

Category number		Description of verbal behavior
1	TEACHER TALK	*Accepts feeling:* accepts and clarifies the feeling tone of students in a nonthreatening manner. Feelings may be positive or negative. Predicting and recalling feelings are also included.
2		*Praises or encourages:* praises or encourages student action or behavior. Jokes that release tension, not at the expense of another individual, nodding head or saying "uh-huh" or "go on" are included.
3		*Accepts or uses ideas of student:* clarifying, building on, developing and accepting ideas of students.
4		*Asks questions:* asking a question about content or procedure with the intent that the student should answer.
5		*Lectures:* giving facts or opinions about content or procedure; expressing his own ideas; asking rhetorical questions.
6		*Answers student questions:* direct answers to questions regarding content or procedure asked by students.
7		*Gives directions:* directions, commands, or orders to which a student is expected to comply.
8		*Criticizes or justifies authority:* statements intended to change student behavior from a nonacceptable to an acceptable pattern; bawling out someone; stating why the teacher is doing what he is doing so as to achieve or maintain control; rejecting or criticizing a student's opinion or judgment.

* The categories of verbal behavior used in this system are basically those used by Flanders in his ten-category system of interaction analysis. Categories 6, 9 and 12 represent additions to Flanders' category system.

ence, Pupil Attitudes and Achievement (1965a). The modifications of the Flanders system that were used in this study include the following: (a) a sub-classification of Flanders' category 9 to distinguish between student questions and declarative emitted responses, (b) a sub-classification of Flanders' category 5 to distinguish between teacher initiated lecture and teacher lecture as an answer to student questions, (c) a sub-classification of Flanders' category 7 to distinguish between corrective feedback and personalized criticism and sarcasm. These categories are taken from an observational system developed by Hough and reported in *An Observational System for the Analysis of Classroom Instruction* (1966). A summary of the category system used in this study may be found in Table 3-24.

The observation of classroom teaching behavior in this study was done by five observers who were trained in interaction analysis for several months.

Table 3-24 Continued

Category number		Description of verbal behavior
9	TEACHER TALK	*Corrective feedback:* telling a student that his answer is wrong when the incorrectness of the answer can be established by other than opinion, i.e., empirical validation, definition or custom.
10	STUDENT TALK	*Student talk—response:* talk by students in response to requests or narrow teacher questions. The teacher initiates the contact or solicits student's statement.
11		*Student talk—emitted:* talk by students in response to broad teacher questions which require judgment or opinion. Student declarative statements emitted but not called for by teacher questions.
12		*Student questions:* questions concerning content or procedure that are directed to the teacher.
13		*Silence or confusion:* pauses, short periods of silence, and periods of confusion in which communication cannot be understood by the observer.

$$\text{Indirect–direct ratio} = \frac{\text{categories } 1, 2, 3, 4, 6}{\text{categories } 5, 7, 8, 9}$$

$$\text{Revised indirect–direct ratio} = \frac{\text{categories } 1, 2, 3}{\text{categories } 7, 8, 9}$$

$$\text{Student–teacher ratio} = \frac{\text{categories } 1, 2, 3, 4, 5, 6, 7, 8, 9}{\text{categories } 10, 11, 12}$$

The inter-observer reliability of the five observers in this study was obtained prior to any gathering of data. The means used to establish inter-observer reliability involved categorization of three tape-recorded classroom situations of 10, 15, and 20 minutes respectively. Each of the tape-recorded classroom episodes contained all of the 13 categories of the observational system used in this study. Inter-observer reliability was computed by a formula suggested by Scott (1955). The coefficients of inter-observer reliability for the five observers are reported in Table 3-25.

Measurement of control variables

The stasis-process factor is related to a person's openness to central dimensions of problems and one's positive feelings of worth. It is assumed that persons at the process end of the stasis-process continuum are more capable of entering into and profiting from human relations training. In this study the stasis-process factor was measured by The College Student Problems Q-Sort developed by Freeze. The procedures used to develop this instrument as well as a report of the instrument's validity and reliability may be found in *A Study of Openness as a Factor in Change of Student Teachers* (Freeze, 1963).

Table 3–25

Inter-observer Reliability Coefficients for Five Observers on Three Tape-Recorded Classroom Situations

Observer	Observer				
	1	2	3	4	5
	Ten-minute tape				
1	1.00	0.81	0.89	0.85	0.91
2		1.00	0.75	0.69	0.80
3			1.00	0.88	0.92
4				1.00	0.86
5					1.00
	Fifteen-minute tape				
1	1.00	0.83	0.86	0.92	0.78
2		1.00	0.85	0.86	0.82
3			1.00	0.92	0.86
4				1.00	0.84
5					1.00
	Twenty-minute tape				
1	1.00	0.86	0.83	0.94	0.85
2		1.00	0.86	0.87	0.77
3			1.00	0.84	0.72
4				1.00	0.79
5					1.00

The relative openness or closedness of a person's belief–disbelief system is related to a person's ability to receive, evaluate and act on relevant information received from the outside on its own intrinsic merits, unencumbered by irrelevant factors in the situation arising from within the person or from the outside. In this study, the relative openness or closedness of the belief–disbelief system was measured by Form E of The Dogmatism Scale developed by Rokeach. The procedures used in the development of this instrument are reported in *The Open and Closed Mind* (Rokeach, 1960). A corrected split half reliability of 0.86 for The Dogmatism Scale is reported by Hough (1965) in a study that involved a population and testing procedures similar to the ones used in this study.

DESIGN

This study employed five treatment groups of eighty-four subjects each. Each treatment group was made up of students from four Education 535 classes (two each during the winter and spring quarters) making a total of twenty classes in all. Three classes were scheduled at each of the following hours: 8:00 a.m., 10:00 a.m., 12:00 m. and 2:00 p.m. Students registered for Education 535 at a given hour were randomly assigned to one of the three classes meeting at that hour.

	Winter quarter		Spring quarter	
A	Treatment 1 12:00 m.	Treatment 3 2:00 p.m.	Treatment 2 8:00 a.m.	Treatment 5 10:00 a.m.
B	Treatment 1 8:00 a.m.	Treatment 2 10:00 a.m.	Treatment 5 12:00 m.	Treatment 4 2:00 p.m.
C	Treatment 3 12:00 m.	Treatment 5 2:00 p.m.	Treatment 4 12:00 m.	Treatment 1 2:00 p.m.
D	Treatment 5 8:00 a.m.	Treatment 4 10:00 a.m.	Treatment 3 10:00 a.m.	Treatment 2 2:00 p.m.
E	Treatment 4 8:00 a.m.	Treatment 2 12:00 m.	Treatment 3 8:00 a.m.	Treatment 1 10:00 a.m.

FIG. 3–8. Illustration of distribution of treatments by instructor, class period, and quarter.

The time of the day that classes met and the influence of individual instructors represent two variables that were considered as significant to control. In order to do this, the five instructors were assigned to class sections so that no instructor taught more than one class associated with any one of the five treatment groups. In addition, treatment types were randomly assigned to classes meeting during the various hours of the day. This purposeful assignment of treatment types to instructors and the time during the day that classes met for the two quarters is presented in Fig. 3–8.

Treatment groups defined

The five treatment groups used in this study differed only with respect to the means of instruction used to teach human relations skills and the analysis of verbal teaching behavior.

HUMAN RELATIONS TRAINING. Three methods were used to teach human relations skill. The first method involved the use of The Human Development Institute's *General Relationship Improvement Program* (Berlin and Wyckoff, 1963). *The Relationship Improvement Program* is a type of dyadic programmed instruction designed to be used by two people for ten hour-long instructional sessions. During these ten sessions, pairs of subjects react to the program and interact with each other by means of structured discussions and role plays based on concepts presented in the program. The objectives of the program are increased awareness of self and others and skill in showing to others the conditions of unconditional positive regard, empathy and congruence.

The Relationship Improvement Program was scheduled for use once each week, with the exception of the first and seventh weeks of the quarter. Two sessions were covered during the eighth and ninth weeks. In this way all ten sessions were used during the ten-week quarter.

The second method used to teach human relations skill employed selected readings on the theory and classroom application of human relations concepts.

These concepts were discussed in class by means of whole class and group discussions. The estimated time spent in reading about and discussing human relations concepts, and their classroom application, was ten hours.

The third method involved pairs of students reading and discussing ten educational case studies of classroom instructional problems. The case studies were discussed by pairs of students during ten separate one-hour sessions. These dyadic case study discussions were distributed throughout the quarter on the same schedule as the use of *The Relationship Improvement Program.*

The second and third methods involving reading about and discussion of human relations concepts and the dyadic case study discussions were used as controls for the first method, i.e., use of *The Relationship Improvement Program,* which by its very nature involves dyadic discussion of human relations concepts.

ANALYSIS OF VERBAL TEACHING BEHAVIOR. Two methods were used to teach the analysis of verbal teaching behavior. The first of these methods employed the Flanders system of interaction analysis. Students were taught the category system to the point of minimum proficiency. Minimum proficiency required that students be able to: (a) tabulate a 12-minute tape recorded classroom situation containing illustrations of all categories at a minimum reliability of 0.60; (b) plot a matrix with no more than 5% error; (c) compute and interpret the meaning of the indirect–direct ratio, the revised indirect–direct ratio and the student–teacher ratio, and (d) read and interpret the meaning of cell loadings in major regions of the matrix. In addition to the skills of tabulation and matrix interpretation, students who were taught interaction analysis also were involved in a series of simulated micro-teaching experiences in which they attempted to replicate their instructional intentions as expressed in models of teaching patterns. During the two weeks of the course that are devoted to observation and participation in public schools, students were encouraged to take interaction analysis on the teachers they were observing and to analyze the teachers' verbal behavior. During their two weeks of observation and participation in the public schools, many students did one or more class periods of exploratory teaching. While they were teaching, another student trained to do so took interaction analysis on their teaching.

The second method of learning to analyze verbal teaching behavior did not use interaction analysis. Students taught under this method listened to tape recordings of classroom incidents and discussed the verbal behavior used in these recorded lessons. During class and small group discussions, categories of verbal behavior similar to those used in the Flanders system of interaction analysis were identified and discussed. The students did not, however, create a formal category system for observational purposes nor, of course, did they engage in matrix plotting or interpretation. In addition to listening to examples of classroom teaching situations and analyzing the verbal behavior used in these recorded lessons, students practiced patterns of teaching in a series of simulated micro-teaching situations. During the two weeks of observation in public schools, students observed teachers and analyzed their teaching by applying

Treatment	Human-relations training	Verbal-teaching-behavior training
One	Readings, lectures and classroom discussion of human relations in teaching	Skill training in interaction analysis as a means of analyzing verbal teaching behavior
Two	Dyadic programmed instruction in human relations skill	Analysis and discussion of verbal teaching behavior but no instruction in the skill of interaction analysis
Three	Readings, lectures and classroom discussion of human relations in teaching	Analysis and discussion of verbal teaching behavior but no instruction in the skill of interaction analysis
Four	Dyadic discussion of educational case studies	Analysis and discussion of verbal teaching behavior but no instruction in the skill of interaction analysis
Five	Dyadic programmed instruction in human relations skill	Skill training in interaction analysis as a means of analyzing verbal teaching behavior

FIG. 3–9. Summary of the five treatments.

knowledge learned about teaching behavior in their college class. They also engaged in one or more periods of exploratory teaching.

The time spent in analysis of teaching behavior under the two methods (including eight hours of observation in the public schools and the time spent in micro-teaching) amounted to approximately 25 hours under each method.

With the exception of the experimental differences mentioned above, all other experiences were equivalent in all classes. These experiences involved such activities as class discussions, lectures and skill sessions on selected instructional principles, lectures and discussions on concepts of measurement, lectures and skill sessions in the stating of behavioral objectives, lectures and discussions on lesson planning, simulated teaching experiences and routine administrative matters and course evaluation procedures not connected with the study.

The treatment groups used in this study involved five combinations of methods of teaching human relations skills and the analysis of verbal teaching behavior. The experimental characteristics of each of the five treatments is summarized in Fig. 3–9.

TESTING PROCEDURES AND DATA ANALYSIS

During the first week of the winter and spring quarters, all students in Education 535 classes were tested on The Dogmatism Scale, The Teaching Situation Reaction Test and The College Student Problems Q-Sort. Data presented in Table 3–26 show that the five treatment groups did not differ significantly on pretest scores on the three control variables.

During the eighth and ninth weeks of the quarter, each student planned, taught and evaluated a half-hour simulated lesson in which members of his

Table 3–26

Analysis of Variance for the Five Treatment Groups on Control Measures

Source of variance	Sum of squares	d.f.	Mean squares	F*
Dogmatism Scale				
Between	663.60	4	165.90	0.39
Within	176,964.48	415	426.42	
Total	177,528.08			
College Student Problems Q-Sort				
Between	427.56	4	106.89	0.77
Within	61,808.04	415	148.93	
Total	62,235.60			
Teaching Situation Reaction Test				
Between	208.32	4	52.08	0.47
Within	45,602.76	415	109.88	
Total	45,811.08			

* F-ratio of 2.39 is significant at the 0.05 level with 4 and 415 d.f.

education class role played typical secondary school students. Students in all treatment groups were restricted to lessons in which at least 20% of all verbal interaction must be student talk and in which no more than 40% of any one classification or type of teacher talk was permitted. A special attempt was made in noninteraction analysis classes to translate this requirement into language that these students would understand.

During the lesson, the student's instructor, a trained observer in interaction analysis, took interaction analysis on the student's lesson.

All students on whom complete data were not available were eliminated from the study. In order to equalize the size of treatment groups to facilitate statistical analysis, subjects were randomly eliminated from the four largest treatment groups to equalize group size at 84 subjects each.

Interaction analysis data for each student were plotted and the appropriate column totals and ratios were computed by means of a specially prepared computer matrix plotting program, using an I.B.M. 7094 computer. All other test data were hand scored and then treated by means of The Ohio State MR-90 computer program.

FINDINGS

Data presented in Table 3–27 show the results of an analysis of variance for the percentages of verbal behavior used by subjects in the five treatment groups during a half-hour teaching simulation in which students in Education 535

Table 3–27

Analysis of Variance for Five Treatment Groups on Percentage of Categories of Verbal Teaching Behavior Used During Simulated Teaching

Source of variance	Sum of squares	d.f.	Mean squares	F	p
		Category #1			
Between	0.134	4	0.033	0.50	
Within	27.470	415	0.066		
Total	27.604				
		Category #2			
Between	124.32	4	31.08	4.90	0.01
Within	2,633.40	415	6.34		
Total	2,757.72				
		Category #3			
Between	416.64	4	104.16	3.68	0.01
Within	11,728.92	415	28.26		
Total	12,145.56				
		Category #4			
Between	336.84	4	84.21	3.45	0.01
Within	10,132.92	415	24.42		
Total	10,469.76				
		Category #5			
Between	790.44	4	197.61	1.24	
Within	66,342.36	415	159.86		
Total	67,112.70				
		Category #6			
Between	316.68	4	79.17	2.52	0.05
Within	13,033.44	415	31.40		
Total	13,350.12				
		Category #7			
Between	140.28	4	35.07	2.39	0.05
Within	6,124.44	415	14.75		
Total	6,264.72				
		Category #8			
Between	2.42	4	0.605	4.14	0.01
Within	60.48	415	0.146		
Total	62.90				
		Category #9			
Between	1.94	4	0.485	1.17	
Within	171.36	415	0.413		
Total	173.30				
		Category #10			
Between	1,635.48	4	408.87	6.86	0.01
Within	24,709.44	415	59.54		
Total	26,344.92				

(continued)

Table 3–27 (continued)

Source of variance	Sum of squares	d.f.	Mean squares	F	p
		Category #11			
Between	1,799.28	4	449.82	3.72	0.01
Within	50,152.20	415	120.85		
Total	51,951.48				
		Category #12			
Between	90.72	4	24.30	2.97	0.05
Within	3,401.16	415	8.19		
Total	3,491.87				
		Category #13			
Between	299.88	4	74.97	2.32	
Within	13,431.60	415	32.36		
Total	13,731.48				

classes played the roles of typical secondary school students. Significant F-ratios were obtained in nine of the 13 analyses. These data show clearly that treatment groups differed with respect to their use of the following teacher verbal behaviors: (a) praise and encouragement, (b) acceptance and clarification of student ideas, (c) questions, (d) answers to student questions, (e) directions and commands, (f) criticism. The percentage of types of student talk used during simulated teaching was also found to differ between treatment groups. Significant F-ratios were obtained in the analyses of all three student-talk categories.

There is some question regarding the appropriateness of further tests following a one-way analysis of variance. Guilford (1956), however, suggests a modified t test following an F test that is designed to ascertain which group means differ significantly from the population mean when a significant F-ratio is obtained. Table 3–28 presents a summary of these tests. Data presented in this table indicate that students in treatment one (the treatment which combined the teaching of interaction analysis with readings and discussion of human relations concepts) used significantly more praise and encouragement and questions and significantly less criticism during their simulated teaching than the total population from which they were drawn. Students in treatment five (the treatment which combined human relations training by means of *The Relationship Improvement Program* with instruction in interaction analysis) used significantly more accepting and clarifying behavior during their simulated teaching and generated significantly more student initiated responses and significantly fewer teacher initiated responses.

Subjects in treatment two (in which the use of *The Relationship Improvement Program* was combined with the teaching of the analysis of verbal behavior without the aid of a formal category system) used significantly more directions and elicited significantly more teacher initiated student responses.

Table 3–28

Treatments that Differ Significantly from the Population on Categories of Verbal Behavior on which Significant F Ratios were Obtained ($N = 84$ in each treatment)

Category of verbal behavior	M_t	Interaction analysis treatments 1 and 5			Noninteraction analysis treatments 2, 3, and 4		
		Treatment	M	d_s	Treatment	M	d_s
Category #1	0.09						
Category #2	3.12	#1	3.98	+0.86*	#3	2.28	−0.84*
Category #3	9.81	#5	11.37	+1.56*	#3	8.33	−1.48†
Category #4	11.11	#1	12.86	+1.75*	#4	12.18	+1.07*
Category #5	31.57						
Category #6	7.15				#2	7.87	−1.20†
					#3	8.43	+1.28†
Category #7	2.36				#2	3.24	+0.88†
Category #8	0.17	#1	0.08	−0.09†	#3	0.28	+0.11†
Category #9	0.50						
Category #10	11.93	#5	9.25	−2.68*	#2	14.43	+2.50*
					#4	9.98	−1.95*
Category #11	10.28	#5	12.65	+2.37†	#3	6.77	−3.51*
Category #12	3.89				#3	6.77	−3.51*
Category #13	7.69						

Significant deviations from the population mean are computed by multiplying $MS_{w/n}$ times the t ratio for a given level of significance and degrees of freedom.
* Significant 0.01 with 419 d.f.
† Significant 0.05 with 419 d.f.

Subjects in treatment four (in which dyadic case study discussions were used in conjunction with a noninteraction-analysis investigation of teacher verbal behavior) used significantly more questions yet generated significantly fewer teacher initiated student responses. Subjects in treatment three (the treatment groups in which human relations content was taught by means of readings and class discussions and in which the analysis of verbal teaching behavior was taught without the aid of a formal category system) used significantly less praise, encouragement, acceptance, and clarification and significantly more directions and corrective feedback. In addition, subjects in this treatment group generated fewer student initiated responses but had significantly more questions asked by students and more teacher answers to student questions.

In summary, data presented in Table 3–28 show a trend toward greater use of categories of indirect influence during simulated teaching by subjects in treatments taught interaction analysis. A similar trend toward the use of more direct influence by subjects in treatment groups in which the analysis of verbal behavior was taught without the aid of a formal category system is also apparent. This is particularly true of treatments two and three.

Table 3–29

Comparison of Combined Interaction Treatment and Combined Noninteraction Analysis Treatments on Percentages of Verbal Behaviors Used during Simulated Teaching

Category of verbal behavior	Interaction analysis treatments (N = 168)		Noninteraction analysis treatments (N = 252)			
	M	S.D.	M	S.D.	t	p
Category #1	0.09	0.20	0.06	0.28	1.32	
Category #2	3.62	2.85	2.79	2.27	3.46	0.01
Category #3	10.42	5.57	9.41	5.08	2.02	0.05
Category #4	11.58	4.63	11.47	5.16	0.23	
Category #5	31.92	12.40	31.33	12.71	0.49	
Category #6	6.87	5.31	7.28	5.28	0.79	
Category #7	1.89	3.09	2.68	4.24	2.19	0.05
Category #8	0.12	0.27	0.21	0.44	2.47	0.05
Category #9	0.43	0.55	0.55	0.68	2.00	0.05
Category #10	11.10	7.23	12.48	8.25	2.46	0.05
Category #11	11.34	12.59	9.56	9.89	1.69	
Category #12	3.58	2.52	4.09	3.06	1.88	
Category #13	7.02	4.53	8.06	6.31	1.92	

Data presented in Table 3–29 show this trend even more clearly. In this table are presented the results of a series of t tests comparing the verbal behaviors used in combined treatment groups in which interaction analysis was taught with combined treatment groups in which instruction in the analysis of verbal teaching behavior did not make use of a formal category system.

Table 3–30 shows the results of a series of t tests comparing the categories of verbal behavior used by subjects in treatment groups taught human relations skills by means of the HDI program and groups in which the program was not used. Only in the use of category three (acceptance and clarification of student ideas) did these two combined groups of subjects differ.

SUMMARY AND DISCUSSION

The research reported in this paper was the culmination of a two year course revision and evaluation project dealing with the introductory professional course in The Ohio State University's program for the preparation of secondary school teachers. Five experimental treatments were used. These five treatments involved various combinations of methods of teaching human relations skills and the analysis of verbal classroom teaching behavior. The methods of instruction used in each of the treatment groups were piloted in classes prior to their use in the study. The five experimental treatments were developed as a result

Table 3–30

Comparison of Combined Groups Using the HDI Relationship-Improvement Program and Combined Groups Not Using the Program on the Percentages of Verbal Behavior Used during Simulated Teaching

Category of verbal behavior	HDI program treatments (N = 168)		NonHDI program treatments (N = 252)			
	M	S.D.	M	S.D.	*t*	p
Category #1	0.08	0.36	0.06	0.15	0.83	
Category #2	3.11	2.43	3.13	2.64	1.09	
Category #3	10.80	5.73	9.15	4.89	3.30	0.01
Category #4	11.15	5.05	11.77	4.89	1.32	
Category #5	31.62	12.28	31.53	12.81	0.07	
Category #6	6.24	4.85	7.70	6.02	0.41	
Category #7	2.49	4.53	2.27	3.31	0.61	
Category #8	0.14	0.31	0.20	0.42	1.66	
Category #9	0.50	0.67	0.51	0.62	0.01	
Category #10	11.84	8.55	11.99	7.42	0.20	
Category #11	11.25	11.93	9.63	10.43	1.80	
Category #12	3.54	2.60	4.12	3.02	0.67	
Category #13	7.19	5.69	7.94	5.68	1.39	

of experiences gained in trying out new teaching techniques in Education 535 classes. Each of the five treatment groups had the same behavioral objectives, i.e., the use, under simulated classroom conditions, of verbal behaviors that have been found to be associated with more positive student attitudes toward school and greater student achievement, i.e., accepting, clarifying and encouraging behavior rather than directive, critical and rejecting behavior.

Data presented in the findings section of this report indicate clear differences with respect to the types of verbal behavior used by students in the different groups during their simulated teaching. Subjects in the treatment groups taught interaction analysis were found to use, in their teaching simulations, significantly more verbal behaviors that have been found to be associated with higher student achievement and more positive student attitudes toward their teachers and school. These same subjects were found to use significantly fewer behaviors that have been found to be associated with lower achievement and less positive attitudes.

That the verbal behavior of students who were taught interaction analysis differed from those not taught this skill is clear. Why they differed presents a different question. One way of viewing these differences relates to an assumption underlying a rationale for teaching interaction analysis to teachers and prospective teachers. It may be assumed that when the skill of interaction analysis is learned, it gives the teacher a feedback mechanism in the form of a category system, that he may use to become more sensitively aware of his own teaching behavior (Flanders, 1961, 1963; Hough and Amidon, 1965). Interaction analysis seems to provide the teacher with a cognitive organizer to more accurately interpret the effects of his behavior on his students. In this way, the teacher becomes more aware of his behavior. If interaction analysis, in fact, functions as a feedback mechanism, then it has the potential to act as a mechanism for the reinforcement of behavior. If this is true, then as students in Education 535 analyzed and experimented with their verbal teaching behavior and analyzed the behavior of other teachers, those students who had been taught interaction analysis had a more adequate cognitive organizer to aid them in interpreting and internalizing what they saw happening to themselves and to other teachers.

In all treatments, students were given a rationale for using acceptance, encouragement and praise and avoiding or judiciously using criticism and directive behaviors that tend to restrict student freedom. In addition, students in all treatment groups were restricted during their simulated teaching (by the objectives of the course) to lessons in which at least 20% of all verbal interaction must be student talk and in which no more than 40% of any one classification or type of teacher talk was permitted. It is assumed that as students experimented with their teaching behavior, those who were taught interaction analysis had a more exacting way of perceiving and conceptualizing those behaviors which have been associated with more positive student achievement and attitudes. As students in Education 535 tried to use these behaviors in microteaching and in exploratory teaching in the public schools, those who had been taught interaction analysis had a more adequate feedback mechanism to receive and interpret the effects of their behavior and the behavior they observed. In this way these behaviors were reinforced and thus became more likely to occur, e.g., in the simulated teaching situation.

The significantly greater use of category three (acceptance and clarification of student ideas) by subjects in treatment five presents a most provocative finding. It was this treatment group that combined instruction in interaction analysis with human relations training by means of the HDI *Relationship Improvement Program.* An inspection of the summary matrices for treatment groups shows that in addition to a greater total percentage of category three, subjects in treatment five used almost two-thirds more extended acceptance and clarification (the 3–3 cell) than subjects in treatment four (the treatment group that rated second highest in its use of extended acceptance and clarification).

CONCLUSIONS AND IMPLICATIONS

The primary purpose of institutional research is to provide the basis for program evaluation and modification. This purpose was achieved by this study. On the basis of findings, and the two years of experience that led to the creation of this study, substantial modifications have been made in the introductory general methods course for the preparation of secondary school teachers at The Ohio State University. Interaction analysis is now taught to all students as a technique for analyzing their own verbal behavior. It should be pointed out that the emphasis is on analysis and not upon evaluation or judgment. We realize that we are a long way from identifying and shaping the behavior of effective teachers let alone identifying prospective good teachers from data gathered on the basis of one or even a few simulated teaching experiences. Indeed, we have not even seriously addressed ourselves to the problem of predicting teacher effectiveness on the basis of performance in pre-service education classes.

Data reported with respect to the effect of the interaction of the three human relations training designs for the analysis of verbal teaching behavior seem to indicate that the combinations of experimental variables produced interactions that should be investigated in future studies. Certainly, the combination of classroom applications of nondirective theory and a social–emotional theory of classroom interaction presents a provocative area of study in educational methodology that needs more rigorous investigation. To draw more than such a recommendation from this data could be presumptuous.

Because of the time lag between when students take Education 535 and the time that they do their student teaching, it may be assumed that students will forget much of what they learned about controlling their verbal behavior. We are, therefore, following a selected population of these students into their student teaching. Our intention is to see if the differences that we found in teacher verbal behavior under simulated conditions will continue to be manifested in student teaching four to twelve months later. In this study, the verbal behavior during student teaching of subjects who were taught interaction analysis is being compared with subjects who were not instructed in this technique for the analysis of verbal teaching behavior.

10

A STUDY OF THE EFFECT OF PRE-SERVICE TRAINING IN INTERACTION ANALYSIS ON THE VERBAL BEHAVIOR OF STUDENT TEACHERS[47]

ERNEST E. LOHMAN, RICHARD OBER, and JOHN B. HOUGH

One of the important functions of pre-service teacher-education experiences is to develop in pre-service teachers an awareness of and skill in the appropriate use of a variety of verbal teaching behaviors.

In a recent study conducted at The Ohio State University two methods were utilized to teach the analysis and control of verbal teaching behavior to pre-service teachers taking a general-methods course (Hough and Ober, 1966). The first method employed the Flanders system of interaction analysis. Students were taught the category system, the skills of tabulation, and matrix interpretation. Interaction analysis was taught as a tool for self-analysis of simulated teaching experiences. It was assumed that learning the skill of interaction analysis would give these pre-service teachers a feedback mechanism that would enable them to interpret the effects of their teaching behavior more accurately than they could without it. It was further assumed that by becoming more aware of their behavior, these pre-service teachers would be able to analyze discrepancies between their intentions and their actions while teaching.

Students taught by the second method discussed and identified verbal behaviors, but did not create or use a formal category system of verbal behaviors. These two experimental approaches were used in the general-methods course that precedes student teaching in The Ohio State University's program for the preparation of secondary school teachers.

STATEMENT OF THE PROBLEM

The purpose of this study was to follow into their student teaching two groups of student teachers who had been instructed in these two methods of analyzing verbal teaching behavior, and to determine whether there would be a difference

---

[47] This paper was prepared specially for this book.

in the verbal behaviors they used during their student teaching experience four to twelve months after instruction.

The general hypotheses tested in this study were as follows:

1. There will be no difference between the percentages of direct teacher talk of student teachers trained in the Flanders system of interaction analysis and the direct teacher talk of student teachers not so trained.

2. There will be no difference between the percentages of indirect teacher talk of student teachers trained in the Flanders system of interaction analysis and the indirect teacher talk of student teachers not so trained.

3. There will be no difference in the percentages of student talk in classes taught by student teachers who have been trained in the Flanders system of interaction analysis and the student talk in classes taught by student teachers not so trained.

4. There will be no difference in the following ratios between student teachers trained in the Flanders system of interaction analysis and student teachers not so trained: (1) S/T ratio, (2) I/D ratio, (3) revised i/d ratio, (4) Student Response I/D ratio, and (5) Teacher Response I/D ratio.

REVIEW OF THE LITERATURE

Literature in the field gives some support to the assumption underlying the purpose of this study. In an initial study of in-service teachers that used interaction analysis as a feedback tool, Flanders (1963) reported that in-service teachers trained in interaction analysis did change their teaching behavior. They became more sensitive to their own classroom teaching and became more independent and self-directing in comparing their intentions with their actions.

Studies by Furst (1965), Hough and Amidon (1963), and Kirk (1964) that used interaction analysis as an instructional-feedback tool, report that pre-service teachers who have been taught interaction analysis do differ significantly from those pre-service teachers who have not been taught interaction analysis. In these studies, pre-service teachers who were trained in interaction analysis used significantly more verbal behaviors that have been found by Flanders (1960), Amidon and Flanders (1961), and La Shier (1966) to be associated with higher student achievement and more positive student attitudes toward their teachers and school. These same subjects were found to use significantly fewer behaviors that have been found to be associated with lower achievement and less positive attitudes. In addition, there is evidence of more student participation— particularly spontaneous student participation—in classes taught by student teachers trained in interaction analysis.

PROCEDURES

The 60 subjects for this study were drawn primarily from a population of students who, during the previous academic year, had taken the general-methods course at The Ohio State University. This student population (420

Table 3–31

Description of Categories for the 13-Category Modifications of Flanders' System of Inter-action Analysis

Category number		Description of verbal behavior
1	TEACHER TALK	*Accepts feeling:* accepts and clarifies the feeling tone of students in a nonthreatening manner. Feelings may be positive or negative. Predicting and recalling feelings are also included.
2		*Praises or encourages:* praises or encourages student action or behavior. Jokes that release tension, not at the expense of another individual, nodding head, or saying ''uh-huh'' or ''go on'' are included.
3		*Accepts or uses ideas of student:* clarifying, building on, developing and accepting ideas of students.
4		*Asks questions:* asking a question about content or pro-cedure with the intent that the student should answer.
5		*Lectures:* giving facts or opinions about content or pro-cedure with the intent that the student should answer.
6		*Answers student questions:* direct answers to questions regarding content or procedure asked by students.
7		*Gives directions:* directions, commands or orders to which a student is expected to comply.
8		*Criticizes or justifies authority:* statements intended to change student behavior from a nonacceptable to an acceptable pattern; bawling out someone; stating why the teacher is doing what he is, doing so as to achieve or maintain control; rejecting or criticizing a student's opinion or judgment.
9		*Corrective feedback:* telling a student that his answer is wrong when the incorrectness of the answer can be established by other than opinion, i.e., empirical valida-tion, definition or custom.

students) served as subjects in the study, *The Effect of Training in Interaction Analysis on the Verbal Behavior of Pre-service Teachers* (Hough and Ober, 1966). This study was the parent study for the research reported here. The parent study used five treatments of 84 subjects each. Subjects in two of the treatment groups were trained in interaction analysis; subjects in three treatment groups were not trained in interaction analysis. In all, 168 subjects were trained in interaction analysis and 252 were trained to analyze verbal teaching behavior without the aid of a formal category system. In the parent study, a 13-category modification of the Flanders system of interaction analysis was used to measure the dependent-variable, verbal behavior of pre-service teachers under simulated conditions of teaching. Table 3–31 contains a description of this 13-category modification of the Flanders system. In the parent study, scores from two tests given prior to instruction were used as control variables. These two tests were The Teaching Situation Reaction Test (TSRT) and

Table 3–31 (continued)

Category number		Description of verbal behavior
10	STUDENT TALK	*Student talk–response:* talk by students in response to requests or narrow teacher questions. The teacher initiates the contact or solicits student's statement.
11		*Student talk emitted:* talk by students in response to broad teacher questions which require judgment or opinion. Student declarative statements emitted but not called for by teacher questions.
12		*Student question:* questions concerning content or procedure that are directed to the teacher.
13		*Silence or confusion:* pauses, short periods of silence, and periods of confusion in which communication cannot be understood by the observer.

$$\text{Indirect--direct ratio} = \frac{\text{categories 1, 2, 3, 4, 6}}{\text{categories 5, 7, 8, 9}}$$

$$\text{Revised indirect--direct ratio} = \frac{\text{categories 1, 2, 3}}{\text{categories 7, 8, 9}}$$

$$\text{Student--teacher ratio} = \frac{\text{categories 10, 11, 12}}{\text{categories 1--9}}$$

$$\text{Student response I/D ratio} = \frac{\text{columns 10, 11, 12; rows 1, 2, 3, 4, 6}}{\text{columns 10, 11, 12; rows 5, 7, 8, 9}}$$

$$\text{Teacher response I/D ratio} = \frac{\text{rows 10, 11, 12; columns 1, 2, 3, 4, 6}}{\text{rows 10, 11, 12; columns 5, 7, 8, 9}}$$

Form E of the Dogmatism Scale (D-Scale). In addition, the Relationship Inventory was also administered as a pre-test. Each of these instruments was again administered as a post-test at the completion of the course experience used in the parent study.

Administration of one of the control measures used in the parent study, The Relationship Inventory, required that subjects be paired with a partner. As a result, in addition to the 420 subjects mentioned above, there were a number of single subjects for whom appropriate data were available, but who were not used in the parent study because the data on their partners were incomplete. In addition, students were available from two class sections taught by the principal investigator of the parent study who were not included as subjects of the parent study. These three sources, then, constituted the pool of subjects available for this study.

From this pool of subjects was selected a sample of 60 on whom data were complete and who were scheduled for student teaching during the 1965–66 academic year. Thirty of these student teachers had received training in interaction analysis in the general methods course during the previous academic year, and 30 had not. As many control variables as was prudent were identified and analyzed to determine if the two groups of 30 student teachers differed.

Table 3–32

A Comparison of the Noninteraction-Analysis Group of Student Teachers and the Interaction-Analysis Group of Student Teachers on Control Variables

Control variables	Noninteraction analysis (N = 30)		Interaction analysis (N = 30)			
	$\overline{X}$	S.D.	$\overline{X}$	S.D.	t	p
TSRT pre-test	82.80	10.53	78.70	10.31	1.49	n.s.
TSRT post-test	81.30	10.25	79.07	10.80	0.808	n.s.
TSRT pre-post change	−1.50	9.85	0.367	6.65	0.157	n.s.
D-Scale pre-test	146.00	20.03	143.60	21.67	0.438	n.s.
D-Scale post-test	150.00	20.96	145.07	22.46	0.863	n.s.
D-Scale pre-post change	2.60	12.19	1.50	15.65	0.081	n.s.
Age	21.50	2.01	21.80	2.99	0.50	n.s.

Table 3–33

Chi-Square Test of Compatibility between Males and Females of 30 Noninteraction-Analysis Student Teachers and 30 Interaction-Analysis Student Teachers

Sex	Fo		Fe		d.f.	χ^2	p
	IA	Non-IA	IA	Non-IA			
Male	17	15	16	16			
Female	13	15	14	14			
Total	30	30	30	30	1	0.267	n.s.

Table 3–34

Chi-Square Test of Compatibility between 30 Noninteraction-Analysis Student Teachers and 30 Interaction-Analysis Student Teachers with Regard to Marital Status

Marital Status	Fo		Fe		d.f.	χ^2	p
	IA	Non-IA	IA	Non-IA			
Married	4	5	4.5	4.5			
Single	26	25	25.5	25.5			
Total	30	30	30	30	1	0.13	n.s.

Table 3–35

Chi-Square Test of Compatibility between 30 Noninteraction-Analysis Student Teachers and 30 Interaction-Analysis Student Teachers with Regard to Instructor in the General Methods Course

Instructor	Fo		Fe		d.f.	χ^2	p
	IA	Non-IA	IA	Non-IA			
A	6	5	5.5	5.5			
B	7	6	6.5	6.5			
C	5	9	7	7			
D	3	7	5	5			
E	7	3	5	5			
F	2	0	1	1			
Total	30	30	30	30	5	4.91	n.s.

Table 3–36

A Comparison of the 30 Noninteraction-Analysis Student Teachers with the 252 Noninteraction-Analysis Subjects of the Parent Study on Several Control Variables

Control variables	Noninteraction analysis (N = 30)		Noninteraction analysis (N = 30)		t	p
	$\bar{X}$	S.D.	$\bar{X}$	S.D.		
TSRT pre-test	146.00	20.03	147.09	20.20	0.62	n.s.
TSRT post-test	150.00	20.96	151.39	19.46	1.01	n.s.
D-Scale pre-test	82.97	10.51	80.85	10.05	0.33	n.s.
D-Scale post-test	81.30	10.25	80.39	10.92	0.04	n.s.
Verbal behaviors:						
Category #1	0.045	0.129	0.058	0.286	0.39	n.s.
Category #2	2.71	2.10	2.80	2.28	0.20	n.s.
Category #3	10.62	5.13	9.42	5.08	1.20	n.s.
Category #4	12.57	3.92	11.47	5.16	1.40	n.s.
Category #5	28.90	10.57	31.33	12.72	1.15	n.s.
Category #6	6.29	4.28	7.28	5.82	1.12	n.s.
Category #7	2.39	2.35	2.68	4.25	0.56	n.s.
Category #8	0.178	0.303	0.211	0.440	0.53	n.s.
Category #9	0.729	0.805	0.552	0.688	1.11	n.s.
Category #10	13.82	6.63	12.48	8.25	1.00	n.s.
Category #11	9.27	8.11	9.57	9.89	0.19	n.s.
Category #12	3.82	2.33	4.10	3.07	0.59	n.s.
Category #13	8.65	6.98	8.06	6.32	0.44	n.s.
I/D ratio	1.14	0.547	1.07	0.690	0.62	n.s.
Revised i/d ratio	9.65	14.80	10.39	14.40	0.25	n.s.
S/T ratio	0.438	0.182	0.43	0.25	0.17	n.s.

Table 3–37

Chi-Square Test of Compatibility between 30 Noninteraction-Analysis Student Teachers and 252 Noninteraction-Analysis Students from Parent Population with Regard to Sex

Sex	Fo		Fe		d.f.	χ^2	p
	Non-IA	252	Non-IA	252			
Male	15	99	12.12	101.87			
Female	15	153	18	150.12			
Total	30	252	30	252	1	1.32	n.s.

Table 3–38

Chi-Square Test of Compatibility between 30 Noninteraction-Analysis Student Teachers and 252 Noninteraction-Analysis Students from Parent Population with Regard to Marital Status

Marital status	Fo		Fe		d.f.	χ^2	p
	Non-IA	252	Non-IA	252			
Married	5	29	3.62	30.38			
Single	25	223	26.38	221.82			
Total	30	252	30	252	1	0.651	n.s.

Table 3–39

Chi-Square Test of Compatibility between 30 Noninteraction-Analysis Student Teachers and 252 Noninteraction-Analysis Students from Parent Population with Respect to Instructor*

Instructor	Non-IA	252	Non-IA	252	d.f.	χ^2	p
A	5	42	5	42			
B	6	44	5.32	44.68			
C	9	62	7.55	63.45			
D	7	60	7.13	59.87			
E	3	44	5	42			
Total	30	252	30	252	5	1.3	n.s.

* Only five instructors are represented, since the principal investigator of the "parent study" did not teach any noninteraction-analysis students.

Findings from the analysis of control data are reported in Tables 3–32, 3–33, 3–34, and 3–35. Data in these tables show that the two groups of student teachers (those who had experienced training in interaction analysis and those who had not) did not differ significantly on any of the following control variables: scores on tests administered in the general-methods course [i.e., The Teaching Situation Reaction Test (TSRT), and the Dogmatism Scale (D-Scale)], age, sex, marital status, or instructors in class sections of the general-methods course.

Table 3–40

A Comparison of the 30 Interaction-Analysis Student Teachers with the 168 Interaction-Analysis Subjects of the Parent Study on Several Control Variables

Control variables	Noninteraction analysis (N = 30)		Noninteraction analysis (N = 30)		t	p
	X̄	S.D.	X̄	S.D.		
TSRT pre-test	143.23	21.89	145.41	21.18	0.50	n.s.
TSRT post-test	145.97	21.18	146.67	20.94	0.17	n.s.
D-Scale pre-test	78.47	10.42	80.91	10.92	1.16	n.s.
D-Scale post-test	78.93	10.94	79.85	11.69	0.41	n.s.
Verbal behaviors:						
Category #1	0.08	0.19	0.086	0.205	0.15	n.s.
Category #2	3.92	2.75	3.61	2.86	1.71	n.s.
Category #3	11.43	5.40	10.40	5.57	0.94	n.s.
Category #4	12.43	4.18	11.58	4.64	0.99	n.s.
Category #5	27.90	12.42	31.92	12.41	1.61	n.s.
Category #6	6.29	4.15	6.87	5.32	0.67	n.s.
Category #7	1.35	1.38	1.89	3.09	1.56	n.s.
Category #8	0.152	0.278	0.121	0.275	1.67	n.s.
Category #9	0.529	0.653	0.43	0.558	0.76	n.s.
Category #10	10.99	5.89	11.10	7.24	0.09	n.s.
Category #11	13.91	12.94	11.34	12.59	0.00	n.s.
Category #12	3.86	2.31	3.58	2.52	0.59	n.s.
Category #13	7.17	4.71	7.03	4.53	0.15	n.s.
I/D ratio	1.34	0.657	1.13	0.629	1.61	n.s.
Revised i/d ratio	13.62	16.02	11.91	14.61	0.54	n.s.
S/T ratio	0.583	0.765	0.46	0.47	0.87	n.s.

In order to establish that the two samples of 30 student teachers each were representative samples of the larger student populations in the parent study from which they were drawn, a number of control variables were also identified and tested for significance. A comparison of 30 noninteraction-analysis student teachers with the 252 noninteraction-analysis subjects of the parent study is reported in Tables 3–36, 3–37, 3–38, and 3–39. These data show that the sample of 30 student teachers did not differ significantly from the larger population from which they were drawn with respect to scores on the Teaching Situation Reaction Test, the Dogmatism Scale, sex, marital status, instructors in Education 535 during the parent study, or on selected verbal behaviors used in simulated teaching during the parent study.

Table 3–41

Chi-Square Test of Compatibility between 30 Interaction-Analysis Student Teachers and 168 Interaction-Analysis Students from Parent Population with Regard to Sex

Sex	Fo		Fe		d.f.	χ^2	p
	IA	168	IA	168			
Male	17	65	12.42	68.56			
Female	13	103	17.07	98.42			
Total	30	168	30	168	1	2.98	n.s.

Table 3–42

Chi-Square Test of Compatibility between 30 Interaction-Analysis Student Teachers and 168 Interaction-Analysis Students from Parent Population with Regard to Marital Status

Marital Status	Fo		Fe		d.f.	χ^2	p
	IA	168	IA	168			
Married	4	17	3.18	17.82			
Single	26	151	26.82	150.18			
Total	30	168	30	168	1	0.284	n.s.

Table 3–43

Chi-Square Test of Compatibility between 30 Interaction-Analysis Student Teachers and 168 Interaction-Analysis Students from Parent Population with Respect to Instructor

Instructor	Fo		Fe		d.f.	χ^2	p
	IA	168	IA	168			
A	6	42	7.27	40.72			
B	7	40	7.12	39.87			
C	5	20	3.79	21.21			
D	3	24	4.09	22.91			
E	7	42	7.42	41.07			
F	2	0	0.33	1.7			
Total	30	168	20	168	5	10.7	n.s.

A comparison of 30 interaction-analysis student teachers with the 168 interaction-analysis subjects of the parent study on the same variables is reported in Tables 3–40, 3–41, 3–42, and 3–43. These data show that the 30 student teachers did not differ significantly from the population of 168 subjects from which they were drawn.

The student teachers included in this study were assigned to their student teaching through the normal procedures established by the Office of Field

Services of The Ohio State University. The students were placed in secondary schools of the city of Columbus, Ohio, the public schools of Franklin County, Ohio, and public schools in the immediate environs. All subjects were apprised of the purposes of the study early in their student teaching assignment and were told that the data gathered would have no effect on their grade and would not be made available to them for self-analysis purposes during their student teaching.

Each student teacher was observed by one of two reliable observers for periods of 20 minutes on each of six different occasions during the ten-week student-teaching experience. The system employed in this study to observe and classify verbal behavior was the same 13-category modification of the Flanders system of interaction analysis used in the parent study (see Table 3–31). Procedures followed in making classroom observations were in general the same as those of other recent studies using interaction analysis. The inter-observer reliability of the two observers was obtained throughout the duration of this study. The means used to establish inter-observer reliability involved the categorization of six tape-recorded classroom situations of ten or twelve minutes each. The mean inter-observer reliability, computed by a formula suggested by Scott (1955), was 0.76.

Interaction analysis data for each subject were plotted and the appropriate column totals and ratios were computed by means of a specially prepared computer-matrix plotting program, using an IBM 7094 computer. All the data needed for testing the hypotheses were treated by means of the Ohio State University MR 90 computer program.

A mean per cent or ratio score for each of the selected verbal behaviors used in this study was calculated for each of the samples. The use of selected verbal behaviors by the two samples was compared by the use of a *t*-test of the difference between means, and the purpose of the comparison was to test the differences between the two samples on each of the selected measures of verbal behavior. An *F* test was made to determine whether the variances of the two groups differed significantly. Where the *F* test showed that variance differed significantly, the *t* table was entered with one-half the usual degrees of freedom.

FINDINGS

Data presented in Tables 3–44 and 3–45 represent a summary of 120 hours of classroom observation by two reliable observers. Tabulating at an average rate of one tally every three seconds, the observers recorded 145,868 tallies for the 60 student teachers used in this study. Data presented in Tables 3–46 and 3–47 show the results of *t*-tests of differences between means of the verbal behaviors used by the student teachers in each of the two groups during their student teaching experience. Significant *t* values were obtained in ten of the 23 analyses conducted in this study. These data clearly show that those student teachers trained in interaction analysis during the general-methods course differed

Table 3–44

Cumulative Matrix for 30 Noninteraction-Analysis Student Teachers

	1	2	3	4	5	6	7	8	9	10	11	12	13
1	0.00	0.00	0.00	0.00	0.01	0.00	0.00	0.00	0.00	0.00	0.00	0.00	0.00
2	0.00	0.03	0.35	0.24	0.41	0.01	0.02	0.01	0.00	0.12	0.07	0.05	0.08
3	0.00	0.36	1.85	1.66	2.12	0.88	0.18	0.03	0.03	1.64	0.28	0.20	0.50
4	0.00	0.04	0.02	4.11	0.67	0.01	0.10	0.03	0.00	5.55	0.14	0.24	1.30
5	0.01	0.09	0.12	3.09	28.03	0.02	0.38	0.08	0.01	0.48	0.58	0.63	1.31
6	0.00	0.01	0.03	0.26	0.50	2.21	0.03	0.02	0.00	0.13	0.22	0.29	0.25
7	0.00	0.01	0.01	0.12	0.24	0.00	0.43	0.03	0.00	0.47	0.04	0.08	0.33
8	0.00	0.00	0.01	0.08	0.10	0.01	0.03	0.11	0.00	0.07	0.06	0.02	0.12
9	0.00	0.00	0.02	0.10	0.16	0.01	0.02	0.01	0.10	0.11	0.04	0.01	0.04
10	0.00	0.65	5.24	1.09	0.82	0.06	0.27	0.12	0.34	8.91	0.17	0.11	0.68
11	0.00	0.15	0.93	0.12	0.21	0.02	0.03	0.03	0.09	0.01	2.01	0.12	0.19
12	0.00	0.02	0.20	0.13	0.03	1.45	0.01	0.01	0.01	0.00	0.05	0.95	0.05
13	0.00	0.04	0.15	1.33	1.52	0.07	0.25	0.13	0.02	0.96	0.26	0.22	5.55
	0.01	1.40	8.93	12.23	34.82	4.75	1.75	0.61	0.61	18.45	3.92	2.92	10.40

Table 3–45

Cumulative Matrix for 30 Interaction-Analysis Student Teachers

	1	2	3	4	5	6	7	8	9	10	11	12	13
1	0.00	0.00	0.00	0.00	0.01	0.00	0.00	0.00	0.00	0.00	0.00	0.00	0.00
2	0.00	0.05	0.59	0.37	0.50	0.01	0.03	0.01	0.01	0.21	0.20	0.07	0.11
3	0.00	0.55	2.49	1.83	2.10	0.11	0.18	0.02	0.02	1.99	0.63	0.25	0.52
4	0.00	0.08	0.03	4.16	0.65	0.01	0.08	0.01	0.00	5.48	0.25	0.23	1.40
5	0.01	0.10	0.13	2.88	20.96	0.04	0.25	0.05	0.01	0.52	0.95	0.62	1.17
6	0.00	0.02	0.04	0.30	0.47	2.83	0.04	0.01	0.00	0.10	0.37	0.42	0.25
7	0.00	0.01	0.01	0.09	0.17	0.00	0.13	0.01	0.00	0.37	0.06	0.05	0.17
8	0.00	0.00	0.01	0.04	0.06	0.01	0.01	0.04	0.00	0.05	0.02	0.01	0.05
9	0.00	0.00	0.02	0.10	0.10	0.01	0.01	0.00	0.05	0.13	0.04	0.02	0.03
10	0.00	0.92	5.49	1.03	0.77	0.08	0.16	0.07	0.37	9.69	0.24	0.12	0.79
11	0.00	0.38	1.46	0.20	0.45	0.04	0.04	0.03	0.12	0.02	4.67	0.16	0.40
12	0.00	0.01	0.24	0.13	0.03	1.65	0.02	0.01	0.00	0.00	0.05	0.84	0.09
13	0.00	0.05	0.17	1.23	1.31	0.09	0.13	0.05	0.02	1.17	0.50	0.27	4.39
	0.01	2.17	10.68	12.36	27.58	4.87	1.08	0.31	0.60	19.73	7.98	3.06	9.37

Table 3–46

A Comparison of the Noninteraction-Analysis Student Teachers and the Interaction-Analysis Student Teachers on Several Dependent Variables

Dependent variables	Noninteraction-analysis student teachers (N = 30)		Interaction-analysis student teachers (N = 30)		t	p*
	$\overline{X}$	S.D.	$\overline{X}$	S.D.		
Category						
1	0.14	0.04	0.26	0.05	1.05	
2	1.41	1.16	2.19	1.11	0.831	
3	8.93	2.57	10.66	2.45	2.64	0.05
4	12.26	3.91	12.37	3.26	0.116	
5	34.69	12.78	27.78	8.38	2.44	0.05†
6	3.95	3.20	4.85	4.49	0.882	
7	1.76	1.57	1.08	0.70	2.14	0.05†
8	0.62	0.93	0.32	0.24	1.67	
9	0.61	0.37	0.60	0.41	0.10	
10	18.45	7.65	19.72	7.51	0.638	
11	3.92	3.31	7.96	6.36	3.04	0.01†
12	2.92	1.94	3.08	2.11	0.283	
13	10.49	5.86	9.41	4.90	0.76	
I/D ratio	0.83	0.48	1.10	0.39	2.37	0.05
i/d ratio	7.07	8.16	8.75	6.60	0.82	
S/T ratio	0.42	0.19	0.54	0.23	0.678	
T/R ratio	5.96	3.86	6.68	3.00	0.79	
S/R ratio	4.15	2.12	4.50	3.36	0.47	

* with 59 d.f.   † t-table entered at one-half the usual d.f.

significantly from those student teachers not so trained in their use of the following teacher verbal behaviors:

1. They used less direct teacher talk.
2. They did less lecturing.
3. They gave fewer directions.
4. They used less extended direct teacher talk.
5. They used more indirect teacher talk.
6. They used more acceptance and clarification of student talk.
7. They used more extended indirect teacher talk.
8. They used more indirect teacher verbal behavior as opposed to direct teacher verbal behavior as revealed in the I/D ratio.

Table 3–47

A Comparison of the Noninteraction-Analysis Student Teachers and the Interaction-Analysis Student Teachers on Several Dependent Variables

Dependent variables	Noninteraction analysis student teachers (N = 30)		Interaction analysis student teachers (N = 30)			
	$\overline{X}$	S.D.	$\overline{X}$	S.D.	t	p^*
Sum of categories 5, 7, 8, 9	37.67	12.08	29.76	8.15	2.93	0.01†
Sum of 5-5, 7-7, 8-8, 9-9 cells	28.50	13.69	21.24	7.59	2.50	0.05†
Sum of categories 1, 2, 3, 4, 6	26.47	6.08	30.05	4.60	2.53	0.05
Sum of 1-1, 2-2, 3-3, 4-4, 6-6 cells	8.10	3.33	0.46	3.85	4.55	0.001
Sum of categories 10, 11, 12	25.28	8.39	30.75	9.02	2.93	0.05
Sum of 10-10, 11-11, 12-12 cells	11.80	7.60	15.14	8.16	1.61	

* with 59 d.f.   † t-table entered at one-half the usual d.f.

In addition, there was significantly more student talk and particularly more spontaneous student talk in classes taught by student teachers trained in the Flanders system of interaction analysis.

A summary of the analysis of data and tests of significance is found in Tables 3–46 and 3–47.

DISCUSSION

Consistent with the findings of other studies, data presented in the findings of this study indicate a clear trend with respect to differences in the types of verbal behaviors used by student teachers trained in interaction analysis. Student teachers who were taught interaction analysis four to twelve months earlier in a general-methods course were found to use more indirect teacher verbal behavior and less direct teacher verbal behavior in their student teaching experience. In addition, there was more student-initiated talk in classes taught by student teachers who had been trained in the Flanders system of interaction analysis.

It is apparent that the student teachers trained in interaction analysis used more verbal behaviors that have been found to be associated with higher student achievement and more positive student attitudes toward school. These same student teachers were also found to use fewer behaviors that have been found to be associated with lower achievement and less positive attitudes.

At the conclusion of the parent study, using simulated teaching behavior as the criterion measure, significant differences were found to exist between the verbal behaviors of those pre-service teachers trained in interaction analysis and those pre-service teachers not so trained (Hough and Ober, 1966). Four to twelve months later these same differences were, in general, found to exist in a selected, representative sample who were followed into their student-teaching experience. Earlier in this paper it was suggested that when the skill of inter- action analysis is learned, it may give the teacher a feedback mechanism that he can use both to become more sensitive to his own teaching behavior and to become more aware of the effect of his behavior on others. Certainly this assumption should be tested directly in future research, but the findings from this study give further evidence that learning a category system such as the Flanders system of interaction analysis seems to help the pre-service teacher assess and analyze his teaching behavior. It seems to provide him with an opportunity to identify his own teaching-behavior problems, to generate predictions or teaching principles about his teaching behaviors, and to gather empirical evidence about his ability to control his verbal behavior. Certainly, the learning of a formal category system seems to be related to the use by student teachers of verbal behaviors that have been associated with more effec- tive teaching as measured by student attitudes and achievement.

SUMMARY

This study followed 30 student teachers who had been trained in interaction analysis prior to student teaching and 30 student teachers who had not been so trained into their student-teaching experience four to twelve months later. Utilizing a 13-category modification of the Flanders system of interaction analysis as an observational tool, observers found that the two groups of student teachers differed significantly in their use of verbal behaviors. Student teachers who were taught interaction analysis were found to use more indirect teacher verbal behavior and less direct teacher verbal behavior in their student teaching experience. In addition, there was more student-initiated talk in classes taught by student teachers who had been trained in the Flanders system of interaction analysis.

11

INTERACTION MODELS
OF CRITICAL
TEACHING BEHAVIORS[48]

NED A. FLANDERS

This paper consists of an exposition of my convictions about teacher education based on my own research which has attempted to assess the social skills used by teachers in the classroom. Inferences about social skills are made from an analysis of the spontaneous verbal statements which occur in classroom discourse.

THE PROBLEM

We are here to discuss teacher education and research on teacher education. To do this we must consider what is said in terms of the purposes of teacher education.

The purpose of teacher education is to start with an average college student and produce a beginning teacher who can, at some minimal level:

a) Accept the need to control his own behavior for professional purposes,

b) Identify the range of teaching behaviors that are required in teaching,

c) Perform these behaviors at appropriate moments in spontaneous situations,

d) Predict the consequences of providing various teaching behaviors under specified conditions,

e) Plan a strategy of teaching behaviors for specified purposes and situations,

f) Collect information about his own behavior and the consequences of his behavior in classroom settings,

g) Achieve those resources necessary to continue his professional growth on the job,

h) Identify his own preferred outcomes of classroom instruction as functions of his own behavior.

---

[48] Taken from Frederick Cyphert and Ernest Spaights, *An Analysis and Projection of Research in Teacher Education.* Cooperative Research Project, No. F-015, U.S. Office of Education, 1964. Reprinted by permission of the author.

The purposes listed above refer to the professional training of a teacher. The fact that a teacher *must* know the content he is to reach is so self-evident that it hardly seems worth mentioning.

CRITICAL TEACHING BEHAVIORS

THE USE OF INTERACTION ANALYSIS. The critical teaching behaviors to be described will make use of interaction analysis categories that have been used in my own research. There are, of course, other category systems. For those readers who are unfamiliar with this technique, earlier parts of this book, or Chapter Six in the *Handbook of Research on Teaching* by Gage may be useful. Following the University of Minnesota adage, "If you can't measure it it's not worth talking about," the critical teaching behaviors to be discussed in this section will make use of the matrix technique of tabulating interaction analysis data. An understanding of this technique is essential to reading the material which follows.

Much of what I have written on teacher education has placed considerable emphasis on overt behavior. This emphasis has many ramifications. It means that what we teach in teacher education may be understood by incorporating it into the personal overt behavior of the teacher-candidate. It also means that any inconsistency between the teaching methods used by the professor of education and the principles of teaching that he espouses may well produce such an important conflict (between ends and means) for the students that they cannot transform their cognitive understanding into their personal behavior.

The paragraphs to follow, in this section of the paper, will describe critical teaching behaviors. I believe that these critical teaching behaviors can and should be taught in teacher education. Each critical behavior pattern will be illustrated in a matrix, hopefully making clear what overt behaviors are present in each instance.

It is self-evident that if teachers in preparation learn to classify overt behavior by some method like interaction analysis, in turn, they will be in a position to refer the goals of their own training to behavior patterns and to assess their own progress toward these goals.

For my own purposes, I have defined a critical teaching behavior as a pattern of acts that: (a) are logically related to certain educational outcomes, (b) follow a certain sequence with measureable probability, and (c) seem crucial in terms of a theory of teacher influence verified by past research.

The first three behavior patterns to be discussed below are quite typical of common practice in classrooms, according to our research data. These more common practices are presented as models of content exposition by the teacher, teacher directed drill, and giving directions which the students are to carry out. The fourth model is concerned with stimulating more independent thought by students. The fifth model is concerned with the affective aspects that are possible in this particular communication circle. To the right there is a thin arrow going from the 4-8 cell to the 8-8 cell and then back to the 8-5 cell. This

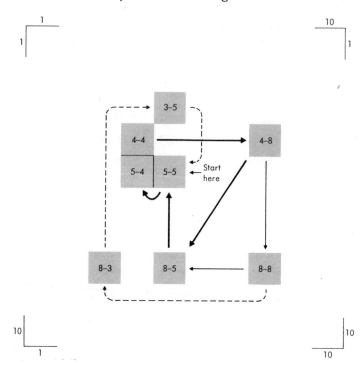

FIG. 3–10. High-content emphasis under close teacher direction.

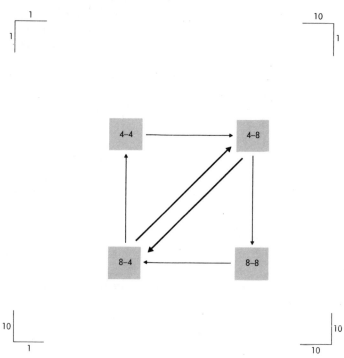

FIG. 3–11. Teacher-directed quick drill.

particular pattern would occur if the answer of the student took longer than three seconds, producing a series of 8's tabulated in the lower right hand 8-8 cell.

The dotted lines in Fig. 3–10 illustrate a second alternative pattern, which is the next most frequent embellishment. When a student takes more than three seconds to answer, and thus produces an 8-8 sequence pair, the teacher sometimes acknowledges the idea expressed by the student very briefly, taking less than three seconds. Thus, a "three" occurs in the sequence pair 8-3. This brief acknowledgement is immediately followed by additional lecturing which produces a tally in the 3-5 cell and the teacher then moves from the 3-5 cell to the 5-5 cell.

Figure 3–10, then, represents a frequently occurring pattern of teaching in which the teacher communicates content and occasionally asks questions to which the students can reply briefly. In the side patterns it is possible for the teacher to acknowledge briefly the contribution of the student, but this is a small part of the total interaction. The central core of the verbal communication is the teacher's expression of content.

Figure 3–11 represents a basic quick drill model in which short questions are asked by the teacher and short responses are given by the pupils. This direct 8-4 to 4-8 communication is shown by the double arrows. There are two side tracks to this basic pattern. In the event that a student requires longer than three seconds to answer a question, an 8-8 sequence pair occurs which is shown in the lower right hand side of the diagram. In the event that the teacher takes longer than three seconds to ask a question a 4-4 sequence pair occurs, shown on the upper left hand side of the diagram.

Figure 3–12 shows a slight embellishment on the basic drill model. In this instance the basic drill relationship between 4-8 and 8-4 is interrupted occasionally by teacher explanation. Most often this break occurs as an 8-5 sequence pair in which a teacher lectures in response to a student statement. The dotted lines show silence following a teacher question, 4-10, and the teacher repeating the question or returning to further lecture; see the 10–4 and 10–5 cells leading to the 5-5 cell. Then the cycle returns to question and answer sequences. Figure 3–12 illustrates a possible variation that typically occurs when Model One is combined with Model Two and might occur when drill is interrupted for explanation by the teacher.

The first three figures are interaction models in which the teacher takes a very active and direct supervisory role. Most of the communication is controlled by the teacher because the pupils speak to the teacher and less frequently to each other. Most questions are referred to the teacher for his judgment and the students see their role as responding to the teacher and to his ideas.

Figure 3–13 shows a typical direction-giving model. The sustained giving of directions by the teacher occurs as sequence pairs in the 6-6 cell. Most often two events are likely to follow; first, direction giving can be followed by silence shown by the 6-10 cell; and second, direction giving can be followed by student initiation shown by the 6-9 cell. Most often, in these latter instances, the student initiated comment is a request for clarification and occasionally an expression of resistance to the directions given by the teacher.

364

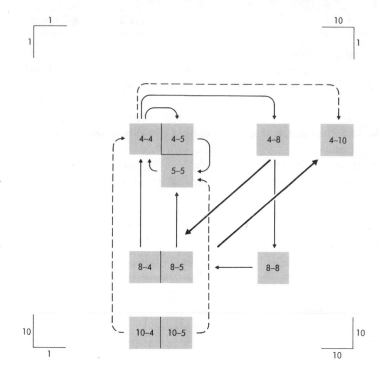

FIG. 3–12. Drill combined with lecture demonstration.

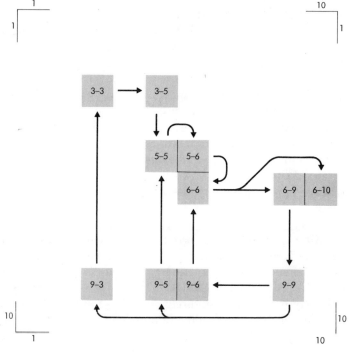

FIG. 3–13. Teacher gives directions with some clarification.

A sub-pattern, not illustrated in Fig. 3–13, appears as high frequencies in the 6-7 and 7-6 transition cells, whereby a teacher turns from giving directions to criticisms and then returns to giving directions. This in combination with a high loading on the 6-9 cell, is a pretty clear indication of student resistance to the directions the teacher has given. A teacher normally expects compliance to the giving of directions and in many instances of cooperation the giving of directions is followed by silence or category eight.

Occasionally the comments of a student are developed into longer statements, which is shown by the arrow from the 6-9 cell down to the 9-9 cell. When sustained student initiation talk indicates difficulty in following directions, the teacher often explains and/or repeats directions making use of the 9-5 or the 9-6 cells. Occasionally the teacher responds to the ideas expressed by the student, which is shown by the arrow leading from the 9-9 cell to the 9-3 cell. This is typically followed by further clarification of the student's idea leading back to lecturing, shown by the 3-5 cell and then sustained lecturing shown by the 5-5 cell and on to giving directions 5-6 to 6-6.

MODELS INVOLVING MORE STUDENT INITIATION. The sustained self-directed inquiry by students with classroom communication that reflects their own ideas requires a different supporting role on the part of the teacher. Figure 3–14 will serve as a model for this type of interaction. In the model the questions asked by the teacher occur in the 4-4 cell because they are longer and often involve more general or abstract concepts. The arrow A_1 going to the 4-9 cell means that the question was sufficiently broad to permit the student to express his own ideas (not the teacher's) in reacting to the question. The A_2 arrow goes down to sustained student participation which frequently follows because broad questions usually take longer than three seconds to answer.

Arrow A_3 is one route in which the teacher decides to respond to student participation by introducing new ideas in the form of questions, see the 9-4 cell. This route continues on A_4 to the 4-4 cell. This basic inner cycle is most often concerned with subject matter content which seems to require guidance and direction from the teacher. The use of category 4 instead of 3 indicates that these questions are new ideas introduced by the teacher. Should the teacher ask a question based on the ideas expressed by the student this would be categorized in category 3.

Part of the time the teacher's reaction to student participation is to clarify or somehow utilize the ideas expressed by the student. This cycle is illustrated in Fig. 3–14 by the outer "B" arrows. It starts with the B_1 arrow leaving the 9-9 cell, going to the 9-3 cell and then on up, along Arrow B_2, to the 3-3 cell. In this model the teacher is likely to elaborate for longer than three seconds in utilizing a student idea and thus, we would expect higher frequencies in the 3-3 cell. If the teacher formulates a question based on student ideas, this is indicated by the B_3 arrow leading to 3-9. The continuing expression of student ideas is illustrated by the B_4 arrow leading down to the 9-9 cell. This model, illustrated by the "B" arrows gives greater emphasis to the ideas expressed by students than the inner "A" route.

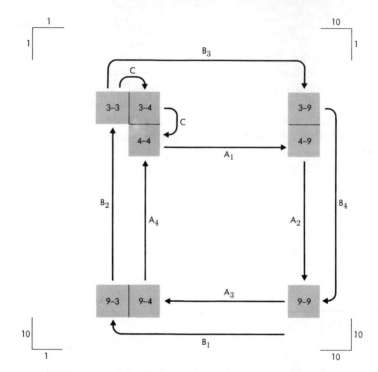

FIG. 3–14. Stimulating independent student thought.

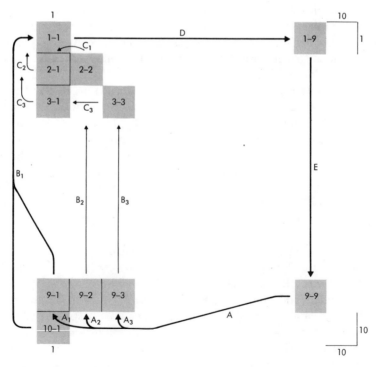

FIG. 3–15. Attending to student feelings.

On some occasions, the teacher may shift to his own ideas in the formulation of a question or in lecture (not shown) which follows the sequence 3-3, 3-4, 4-4 and is indicated by the "C" arrows between these cells.

For the teacher a critical choice is made between the 9-3 and the 9-4 cells shown in the lower left hand side on the diagram. This is a choice in which the teacher must decide whether to clarify the ideas expressed by the student (9-3 cell) or to introduce new ideas of his own by asking further questions (9-4 cell). Similarly another choice point for the teacher occurs when the "C" route is used.

Apparently most of the teachers we have observed do not see much application of this model to most of the classroom learning objectives.

On very rare occasions in the classroom a teacher turns his full attention to the feelings and attitudes expressed by boys and girls in their verbal participation or infers this from some aspect of their behavior. Figure 3–15 shows a typical model of the teacher responding to the affective aspects of student verbalization or behavior in a constructive manner.

This particular cycle begins with the main flow of arrow A from the 9-9 cell to a reaction on the part of the teacher in terms of the pupil's feeling—A_1, giving praise or encouragement—A_2, or the pupil's ideas—A_3. The teacher also might make an inference about the affective aspects of classroom interaction and pick it up as an interpretation during silence shown in that part of the B_1 arrow coming from cell 10-1. The main flow of teacher reaction to feeling would be carried through arrow B_1 into the 1-1 cell where it would be further developed by the teacher. Direct pupil reaction is illustrated by the D arrow leading to the 1-9 cell and then by arrow E to the 9-9 cell.

Critical decisions are required when the teacher makes the transition from the intellectual aspects of what a pupil says to the affective aspects. This is shown in Fig. 3–15 by the B_3 and C_3 arrows. Another route to the interpretation of feeling involves praise and most often occurs when the teacher is attempting to re-enforce positive affective reactions to help motivate students. This latter route is shown by the B_2 and C_2 arrows. Very few teachers find the opportunity or possess the skill to make these transitions. For example, the sum of all tallies falling into the entire category 1 column averages less than one-half of 1% of teacher talk.

A reverse set of critical transition behaviors occurs when the teacher moves from the affective realm to the intellectual realm of classroom communication. The various routes that are possible are shown in Fig. 3–16. Teachers only rarely make these transitions because events in category 1 are so rare.

One of our studies involved two-hour combined English-social studies "core" classes at the seventh-grade level. We were expecting greater use of category 1 in the two-hour classes based on the argument that a teacher who believed in the "core" philosophy would pay more attention to the affective aspects of student behavior than would teachers of eighth grade mathematics. The reverse turned out to be true by a five-to-one ratio. As a hindsight explanation, perhaps students develop more affective reactions trying to learn mathematics and thus confronted, the teacher reacts to student feelings more often. Our data would suggest that the social skills involved in the patterns shown in Figs. 3–15 and 3–16 are needed in all classes and that the more rigorous nature of mathematics is no reason to ignore this aspect of teacher training. Indeed, the reverse reasoning seems more appropriate.

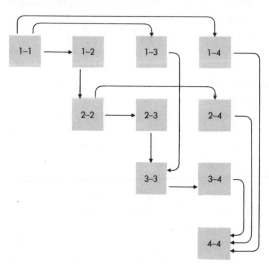

FIG. 3–16. Teacher transitions from an affective to an intellectual emphasis.

A SUMMARY OF THE MODELS OF CRITICAL TEACHING BEHAVIORS. In each of the models so far discussed, decisions are required of the teacher at critical transitions.[49] In Model One, sustained content presentation, the teacher decides when to ask a question which is a transition from category 5 to 4. In Model Two (Fig. 3–12) critical decisions are necessary to decide whether to respond to student talk in terms of further lecture or by asking questions. Similar decisions are required in the model concerned with giving directions.

The fourth and fifth models concerned with developing and maintaining more independent student thought processes and with handling the affective reactions of students, involve even more critical choices for the teacher.

One can summarize these critical decisions by designating certain areas within the matrix. Probably the most important decision area occurs in rows eight and nine, columns one through seven. All tallies in these 14 cells represent the first verbal reaction of the teacher at the moment a student stops talking. When the student stops should the teacher express his own ideas, give directions, or ask further questions to shift the orientation of the student? On the other hand, is more to be gained by expanding the idea expressed by the stu-

---

[49] Transitions are sequence pairs with different numbers; steady-states are sequence pairs with the same number. More than one-half of all sequence pairs, on the average, are steady-state.

dent, praising his contribution, or interpreting the affective aspects of his participation? Once this decision is made, during the spontaneous give and take of a verbal exchange, the effect is to move from one to another of these models.

The second area of critical decisions occurs within the sustained talk of the teacher. Once the teacher commits himself to an initial reaction at the cessation of student talk, transitions are still possible. While lecturing a teacher can shift to questions, or refer back to ideas expressed by students, or praise earlier contributions. These transitions occur in rows and columns one through seven and determine, in the final analysis, the opportunity for student reactions when the teacher stops talking. The last thing said by a teacher, just before the student starts to talk, is clearly indicated by the cell frequencies in columns eight and nine, rows one through seven. The proportional frequencies in these cells will reflect the decisions made by the teacher, just before student talk.

One might ask whether anything new or unusual is being said in this summary concerning critical decisions. Surely, to say that how a teacher first reacts to student contributions and how he creates opportunities for student participation are crucial in classroom communication is to say nothing new, at least for the thoughtful observer of the teaching process. Yet, something new is being said here, providing one sets these comments in the context of current, average teacher performance. On the average, teachers do not make these decisions easily; they do not move from one model to another in response to the different purposes of classroom communication.

Given the premise that what has been said is not news and yet average teachers do not exhibit flexible adaptation of their own behavior in guiding class discussion, only one conclusion remains possible. Apparently teachers are aware of the crucial decisions and important models of teacher influence, but they are not able to implement this knowledge. They know, but they can't act out; they have the right intentions, but their actions do not match their intentions.

To accept what has been said in the previous paragraph is tantamount to saying that teacher education must include behavior practice so that what is understood at an intellectual level can be translated into the spontaneous action level, that is, incorporated in one's own behavior. Perhaps the major weakness of teacher education, as we know it today, is that professors of education do not see themselves as the midwives of this kind of personal self-realization. Professors of education consider that their responsibilities are accomplished when the teacher candidate has been exposed to the concepts and principles of teaching and can show his awareness on a test. It matters little that the more enterprising professor of education devises a unique and unusual test which requires that the prospective teacher think through what he "ought" to do, that is, demonstrate that he can "act out" what to do next "in his mind." This indicates both awareness *and* understanding. Nevertheless, the crucial test is whether he can act out in spontaneous interaction and demonstrate, by his own behavior, that he not only understands, but that he can transform this understanding by controlling his spontaneous behavior.

These more difficult objectives of teacher education will require a special contribution from those of us whose research involves the quantification of the qualitative aspects of spontaneous behavior. Our systems of interaction analysis may become techniques of instruction in teacher preparation programs. The education instructor will be more interested in research procedures that have practical applications to teacher training, that can be adapted to education courses at the college level. Systems that are complex and costly to employ, that make use of recorded behavior which can be played again and again for intensive analysis, may contribute to our knowledge about the teaching process, but they will be too clumsy for use in teacher education.

OTHER CATEGORY SYSTEMS
THAT CAN BE ADAPTED TO MATRIX ANALYSIS

Any set of categories used in interaction analysis can be tabulated into a matrix of rows and columns to indicate sequence pairs. Given "N" categories, observed events can be tabulated into a matrix of N^2 categories of paired events at no increase in work beyond keeping the original sequence of events ordered. Before turning to a discussion of the implications of what has been said for teacher education and research on teacher education, I would like to consider, however briefly, a set of categories different from the ten I have been using for over ten years.

Each category system is designed to give emphasis to a particular conceptual framework. Suppose it was of interest to adapt the matrix form of tabulation to a set of categories concerned with the cognitive aspects of logical reasoning as it occurs in classroom discourse. Suppose further, that one's model of cognitive reasoning borrowed some of its concepts from the creative, exciting, and insightful research of Dr. Hilda Taba.[50] One sequence she discusses involves thought development which might occur in a 15- to 30-minute class discussion. First, the elements of a problem are differentiated. Second, the elements are grouped into homogeneous clusters and each cluster is given a label. The label is, by definition, at a higher level of abstraction than the elements making up each set. Third, relationships between clusters can be hypothesized using the shorthand labels. Fourth, generalizations from these relationships are discussed and predictions are made in an effort to apply these relationships in different situations.

Suppose these ideas from Dr. Taba's research were used as the basis of interaction analysis categories with the intent of tabulating them into a matrix. Table 3–48 provides for 21 categories, some of which would probably be used

---

[50] I believe that Dr. Taba's current research on the reasoning processes of elementary school children in class discussions has the potential of making an unusually fine contribution to understanding the teacher's role in logical discourse (Taba, 1963).

Table 3–48

Cognitive Categories for Matrix Interpretation

Behavior description	Category numbers			
	Asking for		Giving	
	Teacher	Student	Teacher	Student
Facts and opinions	1	11	6	16
Explanation-interpretation	2	12	7	17
Group common elements, label	3	13	8	18
Generalizations and predictions	4	14	9	19
Statements, not above	5	15	10	20

No verbal statement is category 21

so infrequently that they could be combined and others eliminated so that the most efficient[51] system could be gradually developed.

Figure 3–17 shows one section of the 21 × 21 matrix that will be used to illustrate some of the inferences that are possible from an analysis of the cognitive aspects of classroom discourse. All cells with the letter "A" show a one-to-one correspondence between the level of abstraction of the teacher's inquiry and the initial response made by the student. Cells marked "B" represent responses at a higher level of abstraction than is asked for by the teacher. Cells marked "C" indicate responses which are below the level of abstraction intended by the teacher's inquiry. The proportion of tallies classified into the type A, B, and C cells would provide information about the effectiveness of the teacher's ability to "lift" the level of abstraction. With the B responses

	1 〜 16	17	18	19
1	A	B	B	B
2	C	A	B	B
3	C	C	A	B
4	C	C	C	A

FIG. 3–17. Interpreting a section of a cognitive matrix.

[51] I believe that the most efficient systems contain the fewest number of categories necessary to make the distinctions of interest to the researcher. The difficulties do not arise from the procedures of observation, but in the researcher's statement of the problem. Fewer categories are needed when the research problem is stated with more precision.

greater than C, the students are moving faster than the teacher; the reverse would occur when the teacher was moving too fast. By tabulating matrices separately for the first, second and third ten-minute periods of class discussion, one might trace this development over time. It may be more informative to avoid rigid ten-minute periods and designate the time limits of one matrix, compared with the next, according to the presumed intentions of the individual teacher.

This brief excursion into a different category system illustrates the application of matrix analysis to an area of interest other than social skills.

Incidentally, it is obvious, in these days of computers, that sequences of more than two events could be tabulated in multidimensional matrices. Even though we humans have trouble visualizing a four-dimensional matrix, a computer can do this providing there is enough storage space. For example, a four-dimensional matrix for 21 categories will require 194,481 cells with the number of digits per cell still to be taken into consideration. Our own estimates indicate that sequence pairs (two dimensional) probably account for about 60% of the interdependence between events when our ten categories are involved. It seems likely that even three-dimensional matrices will provide much more precision than is needed for most of the comparisons that we have made concerning the teacher's use of social skills.

THE IMPLICATIONS OF THESE COMMENTS FOR TEACHER EDUCATION AND RESEARCH ON TEACHER EDUCATION

Condensing the four propositions at the beginning of this paper will provide the starting point of this concluding section. These propositions were concerned with the fewest number of concepts necessary to abstract spontaneous classroom behavior with particular emphasis on the teacher influence. Once identified, these concepts can serve as objectives for designing teacher education programs and can help to establish criteria for the evaluation of teacher education programs. To the extent that these "fewest number of concepts" are valid, they may serve equally well as a guide for the professor of education and the classroom teacher. In both cases the understanding of these concepts must find expression in overt, spontaneous behavior in order to have utility.

NOMINATIONS OF CRITICAL BEHAVIORS. There are a number of behavior patterns that occur in teaching at critical decision points. These will now be mentioned in the same order as they were discussed in this paper, an order that is not meant to reflect on how frequently they occur or on their relative importance to effective teaching.

First, teachers must decide when and why they should turn from providing information and begin to invite student verbal participation by the use of questions.

Second, teachers need to know how to ask broad and narrow questions and to predict the consequences of asking either type.

Third, teachers must know when to restrict freedom of student participation by closer supervision and guidance such as occurs in teacher directed drills and in giving assignments and directions

Fourth, teachers must know when to support the expression of student ideas and feelings, how to select particular expressions for further development and application, and how to guide such activities without developing unwanted, excessive dependence. Here, dependence refers to the tendency of students to solicit teacher direction and approval in situations in which more self-directing activities should gradually develop.

Fifth, teachers need to know how to make constructive use of the affective aspects of student behavior. Part of motivation concerns the development and organization of positive attitudes and feelings in relation to educational goals and individual tasks. Part of the problem of establishing a free classroom atmosphere involves an objective analysis of negative feelings should they occur. Both positive and negative feelings are involved.

Behaviors such as these are critical because they involve decisions that will have immediate consequences on subsequent interaction. Further, a series of decisions will create a coherent set of expectations, on the part of students, which will linger long once they are established.

CRITICAL BEHAVIORS AND TEACHER EDUCATION. To the extent that these behaviors are critical in classroom teaching, to this same extent they are crucial in teacher education. The goals of teacher education are revealed as performance in the classroom. The teaching of critical behaviors to prospective teachers will involve at least the following.

a) It will be necessary to conceptualize behavior patterns *and* classroom learning situations.

b) It will be necessary to develop tools for gathering reliable information about behavior and situations.

c) The understanding of these tools and concepts will require practice under conditions which help the prospective teachers transform knowledge into their own spontaneous behavior.

d) Valid principles to guide critical decisions can be discovered once concepts and tools are at hand. Teacher education, in part (or in whole), consists of creating situations in which education students can discover these principles.

RESEARCH ON TEACHER EDUCATION. The most informative research on teacher education will be concerned with coordinating some aspect of teacher training with some aspect of teaching performance, that is, with evaluating classroom teaching. Fortunately, knowledge of effective classroom teaching is also applicable to the design of teacher education programs.

Systems of interaction analysis can be used as a research tool in evaluating teaching performance and as a training device for prospective teachers. In both instances what occurs as behavior is the prime object of study.

Any taxonomy of teaching behavior will necessarily consider behavior in terms of the situation in which it occurs and the objectives which are presumed to exist. Such a taxonomy must provide concepts for classifying classroom learning objectives and the students' perceptions of these objectives. Given these, the taxonomy must also include concepts useful for abstracting student behavior.

Research on teacher education that will be of most help in improving our programs will show whether prospective teachers understand concepts for abstracting the characteristics of learning situations, teacher behavior and student behavior. It will show whether or not this understanding can be inferred from the overt classroom behavior of the beginning teacher and whether or not his behavior is consistent or inconsistent with a set of principles of teacher influence. Finally, it will show whether relationships exist between the foregoing desiderata and events that take place in the teacher education programs.

12

CLASSROOM INTERACTION AND THE FACILITATION OF LEARNING: ·THE SOURCE OF INSTRUCTIONAL THEORY[52]

JOHN B. HOUGH

Teaching and learning, though distinctly different processes, are so closely related in the classroom that to attempt to better understand one while failing to give full attention to the other would seem to be an untenable approach to the development of a functional instructional theory. Yet, with few notable exceptions, this is what educators and psychologists have been doing for years. A survey of texts on educational methods on one hand, and texts on educational psychology and learning theory on the other, will serve as *prima facie* evidence to support the contention that educational methodologists have given inadequate attention to the learning process, and that educational psychologists have largely failed to relate their discipline to the realities of classroom teaching in a functional way. An adequate instructional theory has yet to be developed, but it is clear that when such a theory is developed it must relate the two areas of teaching and learning in such a way as to generate principles of instruction that have functional value to teachers. Such principles of instruction must be stated as predictive, cause–effect relationships between teacher and student behavior and student learning. Ultimately, the effect of teacher and student behavior on clearly defined learning outcomes must be measured. It thus becomes evident that teachers must first be able to clearly specify and measure the learning outcomes of instruction.

If such a theory of instruction is to be developed, much more needs to be known about the relationships that exist between teacher and student behaviors and student learning in typical classroom situations. The study of experimental instructional conditions and student learning in a laboratory setting is of considerable value to builders of instructional theory as they generate hypotheses regarding effective instructional behavior. However, hypotheses generated

---

[52] This paper was specially prepared for this book.

from such laboratory experimentation must ultimately be tested in the class-room, where many variables will be found that are difficult, if not impossible, to simulate in the laboratory. In order to test hypotheses regarding the effect of particular teacher and student behavior on learning outcomes in actual class-room settings, one needs a way of precisely describing such behaviors. The recent development of observational systems of the type described in this book makes such hypothesis testing really possible for the first time. With the de-velopment of observational systems, rudimentary and primitive as they are at their present stage of development, the instructional theorist is armed with a tool for objectively describing the cause–act–effect loop of teacher–pupil in-teraction in the classroom. Teacher and student behaviors which are theoreti-cally associated with particular learning outcomes can be at least quantitatively described as being present or absent from the classroom, and the relative ab-sence or presence of such behaviors can then be related to student learning. The possession of such observational tools should provide the means for a significant breakthrough in the development of a functional instructional theory.

It is the purpose of this paper to explore certain hypothesized relation-ships between aspects of learning theory, the classroom behavior of teachers and students, and the facilitation of student learning. This paper is illustrative of what the author feels to be a provocative approach to the development of a theory of instruction useful to classroom teachers. No such complete theory will be delivered here; what will be done is to take a step in what one hopes will prove to be a fruitful direction.

Specifically, the function of this paper will be to: (a) choose a selected area of learning theory and extract from it a number of principles of learning, (b) discuss these principles in terms of teacher and student behavior, (c) pre-sent evidence that certain identifiable teacher and student behaviors consistent with learning theory are related to student classroom learning, (d) show how these behaviors would be categorized and plotted into the matrix of the Ob-servational System for Instructional Analysis (Hough, 1966), and (e) state a series of instructional principles that seem to have support both in theory and research. These instructional principles will be related to teacher and student classroom behaviors that are described by the Observational System for In-structional Analysis.

For the purposes of this paper, principles of learning drawn from rein-forcement theory will be used. This should not be taken to imply that other theoretical orientations to learning are less useful to teachers, or less sound, or that they are inconsistent with the principles presented here. Illustrations from reinforcement theory have been chosen because reinforcement theory is by its very nature behavioristically oriented. Teacher behavior does influence stu-dent learning in many ways. Some teacher behaviors are stimuli which elicit responses from students, while other teacher behaviors are reinforcers of stu-dent behavior. Teachers' behaviors are on occasion aversive stimuli which evoke respondent types of behavior in students, and such respondent behaviors seem to interfere with verbal learning. Teacher behaviors do cause students to be either active or passive, and thus largely determine both overt and covert involvement, i.e., interaction with stimuli. Such teacher and student behaviors are easily identified on the matrix of the Observational System for Instructional Analysis. It is because principles of reinforcement theory and this observational system are so compatible that they have been combined in this paper to illustrate how principles of learning can be translated into instructional principles and described in a matrix. Because of the close parallel between the Observational System for Instructional Analysis and the Flanders system of interaction analysis, it will be possible to at least tentatively support many of the hypothesized instructional principles that will be developed in this paper by making reference to the findings reported in Flanders' study, "Teacher Influence, Pupil Attitudes and Achievement" (Flanders, 1965a).

The central thesis of reinforcement theory is that if a behavior emitted in the presence of a stimulus (or elicited by a stimulus) is contiguously reinforced, it will, on later presentation of a similar or analogous stimulus, be emitted or elicited with greater probability than if it had not been reinforced. This statement is perhaps clarified by six subsidiary principles of reinforcement theory, each of which is related to parts of the central thesis stated above:

1. A reinforcing stimulus has been by definition a reinforcer if it increases the probability that the response for which it is intended as a reinforcer will be made in the future, or if it increases the rate of the response.

2. Stimuli are the cause of behavior in at least two senses of the word. In one sense they elicit behavior; in a second sense they become the occasion for a behavior to be emitted.[53]

3. The reinforcement must be associated with the behavior for which it is intended as a reinforcer, if the full effect of the reinforcement is to be achieved in regard to that behavior.

4. In order for a reinforcement to be associated with a particular behavior, it should follow that behavior in close temporal contiguity.[54]

5. Repetition of behavior without reinforcement is largely an inefficient and ineffective way to learn.

---

[53] The technical distinction between elicited and emitted responses as defined by Skinner is not being considered here. Elicited responses are defined here as responses which have, as a result of prior conditioning, been associated with a specific stimulus or class of stimuli. Emitted responses are distinguished from elicited responses by the fact that no prior history of conditioning can be traced to the connection between the response and the stimulus which was the occasion for that response to be emitted. It is not denied that, in most cases, prior learning has made the specific emitted response possible.

[54] That the human mind can carry the "image" of a behavior over an extended period of time and that because of this, delayed reinforcement is possible, is not denied. Such delayed reinforcement probably becomes less effective as the complexity of the behavior increases and as the interval between the behavior and the reinforcement increases.

6. For a stimulus to elicit a previously reinforced behavior, the stimulus must be perceived by the behaver as being highly similar to or analogous to the stimulus which last elicited that behavior and/or the stimulus with which that behavior was originally paired.

Added to the central thesis of reinforcement theory, stated and expanded upon above, is a principle regarding the effect of aversive stimulation on the learning of verbal behavior. This principle may be stated as follows:

A stimulus which is perceived by the learner as being an aversive stimulus (e.g., threatening, punishing, etc.) will have variable effects on learning of verbal behavior.[55]

Negative reinforcement (reinforcement which occurs as a result of the withdrawal of a stimulus) often makes use of stimuli which are perceived as being threatening or punishing, i.e., aversive; therefore, prudence seems to dictate that, if maximum learning is to be achieved, a concept of positive reinforcement should be used in formal educational settings wherever possible.

Positive reinforcers may be seen in the classroom in the form of rewards, praise, encouragement, acceptance and clarification of ideas, i.e., feedback. Each of these forms of reinforcement will by definition increase the probability that the behaviors for which they are reinforcers will be elicited in the future. But might not such reinforcers have differential effects on behavior? For example, would not the use of teacher acceptance and clarification of a student's ideas ("3")[56] have a different effect on student behavior than would a teacher comment, "Right, Bill. Very good." ("2")? Would not teacher encouragement of student behavior without reference to the value of that behavior ("1") have a different effect on that student's future behavior than would praise in the form of such a statement as "Good. That's the right answer." ("2")?

It seems, in fact, that different types of reinforcers would have differential effects on behavior. Reinforcers in the form of "That's right, Bill. Very good." ("2") and "Good, that's the right answer." ("2") seem to have their primary effect on the specific response for which they are intended as reinforcers. Further, they seem to function in such a way as to temporarily terminate behavior for those students whose need to receive praise is great, in classrooms where the teacher's pattern is to call on a number of students sequentially or randomly during a period. Students in such classes, having once been reinforced, typically reduce activity until they think their turn is about

---

[55] Aversive stimuli elicit respondent behaviors which are observable in the form of such overt behavior as withdrawal, avoidance, and attack. So long as respondent behavior and its observable behavioral manifestations persist, a condition exists which often seems to interfere with the learning of verbal behavior characteristic of school learning.

[56] ("3") means category 3 of the Observational System for Instructional Analysis. For a discussion of this observational system see (Hough, 1966).

to come up again. This seems to be the pattern of behavior under a schedule of fixed-interval reinforcement and, to a lesser degree, under variable-interval reinforcement schedules. Yet, the use of praise or other forms of reward that focus on a specific response seems to be appropriate for the reinforcement of specific responses to stimuli of the paired-associate type, so long as the teacher uses other motivational techniques to maintain a relatively high level of attention for students who are not overtly responding.

On the other hand, to encourage a student for good thinking by using such statements as, "That's a very interesting way of arriving at the answer," ("1") or by accepting a student response at face value but asking the student to further clarify or justify what he means [e.g., "O.K., but why do you think that a fair housing bill is necessary?" ("3")] seems to act as reinforcement not only for the specific emitted response, but for the entire class of behaviors (i.e., intellectual processes) that led to the response. Such reinforcers, and particularly the type associated with clarification of student responses ("3") seem to keep the student actively involved for longer periods of time than reinforcers that terminate behavior by placing a positive value judgment on specific responses. Hypotheses generated from the theoretical discussion above may be tested, in part, by analyzing student achievement under various classroom reinforcement schedules described by the Observational System for Instructional Analysis.

Teachers should recognize that reinforcements in the form of praise or reward ("2") place a value on the student response which is given by an external authority, i.e., the teacher. When the content of the lesson deals with definitions and facts that are true by definition or tradition, or that can be empirically validated, the teacher simply becomes a substitute for another external authority. In such cases it is probably desirable for the teacher to assume this authority role for purposes of expediency, so long as he makes it clear to his students that he represents a substitute for that authority. On the other hand, when the content of the lesson is in the realm of opinion or judgment, or when more than one response is equally appropriate, for the teacher to place a value judgment on a specific response may tend to develop dependence on the teacher as *the* authority in areas in which independence of thought and justification of appropriate answers are more desirable than correct answers.

Of course, student responses are not always either correct or appropriate, and the processes used to arrive at such responses are not always functional. In the classroom, teacher responses to such statements may range from criticism ("9") to comments designed to inform the student that his response has been incorrect or inappropriate ("7") and/or to help the student see why. Teacher criticism or ridicule ("9"), when perceived as such by the student, may be classified as aversive stimulation which, as has been previously said, results in respondent behavior (e.g., withdrawal, attack, etc.) and interference with the learning of verbal behaviors. The result of such teacher behavior may well be that the student may not learn why his response was wrong or inappropriate and, so long as the effect of the aversive stimulus remains, may not learn what would have been a correct or appropriate response. Certainly there seem to be exceptions to the above statement, but such exceptions probably represent highly motivated students with a self-concept positive enough to withstand such threats to the self. It is more probable that for such students, teacher criticism or sarcasm represents a less intense aversive stimulus. On the other hand, when student responses are incorrect by definition, custom, or empirically validatable fact, failure to point out to the student that his response has been incorrect may simply serve to perpetuate the error. By means of such statements as, "No, Betty, an acute angle is not greater than ninety degrees; that's an obtuse angle," the teacher points out that the student's response has been incorrect ("7") and informs the student what the correct response is ("6"). If said in a positive and supportive tone, such a teacher statement would probably not be an aversive stimulus for most students. The teacher, of course, does not always have to function as the authority for the correctness of a response, nor does he always have to be the source for the correct answer. Involving other students or getting the student to see for himself why his response was incorrect are equally appropriate measures. For example, the teacher could respond to an incorrect definition of an acute angle by saying, "If a right angle is ninety degrees, and an obtuse angle is greater than ninety degrees, an acute angle would have how many degrees?" ("3") By using such a statement the teacher pushes the clarification of an incorrect response back onto the student who gave it.

Often students arrive at answers without knowing why they are correct or appropriate. They guess and are lucky, or they respond as a result of previous conditioning without much understanding. For the teacher to reinforce such responses with reward or praise may terminate behavior in regard to the problem, and the student may never be taken beyond a simple paired-associate type of learning. It seems, therefore, that when student responses to questions represent answers for which there is some rationale, teacher responses in turn should be designed to take the student into intellectual activity which will lead to real understanding, thus providing the conditions for self-reinforcement. Such teacher comments as, "That's correct; how did you arrive at that answer?" (combination of "2" and "3") seem not only to reinforce the correct response but at the same time to probe the student's thinking process to find out whether he really understands, and if not, to help him develop such understanding.

Thus far in this discussion of reinforcement theory and its application to classroom behavior, the primary focus has been on the act of reinforcement. Implied in this discussion have been two other components of the instructional situation which are no less important. These two components are, of course, the stimulus and the response. Let us look at each of these in turn in an attempt to see how they relate to classroom instruction.

In reinforcement theory, stimuli may be seen as either calling forth elicited responses ("10") or being the occasion for an emitted response ("11" or "12"). The distinction between elicited and emitted responses has been discussed earlier in this paper. One additional characteristic of the elicited response should be mentioned, however. Whether the elicited response is correct or incorrect, it is still categorized as ("10"). Thus our definition of elicited responses is broadened to include incorrect responses which are a function of associative inhibition. Examples of elicited responses may be found in responses to such questions ("4") and commands ("8") as, "What is the capital of Brazil?" "How many numerals are there in the binary number system?" and "Bill, name three examples of *Genus Rasbora*." It is characteristic of such questions and commands that the student may choose to ignore the restriction that is imposed by the stimulus and respond with an emitted declarative statement ("11") or a question, ("12"), but this is not the intent of the stimulus. The function of such narrow questions and commands is to call out, that is, elicit, previously conditioned responses so that they may be further reinforced.

On the other hand, it is the function of some stimuli to cause students to behave without reference to a prior conditioned association. Such stimuli in the form of broad questions and commands function in a way that is far less restricting to the student's response. Examples of such questions ("4") or commands ("8") would be, "How did you arrive at that answer to the problem?", "What do you think would be a good way to find out whether a gas will expand if it is heated?" and, "Mary, tell me why *you* believe the foreign policy of the present administration has been less or more effective than under the previous administration." The function of such questions or commands is to provide a stimulus that will function as the occasion on which a student will emit a response that is intended to clarify his thinking or express an opinion that is supported by data. Such stimuli are less restricting than the narrow questions and commands mentioned earlier, and seem to have a greater capacity for causing behavior that will ultimately lead to great independence of thought and action so long as the teacher avoids following such responses with judgmental reinforcement ("2" or "7").

Certainly the examples chosen to illustrate stimuli that elicit responses or stimuli that are the occasion for a response to be emitted have been carefully selected to illustrate broad and narrow questions and commands. Not all classroom illustrations are that clear cut. A question such as, "How does the internal combustion engine work?" may serve to elicit a previously associated chain of responses or it may be the occasion for a student to emit, after a good deal of thought, a response that he has never made before. In such an instance it may be difficult to determine whether the response was, by our definition, elicited or emitted. Granting the difficulty in classifying responses in this grey area at the center of the continuum, it is affirmed that the theoretical distinction between elicited and emitted responses is possible and useful in the classification of classroom behavior. The fact that elicited responses ("10") will most often follow narrow questions and commands, and that emitted responses ("11") will most often follow broad questions and commands, allows for an inferential analysis of the type of stimuli the teacher is providing, i.e., broad or narrow.

To deal in any extended way with the response aspect of the stimulus–response–reinforcement chain would be to repeat much of what has already been said in the discussion of the reinforcement of the stimulus. It is appropriate, though perhaps a bit obvious, to assert that there can be no reinforcement of responses unless responses are made. If this seemingly obvious statement were pushed a little further, the conclusion could be drawn that, from the point of view of reinforcement theory, if there were no responding, there would be no learning. It would seem, therefore, that both the quality and quantity of student responses in the classroom have a direct relationship to learning.

Not all student responses have to be overt, but if students do not respond overtly, how shall the teacher know when and how to reinforce? Ideally, students should ultimately learn to give feedback to their own behavior (i.e., test the fit of their behavior against a structure of understanding) but in the early phases of learning a subject, it is not likely that such a structure of understanding will have been developed. It is at this phase of the learning process that overt responding and reinforcement are especially important.

The Observational System for Instructional Analysis includes four categories to describe student overt responses. Three of these categories, elicited responses ("10"), emitted responses ("11") and questions ("12"), describe audible verbal responses. The fourth type of overt response, directed practice ("13"), is used to describe such student overt behavior as writing responses and working problems. In addition, category ("14") is used to describe periods of silence associated with thinking, i.e., covert responding. It should be pointed out, of course, that covert responding can occur at any time, including moments at which the teacher or other students are talking. It has been stated, however, that such responses are difficult to reinforce, since the teacher has little evidence of their occurrence and no real way either of knowing the nature of the response or of dealing with it. Failure to cause such responses to become overt is critical when the response is wrong, for without knowledge of the incorrectness of the response, the teacher cannot give corrective feedback ("7").

It goes without saying that when a teacher spends a great amount of time in class giving information and opinions ("6") he reduces the amount of student covert responding that is possible. Once students have developed a structure of understanding against which to test the fit of their covert responses, a reasonable amount of teacher lecture may be a useful way of further integrating and extending student understanding.

Thus far in this paper, principles of reinforcement theory have been presented and translated into teacher and student classroom behavior. The basic experimentation to support the principles of reinforcement theory presented has largely been that of the laboratory or the controlled classroom. Research designed to precisely describe the behavior of teachers and students in actual classroom situations is a relatively new approach to education research, an approach which has been possible only through the development of classroom observational systems of the type developed by Flanders. Though Flanders' research has not directly addressed itself to testing the relationships between student learning and student and teacher behavior consistent with reinforcement theory, it may with some risk be interpreted in this way. What follows, therefore, must be seen by the reader for what it is, an interpretation of one man's research findings by another man using a different theoretical system.

Table 3–49

A Comparison of the Per Cent of Selected Teacher and Student Behaviors Reported by Flanders for the Most Indirect and Direct Social Studies Teachers*

Flanders IA	Categories	Hough OSIA	Indirect teachers	Direct teachers
1, 2 and 3		1, 2 and 3	9.8%	3.8%
4		4	10.5%	8.3%
7		7 and 9	1.5%	8.7%
8 and 9		10, 11 and 12	25.9%	22.8%

* Flanders, 1965a.

Table 3–50

A Comparison of the Per Cent of Selected Teacher and Student Behaviors Reported by Flanders for the Most Indirect and Direct Mathematics Teachers*

Flanders IA	Categories	Hough OSIA	Indirect teachers	Direct teachers
1, 2 and 3		1, 2 and 3	10.0%	3.0%
4		4	11.7%	6.6%
7		7 and 9	0.9%	5.9%
8 and 9		10, 11 and 12	16.6%	14.1%

* Flanders, 1965a.

Tables 3–49 and 3–50 summarize the percentage of selected teacher and student behaviors reported by Flanders for the most indirect and most direct social studies and mathematics teachers in his study of the effect of teacher influence on student achievement (Flanders, 1965a). The category numbers used in the Flanders system of interaction analysis are reported in the column headed (IA). The category numbers of the Observational System for the Instructional Analysis are reported in the column headed (OSIA). Though in many cases the two systems use different category numbers to refer to similar behaviors, the behaviors described by the categories are basically the same. The reader is, however, encouraged to examine the behaviors described under categories of both systems found elsewhere in this book to note the slight differences which exist between the categories used by the two systems.

Flanders found that the students of the most indirect teachers made significantly greater achievement (Flanders, 1965a) in both mathematics and social studies. An analysis of the data presented in Tables 3–49 and 3–50 shows differences in the percentage of behaviors used by the most indirect and direct teachers in his sample. The differences in percentage are all in the direction that would be predicted by hypotheses generated from the discussion of reinforcement theory presented in this paper. Certainly there are many theoretical assumptions made in the preceding discussion of reinforcement theory and the classroom behavior of teachers and students that were not addressed by Flanders' research, but it has already been stated that Flanders was interested in a different set of theoretical assumptions. Be that as it may, the following general principles seem to be supported by Flanders' findings as interpreted in the light of reinforcement theory presented in this paper:

a) Classrooms in which there is a large percentage of question-asking, student-responding, and teacher-reinforcing have greater achievement than classrooms in which these conditions are present to a lesser extent.

b) Classrooms in which there is a small percentage of criticism, justification of teacher authority and sarcasm (aversive stimulation) have greater achievement than classrooms in which these conditions are present to a greater extent.

Certainly the assumptions inherent in the discussion of reinforcement theory in this paper must be directly tested by empirical research. The use of theory and related research, however, would allow a set of hypothesized instructional principles to be tentatively projected. These instructional principles will involve statements regarding teacher and pupil classroom behavior. These statements may be translated into the categories of the Observational System for Instructional Analysis and ultimately into cells and regions of the matrix of this system. In order to facilitate the discussion of these principles, areas of the matrix will be discussed first. Figure 3–18 shows areas of the matrix that are critical to instruction which is consistent with reinforcement principles of learning.

Area A: Includes teacher statements of extended indirect influence in the classroom. Extended reinforcement in the form of encouragement, praise, reward, acceptance or clarification of student ideas, or answers to student questions, appear in this area of the matrix. With the exception of corrective feedback ("7"), this area includes all instances of extended feedback that exist in a classroom and are designed as reinforcement.

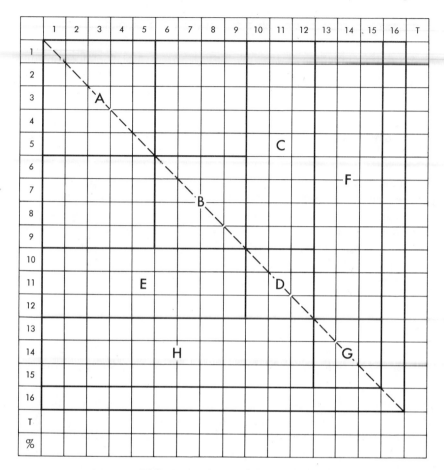

FIG. 3–18. Areas of the matrix.

Area B: Includes teacher statements of extended direct influence in the classroom. Extended information giving, opinion giving, directions and criticism of student behavior, and justification of teacher authority appear in this area. In addition, corrective feedback is included in this area of direct influence rather than in Area A because such teacher behavior moves in the direction of being an aversive stimulus for some students. The rationale for including category ("7") in this area is discussed earlier in this paper.

Area C: Includes the initiation of student responses to teacher stimuli. Included in the cells intersected by rows 1 through 5 and columns 10 through 12 are student overt responses to teacher direct influence. Category 13 is not included in this area because, although it is an overt student response, it is not an audible verbal overt response.

Area D: Includes extended student audible overt responses.

Area E: Includes teacher talk that follows student responses. The cells included in the intersection of rows 10 through 12 and columns 1 through 5, plus 7, represent the initiation of teacher reinforcement and corrective feedback. These 18 cells show if and how a teacher reinforces student verbal behavior in the classroom.

The following is a set of hypothesized principles of instruction which are consistent with a reinforcement theory of learning translated into the teacher and student behavior described by the Observational System for Instructional Analysis.

1. Teachers should maximize the use of indirect influence during the initial stages of instruction on a new topic. Much instructional time should be used in drawing out student understanding of the content to be taught, reinforcing correct elicited responses ("10") with praise and reward ("2"), correcting misconceptions with corrective feedback ("7") and helping students to develop a structure of understanding by encouraging elicited responses ("11") and questions ("12"), and clarifying and extending such responses ("3") and ("5").

2. Direct influence in the form of teacher-initiated information ("6") should be used in the initial stages of instruction of a new unit, primarily to help build a structure of understanding that will lead to student self-reinforcement. As the unit of instruction proceeds, increased use of teacher lecture seems appropriate.

3. Especially during the initial stages of instruction with a new unit, but also at other appropriate times, teachers should consciously predict and be sensitive to student anxiety created by the new or difficult aspects of the unit of study, and should reflect and clarify such feelings ("1") when they are sensed. In so doing, the teacher "bleeds off" anxiety that interferes with learning.

4. During the course of the unit, criticism, sarcasm, and justification of authority ("9") should be avoided, since such behavior represents aversive stimulation and, as such, could interfere with verbal learning.

5. During the course of the unit, the teacher should maintain an optimum amount of overt student behavior by asking questions ("4"), encouraging students ("1"), accepting student responses ("3"), and responding to student questions ("5").

6. As students develop a structure of understanding, teachers should reduce the frequency with which they place themselves in the position of acting as the authority for reinforcement of responses ("2" and "7") but should increasingly encourage students to use their own understandings as a self-reinforcing mechanism by means of acceptance and clarification ("3").

7. Teachers should avoid using praise ("2") and corrective feedback ("7") following emitted student responses ("11") unless such responses are clearly correct or incorrect by definition, custom, or empirical validation.

8. Teachers should make a conscious effort to develop a classroom climate in which students feel free to ask questions of clarification ("12") and state opinions ("11") in order to further their understanding. In order to establish this type of climate, teachers should emphasize the use of encouragement, acceptance and clarification of feeling ("1"), and acceptance of ideas ("3"), and should avoid the use of criticism and sarcasm ("9").

9. Incorrect responses should not go uncorrected, but should either receive corrective feedback ("7") or be thrown back to the student for clarification and correction ("3"). To allow incorrect responses to go unnoticed is to risk the possibility that, for students who have an incomplete or faulty structure of understanding, this will serve as self-reinforcement of incorrect responses.

10. Reinforcement is only possible following a response; this being the case, every attempt should be made to stimulate active involvement (both overt and covert) and to stimulate overt verbal involvement for purposes of reinforcement and corrective feedback in the early phases of a unit.

This paper has been a discussion of the relationship between teacher and student classroom behavior (as described by the Observational System for Instructional Analysis) and principles of learning consistent with reinforcement theory. It has been shown that the research of Flanders offers some support for the theoretical assumptions that have been made. Much more research in actual classroom situations is needed, and more sensitive observational instruments need to be developed before many of the hypotheses stated in this paper can be supported. It has been affirmed, however, that the point of view taken in this paper represents a fruitful direction for research activity of instructional theorists, a direction made possible by the development of observational systems for the more precise description of the classroom behavior of teachers and students.

That predictable cause–effect relationships may be found between patterns of teacher and pupil achievement is not enough. Once such relationships have been clearly established, teachers must be trained to consistently exhibit such behavior in classrooms. In many cases, this will necessitate the retraining of in-service teachers. If the assumptions about reinforcement presented in this paper are correct (i.e., the importance of feedback and knowledge of results), then they are as relevant to the changing of teachers' behavior as to the changing of students' behavior. Not only are observational systems of the type referred to in this paper useful as research tools, but they would seem to be equally useful as feedback mechanisms to aid teachers in learning and relearning effective teaching behavior (Flanders, 1963; Hough and Ober, 1966). It is in this use of observational systems that their greatest potential probably lies. Libraries are full of research findings which have never found their way into teacher behavior. If learning is behavioral change, then it is behavioral change—for both teachers and students—with which we must deal.

13

INTERACTION ANALYSIS:
RECENT DEVELOPMENTS[57]

EDMUND AMIDON and ELIZABETH HUNTER

There are a number of category systems for analyzing verbal interaction in the classroom, and in the past 15 years, the interest shown in category systems as research tools has increased tremendously. In a recent survey, for example, Amidon and Simon (1965) found that educational researchers reported over 20 systems for classifying verbal classroom interaction. We have found that our own colleagues and students are developing category systems at an increasing rate.

Hough (1966), Honigman (1966), Amidon and Hunter (1966), and Simon and Agazarian (1966) have developed systems which include many features of the ten-category system of Flanders, but which also branch out from and differ somewhat from Flanders' interaction analysis. The first issue of The Classroom Interaction Newsletter (1965) presents summaries of a number of studies in which other new category systems have been developed. So many observational systems are now being produced that it is difficult to keep informed about them. While there is a wide field here for innovation and invention, it seems that in order to increase our understanding of classroom verbal interaction and generalize from present findings it would be important to conduct future careful research with presently existing systems or modification of systems that will allow for reference back to current data. The modifications of Flanders' interaction analysis which will be suggested here would allow a researcher to compare any data he collected with that collected using the original system. In addition, the modified system presented here has a unique training potential that allows for a selective analysis of specific aspects of teaching, such as, for example, a teacher's questioning behavior, the type of student talk occurring in the classroom, or the way the teacher uses praise and encouragement in his teaching. This modified system is presented as an example of how the original system of interaction analysis can be expanded to provide a highly flexible research and instructional tool.

---

[57] This paper is based on a paper delivered at the American Educational Research Association convention, February, 1966, in Chicago, Illinois.

Table 3–51

Modified Categories

Teacher talk	1. Accepts feeling	
	2a. Praises	
	2b. Praises using public criteria	
	2c. Praises using private criteria	
	3. Accepts idea through:	a) description
		b) inference
		c) generalization
	4. Asks:	a) cognitive memory question
		b) convergent question
		c) divergent question
		d) evaluative question
	5. Lectures	
	6. Gives direction	
	7a. Criticizes	
	7b. Criticizes using public criteria	
	7c. Criticizes using private criteria	
Student talk	8. Pupil response:	a) description
		b) inference
		c) generalization
	9. Pupil initiation:	a) description
		b) inference
		c) generalization
	10a. Silence	
	10b. Confusion	

The Flanders system as described earlier in this book describes only verbal interaction between teachers and pupils. Only verbal behavior is analyzed because of the difficulty at the present time in reliably categorizing nonverbal behavior. All teacher–pupil interaction is divided into ten categories, seven of teacher talk, two of student talk, and one of silence or confusion.

The modified system presented in this paper retains the basic ten categories, but includes some ideas of other researchers in the field. Additional categories are added (Table 3–51) so that more data might be collected in classrooms, and also so that student teachers being trained in the use of a category system may look at their classroom verbal interaction more discriminatingly and may thus gain more insight into their own teaching behavior. A wide variety of expansions and contractions of categories are possible to meet specific training or research needs. For example, a teacher who wishes to analyze his own teaching with specific emphasis on patterns of questioning could use a 13-category system composed of the basic ten categories with a category 4 expansion (categories 4a, 4b, 4c, and 4d). A teacher who wished to focus on the effect of clarification on level of student thinking could use the basic ten categories with an expansion of categories 3, 8, and 9. Such an analysis would involve the use of a 16-category system.

PROPOSED MODIFICATION OF
THE FLANDERS SYSTEM OF INTERACTION ANALYSIS

The modification retains the use of the matrix, so that a person using the 24 categories described in this paper would enter data into a 24 by 24 matrix, a 13 by 13 matrix, a 16 by 16 matrix or a matrix of varying size determined by the particular categories being used. In each case, however, the categories may be collapsed back into a 10 by 10 matrix.

In creating the flexible system presented here, the authors have drawn from the work of Marie Hughes, Hilda Taba, and James Gallagher and Mary Jane Aschner. The contribution of each of these people to the flexible category system is presented below.

Category 1, accepts feeling, category 5, lectures, and category 6, gives directions, are left as they are in the Flanders system. Category 2, praises or encourages, is modified by using Marie Hughes' ideas about public and private criteria (Hughes *et al.*, 1959). If a teacher praises by saying, "good," or "fine work," and uses no criteria, then category 2a would be tallied. If a teacher gives the kind of reasons which are logical and explicit, then 2b would be tallied. Examples of 2b would be, "Your report was particularly helpful because you used those graphs to show us exactly how production changed income levels," or "Your quiet voices are helping the rest of us concentrate on our written work." If a teacher gives reasons for praise which involve his own likes and dislikes, 2c, or private criteria would be tallied. Examples of this would be, "I was proud of your behavior in the halls today," or, "A report like John's makes me very happy." These additions should help student teachers think about and use praise in ways which encourage pupils to grow and become more self-directing.

Taba's levels of thinking (Taba, 1964) have suggested the modifications in category 3, accepts ideas. Three sub-categories have been added to category three: describing, inferring, and generalizing. Examples of these sub-categories would be:

Student: "They built their houses out of snow."

Teacher: "So they used snow to provide shelter." (Acceptance through description)

Student: "They had to use snow."

Teacher: "You mean that if they had had wood or stone available they probably would have used that instead." (Acceptance through inference) "People in primitive cultures have to use the materials in their immediate environments for their homes." (Acceptance through generalization)

By dividing acceptance of ideas in this way, student teachers are helped to think about their pupils' levels of thinking, and also to be aware of whether or not their own responses to pupils will be most helpful if kept on the same level, or if moved to another level.

The categories of Gallagher and Aschner (1963) are used in the modifications of Flanders' Category 4, asks questions. Examples of cognitive memory, convergent, divergent, and evaluative questions follow in the order in which they are listed: 4a) "What is the largest city in New York state?" 4b) "What is there about the position of New York City which accounts for its importance?" 4c) "How might the lives of the people of New York City be different if the city were located in the torrid zone?" 4d) "Would you like to live in New York City?" According to Gallagher and Aschner, cognitive memory questions ask for recall and require no additional thinking, convergent questions require some analysis of data, divergent questions call for imagination and a move in new directions, and evaluative questions ask for judgment. By dividing questions into these broad and narrow categories, student teachers are helped to formulate questions in a more varied way than they might otherwise do.

Category 7, criticizes or justifies authority, has been modified in the same way that praise has been, by adding public and private criteria; and for the same reasons, so that pupils will be provided with reasons for criticism when this is appropriate. An example of criticism, 7a, would be, "wrong." 7b, criticism using public criteria, might be, "Your answer is wrong because you divided with a nine instead of a seven." An example of 7c, criticism using private criteria, would be, "I don't like your attitude."

The Flanders categories 8 and 9 have been modified in the same way as category 3, by the addition of the sub-headings, description, inference, and generalization. The reasons for this change are to help student teachers to think about the levels of pupils' contributions, to help them move from one level to another, to back up if necessary, to be aware of what Taba calls "jumpers," (those pupils who may skip levels when others are not ready), and so forth.

The Flanders category 10, silence or confusion, has been divided into two categories. Silence following a question, for example, is quite different from confusion following a question. It would seem helpful for student teachers to learn to allow silence after truly thought-provoking questions.

Obviously, the potential creation of sub-categories is not restricted to those derived from the work of Hughes, Taba, and Gallagher and Aschner. Many other sub-classifications could be created so long as the behaviors categorized can be identified in spontaneous classroom behavior and so long as the categories are mutually exclusive.

The modifications in interaction analysis suggested in this paper result in 24 categories rather than 10. However, there are only 10 main categories, with the others being sub-headings. Thus, the category system would not be difficult to learn, or to use. The system is particularly designed for use as a feedback tool; to analyze one's own teaching, to think about and formulate questions, to role-play behaviors in the college classroom, to observe teaching patterns, and to diagnose teaching problems.

REFERENCES

Adorno, T. W., et al., 1950. *The authoritarian personality*. New York: Harper.

Allport, G. W., 1937. *Personality*. New York: Holt.

Allport, G. W., 1945. "Psychology of participation," *Psychol. Rev.* **52**, 117–132.

Allport, G. W., 1950. *The nature of personality: selected papers*. Reading, Mass.: Addison-Wesley.

Amidon, E. J., 1959. "Dependent-prone students in experimental learning situations." Unpublished doctoral dissertation, University of Minnesota, Minneapolis.

Amidon, E. J., 1966. "Using interaction analysis at Temple University." Paper presented at the conference on the implications of recent research on teaching for teacher education, University of Rochester, Rochester, New York.

*Amidon, E. J., and N. A. Flanders, 1961. "The effects of direct and indirect teacher influence on dependent-prone students learning geometry," *J. educ. Psychol.* **52**, 286–291.

*Amidon, E. J., and N. A. Flanders, 1963. *The role of the teacher in the classroom*. Minneapolis: Amidon and Associates.

Amidon, E. J., and M. M. Giammatteo, 1965. "The verbal behavior of superior teachers," *Elem. sch. J.* **65**, 283–285.

Amidon, E. J., and Elizabeth Hunter, 1966. *Improving teaching: analyzing verbal interaction in the classroom*. New York: Holt, Rinehart, and Winston.

*Amidon, E. J., and Elizabeth Hunter, 1966a. "Verbal interaction in the classroom: The Verbal Interaction Category System." Available from the author (mimeographed): Temple University, Philadelphia.

Amidon, E. J., and Anita Simon, 1965. "Implications for teacher education of interaction analysis research in student teaching." Paper presented at annual meeting of American Educational Research Association, Chicago.

Anderson, H. H., 1937. "An experimental study of dominative and integrative behavior in children of pre-school age." *J. soc. Psychol.* **8**, 335–345.

Anderson, H. H., 1937a. "Domination and integration in the social behavior of young children in an experimental play situation," *Genet. psychol. Monogr.* **19**, 341–408.

* Indicates that this article is reprinted in this book.

*ANDERSON, H. H., 1939. "The measurement of domination and of socially integrative behavior in teachers' contacts with children," *Child Devlpm.* **10**, 73–89.

ANDERSON, H. H., 1939a. "Domination and social integration in the behavior of kindergarten children in an experimental play situation," *J. exp. Educ.* **8**, 123–131.

ANDERSON, H. H., 1943. "Domination and socially integrative behavior." In R. G. BARKER, J. S. KOUNIN and H. F. WRIGHT (Eds.) *Child behavior and development.* New York: McGraw-Hill.

ANDERSON, H. H., and HELEN M. BREWER, 1945. *Studies of teachers' classroom personalities, I. Dominative and socially integrative behavior of kindergarten teachers.* Stanford University Press, Stanford, Cal.

ANDERSON, H. H., and J. E. BREWER, 1946. *Studies of teachers' classroom personalities, II. Effects of dominative and integrative contacts on children's classroom behavior.* Stanford University Press, Stanford, Cal.

ANDERSON, H. H., et al., 1946. *Studies of teachers' classroom personalities, III. Follow-up of the effects of dominative and integrative contacts on children's behavior.* Stanford University Press, Stanford, Cal.

ANDERSON, J. P., 1960. "Student perception of teacher influence." Unpublished doctoral dissertation, University of Minnesota, Minneapolis.

ANGYAL, A., 1941. *Foundations for a science of personality.* New York: Commonwealth Fund.

ASCH, S. E., 1951. "Effects of group pressure upon the modification and distortion of judgments." In H. GUETZKOW (Ed.) *Groups, leadership, and men.* Pittsburgh: Carnegie Press.

ASCHNER, MARY JANE, 1959. "The analysis of classroom discourse: a method and its uses." Unpublished doctoral dissertation, University of Illinois, Urbana.

BALES, R. F., 1950. *Interaction process analysis.* Reading, Mass.: Addison-Wesley.

BALES, R. F., 1950a. "A set of categories for the analysis of small group interaction," *Amer. sociol. Rev.* **15**, 257–263.

BALES, R. F., 1951. "Some statistical problems in small group research," *J. Amer. statist. Assn.* **46**, 311–322.

BALES, R. F., and H. GERBRANDS, 1948. "The interaction recorder; an apparatus and check list for sequential content analysis of social interaction," *Human Relations* **1**, 456–463.

*BALES, R. F., and F. L. STRODTBECK, 1951. "Phases in group problem solving," *J. abnorm. soc. Psychol.* **46**, 458–496.

BARR, A. S., 1946. "The measurement and prediction of teaching efficiency," *Rev. educ. Res.* **16**, 203–208.

BARR, A. S., 1948. "The measurement and prediction of teaching efficiency: A summary of investigations," *J. exp. Educ.* **16**, 203–283.

BERG, P. C., 1963. "Creativity as a dimension of reading performance." In R. STAIGER and C. MELTON (Eds.) *New developments in programs and procedures for college-adult reading.* Twelfth yearbook of the National Reading Conference.

BERLIN, J. I., and B. WYCKOFF, 1963. "The teaching of improved interpersonal relations through programmed instruction for two people working together." Paper read at the annual meeting of The American Psychological Association, Philadelphia.

BETTE, G. L., 1935. "Evaluation through ratings and other measures of success," *Special survey studies, national survey of the education of teachers, V.* Bulletin No. 10, U.S. Office of Education. Washington, D.C.: Government Printing Office.

BOWERS, N. D. and R. S. SOAR, 1961. *Studies of human relations in the teaching–learning process, V; Final report: evaluation of laboratory human relations training for classroom teachers.* Cooperative research project No. 469, U.S. Office of Education.

BROTEMARKLE, R. A., 1947. "Clinical point of view in education," *Training Sch. Bull.* **44**, 102–110.

BRYAN, R. C., and O. YNTEMA, 1939. *A manual on the evaluation of student reactions.* Western State Teachers College, Kalamazoo, Mich.

BURTON, W. H., 1944. *The guidance of learning activities.* New York: Appleton-Century.

CANTOR, N., 1946. *Dynamics of learning.* Buffalo, New York: Foster and Stewart.

CANTOR, N., 1953. *The teaching–learning process.* New York: Dryden.

CASTANEDA, A., *et al.*, 1956. "Complex learning and task difficulty," *Child Devlpm.*, **27**, 327–332.

CATTELL, R. B., 1946. *Description and measurement of personality.* New York: World.

CLARKE, E., 1961. "Some aspects of attitudinal perception in school supervisors." Unpublished doctoral dissertation, Cornell University, Ithaca, N.Y.

Classroom Interaction Newsletter, 1965. Vol. I, ANITA SIMON (Ed.) Temple University, Philadelphia.

COGAN, M. L., 1956. "Theory and design of a study of teacher–pupil interaction," *Harvard educ. Rev.* **26**, 315–342.

COGAN, M. L., 1958. "The relation of the behavior of teachers to the productive behavior of their pupils," *J. exp. Educ.* **27**, 89–124.

COMBS, A., 1958. "Seeing is behaving," *Educ. Leadership* **16**, 21–26.

COOK, W. W., and C. H. LEEDS, 1947. "Measuring the teaching personality," *Educ. psychol Measmt.* **7**, 399–410.

DARWIN, J. H., 1959. "Note on the comparison of several relatizations of a Markoff chain," *Biometrika* **46**, 412–419.

DAVIES, LILLIAN S., 1961. "Some relationships between attitudes, personality characteristics and verbal behavior of selected teachers." Unpublished doctoral dissertation, University of Minnesota, Minneapolis.

DAVIS, W. M., 1952. "Factors of effectiveness in science teaching and their application to the teaching of science in Ohio's public schools." Unpublished doctoral dissertation, The Ohio State University, Columbus.

DELACATO, JANICE F., and C. H. DELACATO, 1952. "A group approach to remedial reading," *Elem. Engl.* **29**, 142–149.

DEWEY, J., 1910. *How we think.* Boston: Heath.

DEWEY, J., 1916. *Democracy in education.* New York: Macmillan.

DEWEY, J., 1938. *Experience and education.* New York: Macmillan.

DEWEY, J., 1946. *Experience and education.* New York: Macmillan.

DOLLARD, J., and N. MILLER, 1950. *Personality and psychotherapy.* New York: McGraw-Hill.

DOMAS, S. J., 1950. *Report of an exploratory study of teacher competence.* Cambridge, Mass.: New England School Development Council, 20 Oxford Street.

DOMAS, S. J., and D. V. TIEDEMAN, 1950. "Teacher competence: an annotated bibliography," *J. exp. Educ.* **19,** 101–218.

DUNHAM, D. R., 1958. "Attitudes of student teachers, college supervisors, and supervising teachers toward youth." Unpublished doctoral dissertation, Indiana University, Bloomington.

ELLIOTT, H. S., 1928. *The process of group thinking.* New York: Association Press.

ENGLE, H. A., 1961. "A study of openness as a factor in change." Unpublished doctoral dissertation, Auburn University, Auburn, Ala.

FARMER, W. A., JR., 1964. "The image of the competent secondary school science teacher as seen by selected groups." Unpublished doctoral dissertation, The Ohio State University, Columbus.

FILSON, T. N., 1957. "Factors influencing the level of dependence in the classroom." Unpublished doctoral dissertation, University of Minnesota, Minneapolis.

FLANAGAN, J. C., 1941. "A preliminary study of the validity of the 1940 edition of the National Teacher Examinations," *Sch. & Soc.* **54,** 59–64.

FLANDERS, N. A., 1951. "Personal–social anxiety as a factor in experimental learning situations," *J. educ. Res.* **45,** 100–110.

FLANDERS, N. A., 1959. "Teacher-pupil contacts and mental hygiene," *J. soc. Issues* **15,** 30–39.

FLANDERS, N. A., 1960. *Teacher influence: pupil attitudes and achievement.* University of Minnesota, Minneapolis.

FLANDERS, N. A., 1960a. "Diagnosing and utilizing social structures in classroom learning." In *The dynamics of instructional groups,* 59th Yearb. nat. Soc. Stud. Educ. Chicago: University of Chicago.

*FLANDERS, N. A., 1960b. *Interaction Analysis in the classroom: a manual for observers,* University of Michigan, Ann Arbor.

FLANDERS, N. A., 1961. "Interaction Analysis: a technique for quantifying teacher influence." Paper read at the annual meeting of The American Educational Research Association, Illinois.

FLANDERS, N. A., 1963. *Helping teachers change their behavior.* University of Michigan, Ann Arbor.

*FLANDERS, N. A., 1963a. "Intent, action and feedback: a preparation for teaching," *J. teach. Educ.* **14,** 251–260.

*FLANDERS, N. A., 1964. "Some relationships between teacher influence, pupil attitudes, and achievement." In B. J. BIDDLE and W. J. ELLENA (Eds.) *Contemporary research on teacher effectiveness.* New York: Holt, Rinehart, and Winston.

FLANDERS, N. A., 1965. "Integrating theory and practice in teacher education." In forty-fourth yearbook of the Association for Student Teaching, *Theoretical bases for professional laboratory experiences in teacher education.* Dubuque, Iowa: Association for Student Teaching.

FLANDERS, N. A., 1965a. *Teacher influence, pupil attitudes, and achievement.* Cooperative research monograph, No. 12. Washington, D.C.: U.S. Government Printing Office.

FLANDERS, N. A., *et al.,* 1960. *Measuring dependence proneness in the classroom.* Bureau of Educational Research, No. Ber 60-6, University of Minnesota, Minneapolis.

FLANDERS, N. A., and S. HAVUMAKI, 1960. "Group compliance to dominative teacher influence," *Human Relations* 13, 67–82.

FLEISHMAN, E. A., 1953. "The description of supervisory behavior," *J. appl. Psychol.* 37, 1–6.

FOWLER, BEVERLY D., 1961. "Relation of teacher personality characteristics and attitudes to teacher–pupil rapport and emotional climate in the elementary classroom." Unpublished doctoral dissertation, University of South Carolina, Columbia.

FREEZE, C. R., 1963. "A study of openness as a factor in change of student teachers." Unpublished doctoral dissertation, University of Alabama, Montgomery.

FURST, NORMA, 1965. "The effects of training in interaction analysis on the behavior of student teachers in secondary schools." Paper read at the annual meeting of the American Educational Research Association, Chicago.

GAGE, N. L., 1960. Address appearing in "Proceedings," *Res. Resume* 16, Burlingame, Cal.: California Teachers Association.

GAGE, N. L., *et al.,* 1956. "Teachers' understanding of their pupils and pupils' ratings of their teachers," *Psychol. Monogr.: Gen. & Appl.* 406, 21.

GALLAGHER, J. J., and MARY JANE ASCHNER, 1963. "A preliminary report: analysis of classroom interaction," *Merrill-Palmer Quart.* 9, 183–194.

GUETZKOW, H. H., and W. HENRY, 1949. *Group projective sketches.* University of Michigan, Ann Arbor.

GUILFORD, J. P., 1956. *Fundamental statistics in psychology and education.* New York: McGraw-Hill.

HEMPHILL, J. K., *et al.,* 1962. *Administrative performance and personality.* Columbia University, New York.

HENRY, N. B. (Ed.), 1942. *The Psychology of Learning.* Forty-First Yearbook of the National Society for the Study of Education, Part II. Public School Publishing Co., Bloomington, Illinois.

HILGARD, E. R., 1948. *Theories of learning.* New York: Appleton Century Crofts.

HONIGMAN, F., 1964. *Synopsis of innovations and revisions to the Flanders system of interaction analysis.* Temple University, Philadelphia.

HONIGMAN, F., 1966. "Testing a three dimensional system for analyzing teachers' influence." Unpublished doctoral dissertation, Temple University, Philadelphia.

HOUGH, J. B., 1965. "The dogmatism factor in the human relations training of pre-service teachers." Paper read at the annual meeting of The American Educational Research Association, Chicago.

HOUGH, J. B., 1965a. "A study of the effect of five experimental treatments on the development of human relations skills and verbal teaching behaviors of pre-service teachers." Unpublished paper, mimeographed copies available from author. College of Education, The Ohio State University, Columbus.

*HOUGH, J. B., 1966. "An observational system for the analysis of classroom instruction." Unpublished paper (mimeographed), The Ohio State University, Columbus.

HOUGH, J. B., and E. J. AMIDON, 1963. *Behavioral change in pre-service teacher preparation: an experimental study.* Temple University, Philadelphia.

*HOUGH, J. B., and E. J. AMIDON, 1964. "An experiment in pre-service teacher education." Paper read at the annual meeting of the American Educational Research Association, Chicago.

HOUGH, J. B., and E. J. AMIDON, 1965. "The relationship of personality structure and training in interaction analysis to attitude change during student teaching." Paper read at the annual meeting of The American Educational Research Association, Chicago.

HOUGH, J. B., and J. K. DUNCAN, 1965. "Exploratory studies of a teaching situation reaction test." Paper read at the annual meeting of The American Educational Research Association, Chicago.

*HOUGH, J. B., and R. OBER, 1966. "The effects of training in interaction analysis on the verbal behavior of pre-service teachers." Paper read at the annual meeting of The American Educational Research Association, Chicago.

HOYT, C., 1941. "Test reliability estimated by analysis of variance," *Psychometrika* **6**, 153–160.

HOYT, C., and C. L. STUNKARD, 1952. "Estimation of test reliability for unrestricted item scoring methods," *Educ. psychol. Measmt.* **12**, 756–758.

HUGHES, MARIE, et al., 1959. *The assessment of the quality of teaching: a research report.* U.S. Office of Education, Cooperative Research Project No. 353, University of Utah, Salt Lake City.

HUGHES, MARIE, et al., 1959a. *Development of the means for assessment of the quality of teaching in the elementary schools.* University of Utah, Salt Lake City.

JERSILD, A. T., et al., 1939. "An evaluation of aspects of the activity program in the New York City public schools," *J. exp. Educ.* **8**, 166–207.

JERSILD, A. T., et al., 1941. "A further comparison of pupils in 'activity' and 'non-activity' schools," *J. exp. Educ.* **9**, 303–309.

JERSILD, A. T., et al., 1941a. "Studies of elementary school classes in action, II: pupil participation and aspects of pupil–teacher relationships," *J. exp. Educ.* **10**, 119–137.

JOHNSON, MARGUERITE WILKER, 1939. "Verbal influences on children's behavior," *Sch. educ. Monogr. Educ.* **1**, University of Michigan, Ann Arbor.

KAGEN, J., and P. MUSSEN, 1956. "Dependency themes on the TAT and group conformity," *J. consult. Psychol.* **20**, 19–27.

KENDALL, M. G., 1943. *The advanced theory of statistics.* London: Lippincott.

KIRK, J., 1964. "Effects of learning the Minnesota system of interaction analysis by student teachers of intermediate grades." Unpublished doctoral dissertation, Temple University, Philadelphia.

LaDuke, C. V., 1945. "The measurement of teaching ability." *J. exp. Educ.* 14, 75–100.

LaShier, W. S., 1966. "An analysis of certain aspects of the verbal behavior of stu dent teachers of eighth grade students participating in a BSCS laboratory block." Paper read at the annual meeting of the American Educational Research Association, Chicago.

Lasker, B., 1949. *Democracy through discussion.* New York: H. W. Wilson.

Lecky, P., 1945. *Self-consistency: a theory of personality.* New York: Island Press.

Leeds, C. H., 1940. "A scale for measuring teacher–pupil attitudes and teacher–pupil rapport," *Psychol. Monogr.* 64, 1–24.

Lewin, K., 1935. *Dynamic theory of personality.* New York: McGraw-Hill.

Lewin, K., 1938. "The conceptual representation and the measurement of psychological forces." *The Duke Univ. contrib. psychol.* 4, 247.

Lewin, K., 1939. "Experiments in social space," *Harvard educ. Rev.* 9, 21–32.

Lewin, K., 1939a. "Field theory and experiment in social psychology," *Amer. J. Sociol.* 44, 868–896.

Lewin, K., 1943. "Psychology and the process of group living," *J. soc. Psychol.* 17, 113–131.

Lewin, K., and R. Lippitt, 1938. "An experimental approach to the study of autocracy and democracy: a preliminary note," *Sociometry,* 292–300.

*Lewin, K., *et al*, 1939. "Patterns of aggressive behavior in experimentally created 'social climates,' " *J. soc. Psychol.* 10, 271–299.

Lewin, K., et al., 1945. *Changing behavior and attitudes.* Massachusetts Institute of Technology, Cambridge, Mass.

Lins, L. J., 1946. "Prediction of teaching efficiency," *J. exp. Educ.* 15, 2–60.

Lippitt, R., 1940. "An experimental study of authoritarian and democratic group atmospheres," *Stud. Child Welfare* 16, 43–195.

Lippitt, R., 1940a. "An analysis of group reaction to three types of experimentally created social climates." Unpublished doctoral dissertation, University of Iowa, Iowa City.

Lippitt, R., and R. K. White, 1943. "The 'social climate' of children's groups." In R. G. Barker, J. S. Kounin and H. F. Wright (Eds.) *Child Behavior and Development.* New York: McGraw-Hill.

Livson, N., and P. Mussen, 1957. "The relation of control to overt aggression and dependency." *J. abnorm. soc. Psychol.* 55, 66–71.

Maslow, A. H., 1943. "The authoritarian character structure," *J. soc. Psychol.* 18, 402–411.

McAulay, J. D., 1960. "How much influence has a co-operating teacher?" *J. teacher Educ.* 11, 79–83.

McCall, W. A., 1952. *Measurement of teacher merit.* Raleigh, N. Carolina: State Superintendent of Public Instruction.

McKeachie, W. J., 1963. "Research on teaching at the college and university level." In N. L. Gage (Ed.), *Handbook of Research on Teaching.* Chicago: Rand McNally.

MEAD, MARGARET (Ed.), 1937. *Cooperation and competition among primitive peoples.* New York: Macmillan.

MEDLEY, D. M., and H. E. MITZEL, 1958. "Technique for measuring classroom behavior," *J. educ. Psychol.* **49**, 86–92.

MEDLEY, D. M., and H. E. MITZEL, 1959. "Some behavioral correlates of teacher effectiveness," *J. educ. Psychol.* **50**, 239–246.

MILLER, N. E., and J. DOLLARD, 1941. *Social learning and imitation.* Yale University, New Haven.

MITZEL, H. E., and W. RABINOWITZ, 1953. *Assessing social-emotional climate in the classroom by Withall's technique. Psychol. Monogr.* **67**, No. 18. Washington, D.C.: Amer. psychol. Assoc.

MORENO, J. L., 1934. *Who shall survive?* Washington, D.C.: Nervous and Mental Disease Publishing Co.

MURRAY, H. A., 1938. *Explorations in personality.* New York: Oxford University Press.

OLSON, W. C. *et al.*, 1938. "Teacher personality as revealed by the amount and kind of verbal direction used in behavior control," *Educ. Admin. Superv.* **24**, 81–93.

OSMON, R. V., 1959. "Associative factors in changes of student teachers' attitudes during student teaching," *Dissert. Abstr.* **20**, 1281.

PERKINS, H. V., 1951. "Climate influences group learning," *J. educ. Res.* **45**, 115–119.

PERKINS, H. V., 1965. "Classroom behavior and under-achievement," *Amer. educ. Res. J.* **2**, 1–12.

PIAGET, J., 1929. *The child's conception of the world.* New York: Harcourt Brace.

PRICE, R. P., 1961. "Influence of supervising teachers," *J. teach-Educ.* **12**, 471–475.

ROGERS, C. R., 1942. *Counseling and psychotherapy; new concepts in practice.* Boston: Houghton Mifflin.

ROGERS, C. R., 1959. "A theory of therapy, personality and interpersonal relationships as developed in the client-centered framework." In S. KOCH (Ed.) *Psychology: a study of Science, III.* New York: McGraw-Hill.

ROGERS, C. R., 1959a. "Significant learning: in therapy and in education," *Educ. Leadership* **16**, 232–242.

ROKEACH, M., 1960. *The open and closed mind.* New York: Basic Books.

ROLFE, J. F., 1945. "The measurement of teaching ability: study number two," *J. exp. Educ.* **14**, 52–74.

ROMNEY, G. P., *et al.*, 1958. *Progress report of the merit study of the Provo City schools.* Provo, Utah.

ROMNEY, G. P., *et al.*, 1961. *Patterns of effective teaching: second progress report of the merit study of the Provo City schools.* Provo, Utah.

ROSS, C. C., and J. C. STANLEY, 1954. *Measurement in today's schools.* New York: Prentice-Hall.

ROSTKER, L. E., 1942. "A method for determining criteria of teaching ability in terms of measurable pupil changes," *Educ. Admin. Superv.* **28**, 1–19.

ROSTKER, L. E., 1945. "The measurement of teaching ability: study number one," *J. exp. Educ.* **14**, 6–51.

RUNKEL, P. J., 1959. "The social-psychological basis of human relations," *Rev. educ. Res.* **28**, 317–331.

RUSSELL, D. H., and H. R. FEA, 1963. "Research on teaching reading." In N. L. GAGE, *Handbook of research on teaching*, Chicago: Rand McNally.

RYANS, D. G., and E. WANDT, 1952. "A factor analysis of observed teacher behaviors in the secondary school: a study of criterion data," *Educ. psychol. Measmt.* **12**, 574–586.

SCOTT, W. A., 1955 "Reliability of content analysis: the case of nominal coding," *Publ. Opin. Quart.* **19**, 321–325.

SHERIF, M., and M. P. WILSON (EDS.) 1953. *Group relations at the crossroad.* New York: Harper.

SIMON, ANITA, and YVONNE AGAZARIAN, 1966. "Sequential analysis of verbal interaction." Unpublished paper (mimeographed), Temple University, Philadelphia.

SMITH, B. O., 1960. "A concept of teaching," *Teach. Coll. Rec.* **61**, 229–241.

SMITH, B. O., M. J. ASCHNER, and M. MEUX, 1962. *A study of the logic of teaching.* University of Illinois, Urbana.

SMITH, D. E. P., 1955. "Fit teaching methods to personality structure," *High Sch. J.* **39**, 167–171.

SNYDER, W. U., 1947. *A casebook of non-directive counseling.* Boston: Houghton Mifflin.

SPORE, L., 1963. "The competences of secondary school science teachers," *Sci. Educ.* **56**, 319–334.

STORLIE, T. R., 1961. "Selected characteristics of teachers whose verbal behavior is influenced by an inservice course in interaction analysis." Unpublished doctoral dissertation, University of Minnesota, Minneapolis.

SWINEFORD, E. J., 1964. "Analysis of teaching improvement suggestions to student teachers," *J. exp. Educ.* **32**, 299–303.

TABA, HILDA, 1962. *Curriculum development—theory and practice.* New York: Harcourt, Brace and World.

TABA, HILDA, 1963. "Teaching strategy and learning," *Calif. J. instructional Improvement*, Dec.

TABA, HILDA, 1964. *Thinking in elementary school children.* San Francisco State College, San Francisco.

THELEN, H. A., 1960. *Education and the human quest.* New York: Harper.

TORRANCE, E. P., 1962. "Cultural discontinuities and the development of originality of thinking," *Exceptional Children* **28**, 2–13.

U.S. BUREAU OF CENSUS. *Statistical abstract of the United States: 1952.* Washington, D.C.: U.S. Gov. Printing Office.

WHIPPLE, GERTRUDE, n.d., "What pupils do in an activity," *Course of study bulletin*, No. 162, Los Angeles City Schools.

WICKMAN, E. K., 1929. *Children's behavior and teachers' attitudes.* New York: Commonwealth Fund.

WILLIAMSON, S. E., 1956. "Personal problems of teachers influencing teacher pupil relationships." Unpublished doctoral dissertation, University of Oregon, Eugene.

WISPE, L. G., 1951. "Evaluating section teaching methods in the introductory course," *J. educ. Res.* **45**, 161–186.

WITHALL, J., 1949. "The development of a technique for the measurement of social–emotional climate in classrooms," *J. exp. Educ.* **17**, 347–361.

WITHALL, J., 1951. "The development of a climate index," *J. educ. Res.* **45**, 93–99.

WRIGHT, E. MURIEL, 1959. "A rationale for direct observation of behaviors in the mathematics class." In R. L. FEIERABEND and P. H. DuBois (Eds.), *Psychological problems and research methods in mathematics training.* Washington University, St. Louis.

ZAHN, R., 1965. "The use of interaction analysis in supervising student teachers." Unpublished doctoral dissertation, Temple University, Philadelphia.

1F2246